D1171703

the 500 Series creates

Meal·In·One™ Microwave Cooking

from LITTON

Litton Microwave Cooking Products, Minneapolis, Minnesota

Greetings from Litton . . .

You now own the most exciting microwave oven on the market – the Litton 500 Series. It is especially designed with a big oven interior so you can microwave up to three different foods all at once – an entire meal. Cook a beef roast, baked potatoes and dessert all together. Heat soup and sandwiches at the same time. Warm rolls while you cook bacon and eggs. It's fantastic – fun.

And, the Litton 500 Series delivers the quality, single-dish cooking you expect from a Litton Variable Power Microwave Oven. Heat a cup of coffee, defrost a pound of ground beef, cook a hearty casserole. Individual recipes, Oven Meals and "ADD-A" Dish combinations have been developed and tested by Litton home economists to make this new microwave oven usable every meal of the day – and between meals.

Tell us how you like it. Your ideas help us continue to develop new products YOU want. Write: Litton Microwave Cooking, 1405 Xenium Lane North, Minneapolis, Minnesota 55441.

Litton Microwave Cooking Center

Copyright© 1977, Litton Systems Inc., 3rd Printing 1978.
Printed in the United States of America

Contents

Pictured on cover: Gala Feast Oven Meal, page 186 – Beef Standing Rib Roast, New Red Potatoes with Parsley Butter, Fruit Mélange.

Photographs in this book illustrate recipes prepared using Oven Meal Variable Power Microwave oven.

4 CUPS
3 CUPS
2 CUPS
32
28
24
20
16
12
8
40
60
80
100
120
140
160
180
200
220
°F

Meet the Microwave Meal Oven

Cook Up to Three Separate Dishes–All at Once

Three-Dish Oven Meals Highlight New Microwave Oven: Microwave potatoes and dessert along with a meatloaf! Cook an omelet, bacon and French toast together! What a microwave breakthrough! This new, versatile counter-top oven's interior is generously designed so that it evenly cooks three different, delicious dishes — all at the same time — like your conventional range does. Its special engineering, plus Variable Power, lets you microwave several foods together on an oven rack and the bottom shelf. Slow-cooking and fast-heating foods come out of the oven together — hot and tasty. There are two different ways to cook more than one food in this microwave oven — OVEN MEALS and "ADD-A." OVEN MEALS are when three foods are cooked at once. The OVEN MEALS chapter, page 174, gives you 60 different three-dish meal combinations to try — and tells you how to develop your own meal trios. The "ADD-A" is when two foods cook at the same time. "ADD-A" recipes throughout the book demonstrate how easy it is to use this oven to add one other food to a meat, fish or main dish entree. Try these "ADD-A" recipes, then develop your own using directions on page 196. And, of course, this Variable Power oven can bake, braise, warm, sauté, melt, simmer or defrost individual foods. But before you begin cooking, read these introductory pages. Find out what makes microwaves the cooking sensation of the century.

Here's How This Big Oven's Made: This is a big oven! The large cooking cavity, bottom shelf and adjustable oven rack allow you to microwave one, two or three foods a complete meal — all at once. Microwaves from the magnetron tube (source of microwave energy) are channeled through a metal wave-guide to metal stirrer blades. The stirrer distributes microwaves in an even cooking pattern.

A bottom shelf, made of a glass material, holds dishes of food above the oven floor. Microwaves can pass through this shelf, "bounce back" and cook from all angles.

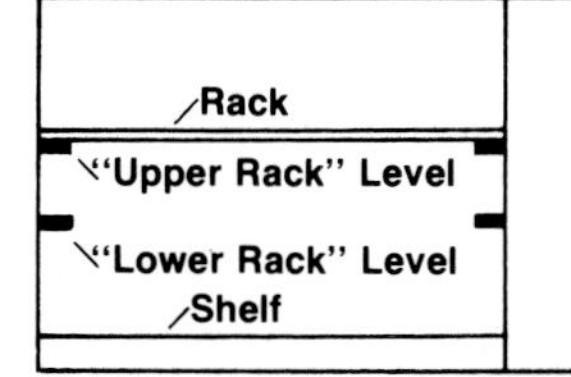

When two or three foods are cooking in the oven, some food is placed on the oven rack and some on the bottom shelf. The bottom shelf receives less microwave energy and food cooks more gently. Food on the rack receives most energy. It cooks more quickly so food that needs longer cooking goes here. The lower rack position is generally used when a large dish needs extra space. *Remove rack when only one food is being cooked, unless otherwise directed in the recipe.*

Microwaves Cook Differently: Whatever the heat source — molecular action within food heats and cooks it. But unlike a gas flame, burning wood, charcoal or electricity, microwaves move directly and quickly into food — right through air and glass, paper or plastic cooking containers. This happens because microwaves are attracted to fat, sugar and liquid (moisture) molecules — causing them to vibrate (heat) at a fantastic rate. Air, glass, paper and plastic do not have these molecules.

Microwaves, however, bounce off metal, cannot pass through it and so are contained with the oven's sealed metal cavity. Here they bounce back and forth, cooking food in

Pictured: Cupboard of microwave cooking supplies to store near a microwave oven.

glass, paper or plastic dishes from all angles. Deep metal dishes are not used for microwave cooking because the waves cannot pass through them and food will microwave only from the top.

Microwave cooking starts with molecule vibration or friction at a food's edges where the waves first make contact. These vibrating molecules bump and rub others, setting up a chain reaction that moves toward the food's center — cooking rapidly as it goes (conduction). Cooking continues for several minutes after food comes from a microwave oven and is taken into consideration (standing time) in microwave recipes.

Microwave Cooking's Really Fast and Cool: Speed is a big advantage of microwave cooking — it's often twice as fast as conventional methods. And, since microwaves move through air and cooking dishes, only the food gets hot — any heat in an oven or a dish comes from hot food during prolonged cooking. Your kitchen stays cool!

Oven Settings: This Variable Power oven has flexible speed control graduated for convenience with six settings — WARM, DEFROST, SIMMER, ROAST, REHEAT and HIGH. Settings denote major cooking techniques for particular microwave speeds; but you can adjust cooking speeds between settings, as with a conventional range. WARM cooks most gently and slowly; HIGH microwaves fastest. Cooking time is expressed in minutes and seconds. Become familiar with all controls on your oven before beginning to cook. See the Use and Care Manual for detailed descriptions.

Here, in brief, is how Variable Power settings are used. Note that when sensitive ingredients are included in food mixtures, a lower setting is usually needed. Refer to individual food chapter introductions for a full explanation of microwave cooking techniques.

- Appetizers — HIGH or ROAST.
- Baked Goods, heat — REHEAT.
- Beverages — HIGH.
- Breads, bake — SIMMER or SIMMER/HIGH.
- Breads, raise dough — WARM.
- Butter, melt — ROAST.
- Cakes — SIMMER/HIGH.
- Candies — ROAST.
- Cheese — ROAST.
- Cookies — SIMMER.
- Custards — SIMMER.
- Eggs — ROAST.
- Fish and Seafood — HIGH.
- Fruits — HIGH or REHEAT.
- Main Dishes — REHEAT, SIMMER or ROAST.
- Meat, braising — HIGH/SIMMER.
- Meat, roasting — HIGH/ROAST or ROAST.
- Meat, small tender cuts — HIGH or ROAST.
- Pasta — HIGH/SIMMER.
- Pie Crusts — ROAST.
- Pies, 1-crust — HIGH or SIMMER.
- Pies, 2-crust — HIGH/Conventional Oven.
- Poultry — HIGH, HIGH/ROAST or ROAST.
- Pudding Mixes — HIGH.
- Salads and Dressings — HIGH or ROAST.
- Sandwiches — HIGH or ROAST.
- Sauces — HIGH or ROAST.
- Soups and Stews — HIGH/SIMMER.
- Vegetables — HIGH or REHEAT.

OVEN MEALS and "ADD-A" recipes are microwaved almost always on HIGH and ROAST.

Do You Want to Defrost, Heat or Cook a Food? A microwave oven will defrost frozen food, heat cooked food or cook food from the raw state. The *DEFROST setting* automatically reduces power to evenly change ice molecules to water without beginning the cooking process. *Heating* occurs when microwaves start food molecules vibrating. Porous food, like bread, heats quickly. Dense food, like cooked meat, should be sliced to heat through without overcooking edges. *Cooking* is prolonged heating that changes food texture from a raw to a cooked state. Since microwaves are attracted to liquid, fat and sugar, Variable Power provides infinite speed control that assures even, quality cooking.

What's Your Food Like? *How much (volume)* food are you cooking? As the volume of food put into the oven increases, the concentration of microwaves in a given food item decreases — cooking time goes up slightly. For example, one sandwich heats faster than two. Oven Meals (page 175) explain techniques for cooking several different foods together. *Starting temperature* determines length of cooking. Cold food takes longer to cook than room temperature or warm food. *More compact (dense)* foods take longer to heat than porous food because microwaves do not penetrate as deeply and food must heat by conduction from the hot outer edges. A slice of meat, for example, heats in 2 to 3 minutes — a slice of bread takes 30 seconds.

What's a Sensitive Ingredient? This term is used throughout the book and refers to food items that microwave very quickly and can overcook, curdle or "pop." These foods are cheese, eggs, cream, sour cream, condensed milk, mayonnaise, snails, oysters, kidney beans and mushrooms. Use lower power settings when sensitive foods are cooked alone or added to a mixture.

Will Food Brown? Microwaved foods are tender, juicy and flavorful because they cook quickly without heating the oven interior (moist heat cooking). Large roasts, turkeys and chickens brown during prolonged cooking because their natural fats attract microwaves. Small food items, such as steaks, chops, hamburgers or fried eggs, will not brown because microwave cooking time is short and there is no drying heat in the oven. Sear, brown, grill and fry these small foods in the oven on a preheated microwave browning grill made of specially formulated ceramic material. Cakes and breads microwave with tender surfaces but do not brown. Recipes suggest ingredients to enhance color.

Dish Size and Shape Are Important: Food volume (amount) should match size of the dish — with some leeway for bubbling. Fill dishes half to two-thirds full. If the dish is too small, food will bubble over edges. If dish is too large, saucy portions will spread out and overcook.

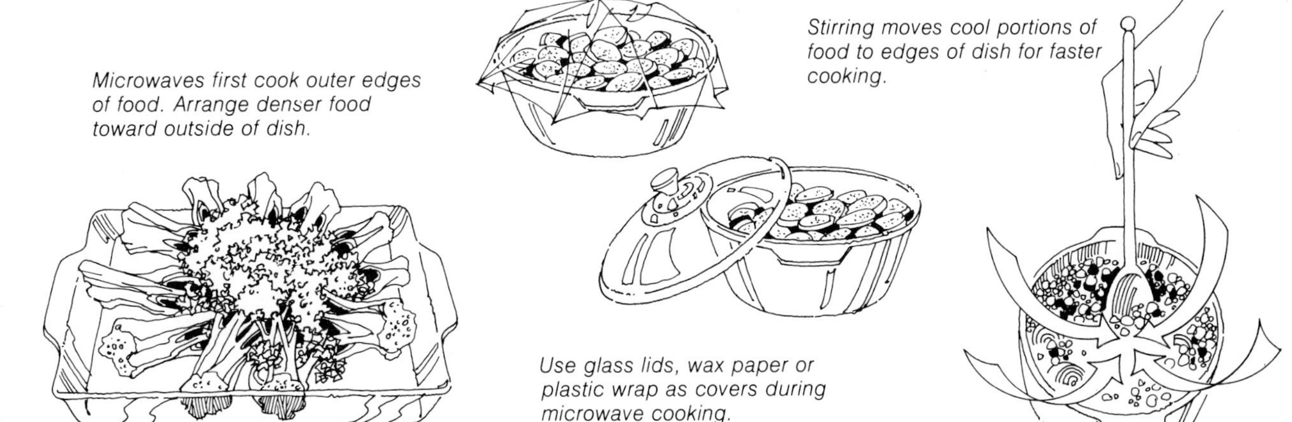

Microwaves first cook outer edges of food. Arrange denser food toward outside of dish.

Use glass lids, wax paper or plastic wrap as covers during microwave cooking.

Stirring moves cool portions of food to edges of dish for faster cooking.

Arrangement Helps Assure Even Doneness: Minimize differences in density, volume or starting temperature when food, such as broccoli or chicken wings, varies in shape or size. Place slow-to-heat dense portion near the outside of the dish where heating takes place first.

Stirring or Turning Help Some Foods Cook Evenly: Variable power and even cooking pattern in this oven keeps stirring at a minimum. However, stirring reduces cooking time for sensitive foods that must cook more slowly — moving cool portions to the edges of the dish where they will cook faster. Meat and other dense pieces of food are turned over once during cooking to assure even doneness.

Covers Trap Steam and Hasten Cooking: Covers, when called for in a recipe, are used to trap steam and hasten cooking. Use glass lids, wax paper, glass plates and saucers without gold, silver, platinum or other metal trim. Tip covers away from hand when removing to prevent steam burns. Plastic wrap may be used as a cover. Pierce it and allow steam to escape before removing. Small pieces of foil may be used to prevent overcooked spots on large pieces of meat, such as a turkey's drumsticks or wing tips.

Standing Time Completes Cooking: Cooking continues after food comes from a microwave oven. It is often advisable to undercook or underthaw food slightly and let the process finish during the standing time designated in recipes.

Is High Altitude Cooking Different? The only change necessary in these microwave recipes may be a slight increase in cooking time.

Adapt Favorite Recipes to Microwave Cooking: Favorite family recipes can be adapted to microwave cooking. Select a similar recipe in this book. Check its chapter introduction for techniques and tips. Always take sensitive ingredients into consideration. Check the Microwave-Conventional Comparison paragraph at the end of each chapter introduction for special tips.

Microwave Ovens Are Safe: A microwave oven is one of the safest appliances in your kitchen. Cooking is done inside a closed, sealed oven cavity — eliminating open burner flames or hot coils. Each microwave oven meets emission safety performance standards of the U.S. Department of Health, Education and Welfare (HEW).

USER INSTRUCTIONS

PRECAUTIONS TO AVOID POSSIBLE EXPOSURE TO EXCESSIVE MICROWAVE ENERGY

(a) Do not attempt to operate this oven with the door open since open-door operation can result in harmful exposure to microwave energy. It is important not to defeat or tamper with the safety interlocks.

(b) Do not place any object between the oven front face and the door to allow soil or cleaner residue to accumulate on sealing surfaces.

(c) Do not operate the oven if it is damaged. It is particularly important that the oven door close properly and that there is no damage to the: (1) door (bent), (2) hinges and latches (broken or loosened), (3) door seals and sealing surfaces.

(d) The oven should not be adjusted or repaired by anyone except properly qualified service personnel.

Internal Temperature Helps Tell When Food Is "Done": Temperatures listed below help you judge when food should be taken from a microwave oven. See recipes and charts for detailed directions. Food continues to cook and temperature will rise 5° F. to 10° F. during standing time. Use a food sensor or microwave food thermometer to measure temperature in the oven during cooking. DO NOT use a conventional meat or candy thermometer during cooking in a microwave oven because mercury in these thermometers reflects microwaves and makes them inaccurate. Insert conventional thermometers only after food is removed from the oven.

Food Sensor Temperature Guide:

Place food sensor in center of food. Food	Internal Temperature
Baked goods, heated	100° F.
Beef roasts, medium	145° F.
Beef roasts, rare	125° F.
Beef roasts, well done	155° F.
Fish, sandwiches, meatloaf	140° F.
Ground beef, precooked main dishes, leftovers, canned vegetables, syrup	150° F.
Ham, fully cooked, Canadian bacon, sausage, fully cooked, wieners	120° F.
Poultry, rabbit, leg of lamb, well done	180° F.
Sauces (or done when thickened at lower temperature)	200° F.
Soups, hot beverages, pork, veal and venison roasts, fresh ham	160° F.

Microwave with Time: Microwave with either time or temperature. If you prefer to use time, set the timer for the shorter time given in the recipe. For instance, many cookbook recipes give a range of time, such as 10 to 12 minutes. You would set the timer for 10 minutes.

Microwave with Temperature, the Food Sensor Way: If you prefer to use temperature, plug the automatic food sensor into the oven and place it into the food with the first half inch of sensor secured in center of food. Note the temperature chart on page 8 and the chart that follows, How to Insert the Food Sensor in Meats. The temperatures printed in some recipes, such as (about 140° F.), indicate the proper setting for the temperature control. Using the food sensor eliminates the need to set the timer. Cooking time is now controlled by internal food temperature. For an example recipe, read Mother's Meatloaf, page 108 in your cookbook.

How to Insert the Food Sensor in Meats:

BONE-IN MEAT CUTS

Insert the food sensor in the fleshy part of the meat. Sensor should not come in contact with bone, marrow or pocket of fat.

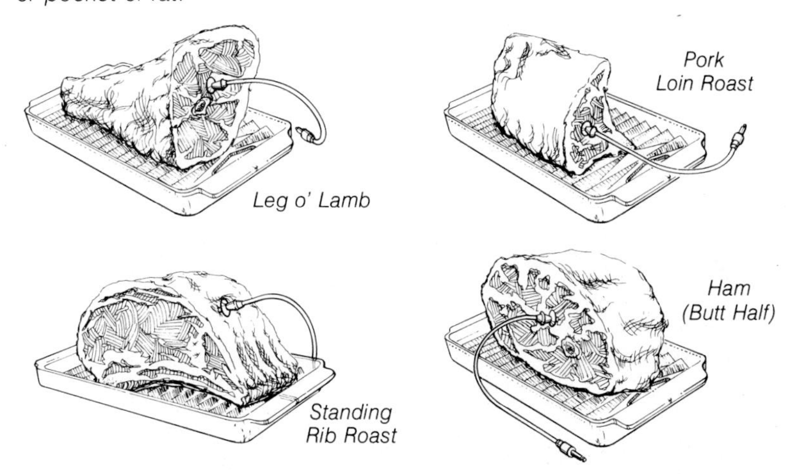

Pork Loin Roast

Leg o' Lamb

Ham (Butt Half)

Standing Rib Roast

BONELESS MEAT CUTS

The food sensor should be placed in the meat from the end and pushed toward center of the fleshy part.

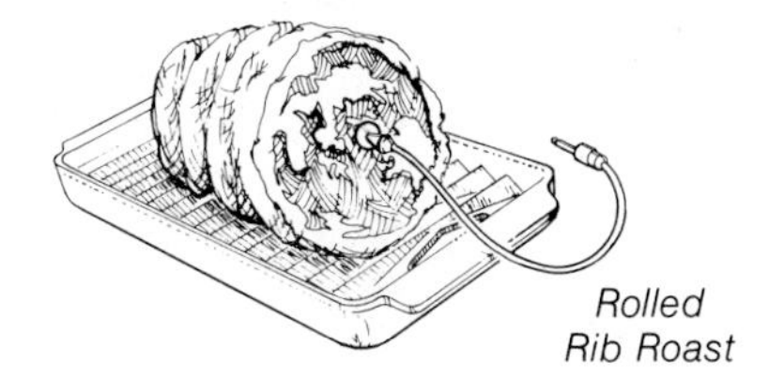

Rolled Rib Roast

Boneless Pork Roast

This is Complete Meal Microwave Cooking: Complete meal microwave cooking is a new cooking dimension; it adds flexibility. You can do one food, two foods, three foods — even a complete meal in the same oven. You can fix a quick cup of coffee; you can scramble an egg; you can microwave a crisp slice of bacon. You can do them separately or together. Sometimes you can put all the foods in at the same time. Sometimes you add a second or third food later — just like you've always done in the conventional oven.

Enjoy Your New Oven: Read and reread this general introduction and the more specific how-to pages that follow. You'll find that this entire section is a handy reference during your first few weeks of microwave cooking. You'll be able to answer your own questions — and those of friends who come to see your new kitchen addition. You'll soon have a working knowledge, a feeling for terms such as food sensor and standing time. You'll know how to cook one, two, even three foods and you'll know how to use your exciting new cookbook.

Using Your New Cookbook

Getting to Know Complete Meal Microwave Cooking: Now that you're the owner of a new microwave countertop oven, we want to help you with this new type of cooking. If you have never cooked with a microwave oven, we want to show you some basic microwave principles. If you are an accomplished microwave cook, we want you to understand the special concepts built into this oven. We want you to feel free to experiment. Try cooking one, two or three foods. As you learn more from your cookbook, you will be just as relaxed and as involved in this kind of cooking as in any other.

Read Your Cookbook: Read your exciting new cookbook to become acquainted with every aspect: the general introduction, the how-to section, the chapter introductions, the recipes, the charts, the index.

Food Chapters in Alphabetical Order: Note that the food chapters are in alphabetical order. There is a great deal of basic microwave information as well as directions and hints for using the special features of this oven.

Look for the Colored Tabs: You'll find illustrations set off in color at the right side of the page to help you identify the food subject of a particular page.

Here's How—and Why Page: Each food chapter is introduced by Here's How — and Why. This section outlines the principles of that particular food cookery. If you have any questions about the how or why of a specific recipe, you may find the answer to your question here.

Note the Microwave/Conventional Comparison: This part of each chapter introduction will help you familiarize yourself with foods that cook as they do conventionally and with those where there are differences.

Check for the * : This symbol at the end of a recipe title is a reminder that two or more power settings are used during cooking. On ovens with a memory these settings can be programmed.

Oven Meal Chapter: The oven meal chapter follows the food chapter, beginning on page 174. The blue charts below each oven meal contain three alternative oven meals that are cooked using the same techniques and placement of foods in the microwave oven as the basic oven meal.

Add-A: Add-A is a term used in the cookbook to describe a two food meal with foods microwaving at the same time. To the main dish, you add a second food — vegetable, dessert or bread. Add-A recipes are highlighted in blue throughout the cookbook.

Daily Heating How-To: The foods in this cookbook chart, page 23, are heated often in the microwave oven. Use the chart frequently as a basic quick reference.

Utensil Chart: Check this chart, page 22, to see whether or not a dish is suitable for use in a microwave oven. Remember that generic or common names are used rather than trademarks.

Convenience Food How-To: Packaged foods are listed in this chart, pages 24-28, by their generic names or common names rather than their trademarks. It's a quick guide to microwaving convenience foods.

Defrosting How-To: This chart, pages 29-31, is your guide to defrosting meat, fish and poultry.

Using the Recipes

Read the Recipes:	Read the recipes carefully then follow the directions step-by-step. Remember that the recipe times have been tested with food at the usual starting temperature: eggs from the refrigerator, breads at room temperature.
Recipe Variations:	Variations follow some recipes. The basic food remains the same and other ingredients are changed to help you adapt foods to your personal taste.
Assemble the Ingredients:	Assemble the ingredients after reading the recipe thoroughly since the starting temperature of food is so important.
Using Utensils:	Glass, straw, paper and dishwasher-safe plastic are suitable utensils for microwave cooking. Do not use metal pots and pans, dishes with gold trim, Melamine dishes, Centura® dinnerware or Corelle® closed-handle cups. For more specific information, read the utensil chart, page 22.
Covering Foods:	Within each recipe you'll find a suggested covering for the food if one is needed. Covers speed cooking time, just as they do in conventional cooking. For more information, see page 12.
Stirring or Turning Foods:	You'll also find a suggested time for stirring or turning foods if such is needed. Stirring helps to distribute heat throughout the food. Turning allows the food to cook more evenly.
What Does Microwave to Desired Doneness Mean:	Perhaps meat is the best example. Some people like rare; others like medium and a few like well-done meat. Therefore, to microwave to desired doneness means that you check the food as you have always done. You open the microwave oven door and look at the food, taste it and decide if the food is cooked to your personal preference.
Cooking with Time or Temperature:	You can microwave with time (i.e., minutes) or temperature. The temperature printed in some recipes, such as (about 140° F.), indicates the internal temperature at which food is done.
Standing Time:	Standing time can take place anywhere while a food continues to cook without the actual microwave energy turned on. Standing time can take place while food sits on the kitchen counter or in the microwave oven. If the recipe reads: let stand, covered — let the food stand with the same cover it had on while cooking.
Open Your Oven; Look at Your Food:	Involve yourself in your cooking just as you've always done. Open your oven anytime. (The microwave energy stops when the oven door is opened.) Look at your food. Stir it. Taste it. Use your own well-developed sense of when food is done.
Adapt Recipes:	Adapt conventional recipes of yours by using similar microwave recipes as a guide. (See page 8.) Adapt microwave recipes to fit your own personal taste judgment. For this cookbook, as any other, is really a guide. Experiment, it's fun. Make your new oven part of your home.
Eating in Shifts:	Microwave ovens give everyone a chance to enjoy the flavor of a freshly cooked meal. You can microwave enough for all ahead of time and let individuals help themselves. If you arrange the food on individual serving plates, remember to put the more dense foods around the outside, the more porous foods near the center.

Beginning Microwave cooking

Microwave Terms & Techniques

To Microwave: The verb microwave means to defrost, heat or cook food in a microwave oven just as you toast in a toaster or blend in a blender.

Power Levels with Variable Power Microwave Oven Control: The variable power feature gives you total flexibility in choosing your speed of cooking very similar to your conventional range infinite oven controls. You can use settings of HIGH, REHEAT, ROAST, SIMMER, DEFROST and WARM or anywhere in between these settings. Take some time to familiarize yourself with this feature.

Food Sensor: This accessory is part of your oven. See detailed description, page 9.

Microwave Food Thermometer: A microwave food thermometer does not automatically shut off the microwave oven when the internal temperature of a food reaches a given point as the food sensor does. It is similar to a conventional meat thermometer and is made of metal that can be used within a microwave oven.

Defrosting: Defrosting is thawing. For details, see pages 24-31.

Reheating: Reheating is bringing food that has already been cooked up to a hot temperature. For time guidelines, see pages 24-28. Foods reheated in the microwave oven retain their moisture and hence their freshly cooked flavor.

Cooking: Cooking changes raw food to a cooked state. It alters the appearance, consistency, flavor or texture of food.

Complementary Cooking: Using both the microwave oven and the conventional oven to prepare one recipe is complementary cooking. Use the microwave oven for speed and the conventional oven for browning.

Volume of Food: As the volume of food increases, the cooking time also increases because the concentration of microwaves in a given food decreases.

Starting Temperature: The starting temperature of food affects the cooking time. Refrigerated food takes longer to microwave than food at room temperature.

Sensitive Ingredients: Sensitive ingredients are foods that microwave very quickly and can overcook, curdle or pop. See page 7.

Root Vegetables: Vegetables vary in density. Root vegetables, like potatoes, are more dense than leafy vegetables and take longer to microwave.

Arranging Food: Place foods in a ring shape to assure more even cooking. Microwaves first cook the outer section of a food and the ring shape creates more area for microwaves to reach.

Covering Food: Food is sometimes covered in the microwave oven to speed the cooking time. Wax paper, paper towels and napkins are *loose covers* used to prevent spattering. Moisture is absorbed by the paper. Plastic wraps and glass lids are *tight covers* used for foods that are kept moist. Tight covers help food cook quickly and more evenly. If you use something other than suggested in the recipe, adjust your cooking time accordingly. Be careful when removing plastic wrap in order to prevent a steam burn.

Stirring: Stirring helps to distribute heat throughout the food. Since microwaves are more attracted to sugar, fat, oil and moisture in food, stirring is recommended to help the food cook more evenly.

Let's Begin with One Food

Let's Fix a Cup of Coffee

Coffee — 1-1½ Minutes: You're excited — you're a little bit afraid — what does it feel like to microwave your first cup of coffee? Relax. Just open your cookbook to beverages, page 38, and follow the chart. You fill a glass or pottery cup without metal trim or a styrofoam® cup with cold coffee — the coffee you made earlier this morning. You set the timer for 1 to 1½ minutes. Don't worry about getting it exact. Some of you like hot, hot coffee. Others like medium hot coffee. A few might like very warm coffee. It may boil over if you give it too much time. So use your own taste judgment and set the timer accordingly. The longer it microwaves, the hotter it gets. Then put the cup on the bottom glass shelf. (It could tip on the metal rack and anyway you should remove the rack when doing only one food.) Set the variable power control on HIGH and close the door. The light comes on when the oven starts; you hear a fan and watch the timer count down.

Cool Cooking: You hear a signal. Your coffee is hot. So is the cup — but not the handle, nor the oven cavity. That's because microwave energy only heats the food, and heat conduction, the heat of the coffee, heated the cup. Now doesn't that reheated coffee taste great?

Let's Try Some Bacon

Bacon — 1 Slice in 1 Minute: So let's try some bacon for a quick snack. It's in the meat chapter, page 97. Again, just follow the directions — or remember that 1 slice takes about 1 minute, 2 slices about 2 minutes and 6 slices about 5 to 6 minutes. The actual volume of food in the oven increases the cooking time.

Using Paper Towels, Paper or Glass Plates: If you use paper towels to absorb the grease and prevent spattering, you might want to put a paper plate underneath the bottom paper towel to keep your hands from getting greasy when the bacon is done. If you use a glass or pottery plate without metal trim or a shallow glass baking dish, also use paper towels to absorb the grease and prevent spattering. Arrange the bacon so that it doesn't overlap; otherwise it will stick together just as it does in a conventional frying pan.

Using a Microwave Roasting Rack: If you use a microwave roasting rack, put the bacon on it crosswise to get more pieces on. After microwaving, the fat is at the bottom, below the rack, and can be used later to season vegetables.

Microwave Time for Bacon Varies: Set the variable power control on HIGH and the timer according to the number of slices you have. Microwave time varies with bacon more than with any other meat because of the different amounts of fat and the different curing processes of different brands. So set the timer for the shortest amount of time first. Then use your personal taste judgment to decide whether or not you want to cook it longer. When you hear a signal, you'll see the bacon — brown, straight and crisp. It really looks beautiful. And it absolutely tastes great.

Let's Scramble Eggs

Scrambling Eggs — 2 Eggs in 2-2½ Minutes: Now let's try some eggs. Turn to the egg and cheese chapter of your cookbook, page 66, and follow the recipe for the number of eggs you want to scramble.

Starting Temperature, An Important Factor: Read the recipe a couple of times before you get the eggs out of the refrigerator. Why? The starting temperature of food is important and eggs warm up quickly sitting on your kitchen counter. If you were to scramble eggs in the microwave oven after they have been sitting out a half hour, you would find them overcooked and rubbery in the suggested cooking time.

Gentle Cooking for Fluffy Eggs: Set the variable power control on ROAST. (Eggs require more delicate cooking.) Set the timer according to the number of eggs you are scrambling.

Stirring Eggs: When you hear the signal, take the eggs out. They won't look like scrambled eggs. They're all one piece and sort of wavy. Pick up a fork to stir gently and you'll find they are wet underneath. Don't put them back in the oven just yet. First try stirring because the stirring helps to make the heat move through the eggs just as it does on the conventional range. That's what heat conduction is all about and you'll see the eggs continue to cook to desired doneness. If they don't put them back into the oven.

Let's Heat Rolls

Sweet Rolls — 2 in 10-15 Seconds: Warming breads is really simple — and such a nice touch for any meal. Sweet rolls, with the higher sugar content and the usual frosting, attract microwaves just like fat does. For instance, the jelly on a roll will be almost too hot to touch after 15 seconds.

Breads — A Porous Food: Breads are also a porous food. They're full of air and have a larger cell structure. Just break open any roll and take a look at it. It's rather airy. Porous food heats faster in a microwave oven, just as it does in a conventional oven. You never reheat or warm a roll for as long as you heat a cup of coffee.

Using Paper Towels: Place the roll on a paper towel or napkin. Otherwise, the roll will be soggy at the bottom because microwave cooking is moist cooking. Set the variable power control on REHEAT and the timer for 10 seconds. Warm, delicious —instantly.

To Microwave One Food: We have given you some extra hints to make your first day with your new microwave easy and fun. We have discussed the preparation of several foods one at a time. Now let's try doing two foods at once.

Let's Try More Than One Food

Let's Cook Bacon & Eggs

Scrambled Eggs and Bacon — 8-8½ Minutes: How about scrambled eggs and bacon for a quick breakfast — your first meal in your new microwave oven. Just turn to Early Morning Breakfast in your cookbook, page 177, and follow the directions.

Note the Diagram: Each of the menus in this section has an illustration of the microwave oven to show you how to position food inside the oven. Generally put the food that takes the longest to cook, the more dense food, on the upper rack. Put the food that takes the shorter time, the quick-cooking or porous food, on the bottom shelf. More microwave energy reaches the food on the upper rack. Foods cook more evenly if they are not placed directly over one another.

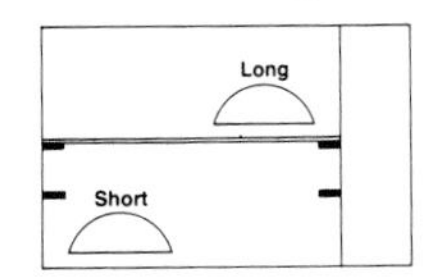

Note the Symbols: Foods in these illustrations are marked with symbols to indicate their cooking times compared to other foods in the meal: Long (L) — foods that generally go on the removable rack. Short (S) — foods that generally go on the glass bottom shelf. Extra-Short (XS) — foods added part way through cooking. Extremely-Short (XXS) — rolls, breads, pastries or frozen brownies added during last 1 or 2 minutes of cooking. Microwave Browning Grill (Mw. Grill) uses the entire bottom shelf — and other foods go on rack. Root vegetables (Root Veg.) such as dense, fresh, uncooked potatoes or carrots — always cook on rack.

Put Eggs on Bottom Shelf and Bacon on Oven Rack: To microwave the eggs and bacon together, set the timer for 8 minutes and turn the variable power control to HIGH. Foods that take longer to cook are put on the removable rack because they will receive more energy. Bacon needs more microwave energy to cook than eggs; therefore, bacon is on the rack and eggs are placed on the bottom shelf.

Use Your Personal Taste Judgment: If your bacon is microwaved to the crispness you like, take it out of the oven. If after stirring the eggs your taste judgment tells you to scramble them longer, set the timer for 30 seconds more; then stir again. What are we really talking about? Getting to know your oven. Getting involved in your cooking just as you always have. Add the seasonings you like. Microwave it. Taste it. Make your new oven part of your kitchen.

Let's Microwave Meatloaf, Baked Potatoes & Green Beans

Meatloaf, Baked Potatoes, Green Beans — 35-40 Minutes: Here's a hearty meal that you can enjoy eating any time of the year. You can feed a family of 4 to 6 in less time, using less energy and keep your kitchen cooler than if cooked conventionally.

Using the Meal-In-One Feature: Turn to the All-American Meatloaf Meal, page 189. Note the menu and the cutaway diagram in the upper left corner of the page. Use these for guidelines as you prepare your first complete meal. For further information, refer to the oven meal chapter introduction, pages 175-176.

Preparing Meatloaf: Prepare the Mother's Meatloaf recipe, page 108, combine the ingredients and put into a (9×5) glass loaf dish. If you want to try one of the other recipe variations — Mexican Meatloaf or Cheesy-Bacon Meatloaf — go ahead. Or if you have your own favorite recipe — try it — but do use 1½ pounds of ground beef. In other words, use the recipes, the seasonings that appeal to you — but try to keep the quantity of food similar as in the meal recipe; otherwise adjust cooking times accordingly.

Baking Potatoes: Let's just bake potatoes for your first meal. Remember to prick each of the 6 potatoes to allow the pressure to escape.

Put Meatloaf and 6 potatoes on Upper Rack: All of these foods go on the upper rack because they are dense foods; they take longer to cook and require more microwave energy.

Adding the Vegetable: You can leave the green beans in the pouch and put the pouch in a dish. Slit the pouch to allow steam pressure to escape. If you are using a frozen block of beans, just put the block in a dish. Either way, the results are excellent. Vegetables prepared in a microwave oven absolutely taste great.

To Microwave Frozen Vegetables: Add the package of frozen green beans to the bottom shelf and set the variable power control on HIGH and the timer for 35 minutes.

To Microwave Until Done: Use your personal judgment to check for doneness. If you used the food sensor for the meatloaf, it should register about 140°F. Remember, the meatloaf will continue to cook during the 5-minute standing time before serving. The meatloaf should be well done in the center. It will be browned but will not have a crisp crust. It will keep its shape, shrinking a little but no more than in a conventional oven. The potatoes will feel somewhat firm but will also continue to cook during the 5-minute standing time. If not completely done after 5 minutes, return the potatoes to the microwave for a couple minutes.

Use Your Own Creativity: This cookbook, as all others, is a guide. This microwave oven has a lot of flexibility built into it. In the blue chart that follows each basic menu, we have suggested some variations and given you some hints and special techniques to use. Now try your own special recipes and menu plans — those that are favorites for you and your family. For the more you involve yourself in your microwave cooking, the more you will truly enjoy the results.

Microwave Cooking Expectations

Differences in Cooking Techniques

Conventional / Microwave

TIME

Food cooks slowly. Five minutes additional time does not change the results much.

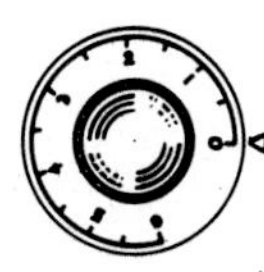

Food can overcook in five extra minutes. When the timer stops, microwave cooking stops immediately. However, food continues to cook while it stands (standing time) because of heat conduction. The food doesn't dry out because there is no heat in the oven.

COVERING

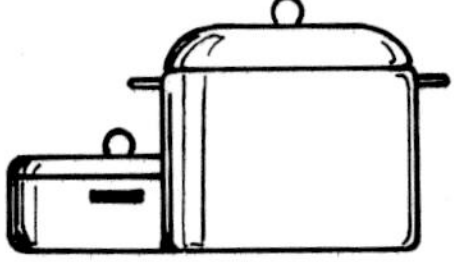

Food can be cooked or heated in covered or uncovered containers. Food can become scorched or dried out because of longer cooking times and direct heat.

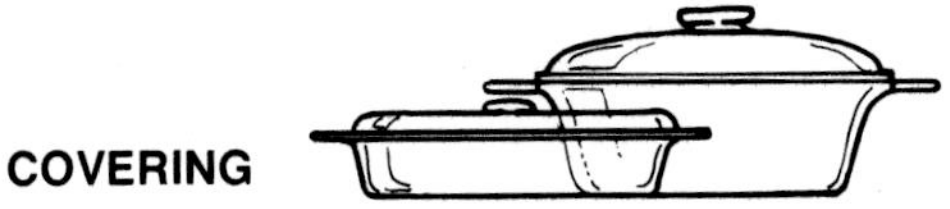

Food microwaved in a covered dish cooks more quickly because of the steam trapped inside the dish. Food microwaved in an uncovered dish takes longer to cook or reheat.

PREHEATING

Preheating is recommended in most cookbooks. Food cooking temperatures vary and you must wait to adjust the temperature when another food is cooked in the same oven.

There is no preheating. The microwave oven is ready to cook when you want to — just set the timer.

DEFROSTING

Frozen food must thaw in the refrigerator for 1 to 24 hours.

Frozen food thaws in just a few minutes. Food continues to thaw after the microwave energy is stopped. Let food stand in order for the ice crystals to melt. Very dense food could need more than one cycle of defrosting.

BROWNING

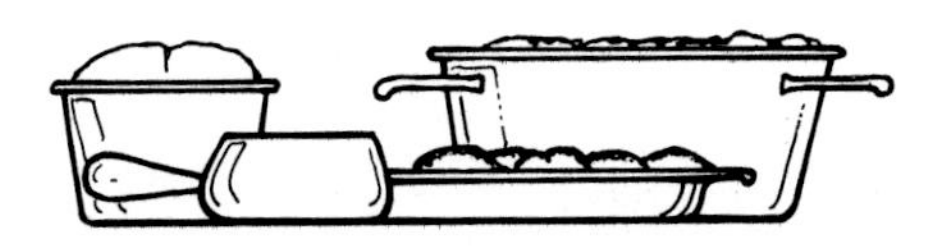

Foods brown because of the dry heat and the length of time in the oven.

Browning occurs on large meat items because the fat naturally available in the food attracts microwaves and reaches a high temperature during cooking. Generally meats cooked less than 10 minutes will not brown. A microwave browning grill is used to sear steaks and chops. Cakes and breads will not brown in the oven but can be browned in the conventional oven if desired. Use your conventional broiler for quick top browning.

Differences in Food Expectations

Conventional		*Microwave*
	APPETIZERS	
Heated dips tend to scorch. Particular care must be given when heating small amounts.		Fondues and heated dips are smooth. Reheating is fast and convenient. Do not assemble canapés until ready to microwave or crackers and toast will be soggy because of lack of dry heat.
	BREADS	
Breads are browned with nicely formed crusts.		Breads do not brown nor form a crisp crust. They look moist. Bread will rise with care in an hour in a microwave oven.
	CAKES	
Cakes are golden brown with a slightly rounded crust.		Cakes are lighter, higher and more tender because there is no crust to restrict them. Tops of cakes will be moist looking. This moisture evaporates during standing time. Cake tops will be flat and do not brown. You cannot bake angel food or chiffon cakes in a microwave oven.
	COOKIES AND CANDIES	
Cookies bake beautifully. Candies can easily scorch.		Cookies spread thin. It is not very convenient to microwave big batches of cookies. Bar cookies that are soft and need no browning microwave well. Candies are beautiful and microwave quickly. They must be watched closely because the high sugar content of these foods attract microwaves and reach desired temperature quickly.

Conventional		*Microwave*
	EGGS AND CHEESE	
Eggs can scorch and are not as fluffy.		Scrambled eggs are wet in the center at the end of the cooking time. Stir to distribute the heat before standing time and they will finish cooking. The high fat content of the yolk will cook faster than the white and tend to pop. Microwave at lower setting when cooking as one food. Do not microwave eggs in the shell or reheat hard-cooked eggs.
Cheese can scorch and must be watched carefully.		Cheese melts beautifully at lower setting. Stir to combine. Process cheese gives better results.
	FISH AND SEAFOOD	
Fish is poached in liquid as it tends to dry out. It is fragile to handle.		Fish and seafood are excellent. They are tender and more moist because of lack of dry heat. Poaching and steaming produce superior results; however crumb coatings do not crisp.
	FRUITS AND VEGETABLES	
Fruits and vegetables can be easily overcooked. They either dry out or become soggy.		Fruits are tender and juicy. Vegetables are tender-crisp. Microwaves cook by using natural moisture in fruits and vegetables. Very little additional water is needed. Steam conducts heat for even cooking with no scorching.
	LEFTOVERS	
Leftovers have a warmed-over taste.		Leftovers taste freshly cooked because of the moist microwave cooking.

Conventional		Microwave
These foods take longer and therefore tend to dry out.	**MAIN DISHES** 	These foods cook quickly with good results. They do not dry out. Use less liquid as no evaporation occurs. Covering traps the steam and speeds the cooking time.
Stew simmers slowly.	**MAIN-DISHES: STEW**	Stew microwaves in minimum time. Use prime quality meat for more tender results. Use less liquid as no evaporation occurs. Cut meat and vegetables into even pieces to insure even cooking.
Roast is excellent but it takes a long time.	**MEATS: ROAST** 	Roast microwaves quickly and easily. It will brown but it will not be as crisp.
Steaks and chops are beautifully browned.	**MEATS: STEAK**	Steaks and chops will not sear without microwave browning grill. The results will be excellent.
Foods such as meatloaf and ham take longer to cook in the conventional oven.	**MEATS: OTHER MEATS**	Meatloaf and ham microwave well. Meatloaf does not become crisp. Watch cured meats, as they tend to overcook in spots containing sugar and salt. Sauces should be added toward the end of cooking.
Pasta and rice require slightly longer hydration time. They tend to stick to the pan if reheated.	**PASTA AND RICE** 	Hydration takes time; thus little time is saved. Pasta and rice reheat beautifully. There is no drying out.

Conventional		Microwave
Pastry crusts are golden brown.	**PIES** 	Pastry crusts are tender and flaky but do not brown. To prevent sogginess, cook crust first before adding high moisture filling like pumpkin. Complementary cooking gives excellent results for double-crust pies. Use the microwave oven for speed; the conventional oven to brown the crust.
Poultry is good with a crisp skin.	**POULTRY** 	Poultry is tender and moist. The skin is golden brown rather than crispy brown. The skin is soft except for more fatty birds, such as duckling. Small poultry microwaves better than larger birds.
Sandwiches and rolls often taste better warmed, but by turning on the conventional oven, you heat the entire kitchen.	**SANDWICHES AND ROLLS** 	These foods heat quickly. Set on a napkin to absorb moisture and prevent sogginess. Do not overheat as bread toughens.
Sauces must be watched constantly.	**SAUCES** 	Sauces are excellent. They do not scorch and you need not stir constantly. Thickening must be well blended as it tends to settle in bottom of dish.

Utensil Chart

Check this chart for the dishes which can or cannot be used in a microwave oven. If in doubt about using any glass, pottery or china utensil without metal trim, place it in the oven on HIGH for 15 to 20 seconds. If the container feels warm when taken from the oven, do not cook or heat in it.

CONTAINER	RECOMMENDED USES
Glass and China	
Baby bottles	Warm formula; lid and nipple may be left in place.
Bone or other fine china	Not recommended.
Centura®·dinnerware	Not recommended. Dishes absorb microwaves; become too hot to handle, and may eventually crack or break.
Clay pot, covered	Presoak in water, as for conventional cooking. Use for braising meats and poultry.
Corelle® Livingware dinnerware	Heat cooked food, beverages, soup. Closed-handle cups should not be used; microwaves may melt adhesives.
Corning® glass ceramic cooking dishes, with glass covers	Cook vegetables, meats, main dishes, desserts. Utensils may also be used for conventional cooking.
Earthenware (ironstone) dinnerware without metal trim*	Heat cooked food and beverages. Dish thickness does not affect microwave penetration. If dish is refrigerated, food takes longer to heat because heavy cold dish absorbs heat from food.
Glass or china dinnerware without metal trim*	Heat cooked food and beverages, usually without affecting dishes. Some paints or glazes used on glass dishes do contain metallic substances and should not be used in a microwave oven. See test in chart introduction.
Lead crystal	Not recommended; metal in this fine glass may cause breakage.
Micro-Browner® grills	Sear, grill and fry small meat items. Special coating on bottom of dishes allow them to absorb microwaves and preheat to high temperatures.
Pottery dishes without metal trim*	Heat cooked food, beverages and soups. Unglazed pottery may absorb moisture and heat up. See test in chart introduction.
Ovenproof Pyrex® and all other ovenproof glass cooking dishes and fitted covers, mixing bowls and measures — without metal trim.*	Cook vegetables, meats, sauces, desserts, main dishes.
Metal	
Foil pie plate	Not recommended if pans are more than ¾ inch deep. Transfer food to glass pie plate.
Foil, sheet	Not recommended in quantity. Foil reflects microwaves and may cause arcing that pits oven interior. Small pieces may be used to cover portions of whole poultry or roasts which appear to be cooking too quickly.
Metal spoons (not silver or gold-colored alloy)	May be left in 1 cup (or more) of sauce or pudding for short cooking periods without causing arcing.
Microwave food thermometer	Use in the microwave oven during cooking to measure temperature of food.
Microwave food sensor	Use in the microwave oven during cooking to measure internal temperature of food.
Pewter or silver dishes	Not recommended; they will tarnish.
Pots and pans	Not recommended. No time saved — metal reflects microwaves so food can only cook from top surface.
Skewers and poultry clamps	Safe in the oven when used with large quantities of food. Do not allow to touch sides of oven or arcing may result.
TV dinner foil trays, up to ¾ inch deep	Heat commercial or homemade frozen dinners. Food depth is shallow enough to heat through from the top.
Twisters for cooking bags	Not recommended; will cause arcing and melt plastic bag or create fire if associated with paper.

CONTAINER	RECOMMENDED USES
Paper	
Fast food cartons with metal handles	Not recommended; handles may cause arcing.
Foil-lined or foil-wrapped containers	Some frozen juice cans are wrapped with foil coated paper; some paper cartons, such as those for egg substitutes, are foil lined. Not recommended; foil reflects microwaves and inhibits heating.
Frozen juice containers	Defrost juice in plain paper containers. Remove one metal end; the other may be left in place during thawing in the oven.
Milk cartons, ½ and 1 pint	Heat milk in opened cartons for short periods of time. Prolonged heating melts carton coating.
Napkins	Heat sandwiches, rolls, doughnuts; absorb excess moisture.
Plates and cups	Heat cooked food and beverages for short periods of time; absorb moisture.
Wax paper	Use to cover cooking dishes and wrap corn on the cob during cooking. Will not adhere to hot food, although hot food may cause wax to partially melt and adhere to dish. Wax is not harmful if eaten.
Towel	Use when heating breads to absorb moisture. Not recommended when cooking more than 4 slices of bacon as some towels are made of recycled materials and may contain metal particles which can cause fire when soaked with fat.
Plastic	
Baby bottles	Warm formula; lid and nipple may be left in place.
Boilable bags	Use when freezing food, then reheating in bag. Slit bag; remove twister.
Cooking pouches	Cook vegetables, rice, meats and other frozen foods. Slit pouch so steam escapes, however, seal on bag is made to withstand low pressure so will not explode if bag is accidently not slit.
Foam cups and dishes	Heat beverages and precooked foods for short periods. Long heating makes food hot and it melts plastic foam.
Melamine dishes	Not recommended. Dishes become hot, often too hot to handle. Food takes longer to cook.
Microwave roasting rack	Roast meat, poultry; heat sandwiches. Holds food above cooking dish moisture and drippings.
Oven film and cooking bags	Film without foil edges is suitable for roasts and stews. Bag, itself, will not cause tenderizing. Use a rubber band in place of metal twister to prevent arcing.
Plastic wrap	Use to cover cooking dishes when a tight covering is needed and a dish has no fitted glass cover. Always puncture wrap and allow steam to escape before removing wrap from a dish of hot food.
Soft plastic, such as dessert topping containers	Use only dishwasherproof containers for storage, then reheating, cooked food. These containers withstand most lower temperatures reached in heating.
Spatulas and spoons	May be left in 1 cup (or more) of food during short-time cooking. Wood handles may become hot.
Tupperware®	Not recommended; it distorts easily.
Straw and Wood	
Baskets, straw or wooden	Use only for short-time heating of breads and rolls.
Cutting boards and bowls, wood	Not recommended. Microwaves cause natural moisture in wood to evaporate, causing drying and cracking.
Spoons, wood	Leave in puddings and sauces when stirring is needed during short cooking. Material can withstand microwaves for a short time.

*Dishes with gold, silver, platinum or other metal trim, including signatures on dish bottoms, should not be used during microwave cooking or they may break.

Daily Heating How-To

These 19 items are heated most often in a microwave oven. See the How to Microwave Precooked Homemade and Commercial Convenience Foods on the following pages for a complete listing. Use the blank space at the bottom of this chart to fill in other items *you* use often.

PRODUCT & SIZE	CONTAINER	SETTING & TIME
Baby Bottle, 1 bottle (8 oz.)	Baby bottle	REHEAT (about 100° F.) 1½ to 2 min.
Baby Food, 1 jar (4 oz.)	Original jar, remove lid	REHEAT 20 to 30 sec.
Bacon, 4 slices	Between paper towels	HIGH 4 to 4½ min.
Buns and Rolls, 2 at room temp.	Paper plate, paper towel or napkin	REHEAT 10 to 15 sec.
Butter, Melt, ½ cup, refrig.	2-cup glass measure	ROAST about 1½ min.
Soften, ½ cup refrig.	Glass or pottery plate (without metal trim)	WARM 1½ to 2 min.
CHICKEN, 9 pcs. fried, room temp.	Original fast food paper box	REHEAT (about 150° F.) 6 to 7 min.
Chocolate, Melt 1-oz. square	1-cup glass measure	HIGH about 2 min.
Coffee, 1 cup reheat	Glass or pottery cup (without metal trim)	HIGH (about 160° F.) 1 to 1½ min.
Eggs, 2 scrambled with 3 tbsps. milk, 2 tsps. butter	Glass or pottery serving bowl (without metal trim)	ROAST 2 to 2½ min.
Hamburger, 1 lb., thaw	Original plastic wrap	DEFROST 8 to 10 min.
Hamburgers or **Sandwiches,** 2 reheated from room temp.	Paper towel or napkin	REHEAT (about 140° F.) 30 to 45 sec.
Hot Dogs, 2, refrig.	Wrap each loosely in paper towel or napkin	REHEAT (about 120° F.) 1 to 1½ min.
Potatoes, 4 baked, pierce skin	—	HIGH 10 to 12 min.
Rice, 1 cup cooked, refrig.	Covered glass casserole	REHEAT 1½ to 2 min.
Sauce, 1 cup sweet or savory without sensitive ingredients, refrig.	Wax-paper-covered glass casserole or 2-cup glass measure	REHEAT (about 150° F.) 3½ to 4 min.
Soup, 2 bowls	Glass or pottery serving bowls (without metal trim)	REHEAT (about 160° F.) 7 to 8 min.
Spaghetti, 1 can (16 oz.), reheat	1-qt. covered glass casserole	REHEAT (about 150° F.) 3 to 4 min.
T.V. Dinner, 2 trays (10 to 11 oz. ea.), frozen	Original ¾ in. foil tray, uncovered, in paper carton	REHEAT 14 to 16 min.
Vegetables, 1 can (16 oz.), undrained	1-qt. covered glass casserole	REHEAT (about 150° F.) 3 to 4 min.

Add items you use daily, below:

Pictured from the top: Wheat Germ Bread, page 43; Biscuit Mix Coffee Cake, chart, page 42.

Convenience Food How-To

Heat, Defrost, Melt or Cook

• Generic names of products are general terms not protected by trademarks. Look for your favorite packaged foods under their common names.

• Precooked foods without sensitive ingredients heat on REHEAT.

• Precooked foods with sensitive ingredients, such as mushrooms, cheese, sour cream or eggs heat on ROAST.

• Large volumes and/or dense precooked foods thaw on DEFROST until icy in the center, then heat as specified above.

• Use glass baking dishes, glass casseroles, glass measures, paper plates, paper towels, paper napkins, glass or pottery serving bowls, or plates without silver or other metal trim. Cover with glass lids or wax paper.

• Most frozen foods can be heated in aluminum foil or plastic trays. Foil trays must be no more than ¾ inch deep.

PRODUCT & SIZE	CONTAINER	SETTING & TIME	SPECIAL TECHNIQUES
APPETIZERS			
Avocado Dip, 6-oz., frozen	Glass or pottery bowl (without metal trim); cover	DEFROST 2 to 3 min.	Stir occasionally. Stand, covered, 5 min.
Egg rolls, 6-oz., frozen	9-inch glass pie plate	ROAST (about 150° F.) 2½ to 3 min.	Stand 1 min.
Fondue, Swiss, 10-oz., frozen	2-qt. (8 x 8) glass baking dish	ROAST (about 150° F.) 5 to 6 min.	Slit plastic pouch. Stir once before serving.
BABY FOOD			
Baby Food, 1 jar (4 oz.), room temp.	Original jar, remove lid	ROAST 25 to 35 sec.	—
1 jar (7 to 8 oz.), room temp.		55 to 65 sec.	—
Milk,	Baby bottle	REHEAT (about 100° F.)	
4-oz.		1 to 1½ min.	—
8-oz.		1½ to 2 min.	—
BEVERAGES			
Coffee or Cocoa, made with water or milk,	Glass or pottery cups (without metal trim)	HIGH (about 160° F.)	Times are for reheating beverages.
1, (8 oz.)		1½ to 2 min.	
2, (8 oz. ea.)		2½ to 3 min.	
4, (8 oz. ea.)		6 to 7 min.	
6, (8 oz. ea.)		7 to 8 min.	
Frozen Juice Concentrate,	Original container; remove lid	DEFROST	Stand 2 to 3 min.
6-oz.		2 to 2½ min.	
12-oz.		5 to 6 min.	
Milk or Chocolate Milk,	Opened wax cartons	HIGH (about 160° F.)	
1, (½ pt.)		1½ to 2 min.	—
2, (½ pt. ea.)		2½ to 3 min.	—
4, (½ pt. ea.)		5½ to 6 min.	—
1 qt.	Glass pitcher	8 to 9 min.	—
Water or Milk, to make tea, instant beverages and breakfasts	Glass or pottery cups (without metal trim)	HIGH (about 160° F.)	Instant coffee or tea will fizz when stirred into hot liquid.
1, (8 oz.)		1½ to 2 min.	
2, (8 oz. ea.)		3 to 3½ min.	
4, (8 oz. ea.)		7 to 8 min.	
6, (8 oz. ea.)		9 to 10 min.	
BREADS			
Bread, frozen, 1 slice	Paper towel or napkin or original plastic bag	DEFROST 15 to 20 sec.	Remove plastic wire twister from bag.
1 loaf (1 lb.)		1½ to 3 min.	Stand 3 min.
Buns and Rolls, hamburger, hot dog, dinner, bagel	Paper plate, towel or napkin	REHEAT	Add about 15 sec. if frozen.
1, room temp.		5 to 10 sec.	
2, room temp.		10 to 15 sec.	
4, room temp.		15 to 20 sec.	
6, room temp.		20 to 25 sec.	
Doughnuts (Cake or Raised), Sweet Rolls, Coffee Cake, Muffins,	Paper plate, towel or napkin	REHEAT	Add about 5 sec. if frozen.
1, room temp.		10 to 15 sec.	
2, room temp.		20 to 25 sec.	
4, room temp.		35 to 40 sec.	
6, room temp.		45 to 50 sec.	
Whole coffee cake, room temp.		REHEAT (about 100° F.) ½ to 1 min.	
Whole coffee cake, frozen		1½ to 2 min.	
French Bread, 1 lb.	Paper plate, towel or napkin	REHEAT (about 100° F.)	
Room temp.		20 to 30 sec.	—
Frozen		1½ to 2 min.	—
Pancakes, French Toast, Waffles, English Muffins, Popovers,	Paper plate, towel or napkin	REHEAT (about 100° F.)	Add 20 to 35 sec. if frozen.
1, room temp.		10 to 20 sec.	
2, room temp.		15 to 25 sec.	
4, room temp.		25 to 35 sec.	
Pancake Batter, 7-oz., frozen	Original wax carton; open	DEFROST 3 to 4 min.	Shake, let stand 10 min.
16-oz., frozen		6 to 6½ min.	
Quick Bread Mixes			See chart, page 42.
Yeast Bread			See chart, page 42.
BUTTER			
Melting,		ROAST	
2 tbsps. to ¼ cup, refrig.	1-cup glass measure	about 1 min.	
⅓ cup to ½ cup, refrig.		about 1½ min.	
½ cup, frozen		about 3 min.	
1 cup, refrig.	2-cup glass measure	about 2½ min.	
Softening, for table use,	Glass plate (without metal trim)	WARM	
½ cup, refrig. or frozen		1½ to 2 min.	
1 cup, refrig.		1½ to 2 min.	
1 cup, frozen		2 to 2½ min.	
CAKES			
Cake, frozen, 12 to 17-oz.	Paper plate, towel or napkin	DEFROST 2 to 3 min.	Remove from paper carton to thaw; stand 5 min.
13 x 9-inch		3 to 4 min.	

PRODUCT & SIZE	CONTAINER	SETTING & TIME	SPECIAL TECHNIQUES
CANDY			
Caramel Apples, with caramel sheets,	On sheet of paper in package	ROAST	
1		20 to 30 sec.	—
4		45 to 55 sec.	—
Melting Caramel Bar, 28-oz. ½ bar	1½-quart covered glass casserole	4 to 5 min.	Add water as pkg.directs. Stir.
CEREAL, QUICK-COOKING			See chart, page 120.
CHEESE			
Cheese spread, soften, 8-oz., refrig.	Glass container; remove lid	WARM (about 80° F.) 4 to 4½ min.	—
Cream cheese, soften, 3-oz., refrig.	Remove from original foil package; place on glass or pottery plate (without metal trim)	(about 80° F.) WARM 2 to 2½ min.	—
3-oz., frozen		DEFROST 2 to 2½ min.	—
8-oz., refrig.		WARM 4 to 4½ min.	—
8-oz., frozen		DEFROST 3 to 4 min.	—
CHOCOLATE, MELTED			
Chips, 6-oz. pkg.	2-cup glass measure	HIGH 2 to 2½ min.	Stir to blend
12-oz. pkg.	4-cup glass measure	2½ to 3 min.	Stir to blend
Squares, 1 or 2 (1 oz. ea.)	1-cup glass measure	HIGH about 2 min.	
COOKIES AND BARS			
Bar Mixes			See chart, page 54.
Brownies and Other Bars, frosted, (12 to 13 oz.), frozen.	Original ¾-in. foil tray; remove lid	DEFROST (about 100° F.) 2 to 3 min.	Stand 5 min.
Cookies, frozen,	Paper plate, towel or napkin	DEFROST (about 100° F.)	
2		30 to 35 sec.	
6		50 to 55 sec.	—
12		1½ to 2 min.	—
DESSERTS			
Custard Mix			See chart, page 61.
Dessert Cups, 3½-oz., frozen, 2 containers	Original plastic cup; remove lid	DEFROST 1½ to 2 min.	—
Puddings, 2 cups (3-oz. ea.), frozen	Original plastic cup; remove lid	DEFROST 4 to 5 min.	Stir to blend, stand 2 min.
17½-oz., frozen		7 to 9 min.	
Dry Mixes			See chart, page 61.
EGGS			
Egg Substitute, 8-oz., frozen	Opened wax carton	DEFROST 4 to 4½ min.	Stand 3 min.; shake well.
10 to 11-oz		7 to 8 min.	Cook as scrambled eggs, chart, page 66.
Omelette, 10-oz., frozen	Glass plate; cover.	ROAST 4 to 5 min.	
TV Breakfasts			See Meals.

PRODUCT & SIZE	CONTAINER	SETTING & TIME	SPECIAL TECHNIQUES
FAST FOODS			See Main Dishes, Meats, Poultry or Sandwiches.
FISH			
Fish Patties, (round) or Fillets (square), breaded, frozen	Glass or pottery serving plate (without metal trim)	REHEAT (about 120° F.)	
1		1 to 2 min.	Stand 2 min.
2		3 to 4 min.	Stand 2 min.
6		5 to 6 min.	Stand 3 min.
Fish Sticks, breaded, frozen	Glass or pottery serving plate (without metal trim)	REHEAT (about 120° F.)	Arrange "spoke-fashion" on round plate.
4		2 to 3 min.	Stand 3 min.
8		3½ to 4½ min.	
12		4½ to 5½ min.	
Seafood			See Seafood.
FRUITS			
Frozen Juice Concentrate			See Beverages.
Fruits, frozen	Original paper container: Remove top or lid. Plastic pouch: Slit and place in glass dish. Plastic bag: Remove fruit and place in glass casserole, cover.	DEFROST	Fruit will remain icy in center; stir to loosen fruit.
10-oz.		3 to 5 min.	
16-oz.		7 to 9 min.	
GRAVY			See Sauces.
ICE CREAM			
Soften, ½ gal.	Original carton, opened	WARM 1½ to 2 min.	—
LEFTOVERS			See Main Dishes, Meals, Meats or Sandwiches.
MAIN DISHES			
Baked Beans			See Vegetables.
Chili with Beans, canned	1-qt. covered casserole	ROAST (about 150° F.)	
15-oz.		5 to 6 min.	Stand, covered, 3 min.
40-oz.		10 to 12 min.	
Chow Mein, 42-oz. beef, canned	2-qt. covered glass casserole	REHEAT (about 150° F.) 8 to 10 min.	Combine both cans and heat.
24-oz. chicken, canned		7 to 8 min.	Stand, covered, 3 min.
32-oz. chicken, frozen	2-qt. (12 x 7) glass baking dish covered with wax paper	25 to 27 min.	Remove from foil tray if deeper than ¾-in. Stand 3 min.
Corned Beef Hash, 15-oz., canned	1-qt. casserole	REHEAT (about 150° F.) 5 to 6 min.	Stand 3 min.
Creamed Chicken, 2 pkgs. (6½ oz. ea.), frozen	2-qt. (12 x 7) glass baking dish	REHEAT (about 150° F.) 6 to 7 min.	Slit plastic pouch. Heat; stand 3 min.
Enchiladas, 18-oz., canned	3-qt. (13 x 9) glass baking dish, covered	REHEAT (about 150° F.) 6 to 8 min.	Let stand, covered, 3 min.
12-oz., frozen	2-qt. (8 x 8) glass baking dish	ROAST (about 150° F.) 8 to 10 min.	Slit pouch or remove from aluminum tray. Let stand 3 min.
22-oz., frozen		18 to 20 min.	
Fish Sticks			See Fish.
Hamburgers			See Sandwiches.

(Continued, next page.)

PRODUCT & SIZE	CONTAINER	SETTING & TIME	SPECIAL TECHNIQUES
Hamburger Main Dish Mixes, *	2½-qt. covered glass casserole		Brown hamburger for HIGH time. Add dry mix envelopes and bring to a boil on HIGH, then SIMMER. Let stand, covered, 5 min. before serving.
Potato (7 oz.), 1 lb. hamburger		HIGH about 5 min.	
mix		HIGH 5 min. SIMMER 15 to 22 min.	
Macaroni or Noodle, (7 to 8 oz.), 1 lb. hamburger		HIGH about 5 min.	
mix		HIGH 5 min. SIMMER 10 to 14 min.	
Rice (7 oz.) 1 lb. hamburger		HIGH about 5 min.	
mix		HIGH about 5 min.	
Lasagna,	Remove from foil tray to 2-qt. (12 x 7) glass baking dish, covered	ROAST (about 150° F.)	Stand, covered, 5 min.
21-oz.,frozen		18 to 20 min.	
50-oz., frozen		28 to 30 min.	
Macaroni and Cheese, 14 to 15-oz., canned	1-qt. covered glass casserole	REHEAT (about 150° F.) 3 to 4 min.	Stand, covered, 3 min.
7¼-oz., dry mix, * 2 cups water	2-qt. covered glass casserole	HIGH (about 200°F.) 4 to 5 min.	Stir mix into boiling water. Stand, covered, 3 min.
mix		SIMMER 10 to 12 min.	
8-oz., frozen	2-qt. (8 x 8) glass baking dish	ROAST (about 150° F.) 5½ to 6½ min.	Slit plastic pouch
Main Dishes, Homemade or Commercial, Meat and vegetables in sauce, canned	1½-qt. covered glass casserole	REHEAT (about 150° F.)	Stand, covered, 3 min.
15 to 16-oz.		5 to 7 min.	
31 to 42-oz.		9 to 10 min.	
Precooked, frozen, *	Covered glass casserole or glass baking dish	(about 150° F.)	
2 cups		DEFROST 3 min. REHEAT 5 to 6 min.	Stand, covered, 3 min.
1-qt.		DEFROST 8 min. REHEAT 18 to 20 min.	Stir during REHEAT time. Stand 5 min.
2-qt.		DEFROST 12 min. REHEAT 20 to 22 min.	
Precooked, refrig.	Covered glass casserole	REHEAT (about 150° F.)	
2 cups		4 to 5 min.	Stand, covered, 3 min.
1-qt.		10 to 12 min.	Stand, covered, 5 min.
2-qt.		14 to 16 min.	Stand, covered, 5 min.
Meat Pies, 8-oz., frozen	Ovenproof glass or pottery plate (without metal trim)	HIGH	Brown in preheated 425° F. oven after thawing in microwave.
2 pies		7 to 8 min.	
4 pies		8 to 9 min.	

The " * " at the end of a recipe title reminds you that there are two or more power settings during cooking.

PRODUCT & SIZE	CONTAINER	SETTING & TIME	SPECIAL TECHNIQUES
Meatballs			See Meats.
Pizza, reheat, 1 to 2 pcs., refrig.	Paper plate, paper towel or napkin	ROAST (about 140° F.) 1 to 1½ min.	—
1 medium, 12-in., room temp.	Paper board	3½ to 4 min.	—
Plates of Food			See Meals.
Pork and Beans			See Vegetables.
Rice and Macaroni Main Dish Mix, water and rice mix	2-qt. covered glass casserole	HIGH 4 to 5 min. SIMMER 13 to 15 min.	Combine rice mix and water; boil on HIGH, then SIMMER. Stand, covered, 3 min.
Salisbury Steak			See Meats.
Shrimp Newburg			See Seafood.
Spaghetti, 14 to 15-oz., canned	1-qt. covered glass casserole	REHEAT (about 150° F.) 3 to 4 min.	Stand, covered, 3 min.
26-oz., canned	1½-qt. covered glass casserole	8 to 10 min.	
8-oz. dry mix, * 4 cups water	3-qt. covered glass casserole	HIGH (about 200° F.) 7 to 8 min.	
add spaghetti		SIMMER 10 to 12 min.	
sauce	1-qt. covered glass casserole	SIMMER 5 to 6 min.	
8-oz., frozen	2-qt. (8 x 8) glass baking dish	REHEAT (about 150° F.) 4 to 5 min.	Slit pouch.
Spaghetti Sauce, 15½-oz., canned	1-qt. covered glass casserole	REHEAT (about 150° F.) 6 to 7 min.	Stir once. Stand, covered, 3 min.
32-oz., canned	1½-qt. covered glass casserole	8 to 10 min.	Stir during heating.
1½-oz., dry mix *	1½-qt. covered glass casserole	HIGH 4 min. SIMMER 5 to 8 min.	Prepare as pkg. directs; cook. Stand, covered, 3 min.
Stews			See Stews.
Stuffed Cabbage Roll, 14-oz., frozen	1-qt. covered glass casserole	REHEAT (about 150° F.) 12 to 13 min.	Stand, covered, 3 min.
Tuna Main Dish Mixes, * Macaroni, noodle (7 to 9 oz.) or Rice (8 to 9 oz.)	2½-qt. covered glass casserole	HIGH 5 min. SIMMER 12 to 18 min.	Combine tuna, liquid and mixes; boil on HIGH, then SIMMER. Stand, covered, 5 min.
Turkey Slices and Giblet Gravy, 32-oz., frozen	2-qt. (12 x 7) glass baking dish; cover with wax paper	REHEAT (about 150° F.) 25 to 27 min.	Remove from foil tray higher than ¾-in. Stand, covered, 3 min.
T.V. Dinners			See Meals.
Welsh Rarebit, 10-oz., frozen	1½-quart covered glass casserole	ROAST (about 150° F.) 6 to 7 min.	Stir during cooking. Let stand 3 min.
MARSHMALLOWS			
1 bag (10 oz.), freshen	Plastic bag, opened	WARM 4 to 5 min.	Softens dry marshmallows.
MEALS			
Casserole Dishes, leftovers			See Main Dishes, precooked, refrig.

PRODUCT & SIZE	CONTAINER	SETTING & TIME	SPECIAL TECHNIQUES
Plates of Food, reheated 1, refrig. 1, room temp. 2, refrig. 2, room temp.	Glass or pottery plates (without metal trim); cover with wax paper	REHEAT (about 150° F.) 4 to 5 min. 3 to 4 min. 7 to 10 min. 5 to 8 min.	Place 1 plate on upper rack of oven and 1 on bottom shelf. Plate on upper rack of oven will be hot in 5 to 7 min. Continue heating plate on bottom shelf for 1 to 2 min. Let stand, covered, 3 min.
T.V. Dinners, frozen			
Diet Meals and Meat with 2 to 3 Other Foods 1 (8 to 11 oz.) tray 2 (8 to 11 oz. ea.) trays 1 (15 to 16 oz.) tray 2 (15 to 16 oz. ea.) trays	Foil tray, uncovered, in carton or covered with wax paper	REHEAT (about 150° F.) 8 to 10 min. 14 to 16 min. 10 to 12 min. 18 to 20 min.	Foil tray should be no more than ¾-in. deep. Remove foil covers. Remove rolls or bread; return to tray during last 20 sec. of cooking. Stand, covered, 3 min.
Meat Entrees with Sensitive Ingred. 2 trays (10 to 11 oz. ea.)		ROAST (about 150° F.) 12 to 14 min.	
Scrambled Eggs and Sausage, 1 tray, (6¼ oz.)		ROAST (about 150° F.) 5 to 7 min.	
MEATS			
Chicken			See Poultry.
Corn Dogs, frozen 2 4	2-qt. (8 x 8) glass baking dish, cover with wax paper	ROAST (about 140° F.) 2 to 2½ min. 3 to 4 min.	 — —
Cube Steaks, cooked and frozen 1 2	Glass or pottery plate without metal trim; cover with wax paper	REHEAT (about 150° F.) 3 to 3½ min. 4 to 5 min.	Separate steaks during reheating.
Diced Cooked Meat, frozen 1 cup 2 cups	Paper or glass plate (without metal trim); cover	DEFROST 2½ to 3 min. 4 to 5 min.	Use in casseroles, cream sauces.
Hamburger Patties, cooked and frozen 1 2 6 With Bun	Glass or pottery plate (without metal trim); cover with wax paper	REHEAT (about 150° F.) 1 to 1½ min. 1½ to 2½ min. 5 to 6 min.	 — — — See Sandwiches.
Luncheon Meat, 12-oz., canned	Glass plate (without metal trim)	REHEAT (about 120° F.) 10 to 12 min.	—
Meatballs, 6-oz., frozen	2-qt. (8 x 8) glass baking dish, cover with wax paper	ROAST (about 150° F.) 4 to 5 min.	Stand, covered, 3 min.
Salisbury Steak, 32-oz., frozen	2-qt. (12 x 7) glass baking dish; cover with wax paper	REHEAT (about 150°F.) 14 to 18 min.	Separate steaks after 10 min. of cooking. Stand, covered, 3 min.
Sausage, Pork, precooked links or patties (8-oz.) frozen refrig.	Glass pie plate; cover with wax paper	REHEAT (about 120° F.) 3 to 4 min. 1 to 2 min.	 — —

PRODUCT & SIZE	CONTAINER	SETTING & TIME	SPECIAL TECHNIQUES
Sliced Cooked Meat, frozen 1 slice 4 slices 8 slices	Glass or pottery plate (without metal trim); cover with wax paper	REHEAT 2 to 4 min. 6 to 8 min. 8 to 10 min.	Stand, covered, 2 min.
PASTA			See How To Cook Chart, page 118.
Frozen Egg Noodles, ✻ (10 oz.), plus 6 cups water	3-qt. covered glass casserole	HIGH 7 to 8 min. SIMMER 18 to 20 min.	Prepare according to package directions.
PIES AND TARTS			
Custard Pie, 1 crust 9-in. pie	9-in. glass pie plate	ROAST 4½ to 5½ min.	—
1 pc. pie 2 pcs. pie	Glass plate (without metal trim)	40 to 45 sec. 50 to 55 sec.	— —
Fruit Pie, 2 crust 9-in. pie (33 oz.), uncooked and frozen	9-in. glass pie plate	HIGH 13 to 14 min.	Defrost in microwave; transfer to preheated 425°F. conventional oven. Bake 8 to 10 min. to brown.
9-in. pie, refrig.		REHEAT 4 to 4½ min.	
1 pc. pie, refrig. 2 pcs. pie, refrig.	Glass plate (without metal trim)	35 to 40 sec. 65 to 70 sec.	
Pastry Shell, 9-in., frozen	9-in. glass pie plate	ROAST 5 to 6 min.	Prick bottom and sides of shell.
POULTRY			
Breaded Chicken, precooked 1 pc., refrig. 4 pcs., refrig.		REHEAT (about 150° F.) 1 to 1½ min. 2 to 2½ min.	 — —
2½ to 3 lbs. or 32-oz., frozen	2-qt. (12 x 7) glass baking dish	10 to 12 min.	Stand 3 min.
9-pc. box (fast food), room temp.	Original paper carton	6 to 7 min.	
Turkey Roast, 2-lb., frozen	(9 x 5) glass loaf dish, cover	ROAST (about 175° F.) 38 to 42 min.	Turn over once halfway through cooking. Stand, covered, 5 min.
PUDDING			
Dry Mixes			See chart, page 61.
Frozen			See Desserts.
RICE			
Cooked, 1 cup, refrig. 2 cups, refrig. 2 cups, frozen	Covered glass casserole	REHEAT (about 150° F.) 1½ to 2 min. 3 to 4 min. 6 to 7 min.	Stand, covered, 2 min.
11-oz. pouch, white and vegetables, or white and wild, frozen	2-qt. (8 x 8) glass baking dish	6 to 7 min.	Slit plastic pouch. Stand 2 min.

(Continued, next page.)

PRODUCT & SIZE	CONTAINER	SETTING & TIME	SPECIAL TECHNIQUES
SANDWICHES			
Fast Food Hamburgers with French Fries, 4 orders	Original paper containers	ROAST 2½ to 3 min.	Place all items on bottom shelf.
Meat Sandwich — Hamburger (including fast food)	Wrap sandwiches in paper towel or napkin	REHEAT (about 140° F.)	Use ROAST setting if sensitive ingredients included. Increase time a few seconds.
1, room temp.		25 to 30 sec.	
1, refrig.		½ to 1 min.	
1, frozen		2½ to 3 min.	
2, room temp.		30 to 45 sec.	
2, refrig.		1½ to 2 min.	
2, frozen		3 to 4 min.	
4, room temp.		50 to 60 sec.	
4, refrig.		3 to 4 min.	
4, frozen		5 to 5½ min.	
SAUCES			
	1-qt. covered glass casserole	REHEAT (about 150° F.)	Use ROAST if sensitive ingredients included, reduce time about 1 min.
1 Cup, refrig.		5 to 5½ min.	
2 Cups, refrig.		6 to 7 min.	
Dessert Sauce, ½ jar, (11 oz.), refrig.	Original glass jar, remove lid	50 to 60 sec.	
1 jar, (11 oz.), room temp.		1 to 1½ min.	
SEAFOOD			
Shrimp, cooked, 6-oz., frozen	1½-qt. covered glass casserole	DEFROST 5 to 6 min.	Let stand, covered, 2 min.
Shrimp Newburg, 6½-oz., frozen	2-qt. (8 x 8) glass baking dish	ROAST (about 150° F.) 4 to 5 min.	Slit plastic pouch. Let stand 3 min.
SNACKS			See Candy.
SOUPS			
Canned			See chart, page 154.
Dry Mixes			See chart, page 154.
Frozen,		REHEAT (about 160° F.)	Use ROAST if sensitive ingredients included.
8-oz.	1-qt. covered glass casserole	4 to 6 min.	
15-oz.	1½-qt. covered glass casserole	11 to 12 min.	Increased time about 1 min.
Refrigerated, Tomato, Cream, Noodle or Vegetable	Glass or pottery bowls (without metal trim)	REHEAT (about 160° F.)	
1 bowl		3½ to 4 min.	—
2 bowls		7 to 8 min.	—
4 bowls		10 to 12 min.	—
Cream of Mushroom, Pea, Bean	Glass or pottery bowls (without metal trim)	ROAST (about 160° F.)	
1 bowl		4 to 5 min.	—
2 bowls		9 to 10 min.	—
4 bowls		12 to 14 min.	—
STEWS			
Canned,		REHEAT (about 150° F.)	Stand, covered, 3 min.
16-oz.	1-qt. covered glass casserole	4 to 5 min.	
40-oz.	2-qt. covered glass casserole	9 to 11 min.	
Frozen, 10-oz.	2-qt. (8 x 8) glass baking dish	REHEAT 6 to 7 min.	Slit plastic pouch.

PRODUCT & SIZE	CONTAINER	SETTING & TIME	SPECIAL TECHNIQUES
SUGAR			
Brown Sugar, soften, 1 lb.	1½-qt. covered glass casserole	WARM 4½ to 5 min.	—
SYRUP 1 cup	2-cup glass measure	REHEAT (about 150° F.) 2 to 2½ min.	—
TAKE OUT FOODS			See Main Dishes, Meats, Poultry and Sandwiches.
TOPPINGS			
Nondairy Creamer, liquid 8-oz., frozen	Original wax carton, opened	DEFROST 3 to 3½ min.	Shake or stir; stand 3 min.
Nondairy Topping, 9 to 14-oz., frozen	Original plastic, remove lid	DEFROST 2 to 4 min.	
T.V. DINNERS			See Meals.
VEGETABLES			Also see chart, page 162.
Au Gratin, 11½-oz., frozen	(9 x 5) loaf dish; cover with wax paper	ROAST (about 150° F.) 10 to 12 min.	Stand, covered, 3 min.
Baked Beans, 20 to 21-oz., canned	1½-qt. covered glass casserole	ROAST (about 150° F.) 7 to 8 min.	Stand, covered, 3 min.
9-oz. pkg., dry * water	3-qt. covered glass casserole	HIGH 7 min.	Add beans to boiling water and SIMMER.
beans		SIMMER 15 to 18 min.	Stand, covered, 3 min.
6-oz., frozen	1½-qt. covered glass casserole	ROAST (about 150° F.) 8 to 10 min.	
Corn, Scalloped, 12-oz., frozen	1-qt. covered glass casserole	ROAST (about 150° F.) 7 to 8 min.	Stand, covered, 3 min.
Potatoes,			
Baked, stuffed with sour cream, chives, cheese, frozen,		ROAST (about 150° F.)	
1 pkg. (12 oz.)	1-qt. covered glass casserole	10 to 12 min.	—
2 pkgs. (12 oz. ea.)	2-qt. covered glass casserole	18 to 20 min.	—
Instant Mashed, 2 servings, water and salt	1-qt. glass casserole	HIGH 2 to 2½ min.	Boil water and salt as pkg. directs — stir potatoes into boiling water.
4 servings, water and salt		3 to 4 min.	
Potato tots,	2-qt. (8 x 8) glass baking dish	REHEAT (about 150° F.)	
16-oz., frozen		9 to 10 min.	—
32-oz., frozen		12 to 14 min.	—
Scalloped, 5 to 6-oz. dry mix	3-qt. covered glass casserole	REHEAT 18 to 20 min.	Prepare as pkg. directs. Stand, covered, 3 min.
4 to 5-oz. dry mix with sour cream, etc.		ROAST 20 to 24 min.	

Defrost How-To

Meat, Fish and Poultry

- Thaw fish, seafood, meat or poultry in original, closed package.
- Metal clip and pop-up timers may be left in poultry. Twisters must be removed from bags and may be replaced with a rubber band.
- Place food in a flat glass baking dish to catch drippings.
- Use DEFROST setting to thaw: All fish, meat weighing up to 4 lbs.; ground meat weight up to 2 lbs.; poultry weighing 4 pounds or less.
- Use HIGH/ROAST to thaw: Large roasts weighing 4 lbs. and over; ground meat, 2 lbs. and over; poultry over 4 lbs. Thaw 1 minute per pound on HIGH, 2 minutes per pound on ROAST.
- Where turning is specified in chart, start defrosting whole poultry breast-side-up; meats tray-side-up.
- Food will be icy in the center when removed from the oven. Edges begin cooking if microwaves thaw meat, fish or seafood completely.
- Chart specifies standing time and standing technique which completes thawing.
- Remove loosened giblets from whole poultry and set aside for gravy or broth.

	CUT AND WEIGHT	FIRST SETTING AND TIME	SECOND SETTING AND TIME	STANDING TIME	SPECIAL TECHNIQUES
FISH	**Fillets**	DEFROST			Carefully separate and rinse under cold running water to finish thawing.
	1-lb. pkg.	9 to 11 min.	—	5 min.	
	2-lb. pkg.	13 to 15 min.	—	5 min.	
	Salmon Steaks	DEFROST			
	3 in 12-oz. pkg.	7 to 8 min.	—	5 min.	See Fillets, above.
	Smelt	DEFROST			
	1-lb. pkg.	7 to 8 min.	—	5 min.	See Fillets, above.
	Whole Fish	DEFROST			
	1½ to 2 lbs.	18 to 20 min.	—	5 min.	See Fillets, above.
MEAT	**Beef**				
	Brisket	HIGH	ROAST		
	2½ to 3½ lbs.	1 min. per lb.	2 min. per lb.	45 min.	—
	Ground Beef				
	1 lb.	DEFROST 8 to 10 min.	—	5 min.	—
	2 lbs.	HIGH 1 min. per lb.	ROAST 2 min. per lb.	5 min.	—
	Roasts	HIGH	ROAST		Over 4 lbs., turn over once.
	chuck, 3 to 5-lb.	1 min. per lb.	2 min. per lb.	10 min.	
	rolled rib,				
	3 to 4-lb.	1 min. per lb.	2 min. per lb.	1 hr.	—
	7 to 8-lb.	1 min. per lb.	2 min. per lb.	1½ hrs.	Turn over once.
	rump,				
	3 to 4-lb.	1 min. per lb.	2 min. per lb.	1 hr.	—
	6 to 7-lb.	1 min. per lb.	2 min. per lb.	1½ hrs.	Turn over once.
	sirloin tip, 4 to 5-lb.	1 min. per lb.	2 min. per lb.	1½ hrs.	Turn over once.
	standing rib, 5 to 6-lb.	1 min. per lb.	2 min. per lb.	1½ hrs.	Turn over once.
	Short Ribs,	DEFROST			
	2 to 3 lbs.	8 to 10 min.	—	5 min.	—
	Steaks	DEFROST			
	cubed, ½ lb.	3 to 4 min.	—	5 min.	—
	flank, 1 to 2-lb.	9 to 10 min.	—	5 min.	—
	rib-eye, 2 to 3 lbs.	8 to 10 min.	—	5 min.	—
	round or sirloin, 1½ to 3 lbs.	12 to 15 min.	—	5 min.	—
	Stew Meat	DEFROST			
	1 to 2 lbs.	8 to 10 min.	—	5 min.	—
	Lamb				
	Cubed	DEFROST			
	1 lb.	7 to 8 min.	—	5 min.	—
	Ground or Patties	DEFROST			
	1 to 1½ lbs.	6 to 8 min.	—	5 min.	—
	Roast, leg or shoulder	HIGH	ROAST		
	3 to 4½-lb.	1 min. per lb.	2 min. per lb.	1 hr.	Turn over once.
	Shanks	DEFROST			
	1 lb.	6 to 8 min.	—	5 min.	—
	Spareribs	DEFROST			
	2 to 2½ lbs.	8 to 10 min.	—	5 min.	—
	Steaks	DEFROST			
	2 to 2½ lbs.	10 to 12 min.	—	5 min.	—

MEAT CONTINUED

CUT AND WEIGHT	FIRST SETTING AND TIME	SECOND SETTING AND TIME	STANDING TIME	SPECIAL TECHNIQUES
Pork				
Bacon 1 lb.	DEFROST 6 to 7 min.	—	5 min.	—
Chops ½ in. thick 1 to 1½ lbs.	DEFROST 10 to 15 min.	—	5 min.	—
1 in. thick (loin) 3 to 3½ lbs.	DEFROST 12 to 15 min.	—	10 min.	—
Cubed 1½ lbs.	DEFROST 8 to 10 min.	—	5 min.	—
Ground, fresh or ham 1 lb.	DEFROST 8 to 10 min.	—	5 min.	—
Ham ✻ 3 to 5 lbs.	HIGH 1 min. per lb.	ROAST 2 min. per lb.	1 hr.	Over 4 lbs., turn over once.
Hocks 1 to 2 lbs.	DEFROST 8 to 10 min.	—	5 min.	—
Roast ✻ 4 to 5-lb.	HIGH 1 min. per lb.	ROAST 2 min. per lb.	1 hr.	Turn over once.
Sausage fresh ground, 12-oz. bulk 1 lb. bulk	DEFROST 5 to 6 min. 6 to 7 min.	 — —	 5 min. 5 min.	 — —
links, precooked, ½ lb. 12-oz.	 3 to 4 min. 4 to 5 min.	 — —	 5 min. 5 min.	 — —
links, uncooked, 1 lb.	4 to 5 min.	—	5 min.	—
patties, precooked, ½ lb.	3 to 4 min.	—	5 min.	—
Spareribs and Country Style Ribs 2 to 3 lbs.	DEFROST 15 to 18 min.	—	5 min.	—
Steaks, blade or shoulder 1 to 2½ lbs.	DEFROST 8 to 10 min.	—	5 min.	—
Tenderloin 1½ to 2-lb.	DEFROST 12 to 15 min.	—	5 min.	—
Wieners ½ lb. 1 lb.	DEFROST 2 to 3 min. 5 to 6 min.	 — —	 5 min. 5 min.	 — —
Rabbit, ✻ cut up 2 to 2½-lb.	HIGH 1 min. per lb.	ROAST 2 min. per lb.	30 min.	—
Variety Meats				
Kidney 2-lb.	DEFROST 7 to 8 min.	—	5 min.	—
Liver 8 oz. 1 lb.	DEFROST 5 to 6 min. 7 to 8 min.	 — —	 5 min. 5 min.	 — —
Tongue 2 to 2½-lb.	DEFROST 15 to 16 min.	—	5 min.	—
Veal				
Chops 1 to 2 lbs.	DEFROST 12 to 15 min.	—	5 min.	—
Ground 1 lb.	DEFROST 7 to 8 min.	—	5 min.	—
Rump Roast ✻ 2½ to 3-lb. 4 to 6-lb.	HIGH 1 min. per lb. 1 min. per lb.	ROAST 2 min. per lb. 2 min. per lb.	 30 min. 1 hr.	— Turn over once.
Steak 1-lb.	DEFROST 7 to 8 min.	—	5 min.	—
Venison				
Chops 1 to 1½ lbs.	DEFROST 7 to 8 min.	—	5 min.	—
Rump Roast ✻ 3 to 3½-lb.	HIGH 1 min. per lb.	ROAST 2 min. per lb.	1 hr.	—
Stew Meat 1 to 1½ lbs.	DEFROST 7 to 8 min.	—	5 min.	—

Pictured: Commercial and "made-at-home" frozen foods.

The " ✻ " at the end of a recipe title reminds you that there are two or more power settings during cooking.

	CUT AND WEIGHT	FIRST SETTING AND TIME	SECOND SETTING AND TIME	STANDING TIME	SPECIAL TECHNIQUES
POULTRY	**Capon,** ✱ whole 6 to 8-lb.	HIGH 1 min. per lb.	ROAST 2 min. per lb.	1 hr.	Stand in original container in cold water.
	Chicken	DEFROST			
	Fryer, whole, 2 to 3-lb.	20 to 25 min.	—	30 min.	See Capon, above.
	Fryer, quarters 2½ to 3 lbs.	14 to 16 min.	—	30 min.	See Capon, above.
	Fryer half, quartered 1 to 1½ lbs.	7 to 8 min.	—	—	—
	Roasting, whole 3 to 4 lbs.	25 to 30 min.	—	30 min.	See Capon, above.
	Stewing hen, half 2½ to 3 lbs.	25 to 30 min.	—	30 min.	See Capon, above.
	Breasts, 1½ to 2 lbs.	15 to 17 min.	—	15 min.	—
	Drumsticks or thighs, 1 lb.	7 to 8 min.	—	15 min.	—
	Liver and/or hearts,				
	½ lb.	5 to 6 min.	—	5 min.	—
	2 lbs.	9 to 10 min.	—	5 min.	—
	Wings, 1½ lbs.	6 to 8 min.	—	15 min.	—
	Duckling, ✱ whole 4 to 5-lb.	HIGH 1 min. per lb.	ROAST 2 min. per lb.	30 min.	See Capon, above.
	Goose, ✱ whole 9 to 11-lb.	HIGH 1 min. per lb.	ROAST 2 min. per lb.	1 hr.	See Capon, above.
	Pheasant, whole 2 to 3-lb.	DEFROST 14 to 16 min.	—	20 min.	See Capon, above.
	Rock Cornish Game Hen, whole	DEFROST			
	2 (12 oz. ea.)	15 to 17 min.	—	15 min.	—
	4 (12 oz. ea.)	20 to 22 min.	—	30 min.	—
	Turkey ✱				
	Breast, bone-in 4 to 8-lb.	HIGH 1 min. per lb.	ROAST 2 min. per lb.	20 min.	—
	Drumsticks or Thighs	DEFROST			
	1 to 2 lbs.	15 to 18 min.	—	20 min.	—
	2 to 3 lbs.	25 to 28 min.	—	30 min.	—
	Wings 2 to 3 lbs.	DEFROST 18 to 20 min.	—	20 min.	—
	Whole ✱	HIGH	ROAST		
	8 to 12-lb.	1 min. per lb.	2 min. per lb.	1 hr.	Stand in original container in cold water. Turn large birds over once during thawing.
	12 to 20-lb.	1 min. per lb.	2 min. per lb.	1½ to 2 hrs.	
SEAFOOD	**Lobster Tails** 2 in ½-lb. pkg.	DEFROST 6 to 7 min.	—	5 min.	
	Scallops, Bay	DEFROST			
	12-oz. pkg.	5 to 6 min.	—	5 min.	
	1-lb. pkg.	6 to 7 min.	—	5 min.	
	Shrimp	DEFROST			
	½-lb. pkg.	6 to 7 min.	—	5 min.	
	1-lb. pkg.	9 to 10 min.	—	5 min.	

Appetizers & Beverages

Now a Hostess Joins the Party

Here's How — and Why

Power Settings Vary with Appetizer Ingredients: Most appetizers and dips microwave on ROAST because they contain cheese, mayonnaise, mushrooms or meats that need to gentle-cook. Appetizers with non-sensitive ingredients microwave on HIGH. A few need special care — snails in small shells that do not allow much bubbling and may "pop" or ingredients, like liver, that toughen if cooked too fast. Microwave these delicate appetizers on SIMMER — experiment with one canapé before cooking a whole batch.

Use Sturdy Crackers for Appetizer Bases: Choose sturdy, thicker crackers for appetizers because the oven does not "dry" food. Make appetizer fillings ahead of a party but do not mound on crackers until ready to microwave or base becomes soggy.

Rack Lets You Microwave 2 Batches: Microwave two batches of similar appetizers at once, using the oven's convenient rack. Remove appetizers from the oven as they finish cooking. Single batches usually cook on oven's bottom shelf.

Appetizers Microwave in Many Containers: Microwave appetizers and dips in glass casseroles, glass baking dishes, natural shells — even warm them right on glass or pottery serving plates without gold, silver or other metal trim. Microwave bacon-wrapped appetizers on a microwave roasting rack or inverted heatproof glass saucer that drains away drippings.

Heat Beverages on HIGH: Heat beverages on Microwave HIGH almost to a boil for full flavor. Add coffee or tea after water is hot to avoid bitter taste caused if water boils. Note that "instant crystals" fizz when stirred into hot water. Watch milk closely so it does not boil over. See the hot beverage chart in this chapter. Exact heating time depends on beverage's starting temperature, size and number of containers. Microwave beverages on oven's bottom shelf unless otherwise directed.

Heat a Cup or Pitcher of Beverages: A microwave oven's super-convenient for hot drinks. Don't keep a coffee pot plugged in all day — reheat cup-by-cup in a microwave oven — taste stays fresh. Microwave beverages in 1-serving mugs or cups, pitchers, punch bowls — even small milk cartons, paper or styrofoam "hot" cups. Cups, mugs and pitchers should be glass or pottery without metal trim. *Milk cartons should be opened. Do not overheat cartons* or waxed surface dissolves.

Cover When a Recipe Specifies: Cover appetizers, dips and beverages during cooking only when a recipe specifies. Use fitted glass lids or wax paper — lift lids away from arm to prevent steam burns. Plastic wrap may be used as a cover. Pierce it before removing to allow steam to escape.

Microwave-Conventional Comparison: Appetizers are fast, convenient. Fondues and dips reheat smoothly. Crackers and toast mounded with moist mixtures should be sturdy and crisp or they become soggy because oven is not a dry heat source. However, toast and crackers will not burn easily, as they often do in a conventional broiler. Appetizers with pastry crusts do not microwave well — crust is pale. Munchy nut mixtures turn out exceptionally well. Beverages are easy to microwave by the cupful or pitcherful. Coffee reheats without developing a bitter taste. Cups stay cool while beverages get hot. Heating in small milk cartons and paper cups is a time and dish-saver.

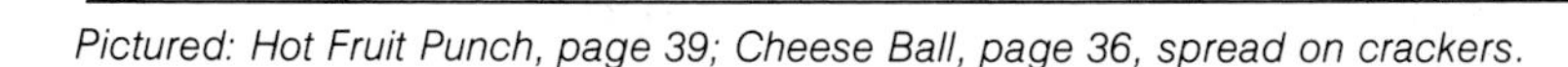

Pictured: Hot Fruit Punch, page 39; Cheese Ball, page 36, spread on crackers.

SPICY FRANKS

- **1 jar (10 oz.) currant jelly**
- **3 tablespoons prepared mustard**
- **1 lb. skinless franks (about 10)**

High-sugar mixtures microwave on ROAST.

1. Combine jelly and mustard in 1½-quart glass casserole.

2. Microwave for about 4 minutes, on ROAST, or until jelly melts. Beat well with rotary beater to blend in mustard.

3. Cut each frank crosswise into 6 pieces. Stir into jelly mixture and continue cooking for 3 to 4 minutes, on HIGH, or until franks are hot. Serve in chafing dish with toothpicks. About 60 Appetizers

TIP: Substitute 2 packages (8 oz. each) cocktail franks for skinless franks.

CHINESE CHICKEN WINGS

- **12 chicken wings**
- **Salt**
- **¼ cup honey**
- **¼ cup prepared mustard**
- **1½ tablespoons orange juice**
- **2 tablespoons sesame seed**
- **¼ teaspoon ginger**
- **1 orange, cut into wedges**
- **Fresh parsley**

Cover holds steam which helps speed cooking.

1. Cut off wing tips of chicken and cut wings in half at the joint. Salt both sides of wings. Place in 2-quart (12 x 7) glass baking dish; set aside. Combine remaining ingredients, except orange and parsley, in small mixing bowl. Pour half of mixture over wings. Cover with wax paper.

2. Microwave for 6 minutes on HIGH. Turn chicken over and brush with remaining sauce. Recover and continue cooking for 6 to 7 minutes, on HIGH, or until chicken is fork tender. Let stand, covered, 5 minutes before serving. Garnish with orange wedges and parsley. 24 Appetizers

SWEET AND SOUR MEATBALLS

- **1 lb. ground beef**
- **¼ cup chopped onion**
- **1 egg, beaten**
- **1 teaspoon salt**
- **¼ teaspoon pepper**
- **2 tablespoons water**

Sauce:

- **1 tablespoon butter or margarine**
- **1 small onion, chopped**
- **1 cup catsup**
- **1½ tablespoons packed brown sugar**
- **1½ tablespoon lemon juice**
- **1 tablespoon soy sauce**

Meatballs microwave evenly on ROAST.

1. Combine all meatball ingredients in medium mixing bowl; mix well. Shape into 20 (1-inch) meatballs. Place in 9-inch round glass baking dish. Cover with wax paper.

2. Microwave for 8 minutes on ROAST; drain. Pour Sauce over meatballs and continue cooking for 3 to 4 minutes, on ROAST, or until hot.

3. **Sauce:** Place butter and onion in 1-quart glass casserole. Microwave for about 2 minutes, on HIGH, or until onion is partly cooked. Stir in remaining ingredients. 20 Meatballs

RECIPE VARIATION

GLAZED MEATBALLS: Substitute 1 package (¾ oz.) brown gravy mix, ½ cup water, ½ cup apple or currant jelly and 2 tablespoons catsup for all Sauce ingredients. Increase final cooking time by 3 to 4 minutes.

SWEET AND SOUR RIBS

- **2 lbs. lean spareribs, sawed and cut into individual rib pieces**
- **Salt**

Sauce:

- **½ green pepper, chopped**
- **½ cup packed brown sugar**
- **½ cup vinegar**
- **1 tablespoon soy sauce**
- **1 can (8 oz.) crushed pineapple, drained**
- **¼ cup dry sherry**

Ask your meat man to saw rack so rib bones are 1½ to 2 inches long.

1. Remove excess fat and arrange ribs in 3-quart (13 x 9) glass baking dish. Sprinkle with salt; cover with wax paper.

2. Microwave for 15 minutes on ROAST. Drain; pour Sauce over ribs. Recover and continue cooking for 10 to 15 minutes, on ROAST, or until fork tender. Let stand, covered, 5 minutes before serving.

3. **Sauce:** Combine all Sauce ingredients in medium mixing bowl. About 4 Servings

RECIPE VARIATIONS

LAMB RIBS: Substitute 2 lbs. sawed and cut lean lamb ribs for pork ribs.

BARBECUE RIBS: Substitute your own barbecue sauce recipe or bottled barbecue sauce for Sauce in the basic recipe.

HOT SARDINE APPETIZERS

Mayonnaise and cheese are sensitive. Microwave on ROAST.

- **2 cans (3¾ oz.) sardines, drained**
- **2 tablespoons mayonnaise or salad dressing**
- **1 tablespoon grated Parmesan cheese**
- **2 teaspoons prepared mustard**
- **Dash hot pepper sauce**
- **Shredded wheat crackers**
- **Hard-cooked egg, sliced, if desired**
- **Fresh parsley, if desired**

1. Mash sardines. Combine remaining ingredients, except crackers, egg slices and parsley, in small mixing bowl; mix well. Spread on crackers. Place in 3-quart (13 x 9) glass baking dish.

2. Microwave for about 6 minutes, on ROAST, or until hot. Garnish with egg slices or fresh sprigs of parsley. About 25 Appetizers

RECIPE VARIATION

SMOKED SALMON APPETIZERS: Substitute 1 can (7¾ oz.) salmon, drained and flaked, for sardines. Increase mayonnaise by 2 tablespoons. Omit mustard and hot pepper sauce. Add 2 green onions, sliced, and 2 teaspoons liquid smoke. Garnish as desired.

MUNCH MIX

Remember, butter melts alone on ROAST to prevent spattering.

- **½ cup butter or margarine**
- **1 package (0.6 oz.) Italian salad dressing mix**
- **2 cups salted peanuts**
- **1 cup pecan halves**
- **2 cups pretzel sticks**
- **2 cups toasted oat cereal**

1. Place butter in 3-quart (13 x 9) glass baking dish.

2. Microwave for about 1½ minutes, on ROAST, or until melted. Stir in seasoning mix and remaining ingredients.

3. Microwave for 2 to 3 minutes, on HIGH, or until heated through. About 7 Cups Mix

TIP: Substitute ½ teaspoon garlic salt, ½ teaspoon celery seed and ½ teaspoon Worcestershire sauce for Italian salad dressing mix.

SWEDISH CRUNCH

Serve salty crunch before dinner – sweet crunch after.

- **1 cup walnut halves**
- **¾ cup almonds**
- **1 egg white**
- **½ cup sugar**
- **Dash salt**
- **¼ cup butter or margarine**

1. Combine walnuts and almonds in 2-quart (12 x 7) glass baking dish.

2. Microwave for about 2 minutes, on HIGH, or until hot. Beat egg white in small mixing bowl until stiff peaks form; beat in sugar and salt. Stir in hot nuts; set aside. Place butter in 2-quart (12 x 7) glass baking dish.

3. Microwave for about 1 minute, on ROAST, or until melted. Spread nut mixture into melted butter.

4. Microwave for 6 minutes on ROAST. Stir well and continue cooking for 5 to 6 minutes, on ROAST, or until glazed. Stir well and let stand 10 minutes until cool and hardened. Break apart to serve. About 2 Cups Nuts

RECIPE VARIATIONS

CINNAMON CRUNCH: Add 1 teaspoon cinnamon with sugar in basic recipe.

CARDAMOM CRUNCH: Add 1 teaspoon ground cardamom with sugar in basic recipe.

CHINESE NUTS: Substitute 1 cup pecan halves for walnuts and add ¾ cup filberts to basic recipe. Omit egg white, sugar and salt. Place butter, 2 tablespoons soy sauce and 1 teaspoon garlic salt in 2-quart (12 x 7) glass baking dish. Microwave for about 1 minute, on ROAST, or until butter is melted. Stir in nuts. Microwave as directed in Step 2. Omit final cooking period in basic recipe. About 3 Cups Nuts

FIESTA NUTS: Substitute ¾ cup filberts for almonds and add ¾ cup pecan halves to basic recipe. Omit egg white, sugar and salt. Place butter, 2 tablespoons Worcestershire sauce and 1 teaspoon onion salt in 2-quart (12 x 7) glass baking dish. Microwave for about 1 minute, on ROAST, or until butter is melted. Stir in nuts. Microwave as directed in Step 2. Omit final cooking period in basic recipe. About 3 Cups Nuts.

CHEESE BALL

Freshen chips and crackers on REHEAT.

- **1 package (8 oz.) cream cheese**
- **2 cups shredded Cheddar cheese**
- **2 ounces Bleu cheese, crumbled**
- **1 green onion, finely sliced**
- **2 tablespoons brandy or apple juice**
- **¼ cup chopped nuts**
- **2 tablespoons dried parsley flakes**

1. Place cream cheese in medium glass mixing bowl.

2. Microwave for about 2 minutes, on ROAST, or until softened. Beat in other cheeses, onion and brandy with wooden spoon or at low speed of electric mixer. Chill slightly for easier shaping. Combine chopped nuts and parsley on wax paper. Form cheese mixture into ball; roll in chopped nut mixture.

About 2-Cup Cheese Ball

RECIPE VARIATION

CHEESE BEEF BALL: Shred 1 jar (2½ oz.) dried beef, using kitchen shears. Combine beef and 1 cup water in 4-cup glass measure. Microwave for 3 to 4 minutes on HIGH; drain. Add beef to cream cheese. Substitute ½ cup grated Parmesan cheese for Cheddar and Bleu cheeses. Substitute 2 tablespoons sour cream for brandy.

HOT ORIENTAL CHESTNUTS

Use inverted heatproof glass saucer if microwave roasting rack is not available.

- **½ cup soy sauce**
- **½ teaspoon ginger**
- **½ can (8 oz.) water chestnuts, cut into halves**
- **6 slices bacon, cut into thirds**
- **Sugar**

1. Combine all ingredients, except bacon and sugar, in 2-cup glass measure. Marinate for 3 to 4 hours.

2. Roll water chestnuts in bacon pieces; coat with sugar and skewer with toothpick. Place on microwave roasting rack in 2-quart (12 x 7) glass baking dish.

3. Microwave for 7 to 8 minutes, on HIGH, or until bacon is crisp.

18 Appetizers

RECIPE VARIATIONS

DATE ROLL-UPS: Substitute 18 dates and 18 pecan halves for soy sauce, ginger and water chestnuts. Stuff dates with pecan halves; roll in pieces of bacon and coat with sugar, as directed in basic recipe. Decrease cooking time by 2 to 3 minutes.

HAWAIIAN ROLL-UPS: Cut bacon slices in half. Substitute ½ cup dry sherry, 1 can (8 oz.) pineapple chunks, drained, and 12 almonds for soy sauce, ginger and water chestnuts. Marinate as directed in basic recipe. Roll 1 pineapple chunk and 1 almond in half slice of bacon. Omit sugar. Increase cooking time by 1 minute.

RUMAKI: Cut bacon slices in half. Substitute 6 chicken livers, 2 tablespoons prepared mustard and 2 olives, chopped, for soy sauce, ginger and water chestnuts. Substitute soda cracker crumbs for sugar. Cut chicken livers in half; top with mixture of mustard and olives. Roll each liver in half slice of bacon; coat with cracker crumbs. Microwave for 15 to 18 minutes, on SIMMER, or until liver is done.

Pictured: Hot Spiced Cider garnished with orange slices, page 38.

ONION CHEESE FONDUE

A stirring keeps cheese mixture cooking evenly.

- **3 tablespoons all-purpose flour**
- **¼ teaspoon salt**
- **⅛ teaspoon white pepper**
- **1 cup milk**
- **1 lb. process cheese spread, shredded**
- **2 tablespoons dry onion soup mix**
- **2 tablespoons sliced pimento**
- **1 tablespoon butter or margarine**
- **½ cup beer**

1. Combine flour, seasonings and milk in 1½-quart glass casserole; beat with rotary beater until smooth. Stir in cheese, onion soup mix and pimento. Add butter. Cover with glass lid.

2. Microwave for 5 minutes on ROAST. Stir well and continue cooking for 5 to 6 minutes, on ROAST, or until thickened and smooth (about 180° F.). Stir in beer.

About 3 Cups Fondue

TIP: May be made ahead, refrigerated and reheated. Microwave for about 8 minutes, on ROAST, or until warm (about 120° F.). Stir well and serve.

RECIPE VARIATION

SWISS CHEESE FONDUE: Add ⅛ teaspoon garlic powder with seasonings in basic recipe. Substitute 1 lb. Emmentaler Swiss cheese, shredded, for process cheese spread. Omit dry onion soup mix and pimento. Substitute ½ cup dry white wine for beer.

CREATE-A-HOT-DIP

- **1 package (8 oz.) cream cheese**
- **½ cup mayonnaise or salad dressing**
- **2 green onions, sliced**
- **1 tablespoon dried parsley flakes**

1. Place cream cheese in medium glass mixing bowl.

2. Microwave for about 2 minutes, on ROAST, or until softened. Add mayonnaise, onions, parsley and ingredients as specified in one of the variations.

About 2 Cups Dip

RECIPE VARIATIONS

HOT CRAB DIP: Add 1 can (6 oz.) crabmeat, drained and flaked, ½ cup slivered almonds, 2 tablespoons dry white wine, 1 tablespoon horseradish, and ¼ teaspoon Worcestershire sauce. Microwave for 4 to 5 minutes, on ROAST, or until hot (about 120° F.).

HOT SPINACH DIP: Add 1 package (10 oz.) frozen chopped spinach, thawed and drained well, 6 slices bacon, crisply fried and crumbled, ⅓ cup grated Parmesan cheese and 2 teaspoons lemon juice. Microwave for 3 to 4 minutes, on ROAST, or until hot (about 120° F.).

STUFFED MUSHROOMS

Adapt your own favorite appetizer and dip recipes – use this chapter as a guide.

- **1 lb. large fresh mushrooms**
- **3 green onions, sliced**
- **1 tablespoon butter or margarine**
- **¼ cup sour cream**
- **1 package (8 oz.) cream cheese**

1. Wash mushrooms; remove stem from each cap by twisting. Arrange caps, stem-side-up, in 3-quart (13 x 9) glass baking dish; set aside. Chop stems fine. Place stems, onions and butter in medium glass mixing bowl.

2. Microwave for 3 minutes, on ROAST, or until onions are tender. Stir in sour cream; add cream cheese.

3. Microwave for 2½ minutes, on ROAST, or until cream cheese is softened; stir well. Divide mixture into four (6 oz. each) custard cups. Stir ingredients from one of the variations, below, into each cup. Fill mushroom caps with one of cream cheese mixtures.

4. Microwave for 5 to 6 minutes, on ROAST, or until hot.

About 36 Mushrooms

RECIPE VARIATIONS

MEXICAN MUSHROOMS: Add 1 tablespoon chopped green chilies and ¼ cup shredded Monterey Jack cheese to ¼ of basic recipe. Garnish each mushroom with one strip of pimento.

ITALIAN MUSHROOMS: Add 3 slices crisp bacon, crumbled, 5 black olives, chopped, ¼ teaspoon oregano leaves and ¼ teaspoon sweet basil leaves to ¼ of basic recipe. Garnish each mushroom with dried parsley flakes.

FRENCH MUSHROOMS: Add ¼ cup crumbled Bleu cheese and ⅛ teaspoon tarragon leaves to ¼ of basic recipe. Garnish lightly with tarragon leaves.

INDIAN MUSHROOMS: Add 2 tablespoons flaked coconut and ¼ teaspoon curry powder to ¼ of basic recipe. Garnish with paprika.

CHICKEN LIVER PATE

Microwave liver on SIMMER so it stays tender.

1 lb. chicken livers
⅓ cup finely chopped onion
1 can (4 oz.) mushroom stems and pieces, drained
1 clove garlic, finely chopped
1 teaspoon salt
¼ teaspoon cayenne pepper
2 teaspoons prepared mustard
¼ cup port wine or water
¼ cup butter or margarine

1. Combine all ingredients, except butter, in 1½-quart glass casserole. Add butter; cover with glass lid.

2. Microwave for 18 to 20 minutes, on SIMMER, or until liver is done.

3. Pour into electric blender and blend until smooth or grind to desired consistency. Pour into serving bowl or mold. Cover and chill before serving. About 3 Cups Pâté

POOR MAN'S CAVIAR

1 small eggplant, unpeeled and finely chopped (about 4 cups)
1 medium onion, chopped
¼ cup chopped green pepper
1 can (4 oz.) mushroom stems and pieces, drained
2 cloves garlic, finely chopped
⅓ cup cooking oil
1 teaspoon salt
½ teaspoon pepper
½ teaspoon oregano leaves
1 can (6 oz.) tomato paste
¼ cup water
½ cup chopped stuffed olives
¼ cup capers
2 tablespoons wine vinegar

1. Combine eggplant, onion, green pepper, mushrooms, garlic and oil in 2-quart glass casserole; mix well. Cover with glass lid.

2. Microwave for 10 minutes on ROAST. Stir in remaining ingredients, recover.

3. Microwave for 14 to 16 minutes, on ROAST, or until eggplant is tender (about 200° F.). Serve with corn chips. About 4 Cups Dip

TIP: May also serve hot over fluffy white rice or green noodles. May be made a few hours ahead and refrigerated. Warm dip for about 10 minutes, on REHEAT, or until warm (about 120° F.).

HOW TO MAKE HOT BEVERAGES

- Microwave on HIGH.
- Microwave hot drinks in glass or pottery cups and serving pitchers without silver or other metal trim — on oven's bottom shelf.
- Heat ½ pints of milk in the carton like (8 oz.) cups milk. Open carton to prevent bulging. DO NOT OVERHEAT or waxed surface dissolves.
- Heat liquids almost to a boil for best taste (about 160° F.).
- Note that coffee and tea crystals fizz when stirred into hot liquid.
- WATCH MILK carefully so it does not boil over.
- Add a marshmallow to hot chocolate drinks during the last 10 to 15 seconds of heating.

BEVERAGE	SETTING	6-OZ. SERVING	MINUTES	8-OZ. SERVING	MINUTES
WATER OR MILK to make regular tea, instant beverages or instant breakfasts	HIGH	1 cup	1½ to 2	1 mug	1½ to 2
		2 cups	2½ to 3	2 mugs	3 to 3½
		4 cups	4 to 5	4 mugs	7 to 8
		6 cups	7 to 8	6 mugs	9 to 10
REHEATING COFFEE OR COCOA made with water or milk	HIGH	1 cup	1 to 1½	1 mug	1½ to 2
		2 cups	2 to 2½	2 mugs	2½ to 3
		4 cups	4 to 5	4 mugs	6 to 7
		6 cups	5 to 6	6 mugs	7 to 8

HOT SPICED CIDER

Make for a crowd – or as a single serving.

2 quarts apple cider
4 cinnamon sticks
16 whole allspice
16 whole cloves
2 tablespoons packed brown sugar
2 lemons, sliced
2 oranges, sliced

1. Combine all ingredients in 3-quart glass bowl.

2. Microwave for 14 to 15 minutes, on HIGH, or until hot and bubbly (about 160° F.). Stir; remove spices and serve. About 8 (8 oz.) Servings

TIP: Make 1 serving. Combine ½ cinnamon stick, 2 whole allspice, 2 whole cloves, ½ teaspoon brown sugar, 1 lemon and 1 orange slice in 8 oz. glass mug. Fill with cider. Microwave for 2 to 2½ minutes, on HIGH, or until hot.

HOT FRUIT PUNCH

Fruit juices heat quickly on HIGH.

- **1 jar (32 oz.) cranberry juice cocktail**
- **3 cups water**
- **1 can (6 oz.) frozen orange juice concentrate, thawed**
- **1 package (10 oz.) frozen red raspberries, thawed**
- **2 oranges, sliced**
- **6 sticks cinnamon**
- **12 whole allspice**
- **½ to ¾ cup light rum or water**

1. Combine all ingredients in 4-quart glass bowl or heat-resistant glass punch bowl.

2. Microwave for 12 to 14 minutes, on HIGH, or until hot (about 160° F.). Stir in rum.

25 to 30 (4 oz.) Punch Cups

TOMATO SIPPER

Serve as a stand-up first course with appetizers.

- **1 can (18 oz.) tomato juice**
- **1 can (10½ oz.) condensed beef broth**
- **¼ cup lemon juice**
- **1 teaspoon horseradish**
- **1 teaspoon dried parsley flakes**
- **½ teaspoon celery salt**
- **2 to 4 tablespoons dry sherry or Madeira**

1. Combine all ingredients, except sherry, in 4-cup glass measure.

2. Microwave for 8 to 9 minutes, on HIGH, or until hot (about 160° F.). Pour into six (6 oz.) cups or mugs. Stir 1 to 2 teaspoons sherry into each cup.

About 6 (6 oz.) Servings

FRENCH HOT CHOCOLATE

Chocolate mixture can be made ahead and refrigerated up to a week.

- **½ cup water**
- **3 squares (1 oz. each) unsweetened chocolate**
- **½ cup sugar**
- **Dash salt**
- **½ cup whipping cream, whipped**
- **Milk**

1. Place water and chocolate in 2-cup glass measure.

2. Microwave for about 2 minutes, on HIGH, or until melted. Blend in sugar and salt.

3. Microwave for about 1 minute, on HIGH, or until hot. Cool. Fold in whipped cream. Refrigerate until served.

4. To make 1 serving, combine 3 tablespoons chocolate mixture and desired amount of milk in individual (6 oz.) glass cups or mugs.

5. Microwave for 1½ to 2 minutes, on HIGH, or until hot (about 160° F.).

About 1 Cup Chocolate Mixture Makes About 5 (6 oz.) Servings

TIP: Add a marshmallow during the last 10 to 15 seconds of heating.

RECIPE VARIATIONS

MINTED CHOCOLATE DRINK: Add ⅛ teaspoon peppermint extract to milk. Garnish with peppermint stick.

MOCHA CHOCOLATE DRINK: Add 1 to 2 tablespoons coffee liqueur to milk.

IRISH COFFEE

Do not allow liquid to boil or flavor will become bitter.

- **3½ cups water**
- **2 tablespoons instant coffee**
- **2 tablespoons sugar**
- **⅓ to ½ cup Irish whiskey**
- **¼ cup whipping cream, whipped**

1. Combine all ingredients, except whiskey and whipping cream, in 4-cup glass measure.

2. Microwave for 8 to 9 minutes, on HIGH, or until hot (about 200° F.). Stir in whiskey. Pour into mugs or glasses. Top with dollop of whipped cream.

About 6 (6 oz.) Servings

RECIPE VARIATIONS

SPANISH COFFEE: Add 1 teaspoon grated orange rind with sugar. Substitute ⅓ to ½ cup orange-flavored liqueur for whiskey.

VIENNESE COFFEE: Decrease sugar to 1½ tablespoons; add 2 cinnamon sticks and 8 whole cloves with sugar. Microwave as directed in basic recipe; omit whiskey.

FRENCH COFFEE: Decrease water to 2 cups. Add ½ teaspoon peppermint extract with water; omit sugar. Reduce cooking time 2 to 3 minutes. Substitute 1 cup whipping cream for whiskey. Microwave for an additional 1 to 1½ minutes, on ROAST, or until warm (about 150° F.). Omit dollops of whipped cream.

Breads

Yeast or Quick Tender, Fast-Rising

Here's How — and Why

Yeast Dough Rises Fast on WARM:	Raising yeast dough is fast and successful in a microwave oven on the gentle WARM setting which keeps fragile yeast alive and active. Steps 2, 3 and 4 in the Wheat Germ Bread recipe outline a technique for raising most freshly-mixed yeast doughs. Raise frozen dough as directed in the How to Bake Frozen Bread Dough recipe.
Bake Yeast Breads in a Few Minutes on SIMMER:	Microwave SIMMER bakes yeast breads with even texture, tender edges — no brown crusts.
Microwave Quick Breads on SIMMER/HIGH:	Quick breads from "scratch," biscuit mix or refrigerator biscuits start baking on Microwave SIMMER, finish up on HIGH to set the batter — a technique similar to baking cakes. Top quick breads with spices, brown sugar, cornmeal and/or frosting for most attractive appearance.
Reheat Baked Breads, Rolls, Popovers:	Baked breads, rolls, doughnuts and popovers reheat superbly. See convenience food chart on page 24.
Glass Baking Dishes Are a Must:	Use only glass baking dishes and bowls for breads. Grease yeast bread dishes well. Do not grease dishes for the types of quick breads in this chapter. Batter for quick breads rise high in a microwave oven, so do not fill dishes more than half full.
Microwave All Breads on Bottom Shelf:	Cover yeast dough with wax paper or plastic wrap during raising. Do not cover breads during baking. Raise and bake all breads on the oven's bottom shelf. Remove oven rack.
Standing Time Important to Tender Breads:	Both yeast and quick breads appear moist at the edges when removed from a microwave oven. Bread is cooked, however, if a toothpick inserted in several places in loaf comes out clean. Overcooked bread is tough and dry. Standing time allows bread's bottom surface to set without overcooking. Edges set as bread cools. Follow recipe directions carefully.
The " * " Shows a Setting Change:	The " * " at the end of a recipe title reminds you that there are two or more power settings during cooking.
Microwave-Conventional Comparison:	A microwave oven is a real time-saver when raising and baking yeast doughs. Freshly mixed dough raises twice and bakes in about 1 hour. Freshly frozen bread dough thaws, raises and bakes fast — in 2 to 2½ hours. Microwave breads are truly a new kind of product. They do not brown and kids love the no-crust slices. The breads are ideal for tea sandwiches, toast and French toast. Bread is moist and tender when taken from the oven so handle it carefully. Toppings enhance quick bread appearance. Popovers, which must crust to hold shape, cannot be baked in a microwave oven.

Pictured: Orange Caramel Sticky Buns, recipe below.

ORANGE CARAMEL STICKY BUNS *

½ cup packed brown sugar
2 tablespoons butter or margarine
2 tablespoons frozen orange juice concentrate, undiluted
½ teaspoon rum flavoring
½ cup chopped nuts
1 can (8 oz.) refrigerated biscuits

1. Combine all ingredients, except biscuits, in (9 x 5) glass loaf dish.
2. Microwave for about 1½ minutes, on HIGH, or until butter is melted. Stir well. Open and separate biscuits; place in sugar mixture, turning to coat. Arrange biscuits on their sides.
3. Microwave for 3 minutes on SIMMER.
4. Microwave for 1 to 1½ minutes, on HIGH, or until biscuits are no longer doughy. Let stand 2 minutes. Invert onto plate. About 6 Servings

HOW TO MICROWAVE QUICK BREAD MIXES AND YEAST BREAD

- Prepare quick bread mix as directed on package. Do not grease baking dish.
- Fill glass cooking dish only half full.
- Pour extra batter into paper-lined individual glass custard cups.
- Place bread on bottom shelf.
- Microwave on SIMMER then HIGH when directed on chart. Allow quick breads to stand 2 to 5 minutes.

- Mix yeast bread as directed in a favorite recipe. Raise on WARM using microwave technique in Wheat Germ Bread, page 43.
- Bake 1 or 2 loaves of bread in well-greased glass loaf dish(es) on bottom shelf.
- Microwave on SIMMER as directed in chart.
- Allow yeast breads to stand 5 minutes. Turn out on wire rack to cool before slicing.

QUICK AND YEAST BREADS	SIZE	GLASS CONTAINER	FIRST SETTING AND TIME	SECOND SETTING AND TIME
COFFEE CAKE MIX ✻	19-oz. pkg.	9-in. round dish	SIMMER 7 min.	HIGH 5 to 6 min.
NUT-TYPE BREAD MIX ✻	15 to 17-oz. pkg.	(9 x 5) loaf dish	SIMMER 9 min.	HIGH 5 to 6 min.
CORNBREAD MIX ✻	15-oz. pkg.	2-qt. (8 x 8) dish	SIMMER 10 min.	HIGH 3 to 4 min.
CORN MUFFIN MIX ✻ 6 Muffins	7½ to 8½-oz. pkg.	Cupcake liners in individual custard cups	SIMMER 4 min.	HIGH 1 to 1½ min.
BLUEBERRY MUFFIN MIX ✻ 4 Muffins 6 Muffins	13 to 14-oz. pkg.	Cupcake liners in individual custard cups	SIMMER 2 min. 2 min.	HIGH 1 to 1½ min. 1½ to 2 min.
HOMEMADE YEAST BREAD 1 Loaf 2 Loaves	 1 lb. 1 lb. ea.	(8 x 4) loaf dish or (9 x 5) loaf dish	SIMMER 10 to 11 min. 13 to 15 min.	

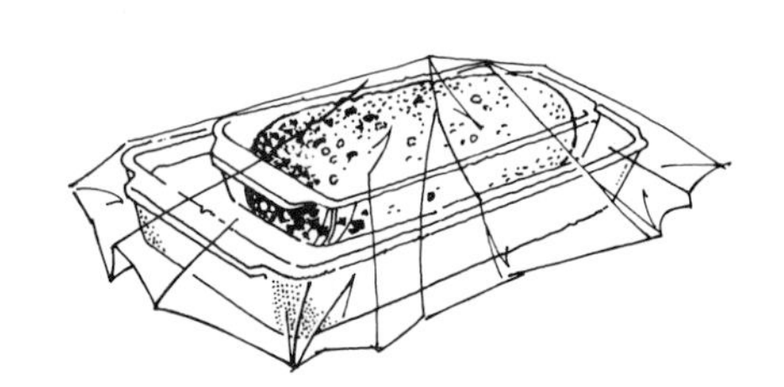

HOW TO BAKE FROZEN BREAD DOUGH ✻

1. Grease one 1-lb. loaf frozen bread dough; place in greased (9 x 5) glass loaf dish. Cover loosely with wax paper. Place dish of dough in 2-quart (12 x 7) glass baking dish. Pour 2 cups hot water (about 130° F.) into baking dish.

2. Microwave for 15 minutes on WARM.

3. Let stand in oven 10 minutes. Repeat these two steps until dough is just above top of dish, about 4 to 5 times. Remove dish of water and uncover bread.

4. Microwave for 10 to 11 minutes, on SIMMER, or until no longer doughy.

1 Loaf Bread

TIP: Frozen bread dough must be fresh or it will not raise fully.

CORNBREAD ✻

Fill quick bread baking dishes no more than half full.

1 cup unsifted all-purpose flour
1 cup cornmeal
3 tablespoons sugar
1 teaspoon salt
1 teaspoon baking powder
½ teaspoon soda
1 cup buttermilk
2 tablespoons cooking oil
2 eggs, slightly beaten

1. Combine dry ingredients in medium mixing bowl. Combine remaining ingredients, add to dry ingredients and stir until smooth. Pour into 2-quart (8 x 8) glass baking dish.

2. Microwave for 10 minutes on SIMMER.

3. Microwave for 2 to 4 minutes, on HIGH, or until toothpick inserted near center comes out clean. Let stand 5 minutes.

About 8 Servings

RECIPE VARIATION

SOUTHERN CORNBREAD: Substitute 2 cups self-rising white cornmeal mix and 1 tablespoon sugar for all dry ingredients. Omit 1 egg, increase buttermilk by ½ cup.

WHEAT GERM BREAD *

Raise any freshly mixed yeast bread using this technique.

1 cup warm water (about 120° F.)
1 package active dry yeast
¼ cup packed brown sugar
1½ teaspoons salt
2 tablespoons cooking oil
1 egg
½ cup wheat germ
1½ cups unsifted all-purpose flour
1 cup unsifted all-purpose flour
Melted butter

1. Combine warm water (about 120° F.) and yeast in large glass mixer bowl. Stir in brown sugar, salt, oil, egg, wheat germ and 1½ cups flour. Beat about 3 minutes at medium speed with electric mixer. Stir in remaining 1 cup flour to form a stiff dough. Knead on floured surface until smooth and elastic, 5 to 8 minutes.

2. **Raising:** Place dough in greased large glass bowl; brush with melted butter and cover loosely with wax paper. Place bowl of dough in 3-quart (13 x 9) glass baking dish containing 3 cups hot water (about 130° F.).

3. Microwave for 10 minutes on WARM. Let stand in oven 15 minutes or until dough is doubled in size. Punch down dough. Shape into a loaf and place in greased (9 x 5) glass loaf dish. Brush top with melted butter. Cover loosely with wax paper. Return to dish with hot water.

4. Microwave for 5 minutes on WARM. Let stand in oven 10 minutes, or until doubled in size. Remove dish of water and uncover bread.

5. **Baking:** Microwave for 10 to 11 minutes, on SIMMER, or until no longer doughy. Let stand 5 minutes. Turn out on rack to cool. 1 Loaf Bread

GARLIC BREAD

Melt butter in a glass pie plate and dip slices into it for even buttering.

½ cup butter or margarine
½ teaspoon garlic powder
1 loaf (1 lb.) French bread, cut crosswise in half

1. Place butter in small glass bowl.

2. Microwave for about 1½ minutes, on ROAST, or until melted. Stir in garlic powder. Slice French bread diagonally into 1-inch slices. Brush butter mixture on both sides of slices with pastry brush; re-form into 2 half loaves. Wrap each loosely in paper towels or paper napkins.

3. Microwave for 1½ to 2 minutes, on REHEAT, or until warmed (about 120° F.). 1 Loaf Bread

QUICK COFFEE CAKE *

Quick bread and cake techniques are similar.

2 cups biscuit mix
2 tablespoons sugar
1 carton (8 oz.) sour cream
1 egg
1 tablespoon sugar
½ teaspoon cinnamon

Filling:
¼ cup biscuit mix
¼ cup packed brown sugar
2 tablespoons butter or margarine
¼ cup chopped nuts

1. Combine all coffee cake ingredients, except 1 tablespoon sugar and cinnamon, in medium mixing bowl; mix well. Divide dough in half; spread half in 9-inch round glass baking dish. Sprinkle Filling over top. Drop remaining dough by teaspoonfuls over Filling (filling will show through). Combine 1 tablespoon sugar and cinnamon; sprinkle over top.

2. Microwave for 8 minutes on SIMMER.

3. Microwave for 4 to 4½ minutes, on HIGH, or until toothpick inserted near center comes out clean. Let stand 2 minutes.

4. **Filling:** Combine biscuit mix and brown sugar in small mixing bowl; cut in butter. Stir in nuts. About 6 Servings

RECIPE VARIATION

APPLE COFFEE CAKE: Substitute 1 carton (8 oz.) spicy apple yogurt for sour cream.

APRICOT NUT BREAD *

Quick breads raise on SIMMER, set on HIGH.

¾ cup water
¾ cup chopped, dried apricots
⅓ cup raisins
¾ cup packed brown sugar
3 tablespoons cooking oil
1 egg, slightly beaten
½ cup chopped nuts
1½ cups unsifted all-purpose flour
1 teaspoon soda
½ teaspoon salt

1. Combine water, apricots and raisins in 2-cup glass measure.

2. Microwave for about 2 minutes, on HIGH, or until boiling.

3. Combine brown sugar, oil and egg; mix well. Stir in fruit mixture and nuts. Add remaining ingredients; stir; pour into (9 x 5) glass loaf dish.

4. Microwave for 6 minutes on SIMMER.

5. Microwave for 3 to 3½ minutes, on HIGH, or until toothpick inserted near center comes out clean. Let stand 5 minutes. 1 Loaf Bread

RECIPE VARIATION

ZUCCHINI NUT BREAD: Substitute 2 teaspoons grated lemon rind for apricots. Decrease water by ¼ cup. Add ¾ cup shredded zucchini with nuts.

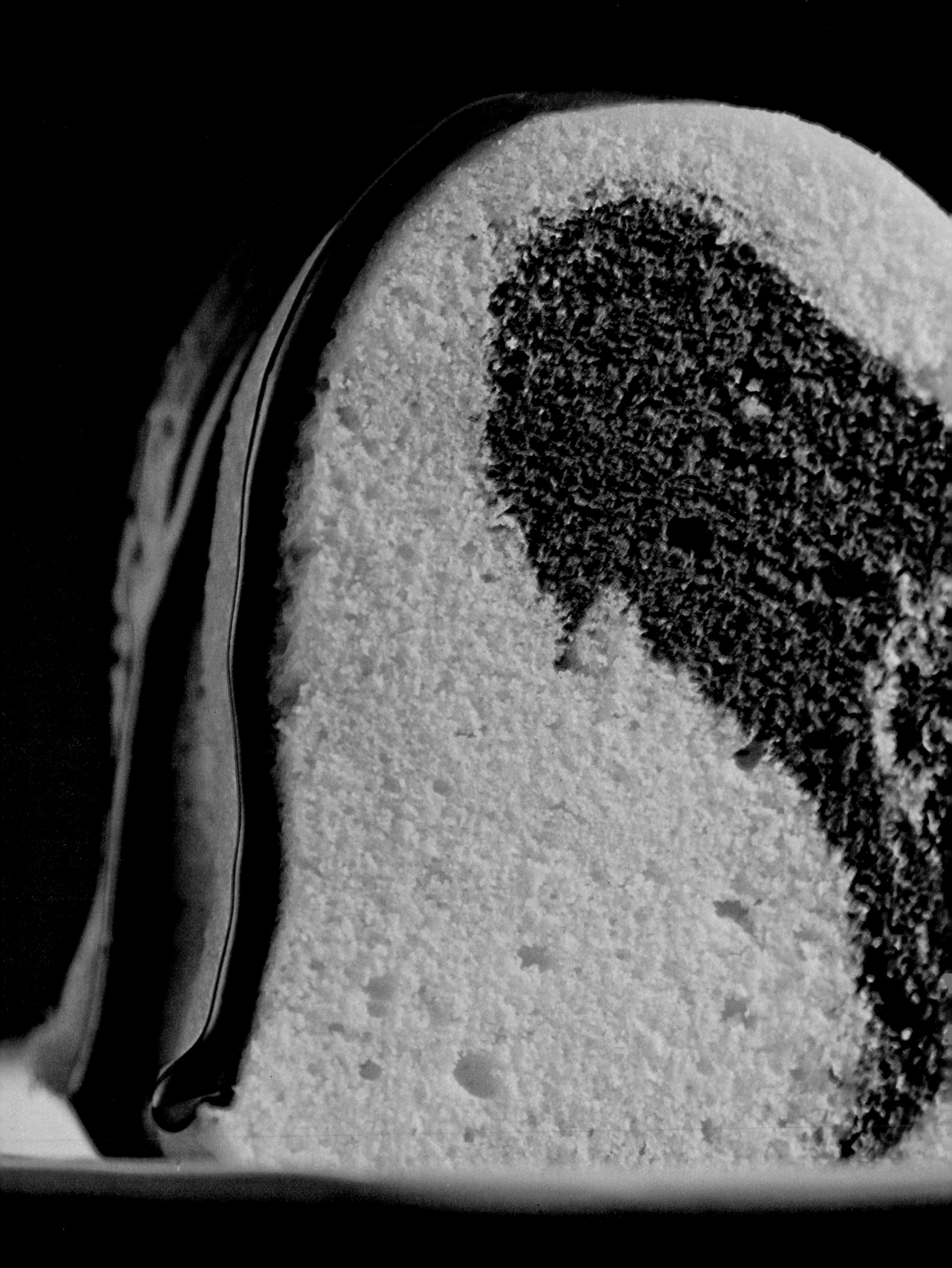

Cakes, Frostings & Fillings

Airy, Fluffy—Moist and Fast

Here's How — and Why

Cakes Rise to Any Occasion — Fast — on SIMMER/HIGH: Microwave cakes rise high, light, tender. AND, you can bake 2 layers at once! Start cooking on SIMMER setting to raise batter; finish up on HIGH to set cake. Fruit cake microwaves on DEFROST because the batter is dense, with a high concentration of sugary fruit.

Round Dishes Work Especially Well: Round, rectangular and square glass dishes work for cake, but round shapes work especially well — layers, ceramic bundt-type dishes or large mixing bowls with a glass set in the center. Insert glass in bowl open-end-up, to create a tube dish, which helps bake center thoroughly.

How to Fill a Baking Dish: It is not necessary to grease and flour baking dishes, but if cake is to be unmolded, line bottom of baking dish with wax paper. Microwave cakes rise high, so fill baking dishes only half full. Use extra batter for cupcakes.

When to Use Oven Rack: Cakes bake on the oven's bottom shelf — including 2 layers baked at once — unless otherwise specified. A few commercial mixes microwave better on the lower rack; see chart.

Standing Time Sets Cake Surface: Cake will test done when a toothpick inserted near center comes out clean, yet surface will still appear moist. Standing time sets and dries cake surface.

Ingredients Are Key to Frosting Cooking Time: Microwaved frostings are airy-light and spreadable. Microwave high-sugar frostings, which are much like rich candy syrups, on ROAST. Microwave simple sweet sauce frostings, which have less sugar and some thickening, on HIGH. Cook frostings on oven's bottom shelf; remove rack.

Fillings, Like Sweet Sauces, Microwave on HIGH: Cake fillings are essentially thick sweet sauces made with cornstarch or other thickening — cook quickly on Microwave HIGH. Some fillings are made with eggs, cream or condensed milk — microwave on ROAST. Cook fillings on oven's bottom shelf; remove rack.

Frostings and Fillings Microwave in a Glass Measure: Measure, mix and microwave frostings or fillings in a glass measure or mixing bowl large enough to hold twice the ingredient volume to prevent bubble-overs.

Beat Frostings and Fillings as a Recipe Directs: Microwaved frostings should be fluffy, so are usually beaten with an electric mixer after cooking. Fillings are beaten to keep them smooth. If a filling curdles, whirl it smooth in an electric blender. Cool frostings and fillings before spreading.

The " * " Notes Change in Cooking Speed: The " * " at the end of a recipe title tells you that 2 or more power settings are used during cooking.

Microwave-Conventional Comparison: Microwave cakes are lighter, higher and more tender than conventional cakes because there is no crust to restrict raising. Surfaces do not brown. Cooked cake surface should appear moist — it sets as cake stands and cools. Cooking times and toothpick doneness test should be observed carefully because microwave cakes overcook easily and toughen. Fruitcake microwaves superbly because surfaces do not burn easily as in a conventional oven. Cake mixes rise higher in a microwave oven — giving cake and cupcakes from one mix. When adapting conventional cake recipes, reduce leavening by ¼ to ⅓. Since cake surface remains tender, frostings and fillings should be fluffy, spreadable.

Pictured: Bundt-Type Cake Mix glazed with chocolate frosting, chart, page 46.

HOW TO BAKE CAKE

• Prepare batter as directed in recipe or on cake mix package.

• Use glass dish specified in chart. It will not always be the same as suggested on the recipe or package.

• Do not fill dish more than half full.

• Use extra batter to make cupcakes, as directed in chart.

• Line bottom of flat dishes with wax paper if cake is to be unmolded.

• Place most cakes on bottom shelf of oven. Follow chart for exceptions due to brand and type of product, when cake should be baked on lower rack.

• Bake 1 or 2 layers at a time — layers baked 1 at a time have most even surface.

• When cake batter is cooked in a large bowl, press a glass into the center of the batter, open end up. Or, use a ceramic bundt-type dish.

• Cake is done when a toothpick inserted near center comes out clean.

• Let cake stand 5 minutes to set.

• Turn out on serving plate to cool or cool in dish on wire rack.

CAKE	GLASS CONTAINER	POSITION	FIRST SETTING AND TIME	SECOND SETTING AND TIME
CAKE MIX *				
9-oz. pkg. 1 layer	9 in. round dish	Bottom shelf	SIMMER 7 min.	HIGH 2 to 3 min.
17 to 18½-oz. pkg. 1 layer	9 in. round dishes	Bottom shelf	SIMMER 7 min.	HIGH 2 to 3 min.
2 layers (both)		Bottom shelf	9 min.	6 to 7 min.
1 cake	2-qt. (12 x 7) baking dish	Bottom shelf	9 min.	3 to 4 min.
1 cake	3-qt. (13 x 9) baking dish	Bottom shelf	9 min.	6 to 7 min.
			SIMMER	HIGH
2 cupcakes	Paper cupcake liners in individual custard cups	Bottom shelf	1 min.	15 to 30 sec.
4 cupcakes			3 min.	30 to 45 sec.
6 cupcakes			4 min.	1 to 1½ min.
8 cupcakes			5 min.	1½ to 2 min.
SNACK-TYPE MIX * 14.5-oz. pkg. 1 layer	9-in. round dish	Lower rack	SIMMER 8 min.	HIGH 3 to 4 min.
BUNDT-TYPE MIX * 18.5-oz. pkg.	Ceramic bundt dish (greased)	Lower rack	SIMMER 9 min.	HIGH 5 to 6 min.
POUND CAKE MIX * 14-oz. pkg.	(9 x 5) loaf dish	Lower rack	SIMMER 9 min.	HIGH 5 to 6 min.
CAKE AND FROSTING MIX * 13.5-oz. pkg.	(5 x 7) foil lined pan (in box)	Bottom shelf	SIMMER 5 min.	HIGH 2 to 3 min.
PINEAPPLE UPSIDE DOWN CAKE MIX * 21.5-oz. pkg. 1 layer	9-in. round dish	Bottom shelf	SIMMER 7 min.	HIGH 5 to 6 min.
GINGERBREAD MIX * 14.5 to 15-oz. pkg.	2-qt. (8 x 8) baking dish	Bottom shelf	SIMMER 7 min.	HIGH 5 to 6 min.
HOMEMADE CAKE *			SIMMER	HIGH
1 layer	9-in. round dish	Bottom shelf	7 min.	2 to 3 min.
2 layers			9 min.	6 to 7 min.

BIRTHDAY CAKE CONES *

1 package (9 oz.) cake mix
8 flat-bottom ice cream cones

Cake mix batter will "keep" in a covered dish in the refrigerator up to 1 week.

1. Prepare cake mix as directed on package. Spoon about 2 tablespoons batter into each ice cream cone. Place cones in oven.

2. Microwave on SIMMER then HIGH:

	SIMMER	HIGH
1 cone	30 seconds	15 to 30 seconds
2 cones	1 minute	15 to 30 seconds
4 cones	2 minutes	30 to 45 seconds
6 cones	3 minutes	1 to 1½ minutes
8 cones	4 minutes	1½ to 2 minutes

Cake Cones are done when toothpick inserted near center of each cake comes out clean. Cake will be slightly soft around edges when cones come from oven. Cool on wire rack. Frost. About 8 Cake Cones

TIP: Top each Cake Cone with a scoop of ice cream and use colored gumdrops to make face on ice cream "head."

PARTY CAKE IN A BOWL *

1 package (18½ oz.) cake mix

A glass in a bowl creates a tube dish or use a ceramic bundt-type dish.

1. Prepare cake mix, as directed on package, in a large glass mixer bowl; beat well. Push a water glass, open-end-up, into center of batter.

2. Microwave for 9 minutes on SIMMER.

3. Microwave for 5 to 6 minutes, on HIGH, or until toothpick inserted near center comes out clean. Let stand in bowl 5 minutes. Remove glass with a twisting motion and invert cake on serving platter. Frost or sprinkle with powdered sugar. About 12 Servings

COCONUT LOAF CAKE *

½ cup butter or margarine
1 cup sugar
3 eggs
½ teaspoon grated lemon rind
1½ cups unsifted all-purpose flour
2 teaspoons baking powder
¼ teaspoon salt
½ cup milk
½ cup flaked coconut

Microwave cakes bake in less than 20 minutes.

1. Place butter in large mixing bowl.

2. Microwave for about 30 seconds, on ROAST, or until softened. Beat in sugar, eggs and lemon rind until light and fluffy. Stir in dry ingredients alternately with milk; mix well after each addition. Fold in coconut. Line bottom of (9 x 5) glass loaf dish with wax paper. Pour batter into dish.

3. Microwave for 9 minutes on SIMMER.

4. Microwave for 4 to 5 minutes, on HIGH, or until toothpick inserted near center comes out clean. Let stand in dish 5 minutes. Turn out on rack to cool. 1 (9 x 5) Loaf Cake

OATMEAL APPLE CAKE *

¼ cup butter or margarine
¾ cup packed brown sugar
2 eggs
¼ teaspoon vanilla
½ cup unsifted all-purpose flour
¼ teaspoon soda
½ teaspoon salt
½ teaspoon cinnamon
1 cup quick-cooking rolled oats
¼ cup water
1 cup chopped peeled cooking apples

Topping:
¼ cup sugar
1 teaspoon cinnamon
¼ cup chopped nuts

SIMMER/HIGH baking raises, then sets batter.

1. Place butter in large mixing bowl.

2. Microwave for about 20 seconds, on ROAST, or until softened. Beat in brown sugar, eggs and vanilla until light and fluffy. Add flour, soda, salt, cinnamon and oatmeal; mix well. Stir in water and apple. Pour into 9-inch round glass baking dish. Sprinkle Topping over batter.

3. Microwave for 7 minutes on SIMMER.

4. Microwave for 4 to 5 minutes, on HIGH, or until toothpick inserted near center comes out clean. Let stand 2 minutes. Cool in dish on rack or serve warm.

5. **Topping:** Combine sugar and cinnamon in small bowl; stir in nuts. 6 to 8 Servings

Pictured: Cake Made from a Mix, chart, page 46; Lemon Filling, page 51; Five-Minute Snowy White Frosting, page 51.

See Sauce chapter for sweet sauce recipes.

HEATING CANNED PLUM PUDDING

1. Remove 1 can (15 oz.) plum pudding from can. Place on glass platter.

2. Microwave for 2 to 4 minutes, on REHEAT, or until heated through (about 120° F.). Serve with rum or brandy-flavored vanilla sauce.

4 to 6 Servings

SPICY CARROT CAKE ✻

2 eggs
2 medium carrots, peeled and cut into pieces
½ cup butter or margarine
½ cup honey
½ teaspoon vanilla
1 cup unsifted all-purpose flour
½ teaspoon soda
½ teaspoon salt
½ teaspoon cinnamon
½ teaspoon nutmeg
½ cup chopped nuts
Whipped cream, if desired

Sauce:
¼ cup orange juice
¼ cup honey
¼ cup butter or margarine
1 to 2 tablespoons orange liqueur, if desired

Sauces absorb quickly into moist-top cakes.

1. Place eggs and carrots in blender container; blend until carrots are in fine pieces; set aside. Place butter in large glass mixing bowl.

2. Microwave for about 30 seconds, on ROAST, or until softened. Blend in honey and vanilla; beat in carrot mixture. Stir in remaining ingredients, except whipped cream. Pour into 2-quart (8 x 8) glass baking dish.

3. Microwave for 9 minutes on SIMMER.

4. Microwave for 3 to 4 minutes, on HIGH, or until toothpick inserted near center comes out clean. Pour warm Sauce over cake; cool. Top with whipped cream.

5. Sauce: Combine all ingredients, except liqueur, in 2-cup glass measure.

6. Microwave for 1½ to 2 minutes, on HIGH, or until the mixture boils (about 200° F.). Stir in liqueur.

About 6 Servings

TIP: If you don't have a blender, grate the carrot before adding to the butter-egg mixture.

PEACH SPICE CAKE ✻

1 can (16 oz.) sliced peaches, drained
2 tablespoons sugar
½ teaspoon cinnamon
1 package (9 oz.) white cake mix
1 teaspoon cinnamon
¼ teaspoon cloves

1. Drain peaches on paper towel. Combine sugar and ½ teaspoon cinnamon; sprinkle over bottom of 9-inch round glass baking dish. Arrange peach slices over sugar mixture; set aside.

2. Combine cake mix and spices in medium mixing bowl. Prepare cake mixture as directed on package. Pour over peaches.

3. Microwave for 7 minutes on SIMMER.

4. Microwave for 6 to 7 minutes, on HIGH, or until toothpick inserted near center comes out clean. Let stand in dish 1 minute. Turn out onto platter and serve warm or cool.

About 6 Servings

FRUITCAKE

¼ cup butter or margarine
¼ cup packed brown sugar
¼ cup dark molasses
2 eggs
1 cup unsifted all-purpose flour
½ teaspoon baking powder
¼ teaspoon salt
¼ teaspoon nutmeg
2 tablespoons cherry brandy or orange juice
1 jar (10 oz.) pickled watermelon rind, drained
1 cup red candied cherries
1 cup dried apricots
1 cup raisins
1 cup whole unpeeled almonds

Fruit may be left whole or chopped.

1. Place butter in large glass mixing bowl.

2. Microwave for about 20 seconds, on ROAST, or until softened. Beat in sugar, molasses and eggs. Stir in dry ingredients alternately with brandy; mix well after each addition. Stir in watermelon rind, fruits and nuts. Line bottom and sides of (9 x 5) glass loaf dish with wax paper. Paper should extend at least 2 to 3 inches above sides of dish. Pour batter into dish.

3. Microwave for 35 to 40 minutes, on DEFROST, or until toothpick inserted near center comes out clean. Let stand in dish 5 minutes. Lift out on rack to cool.

18 to 20 Slices

TIP: Fruit toughens if not stored properly. Wrap cake in several layers of clean cheese cloth. Soak with ¼ cup cherry brandy or rum. Store in tightly sealed container to hold moisture.

OLD-FASHIONED SHORTCAKE *

Remove individual cakes from oven as they finish cooking.

- **2 cups unsifted all-purpose flour**
- **2 tablespoons sugar**
- **2 teaspoons baking powder**
- **½ teaspoon salt**
- **⅓ cup butter or margarine**
- **½ cup milk**
- **1 egg**
- **Sweetened fruit**
- **Whipped cream**

1. Combine flour, sugar, baking powder and salt in medium mixing bowl. Cut in butter until crumbly. Measure milk into small bowl and beat in egg; stir into flour mixture. Shape into 5 or 6 balls; place in individual 6-oz. glass custard cups.

2. Microwave for 3 minutes on SIMMER.

3. Microwave for 2 to 3 minutes, on HIGH, or until cake is no longer doughy.

4. Serve warm topped with sweetened fruit and whipped cream.

5 to 6 Servings

TIP: Use 1 package (9 oz.) frozen sweetened fruit. See page 25 for thawing directions.

DATE CARAMEL PUDDING CAKE *

Toppings enhance cake's appearance.

- **1 cup unsifted all-purpose flour**
- **¾ cup sugar**
- **1 teaspoon baking powder**
- **½ teaspoon salt**
- **½ teaspoon cinnamon**
- **½ cup milk**
- **1 egg**
- **2 tablespoons cooking oil**
- **¾ cup chopped dates**
- **½ cup chopped nuts**
- **1 cup packed brown sugar**
- **1 cup water**
- **Whipped cream**

1. Combine flour, sugar, baking powder, salt and cinnamon in 2-quart glass casserole. Blend in milk, egg and oil. Stir in dates and nuts; spread batter evenly in casserole.

2. Sprinkle brown sugar over batter; set aside. Measure water into 2-cup glass measure.

3. Microwave for 2 to 2½ minutes, on HIGH, or until just boiling (about 200° F.). Pour hot water over brown sugar.

4. Microwave for 9 minutes on SIMMER.

5. Microwave for 6 to 7 minutes, on HIGH, or until cake portion is no longer doughy. Serve with whipped cream.

6 to 8 Servings

MINCEMEAT APRICOT PUDDING *

Microwaved steamed puddings are never soggy.

- **⅓ cup butter or margarine**
- **½ cup packed brown sugar**
- **2 eggs**
- **1¼ cups prepared mincemeat**
- **2 cups unsifted all-purpose flour**
- **1½ teaspoons baking powder**
- **½ teaspoon salt**
- **½ cup chopped dried apricots**

Hot Mincemeat Sauce:

- **1 cup whipping cream**
- **½ cup packed brown sugar**
- **½ cup prepared mincemeat**
- **⅓ cup butter or margarine**
- **1 teaspoon vanilla**

1. Place butter in large mixing bowl.

2. Microwave for about 30 seconds, on ROAST, or until softened. Beat in sugar, eggs and mincemeat. Stir in dry ingredients; mix well. Fold in apricots.

3. Spread batter in 1½-quart glass casserole. Cover with glass lid.

4. Microwave for 10 minutes on SIMMER.

5. Microwave for 5 to 6 minutes, on HIGH, or until toothpick inserted near center comes out clean. Remove cover; let stand 5 minutes; unmold. Serve with Hot Mincemeat Sauce.

6. **Hot Mincemeat Sauce:** Combine all ingredients, except butter and vanilla, in 4-cup glass measure; add butter. Microwave for 6 to 7 minutes, on ROAST, or until bubbly (about 200° F.). Stir in vanilla.

8 to 10 Servings

EASY FUDGE FROSTING

Softer frostings spread best on tender cake tops.

- **2 tablespoons butter or margarine**
- **3 squares (1 oz. each) unsweetened chocolate**
- **2¾ cups powdered sugar, sifted**
- **½ teaspoon salt**
- **⅓ cup light cream**
- **1 teaspoon vanilla**

1. Place butter and chocolate in small glass mixing bowl.

2. Microwave for about 2 minutes, on HIGH, or until melted.

3. Meanwhile, combine remaining ingredients in medium mixing bowl; beat well. Slowly beat in chocolate mixture. Beat with electric mixer on medium speed until frosting is spreading consistency.

Frosts 13 x 9-Inch or Two 9-Inch Layers

FIVE-MINUTE SNOWY WHITE FROSTING

- 1 cup sugar
- ½ cup water
- ¼ teaspoon cream of tartar
- Dash salt
- 2 egg whites
- 1 teaspoon vanilla

Candy-syrup-type frostings cook on ROAST.

1. Combine sugar, water, cream of tartar and salt in 2-cup glass measure.

2. Microwave for 4 to 5 minutes, on ROAST, or until mixture boils (about 200° F.).

3. Beat egg whites in small mixer bowl until soft peaks form. Gradually pour in hot syrup; beat about 5 minutes or until thick and fluffy. Blend in vanilla.

Frosts 13 x 9-Inch or Two 9-Inch Layers

CREAMY WHIPPED FROSTING

- ¾ cup sugar
- ¼ cup unsifted all-purpose flour
- ¾ cup milk
- ½ cup butter or margarine
- 1 teaspoon vanilla

A thick sweet-sauce-type frosting cooks on HIGH.

1. Combine sugar and flour in small glass mixer bowl. Stir in milk.

2. Microwave for 2 minutes on HIGH. Beat lightly with electric mixer and continue cooking for 1 to 1½ minutes, on HIGH, or until mixture boils and thickens (about 200° F.). Add butter and beat until smooth. Refrigerate about 2 hours or until chilled and set. Add vanilla and beat with electric mixer at high speed until light and fluffy.

Frosts 13 x 9-Inch or Two 9-Inch Layers

RECIPE VARIATIONS

NUTTY-COCONUT FROSTING: Fold 1⅓ cups flaked coconut and 1 cup chopped nuts into basic recipe after final beating.

LEMON FROSTING: Substitute 2 to 3 teaspoons grated lemon rind for vanilla in basic recipe. Add few drops of yellow food coloring, if desired.

APRICOT FROSTING: Fold 1 cup finely chopped dried apricots or other dried fruit into basic recipe after final beating.

MINT FROSTING: Substitute 1 teaspoon peppermint extract for vanilla in basic recipe. Add few drops of red food coloring, if desired. Garnish with peppermint sticks.

PINEAPPLE FROSTING: Fold 1 can (8 oz.) crushed pineapple, drained, into basic recipe after final beating.

CARAMEL FROSTING: Substitute ¾ cup brown sugar and ¾ cup light cream for sugar and milk in basic recipe. Microwave for 2 minutes on ROAST. Beat well and continue cooking for 1½ to 2 minutes, on ROAST, or until mixture thickens (about 160° F.). Continue as directed in basic recipe.

CARAMEL-RAISIN FROSTING: Fold 1 cup raisins into Caramel Frosting, above, after final beating.

LEMON FILLING

- ½ cup sugar
- 2 tablespoons cornstarch
- ⅛ teaspoon salt
- ⅔ cup water
- 1½ teaspoons grated lemon peel
- 2 tablespoons lemon juice
- 1 tablespoon butter or margarine

Stir a filling, if directed, to keep it smooth.

1. Combine sugar, cornstarch and salt in 2-cup glass measure; stir in water. Add remaining ingredients.

2. Microwave for 2 minutes on HIGH. Stir and continue cooking for 1½ to 2 minutes, on HIGH, or until thickened (about 200° F.). Stir well. Cool and spread on cake.

1 Cup Filling

TIP: Yellow food coloring may be added, if desired.

VANILLA CREAM FILLING

- 1½ cups milk
- ⅓ cup sugar
- 2 tablespoons cornstarch
- ¼ teaspoon salt
- 2 egg yolks
- 2 teaspoons vanilla

Filling with egg yolks cooks on ROAST.

1. Combine all ingredients, except vanilla, in 2-cup glass measure. Beat well with rotary beater.

2. Microwave for 4 minutes on ROAST. Beat and continue cooking for about 3 minutes, on ROAST, or until thickened (about 170° F.). Add vanilla; beat until smooth. Cool; spread on cake.

About 2 Cups Filling

RECIPE VARIATIONS

CHOCOLATE CREAM FILLING: Increase sugar to ½ cup and combine with ¼ cup cocoa. Stir into milk; add other ingredients, and continue as directed in basic recipe.

BUTTERSCOTCH CREAM FILLING: Decrease milk to 1¼ cups. Add ¼ cup dark corn syrup and substitute ⅓ cup brown sugar for sugar.

Cookies, Candies & Snacks

Kids Love to Microwave these Treats

Here's How — and Why

Bake Cookies on SIMMER:	Homemade cookies and cookies made from a mix microwave on SIMMER to prevent overcooking. Commercial slice-and-bake refrigerator roll cookies are not successful in a microwave oven.
Microwave Bar Cookies on SIMMER/HIGH:	Bar cookies, such as Brownies, bake on SIMMER to raise, then on HIGH to set the batter — similar to the cake technique.
Thaw or Freshen Baked Cookies or Bars on REHEAT:	Recapture "just baked" flavor of stored or frozen individual bars or cookies. Place four on a napkin and microwave on REHEAT for about 15 seconds if cookies are at room temperature; about 20 seconds if frozen. Time varies according to fat and sugar content.
Candy Cooks on ROAST:	Microwave candy on ROAST so sugar syrup boils, sugar dissolves and syrup blends into candy.
Sugar-Syrup Snacks Microwave on ROAST:	Snacks in this chapter are made with sugary syrups similar to candy. Microwave on ROAST to prevent boil-overs. Granola heats on ROAST to blend flavors and toast. Popping corn is NOT RECOMMENDED in a microwave oven. See the convenience food chart, page 25, for making caramel apples using sheet caramel.
Microwave Cookies on Wax Paper; Bars, Candy, Snacks in Glass:	Microwave drop cookies on wax or parchment paper; space 1 to 2 inches apart. Do not remove cookies from paper until cool and firm. A little wax from wax paper may stick to cookie bottoms. It is tasteless and not harmful when eaten. Microwave bars in flat glass baking dishes. Grease dish, if desired, but do not flour or a flour-y layer will result on the bottom of bars. Mix and cook candy ingredients in a buttered glass mixing bowl or 4-cup glass measure which is two to three times larger than the ingredient volume — this prevents boil-overs. Mix and cook snacks in glass mixing bowls or glass baking dishes.
Only Candies and Snacks Need a Cover during Cooking:	Cover candy and snacks when specified in a recipe. Use a glass plate or stretch plastic wrap tautly across bowl. Pierce wrap so steam escapes during cooking.
Candy and Snack Syrups Need Stirring, Watching:	Stir candy during cooking so heat is equalized and candy cooks smooth. Do WATCH CANDY CLOSELY because a microwave oven cooks fast. Check temperature with a candy thermometer. Remove candy from oven before inserting the thermometer — it is not accurate if used during cooking and will be damaged.
The "✱" Is a Reminder that Settings Change:	The "✱" in a recipe reminds you that the oven setting changes during cooking. Stirring at this time is convenient.
Microwave-Conventional Comparison:	Cookies, candies and snacks are a big time-saver because they cook so much faster than with a conventional range. None of these sweets brown — great for sugar and butter cookies which should not brown. Many cookies spread to big, thin crunchy wafers. Some are great "dunkers." Candy must be carefully watched because it cooks very quickly.

Date Bark, page 57; Peanut Brittle, page 56; Sugar Cookies, Krispie Marshmallow Treats, page 55; Fudge Brownies, page 54.

HOW TO MICROWAVE COOKIES AND BARS

- Prepare bar mix as directed on package.
- Grease baking dish, if desired, but do not flour as it will layer on bottom of bar.
- Microwave bars, uncovered, in a glass baking dish.
- Cool and cut bars as directed on package.
- Frost or glaze before cutting. Bars have a slightly irregular top.
- Mix cookies according to package or recipe directions.
- Microwave cookies on wax or parchment paper placed on oven floor.
- Allow enough space between cookies because they spread during cooking.
- Allow cookies to cool on wax paper; remove, and store.

COOKIE OR BAR	PACKAGE SIZE	CONTAINER	FIRST SETTING AND TIME	SECOND SETTING AND TIME
BROWNIE MIX *			SIMMER	HIGH
	16-oz.	Glass (8 x 8)	7 min.	3 to 4 min.
	22.5-oz.	Glass (13 x 9)	7 min.	5 to 6 min.
DATE BAR MIX *	14-oz.	Glass (8 x 8)	SIMMER 12 min.	HIGH 2 to 3 min.
COOKIE MIX	12-oz.	Parchment or wax paper	SIMMER	
4 Cookies			3½ to 4 min.	—
6 Cookies			5 to 5½ min.	—
12 Cookies			7 to 7½ min.	—
HOMEMADE COOKIES		Parchment or wax paper	SIMMER	
4 Cookies			2 to 3 min.	—
6 Cookies			3 to 4 min.	—
12 Cookies			5 to 6 min.	—

FUDGY BROWNIES *

3 squares (1 oz. ea.) or envelopes unsweetened chocolate
½ cup butter or margarine
1½ cups sugar
3 eggs
1¼ cup unsifted all-purpose flour
⅛ teaspoon salt
1 teaspoon vanilla
½ cup chopped nuts

Microwave bars using SIMMER/HIGH cake technique.

1. Place chocolate and butter in medium glass mixing bowl.
2. Microwave for 2 to 2½ minutes, on ROAST, or until melted. Stir in sugar; beat in eggs. Stir in remaining ingredients. Spread batter into 2-quart (8 x 8) glass baking dish.
3. Microwave for 7 minutes on SIMMER.
4. Microwave for 3 to 4 minutes, on HIGH, or until puffed and dry on top. Cool until set; cut into bars. About 24 Bars

TIP: Top brownie squares with ice cream and chocolate sauce for a quick dessert.

CARAMEL APPLES

1 package (14 oz.) caramels
2 tablespoons hot water
6 medium apples
6 wooden sticks

Buttering sheet or paper keeps caramel from sticking.

1. Place unwapped caramels in buttered, deep, medium glass bowl; add water. Cover with wax paper.
2. Microwave for 3 minutes on ROAST. Stir; recover, and continue cooking for about 2 minutes, on ROAST, or until melted.
3. Skewer each apple with wooden stick. Dip each apple in melted caramel mixture; turn to coat evenly. Place dipped apples on buttered cookie sheet or buttered wax paper. 6 Apples

TIP: If caramel mixture thickens while dipping apples, return to oven and resoften, covered, on ROAST.

RECIPE VARIATION

CHOCOLATE CARAMEL APPLES: Add 1 package (6 oz.) "real" chocolate chips, ¼ teaspoon ground cinnamon and dash of cloves to caramels; increase water to ¼ cup.

SUGAR COOKIES

Soften 1 cup butter for 1½ to 2 minutes on WARM.

- **1 cup butter or margarine, softened**
- **1 cup sugar**
- **2 eggs**
- **3 cups unsifted all-purpose flour**
- **1 teaspoon cream of tartar**
- **½ teaspoon soda**
- **½ teaspoon salt**
- **1 teaspoon almond extract**

1. Cream butter in large mixer bowl until fluffy. Beat in sugar and eggs until well blended. Stir in remaining ingredients and chill. Shape into 1-inch balls; place on wax paper, 1 inch apart; flatten with glass dipped in water, then sugar. Place cookies on wax paper in the oven.

2. Microwave on SIMMER until tops have set appearance:
4 cookies — 2 to 3 minutes
6 cookies — 3 to 4 minutes
12 cookies — 5 to 6 minutes
Cool on wax paper; remove, and store in tightly covered container.

About 3 Dozen

TIP: Form dough into 2 rolls, 2 inches in diameter, and freeze. Slice ¼ inch thick and place on wax paper. Microwave 9 cookies for about 4 to 5 minutes, on SIMMER, or until tops have set appearance.

RECIPE VARIATION

SOUR CREAM SUGAR COOKIES: Increase sugar to 2 cups. Add 1 carton (8 oz.) sour cream to eggs. Increase flour to 4 cups and soda to 1 teaspoon.

KRISPIE MARSHMALLOW TREATS

ROAST setting helps prevent boil-overs.

- **¼ cup butter or margarine**
- **5 cups miniature or 40 large marshmallows**
- **5 cups crispy rice cereal**

1. Place butter in 2-quart (12 x 7) glass baking dish.

2. Microwave for about 1 minute, on ROAST, or until melted. Stir in marshmallows.

3. Microwave for 1 minute on ROAST. Stir and continue cooking for about 1½ minutes, on ROAST, or until marshmallows are softened. Stir until smooth. Mix in cereal. Press into baking dish. Cool until set; cut into squares.

24 to 30 Krispie Squares

RECIPE VARIATIONS

BUTTERSCOTCH KRISPIE TREATS: Add 1 package (6 oz.) butterscotch pieces to butter. Microwave for about 2 minutes, on ROAST, or until melted. Increase cereal to 6 cups; add 1 cup salted peanuts with cereal.

MINT CHOCOLATE KRISPIE TREATS: Add 1 package (6 oz.) "real" chocolate pieces to butter. Microwave for about 2 minutes, on ROAST, or until melted. Stir ¼ to ½ teaspoon peppermint extract into melted marshmallows. Increase cereal to 6 cups.

Pictured: Caramel Apples, page 54; Cookie Bars from a Mix, chart opposite.

POPCORN BALLS

- 2½ quarts popped corn
- 1 cup sugar
- ½ cup water
- ¼ cup dark corn syrup
- ½ teaspoon salt
- 1 teaspoon vinegar
- 1 teaspoon vanilla
- Butter or margarine

Popping corn in the microwave oven is not recommended.

1. Place popcorn in buttered jelly roll pan.

2. Combine remaining ingredients, except vanilla and butter, in buttered, medium glass mixing bowl; mix well.

3. Microwave for 16 to 18 minutes, on ROAST, or until candy forms a hard ball in cold water (260° F.). Stir in vanilla. Pour in thin stream over popped corn; mix well. Butter hands lightly and shape into balls.

About 12 Balls

RECIPE VARIATION

CARAMEL CORN: Substitute 1 cup packed brown sugar for sugar. Add 1 cup pecans and ½ cup almonds to popped corn. Pour candy syrup in thin stream over popped corn mixture; mix well.

Make popcorn using a conventional method.

POPCORN: Cooking popcorn in a microwave oven is not recommended. There are too many variables — things such as time, temperature and age of popcorn.

Regardless of popcorn age, microwaves pop too few kernels to make the technique successful. Prolonged cooking does not yield any more popped corn, but can cause fire or make the cooking dish too hot to handle and even break.

Never attempt to pop corn in a paper bag. Oil plus extended cooking can cause smoking and, eventually, fire.

GRANOLA

- 4 cups quick-cooking rolled oats
- 1 cup sunflower nuts
- ¾ cup wheat germ
- ½ cup shredded coconut
- ½ cup packed brown sugar
- ⅓ cup sesame seeds
- ⅓ cup honey
- ⅓ cup cooking oil
- ½ teaspoon vanilla

Stirring heats and blends mixture evenly.

1. Combine all ingredients in large mixing bowl; mix well. Pour into 3-quart (13 x 9) glass baking dish.

2. Microwave for 8 minutes on ROAST. Stir and continue cooking for 4 minutes on ROAST. Stir again and continue cooking for 4 to 5 minutes, on ROAST, or until slightly crisp and flavors blend. Cool.

About 8 Cups Granola

RECIPE VARIATION

APRICOT GRANOLA: Substitute ½ cup chopped, dried apricots and 1 cup pumpkin seeds for sunflower nuts and sesame seeds. Stir 3 to 4 times during cooking.

PEANUT BRITTLE

- 2 cups sugar
- 1 cup light corn syrup
- ½ cup water
- 1½ cups raw Spanish peanuts
- ½ teaspoon salt
- 2 tablespoons butter or margarine
- 2 teaspoons vanilla
- 2 teaspoons soda

Use candy thermometer after removing dish from oven.

1. Combine sugar, corn syrup and water in buttered large glass mixing bowl; mix well.

2. Microwave for 24 minutes, on ROAST, or until a soft ball forms in cold water (240° F.). Stir in peanuts and continue cooking for 12 to 15 minutes, on ROAST, or until candy forms hard, brittle threads in cold water (300° F.). Stir in remaining ingredients until smooth. Divide mixture in half; pour each half on buttered baking sheet. Spread quickly into thin layer. Cool; break into pieces.

About 2 Pounds Candy

S'MORES

Dry marshmallows may take slightly longer to melt.

- **12 graham cracker squares**
- **2 bars (1.2 oz. each) milk chocolate**
- **6 large marshmallows**

1. Place 6 cracker squares on paper towel. Top each with ⅓ chocolate bar, 1 marshmallow and 1 cracker square.

2. Microwave on HIGH until marshmallow(s) puffs. Serve immediately.

1 S'More — 15 to 20 seconds
2 S'Mores — 25 to 30 seconds
3 S'Mores — 30 to 35 seconds
4 S'Mores — 35 to 40 seconds
6 S'Mores — 45 to 50 seconds

6 S'Mores

RECIPE VARIATIONS

BANANA S'MORES: Place 3 slices banana on each chocolate bar; top with marshmallow and cracker square.

PEANUT BUTTER S'MORES: Spread each of 6 graham cracker squares with peanut butter before topping with chocolate bar.

CRYSTALLIZED ORANGE NUTS

Sugar syrup microwaves on ROAST to boil and crystallize.

- **¼ cup orange juice**
- **1 cup sugar**
- **2 cups pecan halves**

1. Combine orange juice and sugar in 2-quart (12 x 7) glass baking dish; mix well. Stir in pecans.

2. Microwave for 6 minutes on ROAST. Stir and continue cooking for 8 to 10 minutes, on ROAST, or until syrup crystallizes. Spread, separate and cool glazed nuts on buttered cookie sheet.

About 3 Cups Nuts

FUDGE

ROAST setting boils syrup, dissolves sugar.

- **1⅔ cups sugar**
- **½ cup evaporated milk**
- **2 cups miniature marshmallows**
- **1 package (12 oz.) "real" chocolate pieces**
- **1 teaspoon vanilla**
- **Dash salt**
- **½ cup chopped nuts, if desired**

1. Combine sugar and milk in large glass mixing bowl.

2. Microwave for 4 minutes on ROAST. Stir well and continue cooking for 2 to 3 minutes, on ROAST, or until boiling and sugar dissolves. Stir in remaining ingredients until melted. Pour into buttered 2-qt. (8 x 8) glass baking dish. Cool; cut into squares.

About 3 Dozen Fudge Squares

ALMOND BARK SUPREME

ROAST setting melts chocolate evenly – no burning.

- **1 to 1½ lbs. white chocolate**
- **1 cup red cinnamon-flavored candies**
- **¾ cup whole almonds**

1. Place white chocolate and candies in 3-quart (13 x 9) glass baking dish.

2. Microwave for 3 minutes on ROAST. Stir and continue cooking for 2 to 3 minutes on ROAST. Stir in almonds. Pour immediately onto wax paper and spread into thin layer. Cool; break into pieces.

About 1 Pound Candy

RECIPE VARIATION

DATE BARK: Omit cinnamon candies. Reduce final cooking time to 1 to 2 minutes. Add 1 cup chopped pitted dates with almonds.

MAPLE NUT DIVINITY

Microwave cooking produces foamy-light Divinity.

- **1 cup sugar**
- **1 cup packed brown sugar**
- **½ cup light corn syrup**
- **½ cup water**
- **2 egg whites**
- **1 teaspoon imitation maple flavoring**
- **Dash salt**
- **½ cup chopped nuts**

1. Combine sugars, corn syrup and water in buttered large glass mixing bowl.

2. Microwave for 15 to 17 minutes, on ROAST, or until candy forms a hard ball in cold water (250° F.). Meanwhile beat egg whites in large mixer bowl until stiff peaks form. Pour candy syrup in thin stream into egg whites, beating constantly with mixer. Add maple flavoring and salt, beat until mixture is stiff and dull. Fold in nuts. Drop mixture by teaspoonfuls onto wax paper. Cool.

About 3 Dozen Pieces Candy

Desserts

Fruit, Custard and One-of-a-Kind

Here's How—and Why

Enjoy Tender, Juicy Fruit Desserts — Use HIGH for Fresh, REHEAT for Canned:	Fresh fruits microwave quickly on HIGH — holding shape and retaining full flavor. Use HIGH setting to soften and "plump" dried fruits, too. Canned fruits are already cooked. Use REHEAT to prevent mushing. Microwave desserts on bottom oven shelf unless otherwise directed in recipe.
Microwave Most Pudding and Pie Filling Mixes on HIGH:	A stabilizer in pudding and pie filling mixes keeps these smooth and creamy, even when cooked on HIGH. See chart in this chapter.
SIMMER Baked and Soft Custard Desserts:	Eggs are a major sensitive ingredient in baked and soft custard desserts. Cook these mixtures gently on SIMMER to help prevent curdling.
Combine Microwave Techniques for Fancy Desserts:	Many delectable desserts combine cooking techniques — Trifle, for example, uses a microwaved cake, custard sauce and other ingredients. Use this chapter as a guide for adapting your own recipes.
Microwave in Glass Without Metal Trim:	Desserts cook superbly in the traditional glass baking dishes and glass casseroles, but are often pretty and easy when mixed and microwaved right in glass or pottery serving bowls, casseroles or platters without metal trim. Baked custards microwave best in individual glass cups.
Few Desserts Need Covers:	Most desserts are cooked uncovered. Dried fruits, however, "plump" best when microwaved with a cover — so do dumpling-topped fruits. Use a fitted glass lid or wax paper to cover. Tip lids away from arm when removing them from steamy food. Plastic wrap may be used to cover. Pierce it and allow steam to escape before removing.
When and If to Stir:	Stewed fruits are stirred once to assure even cooking. Fruit desserts with toppings and baked custards are not stirred. Microwaves cook quickly, so stir or beat soft custards, when recipe directs. If a soft custard should curdle, immediately pour into a cool dish and beat with rotary beater. Or, puree in blender.
When Are Desserts "Done"?	Fruit is cooked when it's soft and tender. Standing time is important to assure softening, especially when rehydrating dried fruits. Baked custard should be removed from the microwave oven if the custard center is almost set when the dish is "jiggled" slightly. Custards may microwave at slightly different rates because the amount in each cup tends to vary. Remove custards from the oven as they finish cooking. Baked custards continue to cook during standing time — firming centers and keeping edges tender. Soft custards thicken during cooking and continue thickening slightly during standing and cooling. Microwave to suggested degree temperature, if specified.
Add-A-Dessert to An Entree:	Desserts can often be cooked along with a meat, fish or main dishes. Look for directions in these chapters plus the Oven Meals chapter.
Microwave-Conventional Comparison:	Fruit desserts cook tender and juicy in a few minutes. Dumplings atop fruit are light and tender without the excessive sogginess sometimes found with conventional methods. Dessert toppings do not brown or crisp. Soft and baked custards microwave quickly, but at a gentle setting which prevents scorching. So, baked custards do not have to be set in water to cook and soft custard does not need constant stirring. However, suggested beatings keep soft custard smooth.

Pictured from the top: Creamy Cheesecake, page 62; Chocolate Glazed Fruits, page 60.

FRESH CHERRIES JUBILEE

Fresh fruits microwave quickly and hold shape on HIGH.

- **2 teaspoons cornstarch**
- **¼ cup water**
- **½ cup red currant jelly**
- **2 cups fresh sweet cherries, washed and pitted**
- **¼ cup brandy**
- **Vanilla ice cream**

1. Combine cornstarch and water in 1-quart glass casserole until smooth; stir in jelly and cherries.

2. Microwave for 6 to 7 minutes, on HIGH, or until hot (about 200° F.).

3. Measure brandy into 1-cup glass measure.

4. Microwave for 15 to 20 seconds, on HIGH, or until warm. Pour brandy over cherry sauce and ignite. Immediately spoon sauce over ice cream. About 2 Cups Sauce

RECIPE VARIATIONS

CHERRIES JUBILEE: Omit cornstarch and water in basic recipe. Reduce red currant jelly to ¼ cup; add ½ teaspoon grated orange rind. Substitute 1 can (21 oz.) cherry pie filling for fresh cherries.

APRICOT JUBILEE: Increase cornstarch to 1 tablespoon in basic recipe. Substitute apple jelly for red currant jelly and 1 can (16 oz.) apricot halves, drained, for fresh cherries. Reduce cooking time 1 to 2 minutes.

CHOCOLATE GLAZED FRUITS

Chocolate melting technique is HIGH.

- **1 package (6 oz.) semi-sweet "real" chocolate pieces**
- **1 pint strawberries, with hulls, washed, or other fruits such as cherries with stems or seedless grapes**

1. Place chocolate pieces in 2-cup glass measure.

2. Microwave for 2 to 2½ minutes, on HIGH, or until melted. Stir and dip strawberries in melted chocolate until partially coated. Place on wax paper and chill for about 30 minutes or until chocolate is hardened. Serve as after-dinner dessert. About 24 Pieces Glazed Fruit

TIP: Hulls or stems act as handles.

HOT PINK PEARS

May also be served as an accompaniment for pork roast.

- **6 ripe winter pears**
- **6 whole cloves**
- **1 cup sugar**
- **½ cup sweet vermouth**
- **¼ cup water**
- **½ teaspoon red food coloring**
- **Whipped cream, if desired**

1. Peel pears; leave stem. Stick 1 whole clove into each pear. Combine remaining ingredients, except whipped cream, in 1½-quart glass casserole. Add pears; cover with glass lid.

2. Microwave for 6 minutes on HIGH. Baste pears; turn over, and recover. Continue cooking for 6 to 8 minutes, on HIGH, or until tender. Serve in individual bowls; garnish with whipped cream. 6 Servings

---

BLUEBERRY DUMPLINGS

Dumplings and fruit steam together superbly on HIGH.

- **1 can (14 oz.) water-packed blueberries**
- **⅓ cup sugar**
- **2 tablespoons all-purpose flour**
- **⅛ teaspoon salt**
- **2 tablespoons sugar**
- **1 teaspoon cinnamon**

Dumplings:

- **2 cups biscuit mix**
- **1 tablespoon grated lemon rind**
- **⅔ cup milk**

1. Combine blueberries, ⅓ cup sugar, flour and salt in 1½-quart glass casserole; mix well.

2. Microwave for 5 to 5½ minutes, on HIGH, or until thickened (about 180° F.). Drop dumplings by tablespoonfuls over hot filling. Sprinkle top with mixture of sugar and cinnamon. Cover with glass lid.

3. Microwave for 4 to 4½ minutes, on HIGH, or until dumplings are no longer doughy.

4. **Dumplings:** Combine all Dumpling ingredients in medium mixing bowl; mix well. About 6 Servings

RECIPE VARIATIONS

RHUBARB COBBLER: Substitute 3 cups diced fresh rhubarb, 1 cup sugar, 2 tablespoons all-purpose flour and ¼ cup water for blueberry filling in basic recipe. Substitute 1 tablespoon orange rind for lemon rind in Dumplings; spread Dumpling batter over hot filling. Cover.

CHERRY DUMPLINGS: Substitute 1 can (21 oz.) cherry pie filling for all blueberry filling ingredients. Drop Dumplings over hot filling. Cover.

BANANA ORANGE FLAMBE

Cook on ROAST because of high fat content.

- **¼ cup butter or margarine**
- **⅓ cup packed brown sugar**
- **4 bananas, peeled, halved crosswise, then lengthwise**
- **1 orange, peeled and sliced**
- **2 tablespoons banana liqueur or orange juice**
- **¼ cup orange-flavored liqueur or brandy**
- **Vanilla ice cream**

1. Place butter in 1½-quart glass casserole.

2. Microwave for about 1 minute, on ROAST, or until melted. Stir in brown sugar. Add bananas and orange slices; stir gently to coat. Pour banana liqueur over top.

3. Microwave for 3 to 4 minutes, on ROAST, or until warm (about 110° F.).

4. Measure orange liqueur into 1-cup glass measure.

5. Microwave for 15 to 20 seconds, on HIGH, or until warm. Pour over fruit and ignite. Immediately spoon sauce over ice cream.

About 4 Servings

CHOCOLATE MOUSSE

Soft custards need gentle cooking on SIMMER.

- **2 squares (1 oz. each) semi-sweet chocolate**
- **⅓ cup sugar**
- **1 envelope unflavored gelatin**
- **⅛ teaspoon salt**
- **3 eggs, separated**
- **1 cup milk**
- **1 teaspoon vanilla**
- **⅓ cup sugar**
- **1 cup whipping cream, whipped**

1. Place chocolate in large glass mixing bowl.

2. Microwave for 1 to 2 minutes, on HIGH, or until melted. Stir in ⅓ cup sugar, gelatin, salt, egg yolks and milk. Beat well with rotary beater.

3. Microwave for 4 minutes on SIMMER. Beat and continue cooking for 1 to 2 minutes, on SIMMER, or until slightly thickened. Beat in vanilla; refrigerate until cool.

4. Beat egg whites in small mixing bowl until soft peaks form. Gradually beat in ⅓ cup sugar until stiff peaks form. Fold egg whites and whipped cream into chocolate mixture. Spoon mixture into individual dishes. Chill about 3 hours or until set.

6 to 8 Servings

HOW TO COOK PUDDING AND PIE FILLING MIX

- Prepare mix as directed on package; beat well with rotary beater.
- Microwave on HIGH as directed in chart. Beat lightly once during cooking.
- Pour into serving dishes.
- Chill to set.

DRY MIX	SIZE	GLASS CONTAINER	SETTING	MINUTES
PUDDING AND PIE FILLING MIX				
4 Servings	3¼-oz. pkg.	4-cup measure	HIGH	6 to 7 (about 180° F.)
6 Servings	5½-oz. pkg.	1½-qt. measure	HIGH	8 to 9 (about 180° F.)
GOLDEN EGG CUSTARD MIX				
4 Servings	3-oz. pkg.	4-cup measure	HIGH	5 to 6 (about 160° F.)
	3-oz. pkg. with 1 egg yolk	4-cup measure	HIGH	5 to 6 (about 180° F.)
TAPIOCA PUDDING	3¼-oz. pkg.	4-cup measure	HIGH	5 to 6 (about 180° F.)

Pictured clockwise from the left: Chocolate Mousse garnished with whipped cream, recipe above, Trifle, page 63; Hot Pink Pears, recipe opposite.

CREAMY CHEESECAKE

Microwave cream cheese on WARM to soften for easy mixing.

- **¼ cup butter or margarine**
- **1 cup graham cracker crumbs (about 12 crackers)**
- **2 tablespoons all-purpose flour**
- **2 tablespoons sugar**
- **¼ teaspoon cinnamon**

Filling:

- **2 packages (8 oz. each) cream cheese**
- **1 can (14 oz.) sweetened condensed milk**
- **2 teaspoons vanilla**
- **¼ teaspoon salt**
- **2 eggs**

1. Place butter in 9-inch round glass baking dish.

2. Microwave for about 1 minute, on ROAST, or until melted. Stir in cracker crumbs, flour, sugar and cinnamon. Press mixture over bottom and up sides of dish. Pour Filling into crust.

3. Microwave for 16 to 18 minutes, on SIMMER, or until almost set in center. Chill 2 to 3 hours before serving.

4. Filling: Place cream cheese in medium glass mixing bowl. Microwave for 8 to 9 minutes, on WARM, or until softened; beat with electric mixer until light and fluffy. Beat in milk, vanilla and salt. Add eggs and beat well.

About 8 Servings

VANILLA CUSTARD ICE CREAM

This custard is a sauce for Trifle.

- **2 cups milk**
- **¾ cup sugar**
- **⅛ teaspoon salt**
- **2 eggs**
- **1 tablespoon vanilla**
- **2 cups light cream**

1. Combine milk, sugar and salt in 4-cup glass measure.

2. Microwave for about 3 minutes, on HIGH, or until hot (about 120° F.). Beat eggs and a small amount of hot milk in small bowl with rotary beater; beat into sugar and milk.

3. Microwave for 5 minutes on SIMMER. Beat well and continue cooking for 5 to 6 minutes, on SIMMER, or until mixture comes to a boil and thickens (about 190° F.). Beat lightly; cool completely. Stir in vanilla.

4. Prepare ice cream freezer according to manufacturer's directions. Pour prepared custard into freezer along with cream. Freeze as directed by manufacturer.

2 Quarts Ice Cream

TIP: If custard curdles, the consistency can be greatly improved by beating with a rotary beater or pureeing in a blender.

RECIPE VARIATIONS

CHOCOLATE CUSTARD ICE CREAM: Decrease sugar in basic recipe to ½ cup. Place 1 package (6 oz.) semi-sweet real chocolate pieces in 2-cup glass measure. Microwave for 2 to 2½ minutes, on HIGH, or until melted. Stir into custard sauce just before cooking. Reduce final cooking time 3 to 4 minutes or until mixture comes to a boil and thickens (about 160° F.). Continue as in basic recipe.

STRAWBERRY ICE CREAM: Omit vanilla from basic recipe. Wash, hull and crush 1 pint fresh strawberries; stir in ¼ cup sugar. Add sugared berries to custard sauce with cream. Continue as directed in basic recipe.

BANANA ICE CREAM: Omit vanilla in basic recipe. Add 3 medium bananas, mashed, to custard sauce with cream. May add 5 to 6 drops yellow food coloring if desired. Continue as directed in basic recipe.

BAKED CUSTARD

Baked custards are not stirred.

- **1¾ cups milk**
- **¼ cup sugar**
- **3 eggs**
- **¼ teaspoon salt**
- **½ teaspoon vanilla**
- **Nutmeg**

1. Combine all ingredients, except nutmeg, in 4-cup glass measure; beat well with rotary beater. Pour into four 6-oz. glass custard cups, filling each ¾ full. Sprinkle with nutmeg.

2. Microwave for 15 to 16 minutes, on SIMMER, or until almost set in center. If necessary, remove individual custards as they finish cooking and continue microwaving others until almost set. Let stand 5 minutes before serving.

4 Custards

TIP: Custards may cook at slightly different rates because amount of custard in each cup tends to vary.

RECIPE VARIATION

PEACH CUSTARD: Drain 1 can (16 oz.) peach slices well and divide slices evenly among six 6-oz. custard cups. Pour basic custard recipe over peaches. Increase cooking time 9 to 10 minutes.

6 Custards

CREME BRULEE

A custard with caramelized topping to serve with fresh fruits.

- 1 pint whipping cream
- 7 eggs
- ½ cup sugar
- ½ teaspoon vanilla
- ½ cup packed brown sugar

1. Pour cream into 4-cup glass measure.

2. Microwave for 3 to 3½ minutes, on ROAST, or until hot (about 120° F.). Beat eggs, sugar and vanilla in 1½-quart glass casserole with rotary beater. Gradually beat in hot cream.

3. Microwave for 8 minutes on SIMMER. Beat and continue cooking for 8 to 9 minutes, on SIMMER, or until almost set in center.

4. Chill at least 6 hours. When ready to serve, sprinkle top with brown sugar and broil in conventional range 8 inches from heat until lightly browned.

About 6 Servings

OLD-FASHIONED BREAD PUDDING

A baked custard dessert – microwave uncovered.

- 2 cups milk
- 2 eggs, slightly beaten
- ½ cup sugar
- 1 teaspoon cinnamon
- ¼ teaspoon salt
- 3 cups soft bread cubes
- ½ cup raisins
- 1 tablespoon butter or margarine

1. Combine milk, eggs, sugar, cinnamon and salt in 1½-quart glass casserole; beat with rotary beater. Stir in bread cubes and raisins. Dot with butter.

2. Microwave for 26 to 28 minutes, on SIMMER, or until almost set in center. Let stand 5 minutes before serving.

4 to 6 Servings

TAPIOCA PUDDING

Beat puddings occasionally to keep them smooth.

- 2 cups milk
- ¼ cup sugar
- 2½ tablespoons quick-cooking tapioca
- ¼ teaspoon salt
- 1 teaspoon vanilla
- 2 eggs, separated
- 2 tablespoons sugar

1. Combine milk, ¼ cup sugar, tapioca, salt, vanilla and egg yolks in 4-cup glass measure; beat with rotary beater.

2. Microwave for 8 minutes on SIMMER. Beat well and continue cooking for 6 to 7 minutes, on SIMMER, or until mixture boils (about 190° F.).

3. Beat egg whites in small mixing bowl until frothy. Gradually add 2 tablespoons sugar, beating until mixture forms soft peaks. Fold egg white mixture into pudding. Serve warm or cold.

4 to 6 Servings

RICE PUDDING WITH RAISINS

Take custards from the oven as they finish cooking.

- 2½ cups milk
- 3 eggs, slightly beaten
- ½ cup sugar
- 1 tablespoon cornstarch
- 1 teaspoon vanilla
- ¾ teaspoon salt
- ½ teaspoon nutmeg
- 1½ cups cooked rice
- ½ cup raisins

1. Combine all ingredients in large mixing bowl; stir well. Pour into eight 6-oz. custard cups, filling each ¾ full.

2. Microwave for 24 to 28 minutes, on SIMMER, or until almost set in center. If necessary, remove individual cups as they finish cooking and continue microwaving others until almost set. Let stand 5 minutes before serving.

8 Servings

TRIFLE

Cake and soft custard techniques combine in this recipe.

- 1 layer yellow cake from mix, page 56
- Vanilla Custard Sauce for Ice Cream (through Step 3), page 72
- 1 jar (10 oz.) strawberry preserves
- 1 cup whipping cream, whipped, if desired
- 1 cup fresh strawberries, washed and hulled, if desired

1. Cut cake into 1-inch cubes. Place half of cubes in 2-quart serving bowl. Pour half of Custard Sauce over cake. Spread half of preserves over top; repeat layer once. Chill 1 hour. Garnish with whipped cream and strawberries.

About 8 Servings

RECIPE VARIATION

RASPBERRY TRIFLE: Substitute raspberry preserves for strawberry preserves. Garnish with whipped cream and fresh raspberries.

Eggs & Cheese

Culinary Classics– Separately or Together

Here's How — and Why

Gentle Cooking Produces Tender Results:	Gentle heat is the secret to tender-light egg and cheese dishes. Since both usually cook at the same setting, combination dishes are delicious.
Beaten Eggs and Whole Raw Eggs Cook on ROAST:	Omelets, scrambled eggs and other dishes with beaten egg mixtures microwave on ROAST to cook the center without overcooking outside edges. Whole raw eggs, WITHOUT THE SHELL, bake or poach on ROAST to keep yolks from cooking before the whites. When sliced or chopped hard cooked eggs are mixed into a cream sauce or main dish, cook on a setting no higher than ROAST to preserve egg's tender texture.
Fry Eggs on a Microwave Browning Grill:	Fry eggs quickly in a microwave oven using the microwave browning grill as directed in the chart in this chapter.
Microwave Soufflés on DEFROST:	Soufflés are a delicate affair; microwave very gently on DEFROST because of the delicate egg-foam structure.
Microwave Quiche Lorraine on SIMMER:	Quiche Lorraine filling is like an egg-custard, so use SIMMER setting to prevent curdling.
DO NOT Microwave Eggs in the Shell:	DO NOT microwave eggs in the shell because fat in yolks cooks very fast, builds up pressure and may explode, even when cooked at low settings. Do not reheat whole, hardcooked eggs in a microwave oven because the yolks' high fat content may cause them to explode.
Cheese Melts and Cooks on Microwave ROAST:	Cheese dishes are smooth, cream cheeses and spreads melt beautifully on ROAST which prevents separation and curdling.
Microwave in a Variety of Glass Dishes:	Microwave individual servings of eggs in glass or pottery dishes without silver or metal trim so each egg may be taken from the oven as it reaches desired doneness. Cook several eggs at once in a glass casserole, glass pie plate or on the microwave browning grill. Cheese dishes microwave in glass casseroles, glass baking dishes or glass measures.
Coverings Are Important — Follow Recipes Carefully:	Since egg yolk contains fat which cooks first and can toughen or even "pop," the cover keeps yolks tender while steam cooks the whites. Covering also keeps cheese tender. Use glass lids, saucers without metal trim or wax paper as directed. Tip glass lids to avoid hot steam.
Standing Time Completes Cooking; Keeps Product Tender:	Standing time, when called for in a recipe, is essential to complete cooking and keep food at the edges of the dish tender.
ADD-A-BACON to Speed an Egg Meal:	Microwave regular or Canadian bacon with eggs on HIGH because most microwaves are attracted to bacon fat. However, when eggs cook alone or when other sensitive ingredients are added to them, use ROAST. Cook bacon on upper rack because it takes longer to cook than eggs, and also needs the more intense microwave energy available there. Microwave egg dishes on bottom shelf. Food cooks faster and more evenly if dishes are staggered.
Microwave-Conventional Comparison:	Egg mixtures microwave very light and fluffy. Cook individual egg servings to desired doneness quickly and easily. Scramble eggs with a single stir at the end of cooking — no standing and stirring. Eggs MUST NOT be cooked in the shell or they may explode. Soufflés are very fluffy and delicate with fine texture, but they do not brown. Since microwaves cook from all sides, cheese dishes do not scorch on the bottom as in conventional cooking. However, eggs and cheese toughen if overcooked.

Pictured: Welsh Rarebit, page 69, garnished with cherry tomato.

HOW TO FRY EGGS ON A MICROWAVE BROWNING GRILL

- Preheat microwave browning grill on HIGH, as directed by manufacturer in browner's instruction booklet.
- Melt 1 teaspoon butter on microwave browning grill.
- Break egg(s) on browning grill.
- Microwave on HIGH.

NO. OF EGGS	SETTING	TIME
1	HIGH	45 to 60 sec.
2	HIGH	1 to 1½ min.
4	HIGH	2½ to 3½ min.

HOW TO BAKE EGGS

- Break each egg into a buttered 10-oz. individual glass casserole or custard cup.
- Cover with glass lid or glass saucer without metal trim.
- Microwave on ROAST.
- Let stand, covered, 1 minute before serving.

NO. OF EGGS	SETTING	TIME
1	ROAST	55 to 60 sec.
2	ROAST	1 to 1¼ min.
4	ROAST	2 to 2½ min.

HOW TO SCRAMBLE EGGS

- Break eggs into soup bowl or 20-oz. glass casserole (1-quart size for 4, 5 or 6 eggs). Without metal trim.
- Add milk and beat together with a fork.
- Add butter and other seasonings to taste.
- Cover with glass lid or wax paper.
- Microwave on ROAST.
- Stir gently with a fork before serving.
- If cooking scrambled eggs a while before serving, undercook slightly and warm, on ROAST, when served.
- Soak cooking dish immediately for easy clean-up.

NO. OF EGGS	MILK	BUTTER OR MARGARINE	SETTING	MINUTES
1	1 tbsp.	1 tsp.	ROAST	1 to 1½
2	3 tbsps.	2 tsps.	ROAST	2 to 2½
4	4 tbsps.	4 tsps.	ROAST	4½ to 5
6	6 tbsps.	2 tbsps.	ROAST	7 to 7½

HOW TO POACH EGGS

- When poaching 1 to 3 eggs, use individual 6-oz. glass custard cups. Poach 4 eggs in a 1-quart glass casserole.
- Bring water and ¼ teaspoon vinegar to boil on HIGH.
- Break eggs carefully into hot water.
- Cover tightly with glass lid or wax paper.
- Microwave eggs in boiling water on ROAST.
- Let stand, covered, 1 minute before serving.
- To poach eggs in bouillon, omit vinegar; use ½ cup water per egg plus 1 cube or teaspoon chicken bouillon. Stir after first heating to dissolve bouillon.

WATER	GLASS CONTAINER	WATER SETTING AND TIME	EGGS	EGG SETTING AND TIME
¼ cup	6-oz. custard cup	HIGH 1½ to 2 min.	1	ROAST 30 to 45 sec.
¼ cup ea.	6-oz. custard cups	HIGH 2 to 2½ min.	2	ROAST 45 to 60 sec.
1 cup	1-qt. casserole	HIGH 2½ to 3 min.	4	ROAST 2 to 2½ min.

HOW TO SOFTEN CREAM CHEESE AND SPREADS

- Remove foil wrapper from cream cheese and place in glass bowl or dish to be used in recipe.
- Cheese spreads may be warmed in their original containers after the cap is removed — or in a glass or pottery serving dish which has no silver or other metal trim.
- Microwave on WARM until cheese is soft.

ITEM	SIZE	SETTING	TIME
CREAM CHEESE	3-oz. pkg.	WARM	2 to 2½ min.
	8-oz. pkg.	WARM	4 to 4½ min.
CHEESE SPREAD	5-oz. container	WARM	2½ to 3 min.
	8-oz. container	WARM	4 to 4½ min.

BASIC OMELET

1 tablespoon butter or margarine
3 eggs
3 tablespoons water
½ teaspoon salt
⅛ teaspoon pepper

ROAST cooks center, keeps edges tender when eggs cook alone.

1. Place butter in 9-inch glass pie plate.

2. Microwave for about 1 minute, on ROAST, or until melted. Beat remaining ingredients with fork into melted butter. Cover with wax paper.

3. Microwave for 3 minutes on ROAST. Stir lightly; recover, and continue cooking for 1½ to 2 minutes, on ROAST, or until almost set in center. Let stand, covered, 2 minutes before serving. 1 to 2 Servings

ADD-A-BACON: Prepare Basic Omelet through Step 2; set aside. Place 4 slices Canadian bacon, ¼ inch thick, on a glass plate. Place bacon on upper rack of oven and omelet on bottom shelf. Microwave both for 4 minutes on HIGH. Stir omelet lightly; recover and continue cooking both for 3 to 4 minutes, on HIGH, or until omelet is almost set in center. Let stand, covered, 2 minutes before serving.

RECIPE VARIATIONS

VEGETABLE OMELET: Add 1 cup broccoli flowerettes and 1 small onion, chopped, to butter. Microwave for about 3 minutes, on HIGH, or until vegetables are partly cooked. Beat in remaining egg ingredients with fork and continue as directed in basic recipe.

DENVER OMELET: Add ¼ cup finely chopped green pepper, 1 green onion, finely sliced, and ⅓ cup chopped cooked ham with butter. Microwave for about 2 minutes, on HIGH, or until vegetables are partly cooked. Add ¼ teaspoon basil leaves to remaining ingredients and beat into ham-vegetable mixture with fork. Continue as directed in basic recipe.

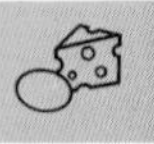

Pictured: Early Morning Breakfast, page 177 – Scrambled Eggs, Bacon, Sweet Rolls.

QUICHE LORRAINE *

Egg-custard filling calls for SIMMER setting.

½ lb. bacon (about 8 slices)
1 (9-inch) Baked Pastry Shell in glass pie plate, page 124.
1 can (4 oz.) mushroom stems and pieces, drained
1½ cups shredded Cheddar cheese
3 green onions, sliced
1¼ cups light cream
3 eggs
½ teaspoon salt
⅛ teaspoon pepper

1. Arrange bacon in single layer in 3-quart (13 x 9) glass baking dish.

2. Microwave for 6 to 7 minutes, on HIGH, or until crisp; cool. Crumble into bottom of baked crust. Sprinkle mushrooms, cheese and onions on top. Beat remaining ingredients in 4-cup glass measure; pour over bacon-cheese mixture.

3. Microwave for 30 to 35 minutes, on SIMMER, or until almost set in center. Let stand 5 minutes before serving. 5 to 6 Servings

RECIPE VARIATIONS

SALMON QUICHE: Substitute 1 can (7¾ oz.) salmon, drained and flaked, for bacon. Omit mushrooms. Substitute 1¼ cups milk for light cream and add ½ teaspoon dry mustard and ¼ teaspoon marjoram leaves with seasonings.

MEXICAN QUICHE: Substitute ½ lb. ground beef for bacon. Crumble ground beef into 1-quart glass casserole. Cover with glass lid. Microwave for 3 to 4 minutes, on HIGH, or until browned. Drain well; sprinkle over bottom of baked crust. Substitute 1 small tomato, chopped, for mushrooms. Reduce light cream to 1 cup and add 2 teaspoons parsley flakes, ½ teaspoon chili powder, ¼ teaspoon garlic powder, ⅛ teaspoon pepper sauce with seasonings.

SEAFOOD SCRAMBLED EGGS

One stir at end of cooking scrambles eggs.

8 eggs
1 can (10¾ oz.) condensed cream of shrimp soup
¼ teaspoon salt
⅛ teaspoon hot pepper sauce
1 can (4 oz.) mushroom stems and pieces, drained
2 green onions, finely sliced

1. Combine eggs, soup and seasonings in 1½-quart glass casserole; beat well. Stir in remaining ingredients. Cover with glass lid.

2. Microwave for 7 minutes on ROAST. Stir; recover, and continue cooking for about 5 minutes, on ROAST, or until mixture is liquid only in the center. Stir gently with fork to scramble and cook excess liquid. Let stand, covered, 3 minutes before serving. 6 to 8 Servings

ADD-A-BACON: Prepare Seafood Scrambled Eggs through Step 1; set aside. Arrange 8 slices of bacon in a single layer in 3-quart (13 x 9) glass baking dish. Place bacon on upper rack of oven and eggs on bottom shelf. Microwave both for 14 minutes on ROAST. Stir eggs; recover, and continue cooking both for 8 to 10 minutes, on ROAST, or until mixture is liquid only in the center. Stir eggs gently with fork to scramble and cook excess liquid. If necessary, continue cooking bacon for 1 to 2 minutes or until crisp. Let eggs stand, covered, 3 minutes before serving.

RECIPE VARIATION

ZUCCHINI SCRAMBLED EGGS: Substitute 1 can (10¾ oz.) condensed cream of mushroom soup for cream of shrimp soup, and ½ teaspoon oregano leaves for hot pepper sauce. Substitute 1 small zucchini, quartered and sliced, and ⅓ cup grated Parmesan cheese for mushrooms and green onion.

BAKED COD FONDUE

Use toasted bread cubes or bread sticks as dippers.

1 lb. frozen cod fillets, thawed and cut into 1-inch pieces
3 green onions, sliced
1 teaspoon salt
½ teaspoon basil leaves
3 peppercorns
1 bay leaf
1 cup milk
3 tablespoons butter or margarine
1½ cups shredded Swiss cheese
½ cup unsifted all-purpose flour
½ cup dry white wine
Paprika

1. Place cod, onions, seasonings and milk in 1½-quart glass casserole. Dot with butter.

2. Microwave for about 10 minutes, on HIGH, or until fish flakes easily (about 140° F.). Drain poaching liquid into small mixing bowl; remove peppercorns and bay leaf. Sprinkle cheese over fish.

3. Combine flour and wine in small bowl until smooth; stir into poaching liquid. Pour over cheese and fish.

4. Microwave for 4 minutes on ROAST. Stir; sprinkle with paprika, and continue cooking for 4 to 5 minutes, on ROAST, or until thickened (about 160° F.). Let stand 5 minutes before serving. About 6 Servings

SAUSAGE EGG NESTS *

- 1 package (12 oz.) bulk pork sausage
- 1 cup shredded Swiss cheese
- 1 tablespoon dried parsley flakes
- 4 eggs
- Salt
- Pepper
- ½ cup light cream

Eggs and cheese cook superbly together on ROAST.

1. Crumble sausage into 2-quart (8 x 8) glass baking dish. Cover with wax paper.

2. Microwave for 5 to 6 minutes, on HIGH, or until browned. Drain well. Stir in ¾ cup of the cheese and parsley. Spread over bottom of dish, making small indentations or nests. Break eggs into indentations. Sprinkle with salt and pepper. Pour cream over top; sprinkle with remaining ¼ cup shredded cheese. Cover with wax paper.

3. Microwave for 8 to 10 minutes, on ROAST, or until eggs are cooked to desired doneness. Let stand, covered, 2 minutes before serving.

About 4 Servings

RECIPE VARIATION

HUNTER'S EGGS: Substitute ½ lb. chicken livers, quartered, for pork sausage. Place in 2-quart (8 x 8) glass baking dish. Cover with wax paper. Microwave for 6 to 7 minutes, on SIMMER, or until partly cooked (still slightly pink). Drain. Stir in cheese and parsley and continue as directed in basic recipe. Substitute ¼ cup catsup and ¼ cup dry white wine for light cream; combine and pour over eggs.

PUFFY CHEESE SOUFFLE *

- 1½ cups milk
- ⅓ cup unsifted all-purpose flour
- ½ teaspoon salt
- 1 teaspoon Worcestershire sauce
- 1½ cups shredded sharp Cheddar cheese
- 2 tablespoons butter or margarine
- 6 eggs, separated
- 1 teaspoon cream of tartar

Top of soufflé looks slightly moist at the end of cooking.

1. Combine milk, flour, salt and Worcestershire sauce in 4-cup glass measure; beat with rotary beater until smooth. Stir in cheese; add butter.

2. Microwave for 5 minutes on ROAST. Beat well and continue cooking for 2 to 3 minutes, on ROAST, or until thickened (about 180° F.); set aside.

3. Beat egg whites and cream of tartar in large mixer bowl until stiff but moist peaks form; set aside. Beat egg yolks in small mixer bowl until thick and lemon colored. Beat thickened cheese sauce into yolks. Spoon mixture over egg whites; fold in gently. Pour into ungreased 2-quart soufflé dish. Place on lower rack of oven.

4. Microwave for 30 to 34 minutes, on DEFROST, or until set. Serve immediately.

4 to 6 Servings

WELSH RAREBIT

- 1 cup milk
- ½ cup beer or milk
- ¼ cup unsifted all-purpose flour
- ½ teaspoon dry mustard
- ¼ teaspoon salt
- ⅛ teaspoon pepper
- 1 cup shredded Cheddar cheese
- 2 tablespoons diced pimento
- ½ teaspoon Worcestershire sauce
- 2 tablespoons butter or margarine
- Toast points

Microwave cheese dishes on ROAST to prevent curdling.

1. Place milk, beer, flour, dry mustard, salt and pepper in 4-cup glass measure; beat with rotary beater until smooth. Stir in cheese, pimento and Worcestershire sauce; add butter.

2. Microwave for 4 minutes on ROAST. Beat well and continue cooking for 3 to 4 minutes, on ROAST, or until thickened (about 190° F.). Beat lightly and serve over toast points.

2 Cups Sauce

CHEESY GRITS *

- 3 cups water
- 1 teaspoon salt
- ¾ cup quick-cooking grits
- 2 eggs, slightly beaten
- 2 cups shredded Cheddar cheese
- 1 tablespoon butter or margarine
- ¼ teaspoon salt
- Dash cayenne pepper

1. Combine water and salt in 2-quart glass casserole. Cover with glass lid.

2. Microwave for 6 to 7 minutes, on HIGH, or until boiling. Stir in grits; recover.

3. Microwave for 3 to 4 minutes, on ROAST, or until thickened. Let stand, covered, 3 minutes to set. Stir in remaining ingredients. Do not cover.

4. Microwave for 22 to 24 minutes, on SIMMER, or until almost set in center. Let stand, 5 minutes, before serving.

About 6 Servings

TIP: Microwave plain grits by following directions in basic recipe through second cooking and standing time.

Fish & Seafood

Moist, Flaky and Delicate in Minutes

Here's How — and Why

Thaw Frozen Fish and Seafood on DEFROST:	Use either fresh or frozen fish or shellfish in a recipe, but always thaw before cooking. Use DEFROST; see chart, pages 17 and 19.
Cook on HIGH Unless Some Ingredients "Sensitive":	Fish and shellfish are tender, delicate foods; cook quickly on HIGH setting. When recipes call for cream, mayonnaise, mushrooms, cheese or eggs, cook food on ROAST to avoid separating and curdling. Microwave snails, clams and oysters on ROAST to prevent "popping."
How Much Does 1 Pound Serve?	When buying fish and shellfish, allow ⅓ to ½ pound of edible flesh per person, depending upon family appetite.
Oven-Bake, Poach or Steam:	Fish and shellfish can be oven-cooked without liquid or with seasoned butter; poached or steamed in liquid such as water, wine or cream.
Most Any Kind of Fish Microwaves Tender and Flaky:	Both fresh and salt water fish and shellfish microwave well. Whole fish should be cleaned and eviscerated. Steaks and fillets may be interchanged in these recipes. Increase cooking time slightly when substituting steaks for fillets. You may also substitute one fish for another.
Dish Shape and Covering Assure Success:	Glass baking dishes or casseroles without metal trim are the usual cooking dishes. However, snail shells and other bowl-shaped natural shells are safe, attractive cooking containers. Use a fitted glass lid or tightly-tucked wax paper to cover. Tip lids away from arm when lifting off steamy food. Plastic wrap may also be used as a cover; pierce before removing.
Arrange Large Pieces at Outer Edges of Dish:	Arrange large pieces and thick edges of fish at the outside edges of the cooking dish where food cooks sooner. Place small whole fish with tail ends toward center of baking dish. Microwave fish on bottom shelf of oven, unless otherwise specified in a recipe. Remove rack from oven.
Don't Overcook Fish or Shellfish:	Fish and shellfish microwave quickly. They're done when flesh loses its translucence, becomes opaque and flakes near the center if lifted gently with a fork. Shellfish with or without a shell cook in the same time.
	Overcooked fish is dry, crumbly, very firm. Cook fish or shellfish last when serving with microwaved vegetables or rice; the latter hold heat longer.
Cooking Continues During Standing Time:	Fish's internal temperature rises about 10° F. after it is taken from the oven. So standing time cooks center while edges stay moist.
Cook More Than One Food at a Time:	Some recipes suggest microwaving a sauce, vegetable or dessert along with a fish dish. Generally, when you "Add-A-" dish, fish is cooked on the bottom shelf because it is less dense. Dishes of food with a few sensitive ingredients, microwave on HIGH when cooked with other foods because each absorbs less microwaves.
Look for the "✻":	The "✻" at the end of a recipe title is a reminder that the food is cooked with two or more power settings. Stir here when suggested.
Microwave-Conventional Comparison:	A microwave oven steams, poaches and bakes fish and delicate shellfish more easily than conventional methods because microwaves penetrate all sides of a dish and little cooking liquid is needed to produce tender, flaky results. One pound of fish fillet, for example, microwaves on HIGH in 6 to 7 minutes. Fish in creamy sauces will not scorch. Microwave speed and moist heat cooking do not crisp crumb coatings of fish. When adapting conventional recipes, use less moisture and butter, and shorten cooking time. Use similar recipes in this chapter as guides.

Pictured from the top: Parsley Butter, page 150; Trout Amandine, page 74, garnished with fresh parsley.

HOW TO COOK FRESH FISH AND SEAFOOD

- Clean and rinse fresh fish and seafood before cooking.
- Always thaw frozen fish or seafood before cooking. Use defrosting chart, pages 29 and 31. Complete thawing under cold, running water.
- Cook fish or seafood in a glass baking dish or casserole. Glass or pottery serving platters may be used if they do not have gold, silver, platinum or other metal trim.
- Place steaks and fillets in baking dish with thicker edges and larger pieces toward outside of baking dish. Arrange small whole fish with tail ends toward center of baking dish.
- Cover cooking dish with a fitted glass lid or wax paper tucked tightly across the top.
- Quick-cook on Microwave HIGH to about 140° F.
- Let fish stand, covered, for 5 minutes to complete cooking. Temperature will increase to about 150° F.
- Fish is done if it flakes when lifted gently with a fork near center.

FISH/SEAFOOD	WEIGHT	GLASS CONTAINER	MINUTES	INTERNAL TEMPERATURE
FILLETS: Sole, Halibut, Perch,	1 lb.	2-qt. (12 x 7) baking dish	6 to 7	140° F.
Pike, Whitefish, Flounder, Snapper	2 lbs.		8 to 9	140° F.
WHOLE FISH	1½ to 1¾ lbs.	3-qt. (13 x 9) baking dish	10 to 12	140° F.
SHRIMP OR BAY SCALLOPS	½ lb.	1-qt. casserole	4 to 5	
SALMON STEAKS (3)	12-oz. pkg.	2-qt. (12 x 7) baking dish	5 to 6	140° F.
LOBSTER TAILS (2 to 3)	8-oz. pkg.	2-qt. (12 x 7) baking dish	4 to 5	

HERB FILLETS

2 tablespoons butter or margarine
1 clove garlic, finely chopped
¼ cup finely chopped onion
1 tablespoon lemon juice
2 teaspoons dried parsley flakes
½ teaspoon salt
¼ teaspoon tarragon leaves
⅛ teaspoon chervil leaves or thyme leaves
1 lb. frozen fish fillets, thawed
¼ cup dry bread crumbs

Oven-bake fish on HIGH.

1. Place butter, garlic and onion in small glass mixing bowl.
2. Microwave for 1 to 2 minutes, on HIGH, or until onion is partly cooked. Stir in remaining ingredients, except fish and bread crumbs.
3. Arrange fillets in 2-quart (12 x 7) glass baking dish with thick edges toward outside of dish. Spoon about ½ of butter mixture over fillets. Stir bread crumbs into remaining butter mixture; sprinkle on top of fillets.
4. Microwave for 7 to 8 minutes, on HIGH, or until fish flakes easily (about 140° F.). Let stand 5 minutes before serving. About 4 Servings

ADD-A-VEGETABLE: Prepare Herb Fillets through Step 3. Place 1 package (10 oz.) frozen peas in 1½-quart glass casserole; cover with glass lid. Place vegetable on upper rack of oven and fish on bottom shelf. Microwave both for 13 to 15 minutes, on HIGH, or until vegetable is tender-crisp. Let stand 5 minutes before serving.

FILETS DE SOLE BONNE FEMME

2 lbs. fresh sole fillets
1 green onion, sliced
½ teaspoon salt
¼ teaspoon pepper
½ cup dry white wine
3 tablespoons butter or margarine
¼ lb. fresh mushroom caps
1 tablespoon butter or margarine

Sauce:
¼ cup milk
3 tablespoons all-purpose flour
¼ teaspoon salt
Dash pepper
1 cup reserved poaching liquid
2 tablespoons lemon juice
1 tablespoon dried parsley flakes

Thawed frozen fish may be used.

1. Arrange fillets in 2-quart (12 x 7) glass baking dish with thick edges toward outside of dish. Sprinkle green onion, seasonings and wine over fillets. Dot with butter; cover with wax paper.
2. Microwave for 10 to 12 minutes, on HIGH, or until fish flakes easily (about 140° F.). Drain, reserving 1 cup poaching liquid for Sauce.
3. Place mushroom caps and 1 tablespoon butter in medium glass mixing bowl.
4. Microwave for about 3 minutes, on ROAST, or until cooked. Arrange mushroom caps over fillets. Serve Sauce over fish and mushroom caps.
5. **Sauce:** Combine milk, flour and seasonings in 4-cup glass measure; beat with rotary beater until smooth. Beat in 1 cup reserved poaching liquid. Microwave for about 3 minutes, on HIGH, or until thickened (about 175° F.). Beat in lemon juice and parsley. 6 to 8 Servings

STUFFED SOLE

Buy less expensive broken shrimp for a more economical dish.

- 2 tablespoons butter or margarine
- 3 green onions, sliced
- 1 clove garlic, finely chopped
- 1 can (6½ oz.) broken shrimp, drained
- ¼ cup soda cracker crumbs
- ½ teaspoon salt
- ⅛ teaspoon pepper
- Salt
- 2 lbs. frozen sole fillets, thawed
- ½ cup chicken broth
- ½ cup dry white wine or water
- 3 tablespoons butter or margarine

Sauce:

- ¼ cup milk
- 2 tablespoons cornstarch
- 1 tablespoon dried parsley flakes
- 1 cup reserved poaching liquid

1. Place butter, onions, garlic and shrimp in 1½-quart glass casserole.

2. Microwave for 3 to 4 minutes, on HIGH, or until onion is partly cooked. Stir in crumbs, ½ teaspoon salt and pepper.

3. Sprinkle salt over fillets. Evenly divide shrimp mixture among fillets; spread on each fillet. Roll up each fillet jelly roll fashion; secure with toothpicks and place in 2-quart (12 x 7) glass baking dish. Pour chicken broth and wine over fish; dot with butter. Cover with wax paper.

4. Microwave for 9 to 10 minutes, on HIGH, or until fish flakes easily (about 140° F.). Drain, reserving 1 cup poaching liquid for Sauce. Let fish stand, covered, 5 minutes before serving. Remove toothpicks and pour Sauce over fish to serve.

5. Sauce: Combine milk, cornstarch and parsley in 4-cup glass measure; beat with rotary beater until smooth. Beat in 1 cup reserved poaching liquid.

6. Microwave about 3 minutes, on HIGH, or until thickened (about 175° F.). Beat lightly. About 6 Servings

FISH PROVENCALE

Mushrooms are sensitive – microwave on ROAST.

- 2 lbs. frozen fish fillets, thawed
- 4 green onions, sliced
- 1 cup sliced fresh mushrooms
- 2 tomatoes, peeled and cut into eighths
- 1 teaspoon salt
- ⅓ cup dry white wine or water
- 1 tablespoon lemon juice
- 3 tablespoons butter or margarine

Sauce:

- ¼ cup water
- 2 tablespoons cornstarch
- 1 tablespoon dried parsley flakes
- 1 cup poaching liquid

1. Arrange fillets in 3-quart (13 x 9) glass baking dish with thick edges toward outside of dish. Sprinkle on remaining ingredients, except butter. Dot with butter; cover with wax paper.

2. Microwave for 15 to 17 minutes, on ROAST, or until fish flakes easily (about 140° F.). Drain, reserving 1 cup poaching liquid for Sauce. Let fish stand, covered, 5 minutes before serving. Pour Sauce over fish and vegetables to serve.

3. Sauce: Combine water, cornstarch and parsley in 4-cup glass measure; beat with rotary beater until smooth. Beat in 1 cup reserved poaching liquid. Microwave for about 3 minutes, on HIGH, or until thickened (about 175° F.). Beat lightly. 6 to 8 Servings

WILD FISH BAKE *

Setting must be reduced to ROAST when sensitive sour cream sauce is put on fish.

- 2 packages (11 oz. each) frozen white and wild rice mix
- 1 lb. frozen fish fillets, thawed
- ½ cup mayonnaise or salad dressing
- ½ cup sour cream
- 2 tablespoons prepared mustard
- ½ teaspoon salt
- ½ teaspoon dill weed

1. Place rice pouches in 2-quart (12 x 7) glass baking dish; slit pouches.

2. Microwave for about 5 minutes, on HIGH, or until thawed. Empty pouches into dish; spread over bottom of dish. Arrange fillets over rice with thick edges toward outside of dish. Cover with wax paper.

3. Microwave for 7 minutes on HIGH. Combine remaining ingredients in small bowl; pour over fish; recover.

4. Microwave for 4 to 5 minutes, on ROAST, or until fish flakes easily (about 140° F.). Let stand, covered, 5 minutes before serving.
About 4 Servings

TIP: Substitue 2½ cups of your own recipe of cooked white and wild rice.

ADD-A-VEGETABLE: Prepare Wild Fish Bake through Step 2. Place 1 package (9 oz.) frozen French-style green beans in 1½-quart glass casserole; cover with glass lid. Place vegetable on upper rack of oven and fish on bottom shelf. Microwave both for 12 minutes on HIGH. Complete fish recipe as directed in Step 3. Microwave both for 6 to 8 minutes, on ROAST, or until fish flakes easily (about 140° F.). Let stand, covered, 5 minutes before serving.

TROUT AMANDINE

Place fish on upper rack in oven because it is a denser food than sauce.

4 (6 to 8 oz. each) frozen trout, thawed
Salt
1 lemon, cut into eighths

Butter Sauce:
⅓ cup butter or margarine
⅓ cup slivered almonds
1 tablespoon dried parsley flakes
1 teaspoon lemon juice

1. Sprinkle inside of trout with salt. Place 2 lemon wedges in each trout cavity. Place trout in 3-quart (13 x 9) glass baking dish with tail ends toward center of dish. Cover with wax paper; set aside.

2. Place Butter Sauce ingredients in 2-cup glass measure.

3. Place fish on upper rack of oven and sauce on bottom shelf.

4. Microwave both for 5 minutes on HIGH. Remove sauce and continue cooking fish for 3 to 4 minutes, on HIGH, or until fish flakes easily (about 140° F.). Let stand, covered, 5 minutes before serving. Stir sauce and pour over trout to serve.
About 4 Servings

TIP: Fresh trout can also be used.

ADD-A-VEGETABLE: Prepare Trout Amandine through Step 2; set aside. Place 1½ lbs. fresh broccoli and ¼ cup water in 2-quart glass casserole; cover with glass lid. Place broccoli on upper rack of oven, fish and Butter Sauce on bottom shelf. Microwave all for 12 minutes, on HIGH, or until butter is melted. Remove Butter Sauce and continue cooking fish and broccoli for about 6 minutes, on HIGH, or until fish flakes easily (about 140° F.). Remove fish and continue cooking broccoli for about 2 minutes, on HIGH, or until tender-crisp.

SALMON STEAKS WITH LEMON DILL SAUCE

May use frozen uncooked salmon steaks, thawed.

4 salmon steaks, ¾ inch thick
1 medium onion, sliced
1 teaspoon instant chicken bouillon
1 teaspoon dill weed
½ teaspoon salt
1 cup water
1 tablespoon lemon juice

Lemon Dill Sauce:
3 tablespoons all-purpose flour
½ cup light cream
½ teaspoon salt
1 tablespoon lemon juice
Reserved poaching liquid
3 tablespoons butter or margarine

1. Arrange salmon steaks in 2-quart (12 x 7) glass baking dish with thick edges toward outside of dish. Top with onion, bouillon, seasonings, water and lemon juice. Cover with wax paper.

2. Microwave for 10 to 12 minutes, on HIGH, or until fish flakes easily (about 140° F.). Drain off poaching liquid; set aside. Let stand, covered, 5 minutes. Pour Lemon Dill Sauce over fish to serve.

3. Lemon Dill Sauce: Combine all sauce ingredients, except poaching liquid and butter, in 4-cup glass measure; beat with rotary beater until smooth. Beat in reserved poaching liquid; add butter. Microwave for about 4 minutes, on ROAST, or until mixture thickens (about 175° F.). Beat lightly.
About 4 Servings

ADD-A-VEGETABLE: Prepare Salmon Steaks with Lemon Dill Sauce through Step 1. Place 1 package (10 oz.) frozen brussels sprouts in 1½-quart glass casserole; cover with glass lid. Place vegetable on upper rack of oven and fish on bottom shelf. Microwave both for 15 to 17 minutes, on HIGH, or until fish flakes easily (about 140° F.) and vegetable is tender-crisp. Drain poaching liquid off fish; set aside. Let stand, covered, 5 minutes before serving. Remove oven rack; make Sauce as directed in Step 3. Pour sauce over fish to serve.

Pictured: Salmon Steaks with Lemon Dill Sauce, recipe above, garnished with parsley.

FISH WITH CUCUMBER SAUCE

Sugar-y dessert microwaves fast – place on bottom shelf.

- 2 lbs. frozen fish fillets, thawed

Cucumber Sauce:

- 1 can (10¾ oz.) condensed cream of shrimp soup
- ½ cup sour cream
- ½ cup finely chopped cucumber
- 2 green onions, sliced
- ½ teaspoon salt
- ⅛ teaspoon pepper

1. Arrange fillets in 2-quart (12 x 7) glass baking dish with thick edges toward outside of dish. Cover with wax paper; set aside.
2. Combine Cucumber Sauce ingredients in small glass mixing bowl.
3. Place fish on upper rack of oven and sauce on bottom shelf.
4. Microwave both for 10 to 12 minutes, on ROAST, or until fish flakes easily (about 140° F.). Stir sauce and let stand 5 minutes before serving. Pour sauce over fish to serve. 6 to 8 Servings

ADD-A-DESSERT: Prepare Fish with Cucumber Sauce through Step 2 and Cherry Crisp, page 185, through Step 1. Place fish and sauce on upper rack of oven and dessert on bottom shelf. Microwave all for 14 to 16 minutes, on HIGH, or until fish flakes easily (about 140° F.) and dessert is hot. Stir sauce and let stand 5 minutes before serving over fish.

TURBAN OF FLOUNDER

- 2 tablespoons butter or margarine
- 2 tablespoons finely chopped onion
- 1 can (4 oz.) mushroom stems and pieces, drained
- 1 cup herb-seasoned stuffing mix
- ¼ cup grated Parmesan cheese
- 1 jar (2 oz.) chopped pimento
- ½ teaspoon celery salt
- ¼ teaspoon pepper
- 1 lb. frozen flounder fillets, thawed
- 1 cup Béchamel Sauce, page 151

1. Place butter, onion and mushrooms in 1½-quart glass casserole.
2. Microwave for about 3 to 4 minutes, on ROAST, or until onion is partly cooked. Stir in remaining ingredients, except fish and Béchamel Sauce; set aside. Lightly butter four 6-oz. custard cups. Coil one fillet around inside of each cup or cut fish to line inside of cup. Evenly divide stuffing among the 4 custard cups. Cover with wax paper.
3. Microwave for 8 to 10 minutes, on ROAST, or until fish flakes easily (about 140° F.). Let stand, covered, 5 minutes before serving. Invert on serving platter. Serve with hot Béchamel Sauce. About 4 Servings

ADD-A-VEGETABLE: Prepare Turban of Flounder through Step 2. Place 1 package (10 oz.) frozen broccoli spears in 1½-quart glass casserole; cover with glass lid. Place vegetable on upper rack of oven and fish on bottom shelf. Microwave both for 15 to 17 minutes, on HIGH, or until vegetable is tender-crisp. Let stand 5 minutes before serving.

SAUCY FISH STICKS

- 2 packages (8 oz. each) frozen fish sticks

Tomato-Bacon Sauce:

- 3 slices bacon
- 1 can (10¾ oz.) condensed tomato soup
- 2 tablespoons water
- ¼ cup chopped celery
- 2 tablespoons chopped onion
- ¼ teaspoon ground oregano
- ⅛ teaspoon garlic powder

1. Arrange frozen fish sticks in 3-quart (13 x 9) glass baking dish; set aside.
2. Arrange bacon in single layer in 1½-quart glass casserole.
3. Microwave for 3 to 3½ minutes, on HIGH, or until bacon is crisp; drain. Crumble bacon. Stir in remaining Tomato-Bacon Sauce ingredients; cover.
4. Place fish on upper rack of oven and sauce on bottom shelf.
5. Microwave both for 10 to 12 minutes, on HIGH, or until fish and sauce are hot (about 160° F.). Stir sauce and let stand 5 minutes before serving. Serve sauce over fish. About 4 Servings

SALMON-RICE LOAF

Foods with sensitive ingredients may be cooked on HIGH when other foods are also cooking in the oven.

- 1 tablespoon butter or margarine
- ¼ cup chopped onion
- ⅓ cup chopped celery
- 1 can (16 oz.) salmon, drained and flaked
- 1 cup cooked rice, page 118
- 2 eggs, beaten
- 1 teaspoon dried parsley flakes
- ½ teaspoon salt
- ¼ teaspoon pepper
- 1 teaspoon lemon juice

1. Place butter, onion and celery in medium glass mixing bowl.
2. Microwave for 2 to 3 minutes, on HIGH, or until vegetables are partly cooked. Add remaining ingredients; mix well. Pat into 9 x 5 glass loaf dish. Cover with wax paper.
3. Microwave for 10 to 12 minutes, on ROAST, or until hot in center (about 160° F.). Let stand, covered, 5 minutes before serving. About 4 Servings

CREAMED TUNA

- 2 tablespoons butter or margarine
- ¼ cup chopped onion
- 2 tablespoons chopped green pepper
- 1 can (6½ oz.) tuna, drained, rinsed and flaked
- ¼ cup unsifted all-purpose flour
- 1½ cups milk
- ¼ teaspoon salt
- ⅛ teaspoon pepper

Melt butter on HIGH when mixed with vegetables for sautéeing.

1. Place butter, onion, green pepper and tuna in 4-cup glass measure.

2. Microwave for 3 minutes on HIGH. Combine remaining ingredients in small bowl until smooth; stir into tuna-vegetable mixture. Continue cooking for 3 to 4 minutes, on HIGH, or until thickened (about 160° F.). Let stand 5 minutes before serving. About 4 Servings

RECIPE VARIATIONS

CREAMED SALMON: Substitute 1 can (6½ oz.) salmon, drained and flaked, for tuna in basic recipe.

EASY CREAMED TUNA: Reduce butter to 1 tablespoon in basic recipe. Substitute 1 can (10¾ oz.) condensed cream of mushroom soup and ¼ cup milk for flour and milk. Stir soup and seasonings into cooked tuna vegetable mixture in Step 2. Microwave for 5 to 6 minutes, on ROAST, or until thickened (about 160° F.). Let stand 5 minutes before serving.

TUNA FISH CAKES

- 2 cans (6½ oz. each) tuna, drained, rinsed and flaked
- ½ cup finely chopped celery
- 1 tablespoon finely chopped onion
- ¼ teaspoon salt
- ⅛ teaspoon pepper
- ⅓ cup mayonnaise or salad dressing
- 1 teaspoon lemon juice
- 2 slices process American cheese, cut in half
- 1 package (2 oz.) seasoned coating mix for fish

1. Combine all ingredients, except cheese and fish coating, in medium mixing bowl; mix well. Shape into 8 patties. Place half a cheese slice on each of 4 patties; cover with remaining patties to make 4 large cakes.

2. Place fish coating mix in shallow dish; coat each cake. Place in 2-quart (12 x 7) glass baking dish.

3. Microwave for 8 to 9 minutes, on ROAST, or until heated through. Let stand 5 minutes before serving. About 4 Servings

RECIPE VARIATIONS

TUNA BUN: Spread 4 split hamburger buns with tartar sauce. Place 1 tuna-fish cake on each bun. Top with sliced dill pickle.

MACKEREL CAKES: Substitute 1 can (15 oz.) mackerel, drained and flaked, for tuna in basic recipe.

STEAMED CLAMS OVER VEGETABLES *

- 1 lb. small new red potatoes, with ½-inch strip of peel removed around center
- 2 small onions, quartered
- 2 medium carrots, cut into pieces
- 1 stalk celery, sliced
- 1 green pepper, cut into strips
- ½ cup water
- 1 teaspoon salt
- ¼ cup butter or margarine
- 12 large fresh clams, soaked and scrubbed

Larger portions of vegetables cook well when immersed in liquid.

1. Combine vegetables and water in 4-quart glass casserole. Sprinkle with salt; dot with butter. Cover with glass lid.

2. Microwave for 12 minutes on HIGH. Place clams over vegetables, hinge down. Recover.

3. Microwave for 12 to 15 minutes, on ROAST, or until vegetables are tender and clams are opened. Lift out opened clams. If necessary, continue cooking unopened clams and vegetables 1 to 2 minutes, on ROAST, or until all clams open. Let stand, covered, 5 minutes before serving. About 3 Servings

TIP: Buy only fresh clams. Shells will be tightly closed. Clams must cook until shell opens or clam is not done.

FRESH LOBSTER

4 cups water
1 to 1½ lbs. fresh lobster, pegged
Melted butter or margarine
Lemon wedges

1. Place water in 10-inch glass skillet. Cover with glass lid.

2. Microwave for 8 to 10 minutes, on HIGH, or until boiling. Place lobster, head first, into boiling water; recover.

3. Microwave for 8 to 10 minutes, on HIGH, or until shell turns red. Split tail; if meat is still translucent in center, continue cooking for 1 to 2 minutes.

4. Remove dark vein and small sac behind head. Crack large claws. Serve with melted or drawn butter and lemon wedges.

1 to 2 Servings

FROZEN LOBSTER TAILS, THAWED

1. Split each 9-oz. tail through top shell. Pull out lobster meat, but leave connected to shell end. Place meat on top of shell. Brush with melted butter or margarine. Sprinkle with paprika. Arrange in 2-quart (12 x 7) glass baking dish. Cover with wax paper.

2. Microwave on HIGH:
1 lobster tail — 3 to 4 minutes
2 lobster tails — 5 to 6 minutes
4 lobster tails — 8 to 10 minutes
Let stand, covered, 5 minutes before serving.

LOBSTER THERMIDOR

Heat cooked food on REHEAT.

¼ cup butter or margarine
2 green onions, sliced
1 cup sliced fresh mushrooms
1 clove garlic, finely chopped
1 can (6½ oz.) cooked lobster meat, drained and diced
3 tablespoons all-purpose flour
1 cup milk
¼ teaspoon salt
¼ teaspoon pepper
½ cup shredded process American cheese
Dash paprika

1. Place butter, onions, mushrooms, garlic and lobster in 1½-quart glass casserole.

2. Microwave for 4 minutes on ROAST. Combine flour, milk and seasonings in small bowl until smooth; stir into lobster-vegetable mixture. Continue cooking 4 to 5 minutes, on ROAST, or until thickened (about 160° F.). Spoon into 4 individual glass casseroles or natural baking shells. Sprinkle each with shredded cheese and paprika.

3. Microwave for 2 to 3 minutes, on REHEAT, or until bubbly. Let stand 5 minutes before serving.

4 Servings

CRAB NEWBURG

Serve in patty shells, or over toast points.

2 tablespoons cornstarch
1½ cups light cream
1 egg yolk
½ teaspoon salt
¼ cup butter or margarine
¼ cup dry sherry or water
2 cans (6½ oz. each) crabmeat, drained and flaked

1. Combine cornstarch, cream, egg yolk and salt in 1½-quart glass casserole; beat with rotary beater until smooth. Add butter.

2. Microwave for 5 minutes on ROAST. Beat well; stir in sherry and crabmeat. Continue cooking for 7 to 8 minutes, on ROAST, or until thickened (about 160° F.). Stir well and let stand 5 minutes before serving.

4 to 5 Servings

SCALLOP KABOBS

May substitute frozen, uncooked sea scallops, thawed, for fresh scallops.

¼ cup cooking oil
2 tablespoons dry onion soup mix
2 tablespoons lemon juice
1 clove garlic, finely chopped
1 teaspoon thyme leaves
1 lb. raw fresh sea scallops
3 ears fresh corn, cut into fourths
12 cherry tomatoes
1 small green pepper, cut into chunks
4 slices bacon, cut into thirds

1. Combine oil, soup mix, lemon juice, garlic and thyme in small mixing bowl. Stir in scallops. Let marinate, covered, in refrigerator for about 2 hours.

2. Alternate scallops on metal skewers with corn, tomatoes, green pepper and loops of sliced bacon; place in 3-quart (13 x 9) glass baking dish. Brush with marinade mixture. Cover with wax paper.

3. Microwave for 10 minutes on HIGH. Rotate and baste kabobs with marinade mixture. Continue cooking for 10 to 12 minutes, on HIGH, or until scallops are tender. Let stand, covered, 5 minutes before serving.

About 4 Servings

SHRIMP JAMBALAYA

2 tablespoons butter or margarine
½ cup chopped onion
½ cup chopped celery
¼ cup chopped green pepper
1 lb. frozen cooked shrimp, thawed
2 cups cubed cooked ham
1 cup quick-cooking rice
2 teaspoons dried parsley flakes
½ teaspoon salt
¼ teaspoon garlic powder
¼ teaspoon thyme leaves
⅛ teaspoon ground cloves
⅛ teaspoon cayenne pepper
1 can (16 oz.) whole tomatoes
½ cup water

1. Place butter, onion, celery and green pepper in 2½-quart glass casserole.

2. Microwave for 4 to 5 minutes, on HIGH, or until vegetables are partly cooked. Stir in remaining ingredients; cover with glass lid.

3. Microwave for 7 minutes on HIGH. Stir and continue cooking for 7 to 8 minutes, on HIGH, or until heated through (about 150° F.). Let stand, covered, 5 minutes before serving.

4 to 6 Servings

ADD-A-DESSERT: Prepare Shrimp Jambalaya through Step 2. Place 2 packages (10 oz. each) frozen mixed fruit in 1½-quart glass casserole; cover with glass lid. Place fish casserole on upper rack of oven and fruit on bottom shelf. Microwave both for 12 minutes on HIGH. Remove fruit and continue cooking fish casserole for 8 to 10 minutes, on HIGH, or until heated through (about 150° F.). Let stand 5 minutes before serving. Serve fruit sauce over ice cream and cake.

SHRIMP ORIENTAL

May substitute frozen uncooked shrimp, thawed, for fresh shrimp.

1 lb. raw fresh shrimp, peeled and deveined
3 tablespoons cooking oil
1 cup chopped celery
1 cup chopped onion
1 medium green pepper, cut into strips
1 can (4 oz.) mushroom stems and pieces, drained
1 package (6 oz.) frozen pea pods
1 jar (2 oz.) sliced pimento, drained
½ cup water
3 tablespoons dry sherry
1 tablespoon soy sauce
2 tablespoons cornstarch
1 teaspoon salt
½ teaspoon ground ginger

1. Place shrimp, oil and vegetables in 3-quart glass casserole. Cover with glass lid.

2. Microwave for 12 minutes on ROAST. Combine remaining ingredients in small bowl until smooth; stir into shrimp vegetable mixture. Recover and continue cooking for 14 to 16 minutes, on ROAST, or until sauce thickens (about 180° F.). Let stand, covered, 5 minutes before serving.

4 to 6 Servings

WINE SCAMPI

Shellfish in the shell cook in the same time as shellfish without a shell.

2 tablespoons butter or margarine
1 clove garlic, finely chopped
3 tablespoons dry white wine
1 lb. raw fresh shrimp or scampi
Parsley, if desired

1. Place butter, garlic and wine in 1½-quart glass casserole.

2. Microwave for 2 minutes on HIGH. Stir in shrimp and continue cooking for about 4 minutes, on HIGH, or until shrimp turns pink. Let stand 5 minutes before serving. Garnish with snipped parsley.

2 to 3 Servings

Pictured: Wine Scampi made with large shrimp, recipe above, garnished with parsley.

COQUILLES ST. JACQUES

- **¼ cup butter or margarine**
- **2 green onions, sliced**
- **1 can (4 oz.) sliced mushrooms, drained**
- **1 lb. raw fresh sea scallops**
- **½ cup dry white wine**
- **1 tablespoon chopped pimento**
- **½ teaspoon salt**
- **⅛ teaspoon pepper**
- **1 bay leaf**
- **3 tablespoons all-purpose flour**
- **¼ cup light cream**
- **¼ cup buttered dry bread crumbs**

May use frozen uncooked sea scallops, thawed instead of fresh.

1. Place butter, onions and mushrooms in 2-quart glass casserole.

2. Microwave for 2 to 3 minutes, on ROAST, or until onion is partly cooked. Stir in scallops, wine, pimento and seasonings.

3. Microwave for 7 minutes on ROAST. Combine flour and cream in small bowl until smooth; stir into scallop mixture. Continue cooking for about 5 minutes, on ROAST, or until scallops are tender and sauce has thickened (about 160° F.). Remove bay leaf. Spoon into 4 natural shells or 1-cup glass sauce dishes. Sprinkle each with bread crumbs.

4. Microwave for 1 to 2 minutes, on REHEAT, or until hot. Let stand 5 minutes before serving. About 4 Servings

TIP: Make buttered bread crumbs by placing 2 tablespoons butter or margarine in 1-cup glass measure. Microwave for about 1 minute on ROAST. Stir in ¼ cup dry bread crumbs.

CRAB-SHRIMP BAKE

- **2 tablespoons butter or margarine**
- **¼ cup finely chopped onion**
- **2 packages (10 oz. each) frozen chopped spinach, thawed**
- **1 can (10¾ oz.) condensed cream of shrimp soup**
- **1 can (6½ oz.) shrimp, drained**
- **1 can (6½ oz.) crabmeat, drained and flaked**
- **1 cup shredded Cheddar cheese**
- **⅛ teaspoon garlic powder**
- **Dash nutmeg**
- **¼ cup cornflake crumbs**

Thaw frozen spinach on HIGH for about 4 minutes.

1. Place butter and onion in 2-quart (8 x 8) glass baking dish.

2. Microwave for 2 to 3 minutes, on HIGH, or until onion is partly cooked. Drain thawed spinach; stir into butter mixture and spread over bottom of dish. Combine remaining ingredients, except cornflake crumbs, in medium mixing bowl; pour over spinach. Sprinkle with cornflake crumbs.

3. Microwave for 15 to 16 minutes, on ROAST, or until heated through (about 150° F.). Let stand 5 minutes before serving. 4 to 6 Servings

ADD-A-DESSERT: Prepare Crab-Shrimp Bake through Step 2 and Strawberry-Rhubarb Sauce, page 188, through Step 1. Place sauce on upper rack of oven and fish on bottom shelf. Microwave both for about 30 minutes, on HIGH, or until rhubarb is tender. Complete sauce as directed and let fish casserole stand 5 minutes before serving. Serve Strawberry-Rhubarb Sauce over cake or ice cream.

OYSTERS ROCKEFELLER

- **1 quart raw oysters in the shell**
- **1 package (10 oz.) frozen chopped spinach**
- **2 tablespoons butter or margarine**
- **2 green onions, finely chopped**
- **2 tablespoons dried parsley flakes**
- **1 tablespoon Worcestershire sauce**
- **½ teaspoon salt**
- **¼ teaspoon pepper**
- **¼ cup light cream**
- **Grated Parmesan cheese**

The natural shells can be used as baking dishes.

1. Remove oysters from shells, rinse off any shell material and pat dry; set aside. Rinse ½ of shells and place, open-side-up, in two 2-quart (12 x 7) glass baking dishes; set aside. Place spinach in 1½-quart glass casserole. Cover with glass lid.

2. Microwave for 8 to 9 minutes, on HIGH, or until partly cooked; drain well. Stir in remaining ingredients, except oysters and Parmesan cheese. Spoon ½ of spinach mixture into shells. Place oysters on spinach and top with remaining spinach mixture. Sprinkle each filled shell with Parmesan cheese; cover with wax paper. Place one dish on upper rack of oven and one on bottom shelf.

3. Microwave both for 6 to 8 minutes, on ROAST, or until oysters are plump and edges curl. Let stand, covered, 5 minutes before serving. About 4 Servings

OYSTER STEW

- **¼ cup butter or margarine**
- **4 green onions, sliced**
- **2 cups milk**
- **1 cup light cream**
- **2 cans (8 oz. each) oysters, undrained**
- **½ teaspoon salt**
- **¼ teaspoon pepper**
- **Dash hot pepper sauce**
- **Oyster crackers**

Both oysters and cream are sensitive ingredients, reduce to ROAST.

1. Place butter and onions in 2-quart glass casserole.

2. Microwave for 2 to 3 minutes, on HIGH, or until onions are partly cooked. Stir in milk, cream, oyster liquid and seasonings.

3. Microwave for 7 minutes on ROAST. Stir in oysters and continue cooking for 5 to 6 minutes, on ROAST, or until hot (about 160° F.). Let stand, covered, 5 minutes before serving. Serve with oyster crackers. 5 to 6 Servings

Main Dishes & Stews

A Nutritious Dinner in a Dish

Here's How — and Why

Main Dishes and Stews Are Convenient, Nutritious:	Meat plus vegetables (and sometimes rice or pasta) combine into main dishes and stews that microwave fast in a single glass dish — let you serve all the nutritious juices along with the meat and vegetables.
Microwave Uncooked Beef, Chicken or Veal Main Dishes on HIGH/SIMMER:	Start microwaving uncooked beef, chicken and veal main dishes on HIGH for fast heat penetration, then on SIMMER to tenderize uncooked meat and vegetables. Brown small slices of meat on the microwave browning grill, preheated as manufacturer's booklet directs, then microwave along with other ingredients on SIMMER to tenderize and complete cooking. See Veal Parmigiana, page 85.
Uncooked Pork or Lamb Main Dishes Cook on ROAST:	Pork and lamb are tender meats, so need the ROAST setting to keep them tender as they cook through.
Uncooked Ground Meat Main Dishes Microwave in Two Steps:	Brown ground meats on HIGH, then change setting depending upon ingredients added: Microwave raw vegetables on HIGH to cook them through; microwave cooked vegetables on REHEAT.
Main Dishes with Cooked Meat or Seafood Microwave on REHEAT:	Generally, all cooked meats, poultry, seafood and vegetable main dishes microwave on REHEAT because heating, not cooking, is required. The small amounts of finely cut uncooked vegetables in these recipes will cook tender-crisp at this setting.
If You Add Rice or Noodles to a Main Dish:	When uncooked noodles or uncooked rice are added to a main dish, cook mixture on SIMMER to allow time for noodles and rice to rehydrate, fluff and/or tenderize. Quick-cooking rice may be added to cooked meat main dishes which do not contain sensitive ingredients — cook such a mixture on HIGH setting.
Stewing Calls for HIGH/SIMMER technique:	First microwave stew meat on HIGH; add vegetables, seasonings and sauce ingredients, and continue heating quickly on HIGH. Use SIMMER setting to finish cooking, tenderizing and blending flavors.
Sensitive Ingredients Microwave on ROAST:	When sensitive ingredients such as eggs, cheese, mayonnaise, salad dressing, sour cream, mushrooms, mushroom soup or kidney beans are added to a main dish or stew, do not microwave at a setting higher than ROAST to prevent "popping," curdling and/or drying.
Microwave in Glass; Cover as Specified:	Use glass casseroles, glass baking dishes, glass ceramic casseroles, skillets or Dutch ovens to microwave main dishes and stews. Cover with glass lids or wax paper when specified in recipes. Tip lids away from hand when removing to prevent steam burns. Plastic wrap may be used as a cover — pierce it and allow steam to escape before removing.
Drain and/or Stir as a Recipe Directs:	Drain off excess fat or liquid, when a recipe directs, to assure good sauce or gravy consistency. Stir mixtures, when directed, to cook ingredients evenly.
Refrigerated Mixtures Cook a Bit Longer:	Main dishes may be mixed ahead of cooking, then refrigerated. Add 5 to 8 minutes to final cooking period when a main dish or stew is microwaved directly from the refrigerator. *(Continued, next page.)*

Pictured: Reuben Casserole, page 88.

The "*" Is a Reminder: Use an "*" in a recipe title as a reminder that the power setting changes during cooking. This is a convenient time to stir or turn food.

"ADD-A-" Recipes Make a Hearty Dinner Easy: Add a vegetable, dessert or salad to main dishes and stews. Presto, you've a hearty meal. Note that power settings usually increase to HIGH when two dishes of food are cooking because microwave intensity to each one is reduced. However, when a sensitive-ingredient-dish is microwaving on ROAST, or a main dish or stew is cooking on SIMMER, the "ADD-A-" dish cooks at ROAST, or SIMMER. Note that "ADD-A-" dishes may cook at slightly different rates; continue cooking one food alone if necessary. Microwave main dishes or stews on the oven's upper rack because the large quantity of food takes longer to cook. Place the second dish of food on the bottom shelf. Stagger dishes for fast even cooking.

Microwave-Conventional Comparison: Main dishes cook quickly in a microwave oven — Tuna Noodle Casserole microwaves in 8 minutes on ROAST versus 30 minutes in a conventional oven. Stews are convenient, but not much faster in a microwave. A frozen block of vegetable may be added to stews or main dishes part way through cooking and stirred in after cooking.

COUNTRY CHICKEN 'N RICE *

1 cup chopped celery
2 medium carrots, peeled and sliced
3 green onions, sliced
1 can (16 oz.) whole tomatoes
1 tablespoon dried parsley flakes
2 teaspoons salt
Dash pepper
2½ to 3-lb. stewing chicken, cut up
3 cups water
1¾ cups uncooked rice

HIGH/SIMMER technique works well with chicken and rice or noodles.

1. Combine all ingredients, except rice, in 3-quart glass casserole. Cover with glass lid.

2. Microwave for 20 minutes on HIGH (about 160°F.). Turn chicken pieces over; recover.

3. Microwave for about 50 minutes, on SIMMER, or until meat cut near bone is no longer pink. Remove chicken from broth; set aside. Stir in rice; recover, and continue cooking both for 15 minutes, on SIMMER, or until rice is cooked. Set aside apples. Continue as directed in basic recipe. Remove chicken from bones. Return meat to broth; mix well, and recover.

4. Microwave for 2 to 3 minutes, on REHEAT, or until hot (160° F.). Let stand, covered, 5 minutes before serving. 4 to 6 Servings

ADD-A-DESSERT: Prepare Country Chicken 'N Rice through Step 1; set aside. Prepare Old-Fashioned Baked Apples, page 181 (recipe variation) through Step 1. Place chicken on upper rack of oven and apples on bottom shelf. Microwave both for 15 minutes on HIGH. Turn chicken pieces over; recover. Microwave for about 50 minutes, on SIMMER, or until meat cut near bone is no longer pink.

COQ AU VIN *

5 slices bacon
1 can (10¾ oz.) condensed cream of onion soup
½ cup dry red wine or water
3 green onions, sliced
1 clove garlic, finely chopped
1½ teaspoons instant chicken bouillon
1 teaspoon salt
1 teaspoon dried parsley flakes
¼ teaspoon thyme leaves
Dash pepper
2½ to 3-lb. frying chicken, cut into pieces
6 small new red potatoes, peeled and cut in half
2 medium carrots, peeled and sliced
8 ozs. fresh mushrooms, washed

Cook on ROAST when sensitive ingredients, like mushrooms, are added.

1. Arrange bacon in single layer in 10-inch glass ceramic skillet.

2. Microwave for about 4½ minutes, on HIGH, or until crisp. Remove bacon; set aside. Drain off fat. Combine soup, wine, onions, garlic, bouillon and seasonings in glass ceramic skillet. Add remaining ingredients, except mushrooms. Cover with glass lid.

3. Microwave for 30 minutes on HIGH. Add mushrooms, crumble bacon over top, and recover.

4. Microwave for 10 to 12 minutes, on ROAST, or until meat cut near bone is no longer pink. Let stand, covered, 5 minutes before serving.
About 6 Servings

CHICKEN 'N DUMPLINGS *

Dumplings cook well in main dishes that finish on SIMMER.

- **2 to 2½-lb. frying chicken, cut into pieces**
- **2½ cups water**
- **½ cup chopped celery**
- **4 carrots, peeled and sliced**
- **1 medium onion, sliced**
- **1 bay leaf**
- **4 peppercorns**
- **1 tablespoon salt**
- **½ cup unsifted all-purpose flour**
- **½ cup water**

Dumplings:

- **1½ cups unsifted all-purpose flour**
- **2 teaspoons baking powder**
- **½ teaspoon salt**
- **½ teaspoon poultry seasoning**
- **⅔ cup milk**
- **1 egg**
- **2 tablespoons cooking oil**

1. Combine all ingredients, except ½ cup flour, ½ cup water and Dumpling ingredients, in 3-quart glass casserole. Cover with glass lid.

2. Microwave for 20 minutes on HIGH (about 160°F.). Combine ½ cup flour and ½ cup water in small bowl until smooth; stir into chicken mixture; recover.

3. Microwave for 30 minutes on SIMMER. Spoon Dumplings over hot chicken mixture. Recover and continue cooking for 10 to 12 minutes, on SIMMER, or until Dumplings are no longer doughy. Let stand, covered, 5 minutes before serving.

4. **Dumplings:** Combine dry ingredients in medium mixing bowl. Blend milk, egg and oil in 2-cup measure; pour into flour mixture. Stir until moistened.

About 6 Servings

BEEF SHORT RIBS AND PARSLEY DUMPLINGS *

Beef starts cooking on HIGH for super-fast heating.

- **2 to 2½ lbs. beef short ribs**
- **1 cup catsup**
- **½ cup water**
- **1 tablespoon sugar**
- **1 tablespoon prepared horseradish**
- **1 tablespoon prepared mustard**
- **1 tablespoon vinegar**
- **1 teaspoon salt**
- **⅛ teaspoon pepper**
- **⅛ teaspoon hot pepper sauce**

Parsley Dumplings:

- **1 cup biscuit mix**
- **1 tablespoon dried parsley flakes**
- **⅓ cup milk**

1. Place ribs, fat-side-down in 10-inch glass ceramic skillet; set aside. Combine remaining ingredients, except dumpling ingredients, in 2-cup glass measure; pour over ribs. Cover with glass lid.

2. Microwave for 10 minutes on HIGH. Turn ribs over; recover.

3. Microwave for 30 minutes on SIMMER. Drop Parsley Dumplings by tablespoonfuls into hot liquid; recover, and continue cooking for 10 to 12 minutes, on SIMMER, or until dumplings are no longer doughy.

4. **Parsley Dumplings:** Combine biscuit mix and parsley flakes in medium mixing bowl; stir in milk.

4 to 6 Servings

SWEET BEEF *

- **2 to 2½ lbs. beef round steak, cut into 1-inch cubes**
- **1 teaspoon salt**
- **¼ teaspoon pepper**
- **2 tablespoons packed brown sugar**
- **1 tablespoon lemon juice**
- **1 can (10½ oz.) condensed onion soup**
- **1 cup pitted whole prunes**
- **1 can (18 oz.) vacuum-packed sweet potatoes**
- **1 envelope (¾ oz.) brown gravy mix**

1. Place beef cubes in 2-quart glass casserole. Stir in seasonings, brown sugar, lemon juice and soup; cover with glass lid.

2. Microwave for 10 minutes on HIGH. Stir in prunes. Top with potatoes. Recover and continue cooking for 35 to 40 minutes, on SIMMER, or until meat is fork tender. Let stand, covered, 5 minutes before serving. Remove meat mixture to serving platter. Add gravy mix to cooking dish; stir well; recover.

3. Microwave for 2 to 4 minutes, on HIGH, or until thickened and hot (about 175° F.). Pour gravy over meat and vegetables and serve.

4 to 6 Servings

LOTS-OF-MEAT MAIN DISH *

- **1 lb. round steak, cut into ½-inch cubes**
- **1 lb. pork steak, cut into ½-inch cubes**
- **1 large onion, chopped**
- **2 cups chopped celery**
- **1 teaspoon sugar**
- **3 tablespoons instant beef bouillon**
- **2 tablespoons soy sauce**
- **1 tablespoon Worcestershire sauce**
- **1 can (8 oz.) tomato sauce**
- **1 can (6 oz.) tomato paste**
- **1 can (17 oz.) whole kernel corn, drained**

Tender pork will not toughen or dry on HIGH because it's cooked in liquid.

1. Combine all ingredients, except corn, in 3-quart glass casserole. Cover with glass lid.

2. Microwave for 10 minutes on HIGH. Stir in corn; recover.

3. Microwave for 35 to 40 minutes, on SIMMER, or until meat is fork tender. Let stand, covered, 5 minutes before serving. 4 to 6 Servings

TIP: Serve Lots-of-Meat Main Dish over rice or noodles.

ADD-A-BREAD: Prepare Lots-of-Meat Main Dish through Step 2. Place main dish on upper rack of oven. Microwave for 22 minutes on SIMMER. During this second cooking time, prepare 1 package (8½ oz.) corn muffin mix according to package directions; spoon into 6 paper-lined custard cups. Place custard cups on bottom shelf. Continue cooking both for 15 to 18 minutes, on SIMMER, or until meat is fork tender and muffins are no longer doughy. Let meat stand, covered, 5 minutes before serving. Split muffins in half; serve Lots-of-Meat Main Dish over muffins.

CHOW MEIN

- **1 lb. coarsely ground beef and pork chow mein meat**
- **2 small onions, chopped**
- **3 stalks celery, chopped**
- **½ medium green pepper, chopped**
- **1 can (4 oz.) mushroom stems and pieces, undrained**
- **1 can (16 oz.) bean sprouts, drained**
- **2 tablespoons cornstarch**
- **¼ cup soy sauce**
- **1 tablespoon dark molasses**
- **Chow mein noodles**

Freshen 4 cups chow mein noodles for 3 to 4 minutes on REHEAT.

1. Place meat in 3-quart glass casserole. Cover with glass lid.

2. Microwave for 10 minutes on HIGH. Stir in onion, celery and green pepper. Drain liquid from mushrooms into small bowl; set aside. Stir mushrooms and bean sprouts into meat mixture. Combine remaining ingredients, except noodles, with drained mushroom liquid in small bowl until smooth; pour over meat; recover.

3. Microwave for 15 to 20 minutes, on SIMMER, or until meat is fork tender. Let stand, covered, 5 minutes before serving. Serve over chow mein noodles. 6 to 8 Servings

PORK 'N BEANS

- **1 lb. lean fresh pork, cut into 1-inch cubes**
- **1 medium onion, chopped**
- **1 can (31 oz.) pork and beans**
- **¼ cup dark molasses**
- **2 tablespoons packed brown sugar**
- **1 tablespoon prepared mustard**
- **2 teaspoons dried parsley flakes**
- **2 teaspoons Worcestershire sauce**

Pork is tender, cook it evenly on ROAST.

1. Place pork and onion in 1½-quart glass casserole. Cover with glass lid.

2. Microwave for about 15 minutes, on ROAST, or until meat is browned; drain. Stir in remaining ingredients. Recover and continue cooking for 10 to 12 minutes, on ROAST, or until hot (about 150° F.). Let stand, covered, 5 minutes before serving. About 4 Servings

ADD-A-DESSERT: Prepare Pork 'n Beans through Step 1; set aside. Prepare Peach Crisp, page 185, through Step 1. Place pork on upper rack of oven and dessert on bottom shelf. Microwave for 12 minutes on HIGH. Drain meat; stir in remaining ingredients. Recover and continue cooking both for 10 to 12 minutes, on HIGH, or until meat dish is hot (about 150° F.). Let meat stand, covered, 5 minutes before serving.

CHILI

- **1 lb. ground beef**
- **1 medium onion, chopped**
- **½ cup chopped green pepper**
- **1 can (6 oz.) tomato paste**
- **1 can (16 oz.) whole tomatoes**
- **1 can (15½ oz.) kidney beans, undrained**
- **½ cup water**
- **1 teaspoon salt**
- **¼ teaspoon garlic powder**
- **2 to 3 teaspoons chili powder**

Covering helps assure even, fast cooking.

1. Crumble ground beef in 2-quart glass casserole. Stir in onion and green pepper. Cover with glass lid.

2. Microwave for about 5 minutes, on HIGH, or until meat is browned. Drain and stir in remaining ingredients; recover.

3. Microwave for 14 to 16 minutes, on ROAST, or until hot (about 150° F.). Let stand, covered, 5 minutes before serving. 4 to 6 Servings

TIP: Sprinkle shredded Cheddar cheese over bowls of chili, if desired.

VEAL PARMIGIANA

Brown pieces of meat quickly on a microwave browning grill.

- **3 tablespoons butter or margarine**
- **⅓ cup grated Parmesan cheese**
- **3 tablespoons corn flake crumbs**
- **½ teaspoon garlic salt**
- **1 lb. veal cutlets or veal round steak, cut ½ inch thick**
- **1 can (8 oz.) tomato sauce**
- **½ teaspoon basil leaves**
- **½ teaspoon oregano leaves**
- **1 teaspoon Worcestershire sauce**
- **2 slices Mozzarella cheese**
- **Hot cooked spaghetti**

1. Place butter in 2-quart (12 x 7) glass baking dish.

2. Microwave for about 1 minute, on ROAST, or until melted. Combine Parmesan cheese, corn flake crumbs and garlic salt in flat dish. Cut veal into serving pieces. Dip each piece into butter; coat both sides with crumb mixture and set aside. Preheat microwave browning grill in oven on HIGH as directed for meats in manufacturer's instruction booklet. Lightly grease grill or spray it with vegetable coating. Place crumb-coated veal on hot grill.

3. Microwave for 2 minutes on HIGH. Turn veal over and continue cooking for 2½ minutes on HIGH. Meanwhile, combine remaining ingredients, except Mozzarella cheese and spaghetti, in greased glass baking dish. Add browned veal, turning to coat with tomato mixture. Cover with wax paper.

4. Microwave for 15 minutes on SIMMER. Place cheese on veal and continue cooking for 3 to 4 minutes, on SIMMER, or until cheese melts. Serve on bed of cooked spaghetti.

4 to 6 Servings

QUICK PIZZA

Heat-sensitive cheese mixtures microwave on ROAST.

- **1 can (6 oz.) tomato paste**
- **⅓ cup catsup**
- **¼ teaspoon garlic salt**
- **¼ teaspoon oregano leaves**
- **4 English muffins, split in half and toasted**
- **1 package (5 oz.) pepperoni, sliced**
- **1 cup shredded Mozzarella cheese**

1. Combine tomato paste, catsup, and seasonings in small bowl; mix well. Divide mixture between English muffin halves; spread over top of each. Place halves in 3-quart (13 x 9) glass baking dish. Place pepperoni slices over tomato sauce mixture; sprinkle with shredded cheese.

2. Microwave for 6 to 8 minutes, on ROAST, or until heated through. Let stand 3 minutes before serving.

8 Pizzas

TIP: Substitute other pizza toppings for pepperoni. Try green pepper rings, mushrooms, anchovies or olives.

CHEESY-BEEF HOT DISH

Ground beef cooks on HIGH; SIMMER is needed to rehydrate noodles.

- **1 lb. ground beef**
- **1 small onion, chopped**
- **1 can (8 oz.) tomato sauce**
- **1½ cups uncooked thin egg noodles**
- **1½ cups water**
- **⅓ cup chili sauce**
- **1 tablespoon packed brown sugar**
- **½ teaspoon salt**
- **¼ teaspoon pepper**
- **1 jar (8 oz.) process cheese spread**

1. Crumble ground beef into 2-quart glass casserole; stir in onion. Cover with glass lid.

2. Microwave for about 5 minutes, on HIGH, or until meat is browned; drain. Stir in remaining ingredients, except cheese spread; recover.

3. Microwave for 20 minutes on SIMMER. Add cheese; recover, and continue cooking for 5 to 10 minutes, on SIMMER, or until cheese is melted. Stir to blend. Let stand, covered, 5 minutes before serving.

4 to 6 Servings

ADD-A-DESSERT: Prepare Cheesy-Beef Hot Dish through Step 2; set aside. Prepare Fudge Sauce, page 150, through Step 1 in 1-quart glass casserole; set aside. Place casserole on upper rack of oven. Microwave for 14 minutes on SIMMER. Place Fudge Sauce on bottom shelf. Continue cooking both for about 6 minutes, on SIMMER, or until chocolate is melted. Add cheese to beef dish; recover. Stir remaining Fudge Sauce ingredients into chocolate; beat with rotary beater until smooth. Microwave both for 6 to 8 minutes, on SIMMER, or until sauce is bubbly (about 200° F.). Stir Fudge Sauce to blend. Let meat dish stand, covered, 5 minutes before serving. Serve Fudge Sauce warm over ice cream.

RECIPE VARIATION

VEGETABLE BEEF HOT DISH: Substitute 2 medium potatoes, cubed, for noodles, water and cheese. Prepare basic recipe, using new ingredients, through Step 2. Change second cooking time to 10 minutes on HIGH. Stir in 1 package (10 oz.) frozen peas; recover, and continue cooking for 5 to 6 minutes, on HIGH, or until hot (about 150° F.). If doing ADD-A-DESSERT with this variation, add Fudge Sauce after 7 minutes of second cooking time.

NUTTY BEEF CASSEROLE

- **1½ lbs. ground beef**
- **1 large onion, chopped**
- **½ cup chopped green pepper**
- **1 can (11 oz.) condensed Cheddar cheese soup**
- **1 can (4 oz.) mushroom stems and pieces, drained**
- **½ cup pimento-stuffed olives**
- **1 teaspoon salt**
- **½ teaspoon basil leaves**
- **¼ teaspoon pepper**
- **½ cup salted Spanish peanuts**

Cheese soup and mushrooms require ROAST setting.

1. Crumble ground beef into 2-quart glass casserole. Stir in onion and green pepper. Cover with glass lid.

2. Microwave for about 6 minutes, on HIGH, or until meat is browned. Drain and stir in remaining ingredients, except nuts; recover.

3. Microwave for 12 to 14 minutes, on ROAST, or until hot (about 150° F.). Let stand, covered, 5 minutes. Sprinkle nuts on top and serve.

4 to 6 Servings

ADD-A-VEGETABLE: Prepare Nutty Beef Casserole through Step 2; set aside. Prepare Spicy-Topped Tomatoes, page 180, through Step 1. Place casserole on upper rack of oven and tomatoes on bottom shelf. Microwave both for 14 to 16 minutes, on ROAST, or until casserole is hot (about 150° F.). Let tomatoes and covered casserole stand 5 minutes. Sprinkle nuts on top of casserole and serve.

Pictured from the top: Nutty Beef Casserole, recipe above; Sweet Beef, page 83.

LASAGNA

- **1 pkg. (12 oz.) bulk pork sausage**
- **1 lb. ground beef**
- **1 can (10¾ oz.) condensed tomato soup**
- **1 can (8 oz.) tomato sauce**
- **1 can (4 oz.) mushroom stems and pieces, drained**
- **1 package (1.5 oz.) dry spaghetti sauce seasoning mix**
- **1 teaspoon salt**
- **1 package (8 oz.) lasagna noodles, cooked**
- **1 carton (12 oz.) creamed cottage cheese**
- **1 package (6 oz.) sliced Mozzarella cheese**
- **½ cup grated Parmesan cheese**

Cheeses require ROAST setting.

1. Crumble sausage and ground beef into 1½-quart glass casserole. Cover with glass lid.

2. Microwave for about 6 minutes, on HIGH, or until meat is browned; drain. Stir in soup, tomato sauce, mushrooms, seasoning mix and salt. Mix well. Layer in 2-quart (12 x 7) glass baking dish: ⅓ cooked noodles, ⅓ meat mixture, ½ cottage cheese and ½ Mozzarella cheese. Repeat layers. On third layer of noodles, spread last ⅓ meat mixture and sprinkle with Parmesan cheese. Cover with wax paper.

3. Microwave for 20 to 25 minutes, on ROAST, or until hot in center (about 150° F.). Let stand, covered, 5 minutes. Cut in squares and serve

6 to 8 Servings

TIP: Make a milder Lasagna by omitting pork sausage and increasing ground beef to 1½ lbs.

ADD-A-BREAD: Prepare Lasagna through Step 2; set aside. Prepare Garlic Bread page 43, through Step 2; set aside. Place Lasagna on upper rack of oven. Microwave for 18 minutes on ROAST. Place bread on bottom shelf of oven. Continue cooking both for 4 to 5 minutes, on ROAST, or until Lasagna is hot in center (about 145° F.) and bread is warm (about 120° F.). Let Lasagna stand, covered, 5 minutes before serving.

TAMALE PIE *

- **1½ lbs. ground beef**
- **4 green onions, sliced**
- **1 can (16 oz.) stewed tomatoes, drained**
- **1 can (12 oz.) whole kernel corn with sweet peppers, drained**
- **1½ teaspoons salt**
- **½ teaspoon chili powder**
- **½ teaspoon oregano leaves**
- **¼ teaspoon pepper**
- **1 cup shredded Cheddar cheese**

Tamale Topping:

- **1½ cups water**
- **1 cup cornmeal**
- **⅔ cup sliced ripe olives**

Cheese melts well on ROAST setting.

1. Crumble ground beef into 2-quart glass casserole; stir in onion. Cover with glass lid.

2. Microwave for about 6 minutes, on HIGH, or until meat is browned; drain. Stir in remaining ingredients, except cheese and topping ingredients. Spread Tamale Topping over top.

3. Microwave for 12 minutes on HIGH. Sprinkle cheese over top.

4. Microwave for 2 to 3 minutes, on ROAST, or until cheese melts. Let stand 5 minutes before serving.

5. **Tamale Topping:** Combine water and cornmeal in 4-cup glass measure.

6. Microwave for 1½ minutes on HIGH. Stir and continue cooking for about 1½ minutes, on HIGH, or until mixture boils and thickens. Stir in olives.

About 6 Servings

PIZZA ROLL-UPS

- **1 package (12 oz.) bulk pork sausage**
- **½ cup chopped green pepper**
- **1 can (8 oz.) tomato sauce**
- **1 cup shredded Mozzarella cheese**
- **1 can (4 oz.) mushroom stems and pieces, drained**
- **½ teaspoon oregano leaves**
- **6 flour tortillas**
- **1 can (10¾ oz.) condensed tomato soup**
- **1 tablespoon dry onion soup mix**
- **1 cup shredded Mozzarella cheese**

Use either frozen tortillas, thawed, or refrigerated tortillas.

1. Crumble sausage into 1½-quart glass casserole; stir in green pepper. Cover with glass lid.

2. Microwave for about 5 minutes, on HIGH, or until meat is browned; drain. Stir in tomato sauce, 1 cup Mozzarella cheese, mushrooms and oregano. Spoon about ¼ cup sausage mixture along center of each tortilla and roll up jelly-roll fashion; place in 2-quart (12 x 7) glass baking dish. Combine soup and dry soup mix in small bowl; pour over tortillas. Sprinkle with 1 cup shredded Mozzarella cheese.

3. Microwave for 14 to 16 minutes, on ROAST, or until hot (about 150° F.).

4 to 6 Servings

RECIPE VARIATION

CHICKEN ROLL-UPS: Substitute 2 cans (5 oz. each) boned chicken and 1 can (10 oz.) mild enchilada sauce for sausage, oregano and tomato sauce. Combine filling ingredients. Microwave for about 6 minutes, on ROAST, or until warm. Spoon mixture along center of tortilla and finish as directed in basic recipe.

SHRIMP CREOLE

Sauté chopped vegetables in butter quickly on HIGH.

2 tablespoons butter or margarine
5 green onions, sliced
½ cup chopped green pepper
1 clove garlic, finely chopped
1 can (16 oz.) whole tomatoes
1 can (6 oz.) tomato paste
1 teaspoon salt
1 teaspoon sugar
2 teaspoons dried parsley flakes
2 teaspoons Worcestershire sauce
¼ teaspoon paprika
⅛ teaspoon hot pepper sauce
1 package (10 oz.) frozen cooked shrimp
Hot cooked rice

1. Place butter, onions, green pepper and garlic in 2-quart glass casserole.

2. Microwave for about 3 minutes, on HIGH, or until vegetables are partly cooked. Stir in remaining ingredients, except cooked rice. Cover with glass lid.

3. Microwave for 5 minutes on REHEAT. Stir, recover and continue cooking for 6 to 7 minutes, on REHEAT, or until hot (about 150° F.). Let stand, covered, 5 minutes before serving. Serve over hot cooked rice.

About 4 Servings

POTATO PORK PIE

1 can (8 oz.) tomato sauce
1½ cups diced cooked pork
1 can (16 oz.) cut green beans, drained
¼ teaspoon garlic salt
⅛ teaspoon pepper
1 (9-inch) Baked Pastry Shell in glass pie plate, page 124

Potato Topping:
1 egg, slightly beaten
1 cup mashed potatoes
½ cup shredded Cheddar cheese

1. Combine tomato sauce, pork, green beans and seasonings in medium mixing bowl. Pour into baked crust in glass pie plate. Spread Potato Topping over pork mixture.

2. Microwave for 18 to 20 minutes, on ROAST, or until set. Let stand 5 minutes before serving.

3. **Potato Topping:** Combine all topping ingredients in small bowl; mix well.

5 to 6 Servings

REUBEN CASSEROLE

1 can (16 oz.) sauerkraut, drained
1 can (12 oz.) corned beef, broken into small pieces
2 cups shredded Swiss cheese
½ cup mayonnaise or salad dressing
¼ cup bottled Thousand Island salad dressing
2 medium tomatoes, sliced
2 tablespoons butter or margarine
¼ cup pumpernickel bread crumbs

1. Place sauerkraut in 1½-quart glass casserole. Top with corned beef, then shredded cheese. Combine mayonnaise and Thousand Island dressing, spread over cheese. Top with tomato slices, set aside. Place butter in small glass bowl.

2. Microwave for about 1 minute, on ROAST, or until melted. Stir in bread crumbs. Sprinkle buttered crumbs over tomato slices.

3. Microwave for 12 to 14 minutes, on ROAST, or until heated through (about 150° F.). Let stand 5 minutes before serving. About 6 Servings

TIP: Crumble about 2 slices dry pumpernickel bread to make crumbs.

CHICKEN A LA KING

Non-sensitive mixtures with cooked meat microwave on REHEAT.

1½ cups milk
¼ cup unsifted all-purpose flour
1 teaspoon salt
Dash pepper
Dash hot pepper sauce
¼ cup butter or margarine
2 cups diced cooked chicken
1 jar (2 oz.) diced pimento, drained
1 tablespoon dried parsley flakes

1. Combine milk, flour and seasonings in 4-cup glass measure; beat with rotary beater until smooth. Add butter.

2. Microwave for 3 minutes on HIGH. Beat well and continue cooking for 2 to 3 minutes, on HIGH, or until thickened (about 180° F.). Stir in remaining ingredients.

3. Microwave for about 2 minutes, on REHEAT, or until hot (about 150° F.). Stir and let stand 3 minutes before serving.

About 3 Cups Chicken à la King

TURKEY TETRAZZINI

- 1 cup chicken broth
- ½ cup whipping cream
- ¼ cup unsifted all-purpose flour
- ½ teaspoon salt
- ½ teaspoon celery seed
- Dash pepper
- ½ cup grated Parmesan cheese
- 3 tablespoons butter or margarine
- 1 can (4 oz.) mushroom stems and pieces, drained
- 2 cups diced cooked turkey
- 4 ozs. spaghetti, cooked
- Grated Parmesan cheese

Substitute 1 cup boiling water and 1 bouillon cube for chicken broth.

1. Combine chicken broth, cream, flour, salt, celery seed, pepper and ½ cup Parmesan cheese in 4-cup glass measure; beat with rotary beater until smooth. Add butter.

2. Microwave for 3 minutes on ROAST. Beat well and continue cooking for 2 to 3 minutes, on ROAST, or until thickened (about 180° F.).

3. Combine sauce and remaining ingredients, except grated Parmesan cheese, in 1½-quart glass casserole; sprinkle with Parmesan cheese.

4. Microwave for 6 to 8 minutes, on ROAST, or until heated through (about 150° F.). Let stand 5 minutes before serving. About 4 Servings

ADD-A-VEGETABLE: Prepare Turkey Tetrazzini through Step 3; set aside. Place 1 can (15 oz.) asparagus spears, undrained, in 1½-quart glass casserole; cover with glass lid. Place casserole on upper rack of oven and vegetable on bottom shelf. Microwave both for 10 to 12 minutes, on HIGH, or until casserole is heated through (about 150° F.). Let casserole and covered vegetable stand 5 minutes before serving.

BEEFED-UP NOODLE DISH

- 1 lb. ground beef
- 1 medium onion, chopped
- 1 clove garlic, finely chopped
- 2 cups cooked noodles
- 1 cup shredded process American cheese
- ½ cup grated Parmesan cheese
- 1 package (3 oz.) cream cheese, softened
- 1 tablespoon dried parsley flakes
- 1 teaspoon salt
- ¼ teaspoon basil leaves
- Dash pepper
- 1 package (10 oz.) frozen chopped spinach
- 1 can (3 oz.) French fried onions

One cup dry noodles equal about 2 cups cooked.

1. Crumble ground beef into 1½-quart glass casserole; stir in onion and garlic. Cover with glass lid.

2. Microwave for about 5 minutes, on HIGH, or until meat is browned. Drain and stir in remaining ingredients, except spinach and onions. Add spinach; recover.

3. Microwave for 15 minutes on ROAST. Stir to combine; top with onions, and continue cooking for 5 to 10 minutes, on ROAST, or until hot (about 150° F.). Let stand 5 minutes before serving. 4 to 6 Servings

ADD-A-SALAD: Prepare Beefed-up Noodle Dish through Step 2; set aside. Prepare Cheese Peaches, page 146, through Step 1; set aside. Place Casserole on upper rack of oven. Microwave for 15 minutes on ROAST. Stir to combine; top with onions. Place peaches on bottom shelf and continue cooking both for 5 to 10 minutes, on ROAST, or until casserole is hot (about 150° F.). Let both stand 5 minutes before serving.

Pictured: Creamy Chicken Stew, page 93, garnished with snipped parsley.

CURRY TURKEY DIVAN

1 package (10 oz.) frozen chopped broccoli
8 to 10 slices cooked turkey
1 can (10¾ oz.) condensed cream of chicken soup
½ soup can water
½ soup can milk
½ cup chopped onion
1 cup quick-cooking rice
1½ cups shredded process American cheese
½ teaspoon salt
1 teaspoon curry powder

1. Place frozen chopped broccoli in 1½-quart glass casserole. Cover with glass lid.

2. Microwave for 8 minutes, on HIGH, or until partly cooked; set aside.

3. Arrange turkey slices in a single layer over bottom of 10-inch glass ceramic skillet. Combine remaining ingredients, except broccoli, in medium mixing bowl; mix well. Pour over turkey slices. Top with cooked broccoli. Cover tightly with glass lid.

4. Microwave for 15 to 17 minutes, on HIGH, or until rice is tender (about 150° F.). Let stand, covered, 5 minutes before serving.

6 to 8 Servings

TUNA NOODLE CASSEROLE

When two foods cook a higher setting may be used.

1 tablespoon butter or margarine
¼ cup chopped onion
½ cup chopped celery
1 can (10¾ oz.) condensed cream of mushroom soup
½ cup mayonnaise or salad dressing
1 can (6½ oz.) tuna, rinsed, drained and flaked
¼ cup sunflower nuts
2 cups cooked egg noodles
¼ cup crushed potato chips

1. Place butter, onion and celery in 1½-quart glass casserole.

2. Microwave for about 3 minutes, on HIGH, or until partly cooked. Stir in remaining ingredients, except potato chips. Sprinkle with crushed potato chips.

3. Microwave for about 8 minutes, on ROAST, or until heated through (about 150° F.). Let stand 5 minutes before serving. 4 to 6 Servings

ADD-A-DESSERT: Prepare Tuna Noodle Casserole through Step 2; set aside. Place 1 package (10 oz.) frozen fruit in 1½-quart glass casserole; slit pouch. Place casserole on upper rack of oven and dessert on bottom shelf. Microwave both for 12 to 14 minutes, on HIGH, or until casserole is heated through (about 150° F.). Let casserole stand 5 minutes before serving.

RECIPE VARIATION

SALMON CHINESE NOODLE CASSEROLE: Increase celery to 1 cup. Substitute 1 can (7¾ oz.) salmon, drained and flaked, for tuna and ½ cup cashews for sunflower nuts. Substitute 1½ cups chow mein noodles for cooked egg noodles and ½ cup chow mein noodles for crushed potato chips.

CHEESY MACARONI-BEEF CASSEROLE

1 jar (2½ oz.) dried beef
1 cup water
1 tablespoon butter or margarine
¼ cup chopped onion
½ cup chopped green pepper
1 can (11 oz.) condensed Cheddar cheese soup
1 cup creamed cottage cheese
2 cups cooked macaroni
¼ teaspoon salt
Dash pepper
2 tablespoons butter or margarine
¼ cup dry bread crumbs

1. Cut dried beef into small pieces, using kitchen shears. Combine beef and water in 4-cup glass measure.

2. Microwave for about 3 minutes on HIGH; drain well; set aside.

3. Place 1 tablespoon butter, onion and green pepper in 1½-quart glass casserole.

4. Microwave for about 3 minutes, on HIGH, or until vegetables are partly cooked. Stir in dried beef and remaining ingredients, except 2 tablespoons butter and bread crumbs; set aside. Place 2 tablespoons butter in small glass bowl.

5. Microwave for about 1 minute, on ROAST, or until melted. Stir in bread crumbs. Sprinkle over casserole mixture.

6. Microwave for 10 to 12 minutes, on ROAST, or until heated through (about 150° F.). Let stand 5 minutes before serving. 4 to 6 Servings

ADD-A-DESSERT: Prepare Chessy Macaroni-Beef Casserole through Step 5; set aside. Remove lid from 1 package (12 oz.) frozen brownies; set aside. Place casserole on upper rack of oven. Microwave for 8 minutes on HIGH. Place brownies on bottom shelf and continue cooking both for 6 to 8 minutes, on HIGH, or until casserole is heated through (about 150° F.). Let stand 5 minutes before serving.

HOME-STYLE BEEF HASH

- **1 tablespoon butter or margarine**
- **½ cup chopped onion**
- **2 cups finely chopped or ground cooked beef**
- **3 cups finely chopped cooked potatoes**
- **1 package (¾ oz.) brown gravy mix**
- **1 cup water**
- **⅓ cup catsup**
- **2 teaspoons Worcestershire sauce**

1. Place butter and onion in 2-quart (8 x 8) glass baking dish.

2. Microwave for about 3 minutes, on HIGH, or until partly cooked. Stir in remaining ingredients. Cover with wax paper.

3. Microwave for 14 to 16 minutes, on REHEAT, or until hot (about 150° F.). Let stand, covered, 5 minutes before serving. About 4 Servings

RECIPE VARIATION

YANKEE RED FLANNEL HASH: Substitute 2 cups ground or finely chopped cooked corned beef for cooked beef. Add 1 can (8 oz.) diced beets, drained, with potatoes. Substitute ½ cup milk for brown gravy mix and water. Omit Worcestershire sauce.

HAM VEGETABLE BAKE

- **1 can (10¾ oz.) condensed cream of celery soup**
- **½ cup milk**
- **½ cup chopped onion**
- **3 medium potatoes, peeled and cubed**
- **2 cups diced cooked ham**
- **1 cup shredded Cheddar cheese**
- **1 jar (2 oz.) sliced pimento, drained**
- **1 package (10 oz.) frozen Brussels sprouts**

1. Combine all ingredients except Brussels sprouts in 2-quart glass casserole; mix well. Cover with glass lid.

2. Microwave for 30 minutes on HIGH. Add Brussels sprouts and recover. Continue cooking for 8 to 10 minutes, on HIGH, or until hot (about 200° F.). Stir to combine Brussels sprouts. Let stand, covered, 5 minutes before serving. 4 to 6 Servings

ADD-A-DESSERT: Prepare Ham Vegetable Bake through Step 1; set aside. Prepare Foamy Applesauce, page 188, (a recipe variation) through Step 1 in a 2-quart (8×8) glass baking dish, cover with wax paper. Place casserole on upper rack of oven and dessert on bottom shelf. Microwave both for 30 minutes on HIGH. Add Brussels sprouts to casserole; recover. Remove apples and continue as directed in Foamy Applesauce recipe. Continue cooking casserole for 8 to 10 minutes, on HIGH, or until hot (about 200° F.). Stir to combine Brussels sprouts. Let casserole stand, covered, 5 minutes before serving.

WIENER HASH-BROWN DISH

- **1 package (24 oz.) frozen shredded hash-brown potatoes**
- **1 can (10¾ oz.) condensed tomato soup**
- **½ cup catsup**
- **½ cup water**
- **1 tablespoon dried parsley flakes**
- **1 can (3 oz.) French Fried onions, slightly crumbled**
- **1 package (1 lb.) wieners**

1. Place frozen hash-brown potatoes in 2-quart (8 x 8) glass baking dish. Cover with wax paper.

2. Microwave for 7 minutes, on HIGH, or until slightly thawed. Combine tomato soup, catsup, water and parsley in 4-cup glass measure, mix well. Stir ½ of soup mixture and ½ of onions into potatoes. Place wieners over potato mixture. Pour remaining soup mixture over wieners; sprinkle with remaining onions.

3. Microwave for 12 to 14 minutes, on REHEAT, or until heated through (about 150° F.). Let stand 5 minutes before serving. 4 to 5 Servings

ADD-A-VEGETABLE: Prepare Wiener Hash-Brown Dish through Step 2; set aside. Place 1 package (10 oz.) frozen peas in 1½-quart glass casserole; cover with glass lid. Place casserole on upper rack of oven and vegetable on bottom shelf. Microwave both for 15 to 16 minutes, on HIGH, or until casserole is heated through (about 150° F.). Let casserole and covered vegetable stand 5 minutes before serving.

IRISH STEW ✻

- 2 lbs. lamb stew meat
- 2 small onions, quartered
- 1 medium carrot, peeled and sliced
- 1 medium turnip, peeled and cubed
- 1 potato, cubed
- 2 teaspoons salt
- 1 tablespoon dried parsley flakes
- 2 teaspoons instant beef bouillon
- 1 teaspoon thyme leaves
- 1 bay leaf
- Dash pepper
- 3 tablespoons cornstarch
- 1 cup water
- 1 package (10 oz.) frozen peas

1. Place lamb stew meat in 3-quart glass casserole. Cover with glass lid.

2. Microwave for 10 minutes on HIGH. Add vegetables and seasonings. Combine cornstarch and water in small bowl until smooth; pour over meat mixture; recover.

3. Microwave for 10 minutes on HIGH (about 160° F.). Stir well and recover.

4. Microwave for 35 minutes, on SIMMER, or until meat is fork tender. Add frozen peas and continue cooking for 5 to 7 minutes, on SIMMER, or until peas are tender crisp. Stir; let stand, covered, 5 minutes before serving.

4 to 6 Servings

TOMATO BEEF STEW ✻

HIGH/SIMMER stewing technique assures tender meat, blended flavors.

- 1½ lbs. beef stew meat
- 1 lb. small new red potatoes, peeled
- ½ lb. pearl onions
- 2 cups frozen crinkle-cut carrots
- 2 cans (10¾ oz. each) condensed tomato soup
- 2 teaspoons salt
- ½ teaspoon tarragon leaves
- ¼ teaspoon pepper
- 1 package (10 oz.) frozen peas
- 1 can (4 oz.) whole mushrooms, drained
- 1 tomato, sliced, if desired

1. Place beef stew meat in 3-quart glass casserole. Cover with glass lid.

2. Microwave for 8 minutes on HIGH. Drain off excess fat. Stir in potatoes, onions, carrots, soup and seasonings; recover.

3. Microwave for 10 minutes on HIGH (about 160° F.). Stir; recover, and continue cooking for 10 minutes on HIGH. Stir in frozen peas and mushroom; recover.

4. Microwave for 45 to 50 minutes on SIMMER, or until meat is fork tender. Let stand, covered, 5 minutes before serving. Garnish with sliced tomato.

4 to 6 Servings

ADD-A-DESSERT: Prepare Tomato Beef Stew through Step 3. Place stew on upper rack of oven. Place 2 packages (10 oz. each) frozen peaches in 1½-quart glass casserole; slit pouches. Place fruit on bottom shelf. Microwave for 15 minutes on SIMMER. Prepare Old-Fashioned Shortcake, page 50, through Step 1; place shortcake in custard cups around fruit on bottom shelf. Continue cooking all for 45 to 50 minutes, on SIMMER, or until meat is fork tender and shortcake is no longer doughy. Let stew stand, covered, 5 minutes before serving.

Pictured: Tomato Beef Stew, recipe above, garnished with sliced tomatoes and parsley.

CREAMY CHICKEN STEW *

2 medium potatoes, cut into small pieces
2 cups thickly sliced carrots
1 cup thickly sliced celery
1 large onion, cut in eighths
2 cans (10¾ oz. each) condensed cream of chicken soup
2 teaspoons salt
1 teaspoon ground sage
⅛ teaspoon pepper
2½ to 3-lb. whole frying chicken, cut up
Parsley

1. Combine all ingredients, except chicken and parsley in 4-quart glass ceramic Dutch oven. Place chicken, skin-side-down and thick edges toward outside of dish, on top of vegetables. Cover tightly with glass lid.

2. Microwave for 25 minutes on HIGH (about 160° F.). Stir well, turning and rearranging chicken; recover.

3. Microwave for 35 to 40 minutes, on SIMMER, or until meat cut near bone is no longer pink. Let stand, covered, 5 minutes before serving. Garnish with snipped parsley. 4 to 6 Servings

PORK AND CORN STEW *

Stir stews once during cooking to assure even tenderness.

1½ lbs. pork stew meat
1 cup chopped onion
1 cup thickly-sliced carrots
1 cup thickly-sliced celery
1 can (17 oz.) cream-style corn
½ cup water
1 package (0.87 oz.) dry pork gravy mix
1½ teaspoons salt
½ teaspoon Italian seasoning
⅛ teaspoon pepper

1. Place pork stew meat in 3-quart glass casserole. Cover with glass lid.

2. Microwave for 8 minutes on HIGH. Stir in remaining ingredients. Recover.

3. Microwave for 15 minutes on HIGH (about 160° F.). Stir and recover.

4. Microwave for 30 to 35 minutes, on SIMMER, or until meat is fork tender. Let stand, covered, 5 minutes before serving. 4 to 6 Servings

ADD-A-BREAD: Prepare Pork and Corn Stew through Step 3. Place stew on upper rack of oven. Microwave for 10 minutes on SIMMER. During this second cooking time, prepare 1 package (7 oz.) bran muffin mix according to package directions; spoon into 6 paperlined custard cups. Place muffins on bottom shelf. Continue cooking both for 20 to 25 minutes, on SIMMER, or until meat is fork tender. Let meat stand, covered, 5 minutes before serving.

VEAL STEW *

Drain off excess fat so gravy retains good consistency.

2 lbs. veal stew meat
¼ lb. bacon, diced
1 medium onion, chopped
2 carrots, peeled and sliced
1 clove garlic, finely chopped
1 can (10¼ oz.) beef gravy
½ cup dry red wine or water
2 teaspoons salt
1 teaspoon tarragon leaves
1 large zucchini, thickly sliced

1. Place veal stew meat and bacon in 3-quart glass casserole. Cover with glass lid.

2. Microwave for 10 minutes on HIGH. Drain off excess fat. Stir in remaining ingredients, except zucchini; recover.

3. Microwave for 10 minutes on HIGH (about 160° F.). Stir and recover.

4. Microwave for 25 minutes on SIMMER. Stir in zucchini; recover. Continue cooking for 15 to 20 minutes, on SIMMER, or until zucchini is tender. Let stand, covered, 5 minutes before serving. About 6 Servings

CHICKEN AND OKRA STEW *

4 slices bacon, diced
1 lb. chicken parts
2 tablespoons cornstarch
1 cup water
1 can (16 oz.) stewed tomatoes
½ cup chopped green pepper
1 teaspoon salt
½ teaspoon oregano leaves
1 package (10 oz.) frozen cut okra

1. Place bacon in 2-quart glass casserole.

2. Microwave for 4 to 4½ minutes, on HIGH, or until crisp. Drain off fat, leaving 2 tablespoons. Combine cornstarch and water in 2-cup measure until smooth; stir it, plus remaining ingredients, except okra, into bacon. Add frozen okra; cover with glass lid.

3. Microwave for 15 minutes on HIGH (about 160° F.). Stir well and recover.

4. Microwave for 25 to 30 minutes, on SIMMER, or until meat cut near bone is no longer pink. Remove chicken from stew; cool. Remove meat from bones and cut into pieces. Return meat to stew; mix well, and recover.

5. Microwave for about 2 minutes, on REHEAT, or until hot (about 160° F.). Let stand, covered, 5 minutes before serving. 4 to 6 Servings

RECIPE VARIATION

CHICKEN AND GREEN BEAN STEW: Substitute 1 package (10 oz.) frozen green beans for okra.

Meats

Thaw, Roast, Braise or Grill in a Lot Less Time

Here's How — and Why

Meat Size and Tenderness Are Keys to Power Settings: Just as in conventional cooking, the size of a meat cut and its tenderness are major factors which determine the power setting used, the length of cooking time, if moisture is added and whether a cover is used. In general, tender meat cuts microwave quickly, uncovered or loosely covered, with no moisture added (dry heat cooking). Less tender meat cooks more slowly, moisture is added and a tight cover used (braising). Small cuts can usually be microwaved quickly; large cuts take longer.

Defrost Most Meat before Cooking; Quick-Cook Some Dishes Using Frozen Meat: Meat cooking charts and basic meat recipes are designed for fresh or completely thawed meats. Defrost meat quickly using the chart on page 29. Some meats, when combined with sauces and/or vegetables will quick-cook from the frozen state — see examples in recipe variations.

Microwave Large Tender Cuts Uncovered on a Microwave Roasting Rack; Use HIGH/ROAST or ROAST: **Beef rib and pork loin roasts** — Microwave on HIGH during first half of cooking to heat meat quickly; then on ROAST to cook meat yet retain tenderness. **Large pieces of cured pork, such as ham, picnics (pork shoulder) or Canadian bacon** — Microwave on ROAST because, although these meats are cooked, the lower setting prevents overcooking and drying on outer edges caused by microwave attraction to the high-sugar content of many cures. **Lamb, veal and venison roasts** — Microwave these large, tender cuts on ROAST to retain juiciness and tenderness in these low-fat meats.

Small Tender Cuts Cook Quickly on HIGH or ROAST: **Beef steaks, chops, cubed steaks, ground beef patties or crumbled ground beef** — Microwave quickly on HIGH to retain juiciness. Use a microwave browning grill when searing is desirable. See meat cooking chart in this chapter. Use ROAST setting when sensitive ingredients such as cream, sour cream, yogurt, cheese or mushrooms are added to these cuts; or when ground meat is formed into meatloaf or meatballs which need even cooking to get the center done. **Fresh pork, lamb, veal and venison chops, steaks, tender cubes, meatballs, meatloaf or pork ribs** — Microwave on ROAST so there is less spattering with fatty meats and low-fat meats stay tender and juicy. **Ground fresh pork or lamb**— Microwave quickly on HIGH when it is crumbled into a glass casserole and browned for use in main dishes because the crumbled meat is less dense so it spatters less. Microwave ground ham dishes on REHEAT because meat is cooked. **Precooked sausage** — Microwave Polish sausage, ring bologna or knockwurst on REHEAT— meat only needs heating. See chart, page 27, for precooked sausage. **Fresh sausage** — Microwave fresh pork sausage patties and bratwurst on ROAST to prevent fat spatters. Grill pork sausage patties using a microwave browning grill and instructions in the meat cooking chart in this chapter, page 100. **Bacon** — Microwave on HIGH to crisp and brown it.

(Continued, next page.)

Pictured: Beef Sirloin Tip Roast, chart, page 100, garnished with corn-on-the -cob and zucchini.

Braise All Less Tender Meat on HIGH/SIMMER:

Rump and shoulder roasts, fresh ham, pork hocks, briskets, short ribs, lamb shanks, round steak, stew meat, liver, tongue — Microwave all less tender meat, large or small, on HIGH to heat it through, then on SIMMER to cook and tenderize. This moist heat technique calls for additional liquid and a tightly covered dish. **Kidney** — Microwave kidneys gently on SIMMER throughout cooking to retain fine texture and flavor.

Cooking Dishes and Covers Vary with Meat Size and Tenderness:

Large tender cuts roast, uncovered, on a microwave roasting rack in a flat glass baking dish. Rack keeps meat above drippings. If edges of roasts start to overcook, use small pieces of foil to cover spots and slow cooking. Do not allow foil to touch oven interior or arcing will result. **Small tender cuts and ground meats** microwave in glass casseroles, glass baking dishes or glass ceramic dishes. Cover with glass lid or wax paper. Tip lids away from arm when removing. Plastic wrap may be used; pierce before removing. Sear small cuts on a microwave browning grill, preheated as directed in manufacturer's instruction booklet. **Large or small less tender cuts** braise best in glass ceramic Dutch ovens, glass ceramic skillets or glass casseroles with tight-fitting glass covers to prevent tenderizing moisture from evaporating. A traditional European covered clay cooking pot may be used to cook and tenderize meat. Presoak pot in water, as when used for conventional cooking.

Meat Size and Tenderness Affect Arrangement, Turning and Draining:

Tender cuts weighing up to 4 lbs. microwave fat-side-up; do not turn these over during cooking. Start cooking meat cuts weighing 4 lbs. or more fat-side-down; turn these over half way through cooking or when power setting changes. Drain fatty meats at this time to remove excess fat and preserve sauce consistency. **Less tender cuts** weighing up to 2 lbs. are braised fat-side-up. Cuts 2 lbs. or over start cooking fat-side-down and are turned over when power setting changes.

Check for Doneness, Then Let Meat Stand to Complete Cooking and Set Juices:

Large tender cuts — Use a food sensor or microwave meat thermometer to check meat doneness. This thermometer may be used in the oven and can be inserted after the meat is turned. DO NOT use a conventional meat thermometer in a microwave oven, insert it as soon as a roast comes from the oven. Internal temperatures will rise up to 15° F. during standing time. Allow roasts over 4 lbs. to stand about 10 minutes. Cover tightly with foil, dull-side-out, during standing. **Small cuts and braised meats** are cooked when thick portion is fork tender; stand, covered, 5 minutes.

"ADD-A-" Vegetable or Dessert to a Meat Dish:

You can easily microwave a vegetable or dessert along with a dish of meat — use recipes in this chapter as guides. Note that power settings do not change, except with ground meat dishes, ham slice, pork chops, luncheon meats, lamb, veal and venison chops or steaks. These small tender cuts usually cook on ROAST to assure juicy tenderness, but may be cooked on HIGH when a second dish of food is added because microwave intensity to each dish is reduced by the increased food load. For this same reason, meat dishes where power settings do not change may need to cook a few minutes longer. "ADD-A-" dishes may cook at slightly different rates. Continue cooking one food alone, if necessary.

Use the Oven Rack When Two Foods Cook:

Microwave smaller cuts of meat on the oven's upper rack when cooking two dishes of food at once. Place large roasts or meat braised in a large 4-quart glass ceramic casserole on the lower rack because more "head room" is needed. Place the second dish of food on the bottom shelf. Food cooks faster and more evenly if dishes are staggered in the oven.

The " ✱ " Tells You When Power Settings Change:

The " ✱ " is a reminder that there are two or more power settings in a recipe. Baste, turn or stir conveniently at this time.

Microwave-Conventional Comparison:

Roasting, braising or grilling — meats cook more quickly in a microwave oven than with a conventional range. A 5-lb. rolled beef rib roast, for example, microwaves to rare doneness in 50 to 55 minutes, but takes about 2½ hours conventionally. Thawing frozen meat is also an amazing time-saver. See the chart on page 29. Small cuts of meat do not brown in a microwave oven, but brown nicely when cooked on a microwave browning grill. Large cuts, which cook longer, will brown. Fat spatters from rapid microwave heating may make "popping" sounds during cooking. Braising sauces never burn or "disappear" during microwave cooking.

HOW TO COOK MEATS

- Microwave fresh or completely thawed frozen meat. Thaw meat using defrosting chart page 29.
- Season meat with salt, pepper and other herbs, if desired.
- Roast a large, tender cut of meat, fat-side-up, on a microwave roasting rack in glass baking dish. Roasts over 4 lbs. should be turned once half way through cooking or after first cooking time; start cooking fat-side-down. Microwave uncovered.
- If the edges of large meats, especially hams, appear to be drying or darkening while microwaving, use small pieces of foil to cover these spots and slow down cooking. Do not allow foil to touch oven walls or microwaves will arc and pit oven surfaces.
- Microwave smaller, tender cuts of meat, fat-side-up, in glass baking dishes, glass ceramic skillets or glass casseroles covered with glass lids or wax paper.
- Braise less tender cuts of meat fat-side-up. Add water and microwave in a glass casserole tightly covered with a glass lid. Meats over 2 lbs. should be turned over after first cooking time; start cooking fat-side-down.
- Grill meats in a microwave oven on a microwave browning grill preheated according to manufacturer's directions. Turn meats over after first cooking time.
- Brown ground meats for casseroles or main dishes by crumbling it into a glass casserole covered with a glass lid or wax paper.
- Use a food sensor or microwave meat thermometer in a microwave oven during cooking. DO NOT use a conventional meat thermometer in a microwave oven; insert it as soon as meat comes from oven.
- Allow large roasts, 4 lbs. or over, to stand, covered tightly with foil, dull-side-out, about 10 minutes after being taken from the oven. Allow smaller cuts of meat to stand, covered, about 5 minutes. Internal temperature will rise as much as 15° F. during standing time.

Microwave-thaw frozen meat as directed in the Defrosting Chart on page 29.

CUT AND AMOUNT	CONTAINER	FIRST SETTING AND TIME	SECOND SETTING AND TIME	SPECIAL TECHNIQUE
BACON				
2 slices	Glass or pottery plate or	HIGH 2 to 2½ min.	—	Microwave 1 to 4 slices of bacon between paper towels to absorb grease.
4 slices	glass baking dish	HIGH 4 to 4½ min.	—	Arrange 4 or more slices in a single layer. Do not use towels. Microwave roasting
6 slices		HIGH 5 to 6 min.	—	rack may be used to hold bacon above drippings.
8 slices		HIGH 6 to 7 min.	—	
Canadian Bacon 1 lb.	2-qt. (8 x 8) glass baking dish	REHEAT 4 to 5 min. (about 120° F.)	—	—
CHOPS				
Lamb Chops 1½ to 2 lbs. (about 6 rib chops)	Microwave browning grill	HIGH 8 min.	HIGH 7 to 8 min.	Cut 1 inch thick; preheat grill. Turn over after first cooking time.
Pork Chops 1 lb.	Microwave browning grill	HIGH 6 min.	HIGH 5 to 6 min.	Cut ½ inch thick; preheat grill. Turn over after first cooking time.
Veal Chops 1½ lbs.	Microwave browning grill	HIGH 2 min.	HIGH 2½ to 3½ min.	Bread chops; preheat grill. Turn over after first cooking time. Follow technique in Veal Parmigiana recipe on page 85.
Venison chops 1 lb.	10-in. glass ceramic skillet	HIGH 5 min. per lb.	SIMMER 15 min. per lb.	Add ¼ cup water; cover tightly with glass lid.
FRANKFURTERS				See Wieners.

(Continued, next page.)

Microwave-thaw frozen meat as directed in the Defrosting Chart on page 29.

CUT AND AMOUNT	CONTAINER	FIRST SETTING AND TIME	SECOND SETTING AND TIME	SPECIAL TECHNIQUE
GROUND MEATS				
Ground Beef Patties				See Hamburger Patties.
Ground Beef 1 lb.	1½-qt. glass casserole	HIGH 5 to 6 min.	—	Crumble into casserole; stir once during cooking.
Ground Lamb Patties 1 to 1½ lbs.	2-qt. (8 x 8) glass baking dish	HIGH 9 to 10 min. per lb.	—	—
Ground Pork 1 lb.	1½-qt. glass casserole	HIGH 6 to 7 min.	—	Crumble into casserole; stir once during cooking.
Meatballs 12 balls, 1½-in. ea.	2-qt. (12 x 7) glass baking dish	ROAST 8 to 10 min.	—	—
Meatloaf 1½ lbs.	(9 x 5) glass loaf dish	ROAST 25 to 30 min. (Medium, about 140° F.)	—	—
HAM & PICNICS				
Bone-in Ham, fully cooked 7 to 8-lb.	3-qt. (13 x 9) glass baking dish with microwave roasting rack	ROAST 8 to 9 min. per lb. (about 120° F.)	—	Turn over once.
Boneless Ham, fully cooked 2 to 3-lb.	2-qt. (12 x 7) glass baking dish with microwave roasting rack	ROAST 11 to 12 min. per lb. (about 120° F.)	—	—
4 to 5-lb.		ROAST 11 to 12 min. per lb. (about 120° F.)	—	Turn over once.
6 to 8-lb.	3-qt. (13 x 9) glass baking dish with microwave roasting rack	ROAST 10 to 11 min. per lb. (about 120° F.)	—	Turn over once.
Canned Ham 3-lb.	2-qt. (12 x 7) glass baking dish with microwave roasting rack	ROAST 10 to 11 min. per lb. (about 120° F.)	—	—
5-lb.		ROAST 11 to 12 min. per lb. (about 120° F.)	—	—
Center Cut Ham Slice 1 to 1½ lbs.	2-qt. (12 x 7) glass baking dish	ROAST 10 to 11 min. per lb. (about 120° F.)	—	—
Cured Picnic (pork shoulder), fully cooked 3 to 5-lb.				Follow technique for boneless ham, fully cooked, above.

Microwave-thaw frozen meat as directed in the Defrosting Chart on page 29.

CUT AND AMOUNT	CONTAINER	FIRST SETTING AND TIME	SECOND SETTING AND TIME	SPECIAL TECHNIQUE
Fresh Ham * 3 to 5-lb.	4-qt. glass ceramic Dutch oven	HIGH 5 min. per lb.	SIMMER 15 to 16 min. per lb. (Well Done, about 160° F.)	Add ¼ cup water; cover tightly with glass lid.
Fresh Picnic * (pork shoulder) 2 to 2½-lb.	10-in. glass ceramic casserole	HIGH 5 min. per lb.	SIMMER 15 min. per lb.	Add ¼ cup water; cover tightly with glass lid. Turn over once.
Southern-type Ham, fully cooked 6 to 8-lb.				Follow technique for boneless ham, fully cooked, above.
HAMBURGER PATTIES				Also see Ground Meat.
1 Patty 4 ozs.	2-qt. (8 x 8) glass baking dish	HIGH 2½ to 3 min.	—	Turn over once.
2 Patties 4 ozs. ea.		HIGH 5 to 5½ min.	—	For grilled patties, see recipe, page 107.
4 Patties 4 ozs. ea.		HIGH 6 to 6½ min.	—	
6 Patties 4 ozs. ea.		HIGH 8 to 8½ min.	—	
HOT DOGS				See Wieners.
RIBS				
Beef Short Ribs * 2 to 3 lbs.	10-in. glass ceramic skillet	HIGH 5 min. per lb.	SIMMER 15 min. per lb.	Add ¼ cup water. Cover tightly with glass lid. Turn over once.
Lamb Spareribs 2 to 2½ lbs.	2-qt. (12 x 7) glass baking dish	ROAST 13 to 14 min. per lb.	—	Brush with barbecue sauce during final cooking time, if desired.
Pork Spareribs 2 to 3 lbs.	3-qt. (13 x 9) glass baking dish	ROAST 15 to 16 min. per lb.	—	Brush with barbecue sauce during final cooking time, if desired.
ROASTS				
Beef Chuck * 2 to 4-lb.	10-in. glass ceramic skillet	HIGH 5 min. per lb.	SIMMER 15 min. per lb.	Add ¼ cup water; cover tightly with glass lid. Turn over once.
Beef Rolled Rib * 3 to 6-lb.	2-qt. (12 x 7) glass baking dish with microwave roasting rack	HIGH 5 min. per lb.	ROAST 3 to 4 min. per lb. (Rare, about 125° F.)	Over 4 lbs., turn over once.
		HIGH 6 min. per lb.	ROAST 4 to 5 min. per lb. (Medium, about 145° F.)	
		HIGH 7 min. per lb.	ROAST 5 to 6 min. per lb. (Well Done, about 155° F.)	
Beef Rump, boneless or bone-in * 3 to 4-lb.	4-qt. glass ceramic casserole	HIGH 5 min. per lb.	SIMMER 15 min. per lb.	Add ¼ cup water; cover tightly with glass lid. Turn over once.

(Continued, next page.)

Microwave-thaw frozen meat as directed in the Defrosting Chart on page 29.

CUT AND AMOUNT	CONTAINER	FIRST SETTING AND TIME	SECOND SETTING AND TIME	SPECIAL TECHNIQUE
Beef Sirloin Tip * 4 to 5-lb.	2-qt. (12 x 7) glass baking dish with microwave roasting rack	HIGH 5 min. per lb.	ROAST 3 to 4 min. per lb. (Rare, about 125° F.)	Turn over once.
		HIGH 6 min. per lb.	ROAST 4 to 5 min. per lb. (Medium, about 145° F.)	
		HIGH 7 min. per lb.	ROAST 5 to 6 min. per lb. (Well Done, about 155° F.)	
Beef Standing Rib * 5 to 6-lb.	2-qt. (12 x 7) glass baking dish with microwave roasting rack	HIGH 5 min. per lb.	ROAST 3 to 4 min. per lb. (Rare, about 125° F.)	Turn over once.
		HIGH 6 min. per lb.	ROAST 4 to 5 min. per lb. (Medium, about 145° F.)	
		HIGH 7 min. per lb.	ROAST 5 to 6 min. per lb. (Well Done, about 155° F.)	
Lamb Leg or Shoulder Roast 4 to 4½-lb.	2-qt. (12 x 7) glass baking dish with microwave roasting rack	ROAST 14 to 15 min. per lb. (Well Done, about 180° F.).	—	For rolled roasts, increase cooking time 1 min. per lb.
Pork Loin Roast, * boneless 4 to 5-lb.	2-qt. (12 x 7) glass baking dish with microwave roasting rack	HIGH 6 min. per lb.	ROAST 5 to 6 min. per lb. (Well Done, about 160° F.)	Turn over once.
Pork Loin, * center rib 4 to 5-lb.	3-qt. (13 x 9) glass baking dish with microwave roasting rack	HIGH 5 min. per lb.	ROAST 4 to 5 min. per lb. (Well Done, about 160° F.)	Turn over once.
Veal Rump 2 to 5-lb.	2-qt. (12 x 7) glass baking dish with microwave roasting rack	ROAST 18 to 19 min. per lb. (Well Done, about 160° F.).	—	Over 4 lbs., turn over once.
Venison Rump 3 to 3½-lb.	2-qt. (12 x 7) glass baking dish with microwave roasting rack	ROAST 12 to 13 min. per lb. (Well Done, about 160° F.).	—	—
SAUSAGE				
Pork 12 ozs. bulk	1½-qt. glass casserole; cover with glass lid	HIGH 5 to 6 min.	—	Crumble into casserole.
16 ozs. bulk		HIGH 6 to 7 min.	—	
Links, fresh 11 links	Microwave browning grill	HIGH 1 min.	HIGH 2 to 3 min.	Preheat grill; turn over after first cooking time.
precooked				See chart, page 27.

Microwave-thaw frozen meat as directed in the Defrosting Chart on page 29.

CUT AND AMOUNT	CONTAINER	FIRST SETTING AND TIME	SECOND SETTING AND TIME	SPECIAL TECHNIQUE
Patties, fresh 12 ozs.	Microwave browning grill	HIGH 1½ min.	HIGH 2½ to 3½ min.	Preheat grill; turn over after first cooking time.
Bratwurst precooked 1 lb.	1½-qt. glass casserole	ROAST 10 to 12 min. (well done, about 170° F.)	—	—
Knockwurst, Ring Bologna and Polish Sausage 1 lb.	1½-qt. glass casserole	REHEAT 4 to 6 min. (about 120° F.)	—	—
STEAKS				
Beef Cubed Steak four, 5 ozs. ea.	2-qt. (12 x 7) glass baking dish	HIGH 10 to 12 min.	—	—
Beef Flank Steak 1½ lbs.	Microwave browning grill	HIGH 3 min.	HIGH 3 to 4 min.	Marinate; preheat grill. Turn over after first cooking time.
Beef Rib-Eye, Sirloin or T-Bone Steak 1½ to 2 lbs.	Microwave browning grill	HIGH 5 min.	HIGH 1 to 2 min.	Preheat grill; turn over after first cooking time.
Beef Round Steak * 1½ to 3 lbs.	10-in. glass ceramic skillet	HIGH 5 min. per lb.	SIMMER 15 min. per lb.	Add ¼ cup water; cover tightly with glass lid. Turn over once.
Beef Top Round Steak 2 lbs.	Microwave browning grill	HIGH 6 min.	HIGH 1½ to 2 min.	Use tenderizer; preheat grill and turn over after first cooking time.
Lamb Steak * 1½ to 2 lbs.	10-in. glass ceramic skillet	HIGH 5 min. per lb.	SIMMER 15 min. per lb.	Add ¼ cup water; cover tightly with glass lid.
Pork Blade Steak * 1 to 1½ lbs.	10-in. glass ceramic skillet	HIGH 5 min. per lb.	SIMMER 15 min. per lb.	Add ¼ cup water; cover tightly with glass lid.
Pork Cubed Steak 1½ lbs.	2-qt. (12 x 7) glass baking dish	HIGH 9 to 10 min. per lb.	—	—
Veal Steak * 1 lb.	10-in. glass ceramic skillet	HIGH 5 min. per lb.	SIMMER 15 min. per lb.	Add ¼ cup water; cover tightly with glass lid.
STEW MEAT				
Beef Stew Meat 1 to 2 lbs.				Follow technique in goulash, page 106.
Pork, cubed 1 lb.				Follow technique in Polynesian pork, page 110.

(Continued, next page.)

Microwave-thaw frozen meat as directed in the Defrosting Chart on page 29.

CUT AND AMOUNT	CONTAINER	FIRST SETTING AND TIME	SECOND SETTING AND TIME	SPECIAL TECHNIQUE
VARIETY MEATS				
Beef Kidney 2 lbs.				Follow technique in recipe, page 115.
Beef Liver * 1 lb.	10-in. glass ceramic casserole	HIGH 5 min. per lb.	SIMMER 15 min. per lb.	Add ¼ cup water; cover tightly with glass lid.
Beef Tongue * 2 to 2½ lbs.	10-in. glass ceramic casserole	HIGH 5 min. per lb.	SIMMER 15 min. per lb.	Add ¼ cup water; cover tightly with glass lid.
WIENERS				
1 wiener	2-qt. (8 x 8) glass baking dish	REHEAT 25 to 30 seconds (about 120° F.)	—	For hot dogs, see recipe, page 111.
2 wieners		REHEAT 35 to 40 seconds (about 120° F.)	—	
4 wieners		REHEAT 50 to 55 seconds (about 120° F.)	—	
6 wieners		REHEAT 1½ to 2 minutes (about 120° F.)	—	
OTHER CUTS				
Beef Brisket, * fresh or corned 2½ to 3½ lbs.	4-qt. glass ceramic Dutch oven	HIGH 5 min. per lb.	SIMMER 15 min. per lb.	Add ¼ cup water; cover tightly with glass lid. Turn over once.
Pork Tenderloin * 1½ to 2 lbs.	2-qt. (12 x 7) glass baking dish with microwave roasting rack	HIGH 8 min. per lb.	ROAST 7 to 8 min. per lb. (well done, about 170° F.)	—
Rabbit, Cut up 2 to 2½-lb.	2-qt. (12 x 7) glass baking dish	HIGH 10 to 11 min. per lb. (about 180° F.)	—	—

BRAISED RUMP ROAST *

Braising requires one turn during cooking for meat 2 lbs. or over.

- **3½ to 4-lb. boneless beef rump roast**
- **1 teaspoon salt**
- **⅛ teaspoon pepper**
- **1 can (10½ oz.) condensed beef broth**
- **½ cup dry red wine or water**

1. Place roast, fat-side-down, in 4-quart glass ceramic Dutch oven. Sprinkle with salt and pepper; add broth and wine. Cover with glass lid.

2. Microwave for 20 minutes on HIGH. Turn fat-side-up; recover.

3. Microwave for 55 to 60 minutes, on SIMMER, or until fork tender. Let stand, covered, 10 minutes before serving. 9 to 12 Servings

ADD-A-DESSERT: Prepare Braised Rump Roast through Step 1; set aside. Prepare Rhubarb-Orange Sauce, page 188 (a recipe variation), through Step 1; set aside. Place roast on lower rack of oven. Microwave for 20 minutes on HIGH. Turn meat fat-side-up; recover. Place dessert on bottom shelf. Microwave both for 55 to 60 minutes, on SIMMER, or until meat is fork tender. Let meat stand, covered, 10 minutes before serving. Complete Rhubarb-Orange Sauce as directed in its basic recipe.

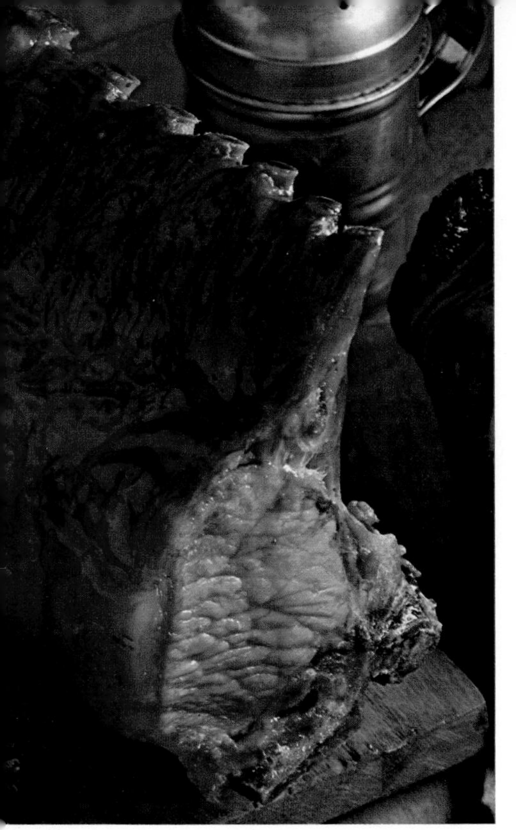

Pictured: Center Rib Pork Roast, chart, page 100.

ROLLED PRIME RIB OF BEEF WITH MUSHROOMS *

4 to 5-lb. rolled beef rib roast

Mushroom Sauce:
½ cup butter or margarine
¼ lb. fresh mushrooms, sliced

1. Place roast, fat-side-down, on microwave roasting rack in a 2-quart (12 x 7) glass baking dish.

2. Microwave for 25 minutes on HIGH. Turn fat-side-up.

3. Microwave for 20 minutes on ROAST. Place Mushroom Sauce on bottom shelf with roast. Continue cooking for 5 to 10 minutes, on ROAST, or until meat reaches rare doneness. Let meat stand, covered with foil, 10 minutes before serving. Serve mushrooms over meat.

4. **Mushroom Sauce:** Place butter and mushrooms in 4-cup glass measure.

4 to 5 Servings

ADD-A-VEGETABLE: Prepare Rolled Prime Rib of Beef with Mushrooms through Step 1; set aside. Prick 6 medium baking potatoes. Place roast on lower rack of oven and potatoes on bottom shelf. Microwave both for 25 minutes on HIGH. Turn meat fat-side-up. Microwave both for 20 minutes on ROAST. Place Mushroom Sauce on lower rack with roast. Continue cooking both for 5 to 10 minutes, on ROAST, or until meat reaches rare doneness and potatoes are tender. Let meat stand, covered with foil, 10 minutes before serving. Serve mushrooms over meat.

RECIPE VARIATION

SIRLOIN TIP WITH GARLIC: Prepare basic recipe using 4 to 5-lb. sirloin tip roast. Substitute 2 cloves garlic, halved, for Mushroom Sauce. Tuck garlic halves into netting around roast. Cook as directed in basic recipe.

POT ROAST WITH BEER *

Roast may be cooked from the frozen state, see variation.

3½ to 4-lb. beef chuck roast
1 can (12 oz.) beer or water
1 large onion, sliced
2 cloves garlic, finely chopped
2 teaspoons salt
½ teaspoon whole black peppercorns
1 bay leaf

1. Place roast in 4-quart glass ceramic Dutch oven; add beer, and sprinkle on remaining ingredients. Cover with glass lid.

2. Microwave for 20 minutes on HIGH. Turn meat over; recover.

3. Microwave for 55 to 60 minutes, on SIMMER, or until meat is fork tender. Let stand, covered, 10 minutes before serving.

6 to 8 Servings

RECIPE VARIATIONS

CHUCK ROAST WITH VEGETABLES: Omit beer, onion and seasonings. Substitute 2-lb. beef chuck roast for 3½ to 4-lb. roast. Add 1 can (10¾ oz.) condensed golden mushroom soup and 1 tablespoon dry onion soup mix to roast; cover. Microwave for 10 minutes on HIGH. Turn meat over; recover. Microwave for 20 minutes on SIMMER. Add 1 can (15 oz.) small whole peeled potatoes, drained, and 1 can (16 oz.) cut green beans, drained; recover. Continue cooking for 15 to 20 minutes, on SIMMER, or until meat is fork tender. Let stand, covered, 5 minutes before serving.

About 4 Servings

TIP: Double recipe for Chuck Roast with Vegetables. Use 3½ to 4 lb. beef chuck roast and cooking times in basic recipe.

QUICK-COOK FROZEN POT ROAST: Place a frozen 3½ to 4-lb. beef chuck roast in 3-quart (13 x 9) glass baking dish; add beer, and sprinkle on remaining ingredients in basic recipe. Cover with wax paper. Microwave for 8 minutes on HIGH. Turn meat over; recover. Microwave for 1¾ to 2 hours, on ROAST, or until meat is fork tender. Let stand, covered, 10 minutes before serving.

Pictured from the top: Home-Style Pot Roast, recipe below; Veal Meatballs in Spicy Sauce, page 115.

HOME-STYLE POT ROAST *

Braising uses HIGH to start cooking and SIMMER to slowly tenderize.

3½ to 4-lb. beef chuck roast
¼ cup water
1 large onion, sliced
1 cup chopped celery
3 medium carrots, peeled and cut into chunks
3 medium potatoes, peeled and quartered
1 can (4 oz.) mushroom stems and pieces
2 teaspoons salt
¼ teaspoon pepper
1 bay leaf

1. Place roast and water in 4-quart glass ceramic Dutch oven; cover with glass lid.

2. Microwave for 20 minutes on HIGH. Turn meat over; add remaining ingredients, and recover.

3. Microwave for 55 to 60 minutes, on SIMMER, or until meat is fork tender. Let stand, covered, 10 minutes before serving. About 6 Servings

BACON-CHEESE TOPPED STEAKS

Do all preparation and cooking in one dish.

2 slices bacon
4 (5 oz. each) cubed steaks
Salt
Pepper
1 medium tomato, sliced
½ cup crumbled Bleu cheese
3 green onions, sliced

1. Arrange bacon in a single layer in 3-quart (13 x 9) glass baking dish.

2. Microwave for 2 to 2½ minutes, on HIGH, or until crisp. Remove bacon and cool; crumble, and set aside. Drain off excess fat. Place steaks in greased baking dish. Sprinkle both sides with salt and pepper.

3. Microwave for 10 to 12 minutes, on HIGH, or until steaks are no longer pink. Top each steak with tomato slice; sprinkle each with mixture of crumbled bacon, cheese and onions.

4. Microwave for 3 to 5 minutes, on ROAST, or until cheese is bubbly. Let stand 5 minutes before serving. 4 Servings

RECIPE VARIATION

QUICK-COOK FROZEN CUBED STEAKS: Place 4 (5 oz. each) frozen cubed steaks in greased 3-quart (13 x 9) glass baking dish. Sprinkle both sides with salt and pepper. Microwave for 16 to 18 minutes, on HIGH, or until steaks are no longer pink. Continue as directed in basic recipe.

PEPPER STEAK

Thaw frozen meat quickly; see defrosting chart, page 29.

1½ lbs. top round steak, cut into thin strips
1 teaspoon salt
⅛ teaspoon pepper
¼ cup soy sauce
2 green peppers, sliced
1 tablespoon cornstarch
¼ cup water
Tomato wedges, if desired

1. Place meat in 2-quart glass casserole. Sprinkle with salt and pepper; add soy sauce. Stir in green pepper. Cover with glass lid or wax paper.

2. Microwave for 14 minutes on HIGH. Combine cornstarch and water in small bowl until smooth; stir into meat mixture. Recover and continue cooking for 2 to 3 minutes, on HIGH, or until thickened. Let stand, covered, 5 minutes before serving. Garnish with fresh tomato wedges. About 4 Servings

ORIENTAL BEEF

ROAST setting in recipe makes chocolate fondue an ideal "ADD-A-".

- **1½ to 2 lbs. beef sirloin steak, cut into thin strips**
- **½ lb. fresh mushrooms, sliced**
- **1 cup chopped onion**
- **1 cup bias-cut celery**
- **1 can (8 oz.) water chestnuts, drained and sliced**
- **2 tablespoons cornstarch**
- **¼ cup soy sauce**
- **1 package (6 oz.) frozen pea pods**

1. Place all ingredients, except cornstarch, soy sauce and pea pods, in 3-quart glass casserole. Combine cornstarch and soy sauce in small bowl until smooth; stir into meat mixture. Cover with glass lid or wax paper.

2. Microwave for 15 minutes on ROAST. Stir; add pea pods. Recover and continue cooking for 5 to 6 minutes, on ROAST, or until meat is fork tender. Stir to combine pea pods. Let stand, covered, 5 minutes before serving.

4 to 6 Servings

ADD-A-DESSERT: Prepare Oriental Beef through Step 1; set aside. Prepare Spiced Chocolate Fondue, page 192 (a recipe variation) through Step 1; set aside. Place beef on upper rack of oven. Microwave for 15 minutes on ROAST. Stir beef and add pea pods; recover. Place fondue on bottom shelf. Continue cooking both for 5 to 6 minutes, on ROAST, or until meat is fork tender. Stir to combine pea pods. Let stand, covered, 5 minutes before serving. Beat fondue until combined and smooth. Keep warm in fondue pot.

BEEF STROGANOFF

Sensitive mushrooms and sour cream change power setting to ROAST.

- **1 to 1½ lbs. beef sirloin steak, cut into cubes**
- **1 medium onion, sliced and separated into rings**
- **1 clove garlic, finely chopped**
- **1 can (10½ oz.) condensed beef broth**
- **1 can (4 oz.) whole mushrooms, drained**
- **1 tablespoon snipped chives**
- **2 tablespoons cornstarch**
- **¼ cup dry red wine or water**
- **1 carton (8 oz.) sour cream**
- **Hot buttered noodles**

1. Place meat, onion and garlic in 10-inch glass ceramic skillet. Cover with glass lid or wax paper.

2. Microwave for 8 minutes on HIGH. Stir in broth, mushrooms and chives. Combine cornstarch and wine in small bowl until smooth; stir into broth. Recover.

3. Microwave for 18 to 20 minutes, on ROAST, or until meat is fork tender. Mix in sour cream; recover, and continue cooking for 3 to 4 minutes, on ROAST, or until heated through. Let stand, covered, 5 minutes. Serve with hot buttered noodles.

About 4 Servings

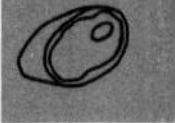

RECIPE VARIATIONS

DILL STROGANOFF: Substitute 1 teaspoon dill weed for chives.

BEEF BURGUNDY: Omit chives and sour cream. Substitute ½ cup beef broth for can of condensed beef broth. Increase dry red wine to ¾ cup. Add 1 medium green pepper, cut into strips, 1 can (16 oz.) whole onions, drained, 1 teaspoon salt and ⅛ teaspoon pepper with mushrooms in basic recipe.

BEEF ROLLS PARMESAN *

Have your meat man slice round steak ¼-inch thick.

- **2 tablespoons butter or margarine**
- **2 tablespoons all-purpose flour**
- **1 can (16 oz.) whole tomatoes**
- **1½ to 2 lbs. beef round steak, ¼-inch thick**
- **⅓ cup grated Parmesan cheese**
- **¼ cup bread crumbs**
- **1 teaspoon garlic salt**
- **1 teaspoon dried parsley flakes**
- **¼ teaspoon marjoram leaves or thyme leaves**
- **3 tablespoons water**
- **1 medium green pepper, cut into thin strips**
- **Hot cooked rice**

1. Place butter in 10-inch glass ceramic skillet.

2. Microwave for about 1 minute, on ROAST, or until melted. Blend in flour; stir in tomatoes; set aside. Trim off fat and cut meat into serving pieces. Combine remaining ingredients, except green pepper, in small mixing bowl; spread on meat pieces. Roll meat up jelly-roll fashion; secure with toothpicks. Place meat in sauce; top with green pepper strips. Cover with glass lid.

3. Microwave for 10 minutes on HIGH.

4. Microwave for 25 to 30 minutes, on SIMMER, or until fork tender. Let stand, covered, 5 minutes. Remove toothpicks and serve with hot rice.

About 6 Servings

ADD-A-RICE: Prepare Beef Rolls Parmesan through Step 2; set aside. Place 2 cups hot tap water, 1 tablespoon butter and 1 teaspoon salt in 2-quart glass casserole; cover with glass lid. Place beef on upper rack of oven and water on bottom shelf. Microwave both for 15 minutes on HIGH. Stir 1 cup raw long grain white rice into water; recover. Microwave both for 35 to 40 minutes, on SIMMER, or until meat is fork tender. Let both stand, covered, 5 minutes before serving. Serve Beef Rolls Parmesan on rice.

SWISS STEAK *

HIGH setting heats meat quickly; SIMMER tenderizes less tender cuts.

2 tablespoons all-purpose flour
1 teaspoon salt
¼ teaspoon pepper
1 to 1½ lbs. beef round steak, cut into serving pieces
1 medium onion, chopped
2 cans (8 oz. each) tomato sauce
1 tablespoon dried parsley flakes

1. Combine flour and seasonings in shallow dish. Coat meat in seasoned flour; pound into meat. Place meat in 10-inch glass ceramic skillet. Place onion over meat pieces. Add tomato sauce; sprinkle with parsley flakes. Cover with glass lid.

2. Microwave for 8 minutes on HIGH.

3. Microwave for 30 to 35 minutes, on SIMMER, or until meat is fork tender. Let stand, covered, 5 minutes before serving. About 4 Servings

ADD-A-VEGETABLE: Prepare Swiss Steak through Step 1; set aside Prepare Parsley Butter Vegetables, page 187, through Step 1; set aside. Place meat on upper rack of oven. Microwave for 8 minutes on HIGH. Place vegetables on bottom shelf. Continue cooking both for 30 to 35 minutes, on SIMMER, or until meat is fork tender. Let both stand, covered, 5 minutes before serving.

RECIPE VARIATION

SAVORY SWISS STEAK: Substitute 1 can (10½ oz.) condensed beef broth for tomato sauce. At end of final cooking period, drain meat, reserving 1½ cups liquid. Combine ¼ cup unsifted all-purpose flour, ⅛ teaspoon salt, dash pepper and ½ cup water in 4-cup glass measure until smooth; beat in 1½ cups reserved broth with rotary beater. Add 3 tablespoons butter or margarine. Microwave for 2 minutes on HIGH. Beat and continue cooking for 1 to 2 minutes, on HIGH, or until thickened (about 200° F.). Serve over meat.

CORNED BEEF 'N CABBAGE *

Brisket is a tougher cut of meat – use the braising technique.

2½ to 3-lb. corned beef brisket with seasonings
1 cup water
2 medium onions, quartered
3 carrots, peeled and thickly sliced
3 turnips, peeled and cut into chunks
1 small cabbage, cut into 8 wedges

1. Place corned beef brisket in 3-quart glass casserole; add water and sprinkle on seasonings included with meat. Cover with glass lid.

2. Microwave for 15 minutes on HIGH.

3. Microwave for 30 minutes on SIMMER. Turn meat over; add remaining ingredients. Recover and continue cooking for 50 to 60 minutes, on SIMMER, or until meat is fork tender. Let stand, covered, 5 minutes before serving. About 6 Servings

TIP: Substitute 1 bay leaf, ½ teaspoon whole plack peppercorns, 2 cloves garlic, finely chopped, and 4 whole cloves for seasoning packet.

RECIPE VARIATION

FRESH BEEF BRISKET: Substitute 2½ to 3-lb. fresh beef brisket for corned beef. Use seasonings in TIP. Substitute 3 medium potatoes, peeled and cut into chunks, for turnips. Omit cabbage.

HUNGARIAN GOULASH *

Tomato, an acid food, helps tenderize.

1½ lbs. beef stew meat
1 medium onion, chopped
½ medium green pepper, chopped
1 medium potato, diced
1 can (10½ oz.) condensed beef broth
1 can (6 oz.) tomato paste
1 tablespoon vinegar
1 teaspoon salt
1 teaspoon paprika
1 teaspoon caraway seeds
¼ teaspoon marjoram leaves or thyme leaves
Cooked noodles, buttered

1. Combine all ingredients, except buttered noodles, in 10-inch glass ceramic skillet. Cover with glass lid.

2. Microwave for 8 minutes on HIGH. Stir well; recover.

3. Microwave for 40 to 45 minutes, on SIMMER, or until meat is fork tender. Let stand, covered, 5 minutes before serving. Serve over buttered noodles. About 4 Servings

ADD-A-VEGETABLE: Prepare Hungarian Goulash through Step 1; set aside. Place 1 package (10 oz.) frozen French-style green beans in 1½-quart glass casserole; cover with glass lid; set aside. Place goulash on upper rack of oven. Microwave for 8 minutes on HIGH. Stir well; recover. Place green beans on bottom shelf. Continue cooking both for 50 to 55 minutes, on SIMMER, or until meat is fork tender. Let both stand, covered, 5 minutes before serving.

GRILLED MEAT PATTIES

1 lb. ground beef
Salt
Pepper

1. Preheat microwave browning grill in oven on HIGH as directed in manufacturer's instruction booklet.

2. Shape ground beef into four patties about ½ inch thick. Place on preheated grill. Season with salt and pepper.

3. Microwave for 4 minutes on HIGH. Turn patties over and continue cooking for 3 to 4 minutes, on HIGH, or until desired doneness.

4 Patties

RECIPE VARIATIONS

ITALIAN PATTIES: Add ½ teaspoon oregano leaves and ¼ teaspoon basil leaves to ground beef. Top cooked patties with shredded Mozzarella cheese.

FRENCH PATTIES: After first cooking time, baste patties with ¼ cup dry red wine; top with 1 can (4 oz.) mushroom stems and pieces, drained. Increase final cooking time by 30 seconds. Garnish with snipped parsley.

CHEDDAR CHEESE PATTIES: After first cooking time, top each patty with 2 tablespoons shredded Cheddar cheese and 1 teaspoon catsup.

HAMBURGERS

For grilled ground beef patties, see recipe, above.

1 lb. ground beef
Salt
Pepper
4 hamburger buns

1. Shape ground beef into 4 patties; season with salt and pepper. Place patties in 2-quart (8 x 8) glass baking dish.

2. Microwave for 3 minutes on HIGH. Turn patties over and continue cooking for 3½ minutes on HIGH. Place cooked patties in split buns; wrap each one loosely in paper napkin or paper towel.

3. Microwave for 45 to 50 seconds on REHEAT. About 4 Servings

TIP: Microwave hamburgers on REHEAT until warm: 1 hamburger 15 to 20 seconds; 2 hamburgers 25 to 30 seconds; 6 hamburgers 1 to 1½ minutes.

RECIPE VARIATION

QUICK-COOK FROZEN HAMBURGERS: Place 4 frozen hamburger patties in 2-quart (8 x 8) glass baking dish. Cover with wax paper. Microwave for 4 minutes on HIGH. Turn patties over; recover, and continue cooking for 5 minutes on HIGH. Continue as directed in basic recipe.

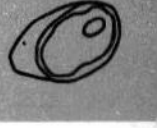

SAUCY MEATBALLS *

1 lb. ground beef
1 medium potato, peeled and shredded
2 tablespoons dry onion soup mix
1 tablespoon dried parsley flakes
1 egg, beaten
2 cups water
1½ tablespoons instant beef bouillon
2 teaspoons Worcestershire sauce
2 tablespoons cornstarch
2 tablespoons water

1. Combine ground beef, potato, soup mix, parsley flakes and egg in medium mixing bowl. Shape into 12 (1½-inch) meatballs; set aside. Combine 2 cups water, bouillon and Worcestershire sauce in 2-quart glass casserole. Cover with glass lid or wax paper.

2. Microwave for 6 to 7 minutes, on HIGH, or until boiling. Add meatballs; recover.

3. Microwave for 8 minutes on ROAST. Combine cornstarch and 2 tablespoons water in small bowl until smooth; stir into meatballs and recover. Continue cooking for 3 to 4 minutes, on ROAST, or until sauce is thickened (about 200° F.). Let stand, covered, 5 minutes before serving.

About 4 Servings

ADD-A-VEGETABLE: Prepare Saucy Meatballs through Step 2; set aside. Place 1 can (16 oz.) cream-style corn in 1-quart glass casserole; top with ¼ cup crushed potato chips. Place meatballs on upper rack of oven and corn on bottom shelf. Microwave both for 6 minutes on HIGH. Combine cornstarch and 2 tablespoons water in small mixing bowl until smooth; stir into meatballs and recover. Continue cooking both for 4 to 5 minutes, on HIGH, or until sauce is thickened (about 200° F.). Let both stand, covered, 5 minutes before serving.

RECIPE VARIATION

ITALIAN MEATBALLS: Substitute ½ cup cracker crumbs, ½ cup grated Parmesan cheese, 1 teaspoon garlic salt, ½ teaspoon ground oregano and dash of pepper for potatoes and soup mix. Substitute 1 can (16 oz.) stewed tomatoes for 2 cups water.

MOTHER'S MEATLOAF

Standing time completes cooking, sets juices.

1½ lbs. ground beef
2 cups soft bread cubes
½ cup finely chopped celery
½ cup chopped onion
¼ cup finely chopped green pepper
1½ teaspoons salt
1 egg
½ cup catsup

1. Combine all ingredients in medium mixing bowl; mix well. Pat into (9 x 5) glass loaf dish.

2. Microwave for 25 to 30 minutes, on ROAST, or until well done in center (about 140° F.). Pour off liquid. Let stand 5 minutes before serving.
5 to 6 Servings

ADD-A-VEGETABLE: Prepare Mother's Meatloaf through Step 1; set aside. Prepare Quick-Bake Potatoes, page 189, through Step 3. Place meatloaf on upper rack of oven and potatoes on bottom shelf. Microwave for 30 to 35 minutes, on HIGH, or until meatloaf is well done in center (about 140° F.). Let both stand 5 minutes before serving.

RECIPE VARIATIONS

MEXICAN MEATLOAF: Substitute ½ cup crushed corn chips, 1 can (8 oz.) whole kernel corn, drained, ½ cup chili sauce and ⅛ teaspoon hot pepper sauce for bread cubes and catsup. Decrease salt to ¼ teaspoon.

CHEESY-BACON MEATLOAF: Combine ingredients in basic recipe. Pat meat mixture into 12 x 9-inch rectangle. Sprinkle 1 cup shredded Swiss cheese and 1 can (4 oz.) mushroom stems and pieces, drained, over meat. Fold narrow ends into center. Seal ends, forming a loaf, and place in (9 x 5) glass loaf dish. Cut 2 slices bacon into fourths; place on meatloaf.

BARBECUED INDIVIDUAL MEAT LOAVES

2 lbs. ground beef
1 cup quick-cooking rolled oats
¾ cup bottled barbecue sauce
1 egg
2 tablespoons bottled Italian salad dressing
1½ teaspoons salt
¼ teaspoon pepper

1. Combine all ingredients in medium mixing bowl. Form into 8 individual meat loaves. Place in 2-quart (12 x 7) glass baking dish.

2. Microwave for 23 to 25 minutes, on ROAST, or until meat is well done (about 140° F.). Let stand 5 minutes before serving. 6 to 8 Servings

RECIPE VARIATION

SALISBURY STEAK: Substitute ¾ cup cooked rice, ¼ cup chopped green pepper and 1 teaspoon dried parsley flakes for oats and barbecue sauce. Shape into 8 patties; place in 2-quart (12 x 7) glass baking dish. Microwave for 12 minutes on ROAST. Combine 1 can (10¾ oz.) condensed beef consommé and 3 tablespoons cornstarch in medium mixing bowl until smooth. Stir in 1 can (4 oz.) mushroom stems and pieces, undrained, ⅓ cup catsup and ¼ teaspoon leaf basil. Pour over patties and continue cooking for 12 to 14 minutes, on ROAST, or until meat is well done. Let stand 5 minutes before serving.

CHEESY BEEF-STUFFED PEPPERS

Cover holds moisture, which helps tenderize.

3 large green peppers, cut in half lengthwise
1 lb. ground beef
1 cup creamed cottage cheese
1 can (8 oz.) tomato sauce
1 small onion, finely chopped
1 egg
⅓ cup bread crumbs
1 tablespoon Worcestershire sauce
2 teaspoons salt
1 cup shredded process American cheese

1. Place peppers in 2-quart (12 x 7) glass baking dish; set aside. Combine remaining ingredients, except shredded cheese, in medium mixing bowl; mix well. Spoon meat mixture into green pepper halves. Cover with wax paper.

2. Microwave for 24 to 26 minutes, on ROAST, or until meat is well done (about 140° F.). Top with shredded cheese and continue cooking on ROAST until cheese is melted. About 6 Servings

RECIPE VARIATION

CABBAGE ROLLS: Substitute 8 large cabbage leaves for green peppers. Wash and stack leaves on glass plate; soften for 3 minutes on HIGH. Substitute ¼ cup wheat germ for bread crumbs; omit shredded American cheese. Divide meat mixture among cabbage leaves; roll up, and place in 2-quart (12 x 7) glass baking dish. Serve topped with your favorite tomato sauce.

PORK ROAST WITH CHERRY SAUCE

4 to 5-lb. pork loin center rib roast

Cherry Sauce:
- ½ cup cherry preserves
- ¼ cup dark corn syrup
- 2 tablespoons vinegar
- ⅛ teaspoon salt
- ⅛ teaspoon nutmeg
- ⅛ teaspoon cinnamon
- ⅛ teaspoon ground cloves
- Dash pepper

1. Place roast, fat-side-down on microwave roasting rack, in 2-quart (12 x 7) glass baking dish.

2. Microwave for 25 minutes on HIGH. Turn fat-side-up.

3. Microwave for 25 to 30 minutes, on ROAST, or until meat registers 165° F. Let stand, covered with foil, 10 minutes before serving. Slash pork roast between ribs; place on serving platter. Pour hot Cherry Sauce over meat.

4. Cherry Sauce: Combine all sauce ingredients in 2-cup glass measure.

5. Microwave for 3 to 4 minutes, on ROAST, or until bubbly (about 150° F.).

6 to 8 Servings

PORK CHOPS WITH WALNUT SAUCE

Recipe variation tells you how to cook chops right from the freezer.

- 6 loin pork chops (about 3 lbs.), cut ¾ inch thick
- ¼ cup finely chopped onion
- ½ teaspoon salt
- ½ teaspoon garlic salt
- ⅛ teaspoon pepper
- ⅛ teaspoon ground cloves
- ⅛ teaspoon cinnamon
- 1 bay leaf
- 1 tablespoon dried parsley flakes
- ½ cup chopped walnuts
- 2 tablespoons cornstarch
- 1 can (10 oz.) condensed beef consommé

1. Place pork chops in 10-inch glass ceramic skillet. Sprinkle with all ingredients, except cornstarch and consommé. Combine cornstarch and consommé in small bowl until smooth; pour over top. Cover with glass lid or wax paper.

2. Microwave for 30 to 35 minutes, on ROAST, or until fork tender. Let stand, covered, 5 minutes before serving.

6 Servings

ADD-A-VEGETABLE: Prepare Pork Chops with Walnut Sauce through Step 1; set aside. Place 2 packages (10 oz. each) frozen carrot nuggets in 2-quart glass casserole; cover with glass lid. Place pork on upper rack of oven and vegetable on bottom shelf. Microwave both for 35 to 40 minutes, on HIGH, or until pork is fork tender. Stir carrots once during cooking. Let both stand, covered, 5 minutes before serving.

STUFFED PORK CHOPS

Cover tightly with glass lid so pork chops do not need turning.

- 4 pork chops (about 2½ lbs.), cut 1 inch thick
- ½ cup orange marmalade

Orange Stuffing:
- 1 tablespoon butter or margarine
- 2 tablespoons orange juice
- 2 green onions, sliced
- 1 cup dry seasoned bread stuffing cubes
- 1 teaspoon dried parsley flakes
- 1 teaspoon grated orange rind
- Dash pepper
- ½ medium orange, chopped

1. Slit into side of each chop to form an opening or pocket. Divide Orange Stuffing among chops; stuff opening. Place chops in 10-inch glass ceramic skillet. Brush with orange marmalade. Cover with glass lid or wax paper.

2. Microwave for 25 to 30 minutes, on ROAST, or until fork tender. Let stand, covered, 5 minutes before serving.

3. Orange Stuffing: Place butter in medium mixing bowl.

4. Microwave for about 1 minute, on ROAST, or until melted. Add remaining ingredients; toss to combine.

4 Servings

ADD-A-DESSERT: Prepare Stuffed Pork Chops through Step 1; set aside. Prepare Crunchy Apple Crisp, page 185, through Step 1. Place pork on upper rack of oven and dessert on bottom shelf. Microwave both for 30 to 35 minutes, on HIGH, or until meat is fork tender. Let meat stand, covered, 5 minutes before serving.

PORK BLADE STEAKS WITH LIMAS

A tight-fitting cover tenderizes fastest.

- 4 pork shoulder steaks (about 1½ lbs.), cut ¾ inch thick
- 1 small onion, chopped
- ¾ cup bottled barbecue sauce
- 1 package (10 oz.) frozen baby lima beans

1. Place pork steaks in 10-inch glass ceramic skillet. Cover with glass lid.

2. Microwave for 8 minutes on HIGH. Drain off fat. Sprinkle steaks with onion; add barbecue sauce, and recover.

3. Microwave for 10 minutes on SIMMER. Add lima beans; recover. Continue cooking for 10 to 15 minutes, on SIMMER, or until meat is fork tender. Stir gently. Let stand, covered, 5 minutes before serving.

4 Servings

GLAZED COUNTRY-STYLE PORK RIBS

Drain off excess fat to preserve sauce consistency.

- **3 lbs. Country-Style pork spareribs**
- **1 cup packed brown sugar**
- **¼ cup vinegar**
- **3 tablespoons Dijon mustard**

1. Arrange ribs in 3-quart (13 x 9) glass baking dish. Cover with wax paper.

2. Microwave for 15 minutes on ROAST. Drain off fat. Combine remaining ingredients in small bowl; mix well, and pour over ribs. Recover and continue cooking for 35 to 40 minutes, on ROAST, or until fork tender. Let stand, covered, 5 minutes before serving.

4 to 6 Servings

BARBECUED SPARERIBS

Pork ribs cook on ROAST because of high fat content.

- **2½ to 3 lbs. pork spareribs, cut into serving pieces**
- **1 medium onion, chopped**
- **½ medium green pepper, chopped**
- **2 cloves garlic, finely chopped**
- **¾ cup catsup**
- **½ cup packed brown sugar**
- **¼ cup dark molasses**
- **¼ cup lemon juice**
- **1 teaspoon dry mustard**

1. Place ribs in 3-quart (13 x 9) glass baking dish. Cover with wax paper.

2. Microwave for 15 minutes on ROAST. Drain and turn ribs over. Sprinkle with onion, green pepper and garlic. Combine remaining ingredients; pour over ribs. Recover and continue cooking for 25 to 30 minutes, on ROAST, or until fork tender. Let stand, covered, 5 minutes before serving.

4 to 6 Servings

TIP: Outdoor barbecuing is fast and easy. Prepare and microwave ribs as directed through first cooking period. Place drained ribs on grill over hot coals. Omit green pepper and finely chop the onion. Make a sauce of remaining ingredients; brush ribs. Turn and continue brushing ribs with sauce until grilled tender.

POLYNESIAN PINEAPPLE PORK

- **1 lb. cubed fresh pork**
- **1 medium onion, sliced and separated into rings**
- **2 fresh pineapples**
- **2 cups fresh broccoli flowerettes**
- **1 cup sliced almonds**
- **1 jar (2 oz.) sliced pimento**
- **2 tablespoons cornstarch**
- **2 tablespoons packed brown sugar**
- **1 teaspoon salt**
- **1 teaspoon ginger**
- **2 tablespoons soy sauce**
- **2 tablespoons dry sherry or water**

1. Place pork and onion in 3-quart glass casserole. Cover with glass lid or wax paper.

2. Microwave for 30 minutes on ROAST.

3. Meanwhile, cut pineapples in half, keeping leaves intact and cutting through them. Loosen and remove pineapple from shells; core and cut into chunks; measure 2 cups of chunks.

4. Stir pineapple chunks, broccoli, almonds and pimento into pork mixture. Combine remaining ingredients in small bowl until smooth; pour over pork mixture. Recover.

5. Microwave for 15 to 20 minutes, on ROAST, or until meat is fork tender. Let stand, covered, 5 minutes. Divide mixture among pineapple shells and serve.

4 Servings

Pictured: Polynesian Pineapple Pork, recipe above.

CANADIAN BACON

Cook meat fat-side-up so it bastes and browns.

- **1½ lbs. whole Canadian-style bacon, fully cooked**
- **Whole cloves**
- **½ cup applesauce**
- **½ teaspoon cinnamon**

1. Score fat on one side of bacon. Place bacon, scored-side-up, in (9 x 5) glass loaf dish. Insert cloves in top of bacon. Combine remaining ingredients and spread over top.

2. Microwave for 20 to 25 minutes, on ROAST, or until meat is heated through (about 120° F.). Let stand 5 minutes. About 7 Servings

PINEAPPLE-GLAZED HAM LOAF

- **1 lb. ground ham**
- **½ lb. ground pork**
- **1½ cups dry bread crumbs**
- **¾ cup milk**
- **2 eggs, beaten**
- **½ teaspoon dry mustard**
- **2 teaspoons dried parsley flakes**

Pineapple Glaze:

- **1 can (8 oz.) crushed pineapple, undrained**
- **¼ cup brown sugar**

1. Combine all ham loaf ingredients in medium mixing bowl; mix well. Pat into (9 x 5) glass loaf dish.

2. Microwave for 30 minutes on ROAST. Pour Pineapple Glaze over ham loaf and continue cooking for 5 to 10 minutes, on ROAST, or until meat is done (about 160° F.). Let stand 5 minutes before serving.

3. Pineapple Glaze: Combine all ingredients in small mixing bowl; mix well. 5 to 6 Servings

HOT DOGS

To warm wieners without buns, see chart on page 102.

- **6 wieners**
- **6 hot dog buns**

1. Place wieners in split hot dog buns; wrap each one loosely in paper napkin or paper towel.

2. Microwave on REHEAT until heated through:

   1 hot dog — 50 to 60 seconds (about 120° F.)
   2 hot dogs — 1 to 1½ minutes (about 120° F.)
   4 hot dogs — 2 to 2½ minutes (about 120° F.)
   6 hot dogs — 2½ to 3 minutes (about 120° F.) 6 Servings

TIP: For assorted hot dog fillings, see Hikers' Hot Dogs, page 168.

RECIPE VARIATION

QUICK-COOK FROZEN WIENERS: Place 4 frozen wieners on glass plate. Microwave for about 4 minutes, on HIGH, or until heated through (about 120° F.). Place in slit hot dog buns.

ZESTY LUNCHEON MEAT

Similar to ham, so microwave on ROAST.

- **1 can (12 oz.) luncheon meat**
- **2 slices process American cheese**
- **2 tablespoons bacon-flavored bits or 2 slices bacon, crisply-fried and crumbled**

1. Place luncheon meat in (9 x 5) glass loaf dish. Cover with wax paper.

2. Microwave for 8 minutes on ROAST. Place cheese slices over meat. Sprinkle with bacon and continue cooking for 1 to 2 minutes, on ROAST, or until cheese is melted. About 4 Servings

ADD-A-VEGETABLE: Prepare Zesty Luncheon Meat through Step 1; set aside. Place 1 can (16 oz.) peas, undrained, in 1-quart glass casserole; cover with glass lid. Place meat on upper rack of oven and peas on bottom shelf. Microwave both for 8 minutes on HIGH. Place cheese slices over meat. Sprinkle with bacon and continue cooking both for 1 to 2 minutes, on HIGH, or until cheese is melted.

RECIPE VARIATION

SAUCY LUNCHEON MEAT: Substitute 1 tablespoon catsup for bacon.

BRATWURST IN BEER

ROAST setting prevents spatters.

- **4 uncooked bratwurst (about 1 lb.)**
- **½ cup finely chopped onion**
- **1 can (12 oz.) beer, room temperature**

1. Place bratwurst in 9-inch round glass baking dish. Add remaining ingredients; cover with wax paper.

2. Microwave for 15 to 16 minutes, on ROAST, or until meat is done (about 170° F.). Let stand, covered, 5 minutes before serving. About 4 Servings

RING BOLOGNA AND SAUERKRAUT

- 1 can (27 oz.) sauerkraut, drained
- 1 medium carrot, shredded
- 1 small onion, chopped
- 1½ teaspoons caraway seeds
- 1 precooked ring bologna (1 to 1½ lbs.)

Standing time completes heating, keeps meat moist.

1. Combine all ingredients, except ring bologna, in 2-quart glass casserole. Place bologna over top. Cover with glass lid or wax paper.

2. Microwave for 8 to 10 minutes, on REHEAT, or until heated through. Let stand, covered, 5 minutes before serving.

About 4 Servings

AUTUMN HAM DINNER

- 2 tablespoons cooking oil
- 1 cup packed brown sugar
- 1 teaspoon cinnamon
- 1 can (3 lb.) ham, fully cooked
- 1 acorn squash, unpeeled and cut into chunks
- 3 small cooking apples, quartered

Braising sauces and vegetables do not dry up in a microwave oven.

1. Combine oil, brown sugar and cinnamon in shallow dish; mix well. Coat ham in ½ of brown sugar mixture, place in 10-inch glass ceramic skillet. Place squash and apple pieces around ham. Sprinkle with remaining brown sugar mixture. Cover with glass lid or wax paper.

2. Microwave for 35 to 40 minutes, on ROAST, or until ham is hot (about 120° F.). Let stand, covered, 5 minutes before serving.

6 to 8 Servings

SOUTHERN BAKED HAM

- 7 to 8-lb. bone-in ham, fully cooked
- ½ cup maple-flavored syrup
- 1 jar (10 oz.) chutney

Cover edges of large ham with small pieces of foil if cooking too fast.

1. Place ham on microwave roasting rack in 3-quart (13 x 9) glass baking dish.

2. Microwave for 35 minutes on ROAST. Turn ham over; continue cooking for 25 minutes on ROAST. Combine remaining ingredients; pour over ham, and continue cooking for 10 to 15 minutes, on ROAST, or until heated through (about 110° F.). Let stand, covered with foil, 10 minutes before serving.

10 to 14 Servings

Pictured: Autumn Ham Dinner, recipe above.

GLAZED HAM SLICE

1½-lb. ham slice, fully cooked, about 1-inch thick

Orange Glaze:
- **¼ cup orange juice**
- **2 tablespoons honey**
- **1 teaspoon grated orange rind**
- **½ teaspoon ginger**

1. Place ham slice in 2-quart (12 x 7) glass baking dish. Pour Orange Glaze over ham. Cover with wax paper.

2. Microwave for 12 to 14 minutes, on ROAST, or until heated through (about 120° F.).

3. **Orange Glaze:** Combine all ingredients in 1-cup measure; mix well.

4 to 6 Servings

ADD-A-VEGETABLE: Prepare Glazed Ham Slice through Step 1; set aside. Prepare Scalloped Potatoes, page 172, through Step 1. Place potatoes on upper rack of oven and ham on bottom shelf. Microwave both for 10 minutes on HIGH. Stir potatoes; sprinkle with buttered bread crumbs, and continue cooking for 20 to 25 minutes, on HIGH, or until potatoes are tender. Let both stand 5 minutes before serving.

RECIPE VARIATION

DILL GLAZED HAM: Substitute 2 tablespoons mayonnaise or salad dressing, 2 tablespoons prepared mustard, 2 green onions, sliced, and ½ teaspoon dill weed for Orange Glaze ingredients.

CURRANT GLAZED LEG OF LAMB

Roasting rack holds meat above pan drippings.

- **4 to 4½-lb. leg of lamb roast**
- **¼ cup red currant jelly**

1. Place roast, fat-side-down on a microwave roasting rack, in a 2-quart (12 x 7) glass baking dish. Spread with ½ of currant jelly.

2. Microwave for 30 minutes on ROAST. Turn meat over and spread with remaining currant jelly. Continue cooking for 30 to 40 minutes, on ROAST, or until meat registers 180° F. Let stand, covered with foil, 10 minutes before serving.

6 to 8 Servings

TIP: Microwave a lamb shoulder roast using the same technique; cook for 14 to 15 minutes per lb. on ROAST.

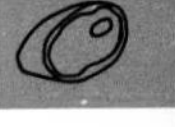

RECIPE VARIATION

ZUCCHINI-STUFFED LEG O'LAMB: Substitute a 4 to 4½-lb. boneless leg of lamb roast for leg of lamb roast. Omit red currant jelly. Remove netting or string and fill center of roast with Zucchini Stuffing. Retie roast; cook as directed in basic recipe.

Zucchini Stuffing: Combine 2 small zucchini, finely chopped, 1 medium onion, finely chopped, ¼ teaspoon garlic powder, ½ teaspoon salt, ¼ teaspoon pepper, ½ teaspoon oregano leaves, ¼ cup catsup; mix well.

HERB LAMB STEAKS *

Small, tender cuts microwave quickly on HIGH.

- **2 tablespoons butter or margarine**
- **2 teaspoons dried parsley flakes**
- **1 teaspoon marjoram leaves**
- **½ teaspoon salt**
- **½ teaspoon rosemary leaves**
- **2 tablespoons water**
- **4 lamb shoulder steaks (1½ to 2 lbs.)**

1. Place butter in small glass bowl; add remaining ingredients, except water and steaks.

2. Microwave for about 1 minute, on HIGH, or until butter is melted. Stir to combine.

3. Place lamb steaks in 10-inch glass ceramic skillet. Brush with herb-butter mixture. Add water; cover with glass lid.

4. Microwave for 10 minutes on HIGH.

5. Microwave for 30 to 35 minutes, on SIMMER, or until fork tender. Let stand, covered, 5 minutes before serving.

About 4 Servings

ADD-A-DESSERT: Prepare Herb Lamb Steaks through Step 3; set aside. Place 1 package (3¼ oz.) tapioca pudding and 2 cups milk in 2-quart glass casserole; mix well, and cover with glass lid. Place lamb on upper rack of oven and dessert on bottom shelf. Microwave both for 10 minutes on HIGH. Beat pudding; recover. Continue cooking both for 30 to 35 minutes, on SIMMER, or until meat is fork tender. Let meat stand, covered, 5 minutes before serving.

DILLED LAMB PATTIES

Ground meats microwave on HIGH when another dish of food is added.

4 ground lamb patties (about 1½ lbs.)
1 carton (8 oz.) plain yogurt
½ teaspoon salt
½ teaspoon dill weed
¼ teaspoon garlic powder
Dash pepper
1 medium tomato, chopped
1 medium onion, chopped

1. Place lamb patties in 2-quart (8 x 8) glass baking dish. Cover with wax paper.

2. Microwave for 15 minutes on ROAST. Drain. Combine remaining ingredients in small bowl and pour over patties. Recover and continue cooking for 4 to 5 minutes, on ROAST, or until meat is done. Let stand, covered, 5 minutes before serving. 4 Servings

ADD-A-VEGETABLE : Prepare Dilled Lamb Patties through Step 1; set aside. Place 1 package (10 oz.) frozen Brussels sprouts in 1½-quart glass casserole; cover with glass lid. Place meat on upper rack of oven and Brussels sprouts on bottom shelf. Microwave both for 13 minutes on HIGH. Drain patties. Combine remaining ingredients for Dilled Lamb Patties in small bowl and pour over lamb. Recover and continue cooking both for 4 to 5 minutes, on ROAST, or until meat is done. Let stand, covered, 5 minutes before serving.

RECIPE VARIATION

CURRIED PATTIES: Substitute 1 teaspoon curry powder for dill weed and 1 medium apple, chopped, for tomato. Increase cooking time 2 to 3 minutes.

VEAL RUMP ROAST *

Turning meat often assures even doneness.

2 to 2½-lb. bone-in veal rump roast
½ cup rosé wine or water
1 medium onion, sliced
1 tablespoon dried parsley flakes
1 teaspoon salt
½ teaspoon celery salt
⅛ teaspoon pepper
½ cup rosé wine or water

1. Place roast, fat-side-down, in 3-quart glass casserole. Sprinkle on onion and seasonings; pour wine over top. Cover with glass lid.

2. Microwave for 12 minutes on HIGH. Turn fat-side-up; recover.

3. Microwave for 40 to 45 minutes, on SIMMER, or until fork tender. Let stand, covered, 5 minutes before serving. About 6 Servings

ADD-A-VEGETABLE: Prepare Veal Rump Roast through Step 1; set aside. Arrange 1 lb. fresh asparagus spears, thick edges toward outside, in 2-quart (12 x 7) glass baking dish; add ¼ cup water, and cover with wax paper. Set aside. Place veal on lower rack of oven. Microwave for 12 minutes on HIGH. Turn meat fat-side-up; recover. Place asparagus on bottom shelf. Microwave for 40 to 45 minutes, on SIMMER, or until veal is fork tender. Let both stand, covered, 5 minutes before serving.

VEAL SCALLOPINI *

1½ lbs. veal round steak, cut into strips
¼ cup butter or margarine
1 can (4 oz.) mushroom stems and pieces, drained
1 small onion, thinly sliced and separated into rings
1 clove garlic, finely chopped
½ teaspoon salt
1 tablespoon cornstarch
½ teaspoon oregano leaves
¼ cup dry sherry or water
2 small tomatoes, cut into wedges

1. Place veal strips, butter, mushrooms, onion, garlic and salt in 10-inch glass ceramic skillet.

2. Microwave for 10 minutes on ROAST. Combine remaining ingredients, except tomatoes, in small bowl until smooth; stir into veal mixture. Add tomatoes. Cover with glass lid or wax paper.

3. Microwave for 15 to 20 minutes, on SIMMER, or until meat is fork tender. Let stand, covered, 5 minutes before serving. 4 to 5 Servings

ADD-A-DESSERT: Prepare Veal Scallopini through Step 1; set aside. Place 1 package (10 oz.) frozen mixed fruit in 1½-quart glass casserole; slit pouch, and set aside. Place veal on upper rack of oven. Microwave for 10 minutes on ROAST. Combine remaining Veal Scallopini ingredients, except tomatoes, in small bowl until smooth; stir into veal mixture. Add tomatoes. Cover with glass lid. Place frozen fruit on bottom shelf. Microwave both for 10 minutes on SIMMER. Remove fruit and continue cooking veal for 5 to 10 minutes, on SIMMER, or until meat is fork tender. Let meat stand, covered, 5 minutes before serving. Serve fruit over ice cream or pound cake.

VEAL MEATBALLS IN SPICY SAUCE

Draining assures good sauce consistency.

2 tablespoons butter or margarine
2 lbs. ground veal
¼ cup dry bread crumbs
1 clove garlic, finely chopped
2 teaspoons prepared mustard
⅛ teaspoon white pepper

Spicy Sauce:
1 can (6 oz.) tomato paste
⅔ cup water
½ cup wine vinegar
¼ cup lemon juice
2 tablespoons Worcestershire sauce
½ cup packed brown sugar
1 teaspoon dry mustard
1 teaspoon salt
¼ teaspoon chili powder

1. Place butter in 2-quart (12 x 7) glass baking dish.

2. Microwave for about 1 minute, on ROAST, or until melted. Combine remaining meatball ingredients in medium mixing bowl. Shape into 18 (1-inch) balls and place in melted butter. Cover with wax paper.

3. Microwave for 8 minutes on ROAST. Drain; pour Spicy Sauce over meatballs. Recover and continue cooking for 8 to 10 minutes, on ROAST, or until meat is well done in center. Let stand, covered, 5 minutes before serving.

4. **Spicy Sauce:** Combine sauce ingredients in 4-cup glass measure, mix well.

4 to 6 Servings

ADD-A-VEGETABLE: Prepare Veal Meatballs in Spicy Sauce through Step 2; set aside. Place 2 packages (10 oz. each) frozen cauliflower in 2-quart glass casserole and cover with glass lid. Place meatballs on upper rack of oven and cauliflower on bottom shelf. Microwave both for 8 minutes on HIGH. Drain meatballs; pour Spicy Sauce over meatballs and recover. Stir cauliflower and continue cooking both for 14 to 16 minutes on HIGH. Let both stand, covered, 5 minutes before serving.

LIVER, BACON AND ONIONS

4 slices bacon
2 medium onions, sliced
1 lb. baby beef liver, sliced
Salt
Pepper

1. Arrange bacon in single layer in 2-quart (12 x 7) glass baking dish.

2. Microwave for 4 to 4½ minutes, on HIGH, or until crisp. Remove bacon; set aside. Coat liver slices with bacon drippings; arrange in baking dish. Add onions. Cover with wax paper.

3. Microwave for 14 to 16 minutes, on SIMMER, or until meat loses pink color. Crumble bacon over top. Let stand, covered, 5 minutes before serving.

About 4 Servings

ADD-A-VEGETABLE: Prepare Liver, Bacon and Onions through Step 2; set aside. Place 1 can (16 oz.) cut green beans, undrained, in 1-quart glass casserole; cover with glass lid. Place liver on upper rack of oven and vegetable on lower rack. Microwave both for 20 to 22 minutes, on SIMMER, or until meat loses pink color. Let both stand, covered, 5 minutes before serving.

CURRIED KIDNEY

SIMMER setting retains kidney flavor and texture.

1 to 1½ lbs. beef kidney, trimmed and cut into small pieces
1 medium onion, chopped
2 tablespoons cornstarch
1 can (13¾ oz.) chicken broth
2 teaspoons curry powder
⅛ teaspoon pepper
Hot cooked rice

1. Wash kidney and place, with onion, in 2-quart glass casserole. Combine remaining ingredients, except hot cooked rice, in small bowl until smooth. Pour over kidney. Cover with glass lid or wax paper.

2. Microwave for 10 minutes on SIMMER. Stir and continue cooking for 10 to 12 minutes, on SIMMER, or until meat loses pink color. Let stand, covered, 5 minutes before serving over hot rice.

4 to 6 Servings

SAVORY VENISON CHOPS

6 venison chops (1½ to 2 lbs.)
1 medium onion, finely chopped
¼ cup chopped celery
¼ cup chopped green pepper
¼ cup chili sauce
¼ cup dry sherry or water
1 teaspoon salt
¼ teaspoon pepper

1. Place chops, onion, celery and green pepper in 2-quart (12 x 7) glass baking dish. Cover with wax paper.

2. Microwave for 10 minutes on HIGH. Drain. Combine remaining ingredients in small bowl; mix well, and pour over chops. Recover and continue cooking for 30 to 35 minutes, on SIMMER, or until fork tender. Let stand, covered, 5 minutes before serving.

3 to 4 Servings

Pastas, Rice & Cereals

Steaming-Hot–
Reheat without Drying

Here's How — and Why

Microwave Tender Rice and Pastas on HIGH/SIMMER: Rice and pastas are the old-fashioned convenience foods that store easily — cook with little effort. Microwave rice or pasta by bringing water, salt and fat to a full, rolling boil on HIGH, then stir in the rice or pasta and microwave on SIMMER to gently rehydrate these dried foods to a light, tender texture. Note that hot tap water comes to a boil fastest — and a small amount of fat added to the water prevents bubble-overs. Wild rice cooks most tender when presoaked two hours before cooking.

Rehydrate Quick-Cooking Rice in a Serving Bowl: Bring water, salt and fat to a boil on HIGH in a glass serving bowl without gold, silver or other metal trim. Stir in quick-cooking rice, cover dish and let stand as package directs. Really simple!

Heat Cooked Rice and Pasta on REHEAT: Microwave cooked rice and pasta in covered dishes until steaming hot on REHEAT setting. If the rice or pasta have been refrigerated, stir once during heating. Thaw 1 cup frozen cooked rice for 5 to 6 minutes on DEFROST.

If a Mixture Contains Cooked Rice or Pasta and Sensitive Ingredients, Use ROAST: When cooked rice or pasta recipes call for sensitive ingredients, such as eggs, cheese, mushrooms, cream, yogurt, sour cream or mayonnaise, microwave on ROAST setting.

Cook in Untrimmed Glass: Cook rice in glass casseroles or serving dishes without metal trim. Since rice expands 2 to 3 times during cooking, use a bowl that's large enough for both rice and bubbling water. Cook pastas in glass casseroles or baking dishes which are large enough so pasta can be covered with water.

Use a Cover: Cover rice and pasta during microwave cooking. Use a glass lid and tip it away from arm when removing, or cover with wax paper. Plastic wrap may be used as a cover. Pierce it and allow steam to escape before removing from hot food.

Rice Needs a Standing Time, Pasta Doesn't: Let rice stand 5 minutes, covered, before serving to absorb moisture and fluff. Toss cooked rice as little as possible so it does not mush. Test to see if pasta is tender before draining; then drain, rinse in hot water and serve.

Microwave Individual Cereal Servings on HIGH: A microwave oven does a great job on quick-cooking or instant cereals in individual glass or pottery serving bowls which do not have gold, silver or other metal trim. Use cereals such as oatmeal, creamy wheat cereal or instant grits. Microwave cereal, water and seasonings on HIGH — and let stand a few minutes to complete cooking. See chart.

Check for the " ✱ ": The " ✱ " at the end of a recipe title or chart item is a reminder that the food cooks at two or more power settings — this is a convenient place to stir, when necessary.

Microwave-Conventional Comparison: There is minimal time saving when cooking rice, pasta or cereal in a microwave oven. However, reheated rice dishes stay fluffier and moister than with conventional reheating. Rice and pasta do not overcook easily, so do not stick to dish bottom. Instant and quick-cooking cereals are conveniently cooked in individual serving bowls. No sticky pans to wash.

Pictured: Buttered Noodles sprinkled with Parmesan cheese, chart, page 118.

HOW TO COOK RICE

- Choose a glass cooking dish two to three times larger than the amount of dry rice to be cooked — rice expands during cooking.
- Add salt as package directs and 1 tablespoon butter or margarine to water for raw rice.
- Bring water and seasonings to a full rolling boil on Microwave HIGH.
- Stir in raw rice and microwave on SIMMER.
- Always cook rice covered. Use a fitted glass lid or dinner plate.
- Let cooked rice stand, covered, 5 minutes after being removed from the oven.
- Cook quick-cooking rice in a glass or pottery serving casserole without silver, gold or other metal trim. Boil water with ½ teaspoon salt and 1½ teaspoons butter or margarine on Microwave HIGH. Stir in quick-cooking rice; cover, and let stand as directed on package.

RICE	COVERED GLASS CASSEROLE	WATER	FIRST SETTING AND TIME	RICE	SECOND SETTING AND TIME
SHORT GRAIN WHITE *	2-qt.	2 cups	HIGH 4 to 5 min.	1 cup	SIMMER 13 to 15 min.
LONG GRAIN WHITE *	2-qt.	2 cups	HIGH 4 to 5 min.	1 cup	SIMMER 15 to 17 min.
WHITE AND WILD MIX *	2-qt.	2½ cups water; add rice and seasonings as package directs	HIGH 5 min.	6-oz. pkg.	SIMMER 20 to 25 min.
BROWN *	3-qt.	3 cups	HIGH 6 to 7 min.	1 cup	SIMMER 35 to 40 min.
WILD RICE, * soaked	3-qt.	3 cups	HIGH 6 to 7 min.	1 cup raw (2 cups soaked)	SIMMER 35 to 40 min.
QUICK-COOKING WHITE	1-qt.	1 cup	HIGH 3 to 4 min.	1 cup	Rest, covered, 5 min. or until all water absorbs
QUICK-COOKING WHITE AND WILD MIX *	2-qt.	2 cups water; add rice as package directs	HIGH 6 to 7 min.	6¼-oz. pkg.	SIMMER 2½ to 3 min.
QUICK-COOKING SEASONED RICE MIX	2-qt.	1 cup water; add rice and seasonings as package directs	HIGH 7 to 8 min.	6-oz. pkg.	Rest, covered, 10 min. or until all water absorbs

HOW TO COOK PASTAS

- Bring water, 1 tablespoon cooking oil and 1 teaspoon salt to a full rolling boil in a 3-quart covered glass casserole on Microwave HIGH. Hot tap water boils fastest.
- Stir in pasta and recover with fitted glass lid or plastic wrap. Pierce plastic wrap before removing and allow steam to escape.
- Microwave on SIMMER. Test for tenderness.
- Drain, rinse with hot water and serve.

PASTA	COVERED GLASS CONTAINER	WATER	FIRST SETTING AND TIME	PASTA	SECOND SETTING AND TIME
SPAGHETTI *	3-qt. casserole	4 cups	HIGH 8 to 10 min.	7-oz. pkg.	SIMMER 8 to 10 min.
MACARONI *	3-qt. casserole	3 cups	HIGH 6 to 8 min.	2 cups	SIMMER 10 to 12 min.
EGG NOODLES *	3-qt. casserole	6 cups	HIGH 10 to 12 min.	4 cups	SIMMER 10 to 12 min.
LASAGNA NOODLES *	3-qt. (13 x 9) baking dish	6 cups	HIGH 10 to 12 min.	8-oz. pkg.	SIMMER 12 to 14 min.

HOW TO PREPARE PASTA OR RICE MIXES

- When preparing pasta or rice box dinner mixes, pour water in glass casserole; cover, and microwave on HIGH until water boils.
- Stir in pasta or rice and seasonings.
- Cover with fitted glass lid or plastic wrap.
- Microwave pastas on SIMMER.
- Follow package directions for dry sauce mixes. Microwave on SIMMER.
- Warm canned sauces in packaged mixes on REHEAT.
- Serve foods directly from the oven.
- If adding 1 lb. crumbled ground beef to a sauce, microwave meat first for 5 to 6 minutes on HIGH.

DEHYDRATED PASTA AND SEASONING MIXES	COVERED GLASS CASSEROLE	WATER	FIRST SETTING AND TIME	PASTA AND SEASONING MIX	SECOND SETTING AND TIME
MACARONI AND CHEESE *	2-qt.	2 cups	HIGH 4 to 5 min.	7¼-oz. pkg.	SIMMER 10 to 12 min.
SPAGHETTI BOX DINNER:					
Spaghetti *	3-qt.	4 cups	HIGH 7 to 8 min.	8-oz. pkg.	SIMMER, 10 to 12 min.
Sauce Mix *	1-qt.	As pkg. directs			SIMMER, 5 to 6 min.
Spaghetti *	3-qt.	4 cups	HIGH 7 to 8 min.	19½-oz. pkg.	SIMMER 10 to 12 min.
Sauce	1-qt.		REHEAT 4 to 5 min.		
SEASONED RICE AND MACARONI MIX *	2-qt.	2 cups (add rice mix)	HIGH 4 to 5 min.	6 to 8-oz. pkg.	SIMMER 13 to 15 min.

HOW TO PREPARE CANNED PASTA

- Remove all processed food from cans and place in glass casserole.
- Cover with fitted glass lid or wax paper.
- Microwave on REHEAT. Stir once during cooking.

CANNED PASTA	SIZE	COVERED GLASS CASSEROLE	SETTING AND TIME
SPAGHETTI	14¾-oz.	1-qt.	REHEAT 3 to 4 min.
MACARONI AND CHEESE	14¾-oz.	1-qt.	REHEAT 3 to 4 min.
MEAT AND NOODLES IN SAUCE	15-oz.	1-qt.	REHEAT 4 to 6 min.

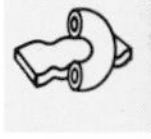

Pictured: Rice Supper Dish, below, garnished with parsley.

RICE SUPPER DISH *

- **¼ cup butter or margarine**
- **⅓ cup chopped onion**
- **½ cup chopped celery**
- **3 cups cooked rice**
- **4 to 5 pre-cooked smoky-flavored breakfast sausage links, sliced**
- **2 medium tomatoes, sliced**

Cook rice as directed on page 118.

1. Place butter, onion and celery in 2-quart glass casserole.
2. Microwave for 3 to 4 minutes, on HIGH, or until vegetables are partly cooked. Stir in rice and sausage. Cover with glass lid.
3. Microwave for 4 to 5 minutes, on REHEAT, or until hot (about 150° F.). Garnish with tomato slices.

4 to 6 Servings

HOW TO MICROWAVE QUICK-COOKING OR INSTANT CEREALS (such as oatmeal or grits)

- Measure water, salt and cereal into individual serving bowls; mix well.
- Microwave on HIGH as directed in chart.
- Stir after cooking.
- Let stand 1 to 2 minutes before serving.

FRUITED CEREALS

Measure water, salt and cereal into individual cereal bowls. Stir in 2 tablespoons of one of the following: raisins, cut-up dry apricots, cut-up dates, cut-up pitted prunes. Cook as directed in cereal chart.

CEREAL TOPPINGS

Garnish and flavor each bowl of cooked cereal with 2 tablespoons of one of the following: applesauce, brown sugar, jam, marmalade, honey, maple syrup or cinnamon.

SERVINGS	WATER	SALT	CEREAL	SETTING AND TIME
1	¾ cup	¼ tsp.	⅓ cup	HIGH 2 to 2½ min.
2	¾ cup each	¼ tsp. ea.	⅓ cup ea.	HIGH 2½ to 3 min.
4	¾ cup each	¼ tsp. ea.	⅓ cup ea.	HIGH 5½ to 6 min.

ITALIAN RICE *

1½ cups water
1 can (10½ oz.) condensed vegetable soup without noodles
1 can (6 oz.) tomato paste
¼ cup finely chopped onion
1 teaspoon salt
1 teaspoon sugar
½ teaspoon sweet basil leaves
¼ teaspoon garlic powder
1 can (4 oz.) mushroom stems and pieces, drained
⅔ cup long grain raw white rice

1. Combine all ingredients, except mushrooms and rice, in 2-quart glass casserole. Cover with glass lid.

2. Microwave for about 5 minutes, on HIGH, or until boiling. Stir in mushrooms and rice, recover.

3. Microwave for 30 to 35 minutes, on SIMMER, or until rice is tender. Let stand, covered, 5 minutes before serving. About 6 Servings

RECIPE VARIATION

SPANISH RICE: Substitute 1 can (16 oz.) whole tomatoes, ¼ cup chopped celery and ½ teaspoon oregano leaves for soup, basil and mushrooms.

RICE PILAF

3 tablespoons butter or margarine
⅓ cup chopped onion
⅓ cup chopped green pepper
⅓ cup shredded carrot
1 cup water
1½ teaspoons instant chicken bouillon
¼ teaspoon salt
¼ teaspoon poultry seasoning
Dash pepper
1 cup quick-cooking rice

1. Combine all ingredients, except rice, in 2-quart glass casserole. Cover with glass lid.

2. Microwave for 5 to 6 minutes, on HIGH, or until boiling. Stir in rice; recover. Rest, covered, 5 minutes or until all water is absorbed. Stir and serve. 4 to 6 Servings

RECIPE VARIATIONS

BROWN RICE PILAF: Omit water, bouillon and quick-cooking rice. Place butter, onion, green pepper and carrot in 2-quart glass casserole. Microwave for 3 to 4 minutes, on HIGH, or until vegetables are partly cooked. Stir in seasonings, 2 cups cooked brown rice, 2 tablespoons chopped pimento and 1 tablespoon soy sauce. Microwave, covered, for 3 to 4 minutes, on REHEAT, or until hot (about 150° F.).

CONFETTI RICE: Omit green pepper, carrot and poultry seasoning. Add 1 package (10 oz.) frozen peas and carrots and 2 teaspoons dried parsley flakes with water in basic recipe. Microwave for 9 to 10 minutes, on HIGH, or until boiling. Increase rice by ½ cup. Stir in rice and continue as directed in basic recipe.

APPLE RICE *

This sweeter rice dish is especially good with duckling and wild game.

4 green onions, sliced
½ cup chopped celery
1 cup apple juice
1 cup water
2 tablespoons butter or margarine
1 teaspoon onion salt
¼ teaspoon cinnamon
1 cup raw white rice
1 medium apple, chopped

1. Combine all ingredients, except rice and apple, in 2-quart glass casserole. Cover with glass lid.

2. Microwave for 6 to 7 minutes, on HIGH, or until boiling. Stir in rice; recover.

3. Microwave for 18 to 20 minutes, on SIMMER, or until rice is tender. Stir in apples; recover.

4. Microwave for 1 to 2 minutes, on REHEAT, or until hot (about 150° F.).

6 to 8 Servings

CHEESY NOODLES

Thaw spinach 6 minutes on DEFROST.

1 carton (8 oz.) sour cream
1 jar (8 oz.) process cheese spread
1 teaspoon onion salt
¼ teaspoon garlic powder
⅛ teaspoon pepper
4 cups cooked egg noodles
1 package (10 oz.) frozen chopped spinach, thawed and drained

1. Combine all ingredients, except noodles and spinach, in 3-quart glass casserole. Stir in noodles and spinach. Cover with glass lid.

2. Microwave for 12 to 14 minutes, on ROAST, or until hot (about 150° F.). Stir to blend. Let stand, covered, 3 minutes before serving.

About 8 Servings

MACARONI AND CHEESE

1 package (7 oz.) macaroni, cooked
1 can (11 oz.) condensed Cheddar cheese soup
1 cup shredded process American cheese
3 green onions, sliced
Salt
Pepper
½ cup milk

1. Place half of cooked macaroni in 2-quart glass casserole. Spoon half of cheese soup over macaroni; sprinkle with half of shredded cheese, green onions. Season with salt and pepper. Repeat layers; pour milk over top. Cover with glass lid.

2. Microwave for 13 to 15 minutes, on ROAST, or until heated through (about 150° F.). Let stand, covered, 3 minutes before serving.

4 to 6 Servings

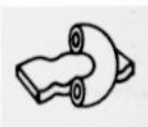

SPICY SPAGHETTI

SIMMER setting blends sauce flavors.

1 lb. ground beef
1 package (12 oz.) bulk pork sausage
½ cup chopped onion
1 clove garlic, finely chopped
1 can (32 oz.) tomato juice
2 cans (6 oz. each) tomato paste
1 tablespoon sugar
1 tablespoon dried parsley flakes
1 teaspoon salt
½ teaspoon ground oregano
¼ teaspoon pepper
Cooked spaghetti
Grated Parmesan cheese

1. Crumble ground beef and sausage into 3-quart glass casserole. Stir in onion and garlic; cover with glass lid.

2. Microwave for 10 minutes on HIGH; drain. Stir in remaining ingredients, except spaghetti and cheese; recover.

3. Microwave for 30 to 35 minutes, on SIMMER, or until hot (about 160° F.). Serve on hot spaghetti; top with Parmesan cheese.

About 8 Servings

RICE YIELDS

1 cup raw white rice = 3 cups cooked rice
1 cup raw brown rice = 4 cups cooked rice
1 cup raw wild rice = 3½ cups cooked rice
1 cup quick-cooking rice = 2 cups cooked rice

PASTA YIELDS

1 package (7 oz.) spaghetti = 4 cups cooked
1 package (7 oz.) macaroni = 4 cups cooked
4 cups egg noodles = 4 cups cooked

Pies

Light, Flaky Crusts Hold Juicy Fruit or Creamy Custards

Here's How — and Why

Pastry and Crumb Crusts Microwave on ROAST: Light-colored, tender pastry shells made with water, and cookie or cracker crumb crusts microwave in a jiffy on ROAST. Pastry shells and crumb crusts must be baked before a filling is added for microwave cooking or refrigeration. Microwave pastry shells that are homemade, made from a mix or frozen, ready-to-bake, in glass pie plates. Remove frozen commercial shells from metal pans before thawing and place in a glass pie plate to thaw; then microwave. Prick pastry shells before cooking. Cool crusts before filling.

Microwave One-Crust Custard Pies on SIMMER: Custard fillings, such as pumpkin or pecan, can be microwaved in baked pie shells. Use SIMMER setting because custard fillings contain eggs which need gentle cooking to prevent curdling and separation.

Open-Face Fruit Pies Microwave on HIGH: One-crust fruit pies, with filling poured into a baked crust, microwave very well on the HIGH setting which cooks the fruit quickly. Sprinkle sugar-butter topping over fruit for flavor and appearance.

Speed-Cook Two-Crust Pies on Microwave HIGH; Brown in a Conventional Oven: Two-crust fruit pies are an outstanding time-saver using both a microwave and conventional oven. Bake either homemade or frozen commercial pies using this technique. Start heating and cooking pies on Microwave HIGH; complete cooking in preheated 425° F. conventional oven to brown.

Pie Fillings Cook on HIGH, Unless Eggs Are Added, then Use Roast: Many pie fillings are cooked, then poured into baked crusts and cooled or refrigerated before serving. Fillings thickened with gelatin, cornstarch or marshmallows microwave on HIGH — but if, or when, eggs are added filling must cook on ROAST to prevent curdling.

Warm Baked Fruit Pie on REHEAT, Custard Pie on ROAST: Enjoy a warm piece of your favorite pie easily and quickly. Slip either whole pies or individual servings into the microwave oven and warm — fruit pies on REHEAT, custard pies on ROAST. See convenience food chart, page 27, for specific directions.

Always Microwave Pies, Uncovered, in Glass Pie Plates: Any time a pastry shell or filled pie goes into a microwave oven it must be in a glass pie plate which allows microwaves to pass through it and cook from all sides. Do not cover pies during baking. Fillings, microwaved separately, are cooked in glass mixing bowls or glass measures.

Standing Time is Especially Important to Custard Pies: Standing time, after pies come from a microwave oven, completes cooking. This time is especially crucial to custard pies which should come from the oven while the center is still slightly moist, thus avoiding overcooked edges or curdling. Custard center will set during standing time specified in recipes.

You Can ADD-A-PIE While Other Foods Cook: This microwave oven's larger size and unique microwave cooking capabilities let you cook several foods at once. See how to ADD-A-PIE to a meat or a complete meal by referring to Meal Variations on page 184.

Microwave-Conventional Comparison: One-crust pies cook well in a microwave oven in precooked shells. The microwave-conventional technique for two-crust fruit pies is a great time-saver and produces a juicy filling and brown, flaky crust — a homemade, two-crust, 9-inch pie cooks in less than 20 minutes. Since microwaves cook from all sides, custard fillings cook evenly without scorching. Baked pie reheats well — either whole or in individual pieces. Microwaved pastry crusts are tender and flaky, but do not brown.

Pictured: Orange Chiffon Pie, page 127, garnished with whipped cream and orange twist.

BAKED PASTRY SHELL

Transfer Frozen Pastry Shells to glass pie plate, then thaw and bake.

½ package (11 oz.) pie crust mix or favorite pie crust recipe

1. Prepare pie crust mix or pie crust recipe as directed on package or in recipe. Line 9-inch glass pie plate. Flute edge; prick bottom and sides of crust with fork.

2. Microwave for 6 to 6½ minutes, on ROAST, or until brown spots just begin to appear in crust. Cool. 9-Inch Pastry Shell

TIP: To enhance crust color, mix 1 or 2 drops of yellow food coloring into water before adding it to dry ingredients.

CHOCOLATE CRUMB CRUST

Crumb crusts are excellent on Microwave ROAST.

¼ cup butter or margarine
2 tablespoons sugar
1¼ cups crushed chocolate wafers (about 20 wafers)

1. Place butter in 9-inch round glass pie plate.

2. Microwave for about 1 minute, on ROAST, or until melted. Stir in remaining ingredients; mix well. Press into bottom and up sides of 9-inch pie plate.

3. Microwave for 1 to 1½ minutes, on ROAST, or until set. Cool before filling. 9-Inch Crumb Crust

TIP: 9-inch glass pie plate may vary in volume; add another ¼ cup crumbs, if necessary.

RECIPE VARIATIONS

VANILLA CRUMB CRUST: Substitute 1¼ cups crushed vanilla wafers (about 30) for chocolate wafers.

GINGER CRUMB CRUST: Substitute 1¼ cups crushed gingersnaps (about 30) for chocolate wafers.

GRAHAM CRUMB CRUST: Substitute 1¼ cups graham crackers, (about 11 rectangles) crushed, for chocolate wafers.

MINCEMEAT PIE

HIGH setting quickly cooks fruit fillings.

1 can (16 oz.) sliced peaches, drained
1 jar (28 oz.) prepared mincemeat
1 (9-inch) Baked Pastry Shell in glass pie plate, page 124

Topping:
½ cup whipping cream
2 tablespoons powdered sugar
½ teaspoon cinnamon

1. Drain peaches well on paper towels. Pour mincemeat into shell; top with peach slices arranged in pinwheel fashion. Push peach slices slightly down into mincemeat.

2. Microwave for 18 to 22 minutes, on HIGH, or until almost set in center. Serve with dollop of Topping.

3. Topping: Whip cream; beat in remaining ingredients. 9-Inch Pie

SHOO-FLY PIE

High sugar content of this pie requires gentle SIMMER cooking.

¾ cup water
½ cup dark molasses
¾ teaspoon soda
¼ teaspoon salt
1 (9-inch) Baked Pastry Shell in glass pie plate, page 124

TOPPING:
1½ cups unsifted all-purpose flour
¾ cup packed brown sugar
½ teaspoon cinnamon
½ cup butter or margarine

1. Measure water into 2-cup glass measure.

2. Microwave for about 2½ minutes, on HIGH, or until boiling (about 200° F.). Stir in remaining pie ingredients, except Baked Pastry Shell. Pour ⅓ of molasses mixture into shell; sprinkle ⅓ of Topping over molasses. Repeat twice.

3. Microwave for 14 to 16 minutes, on SIMMER, or until set. Cool slightly before serving.

4. Topping: Combine dry ingredients in medium mixing bowl; cut in butter. 9-Inch Pie

RHUBARB CUSTARD PIE

Thaw frozen rhubarb for 7 to 9 minutes on DEFROST.

- **2 eggs, slightly beaten**
- **¼ cup light cream**
- **1¼ cups sugar**
- **2 tablespoons all-purpose flour**
- **½ teaspoon cinnamon**
- **½ teaspoon nutmeg**
- **3 cups frozen rhubarb, thawed and chopped**
- **1 (9-inch) Baked Pastry Shell in glass pie plate, page 124**

1. Combine all ingredients, except rhubarb and Baked Pastry Shell, in medium mixing bowl; beat with rotary beater until smooth. Stir in rhubarb; pour into shell.

2. Microwave for 30 to 32 minutes, on SIMMER, or until almost set in center. Let cool and set before serving. 9-Inch Pie

PUMPKIN PIE

Remove custard pies from oven when center looks slightly moist.

- **3 eggs**
- **1 cup packed brown sugar**
- **2 tablespoons all-purpose flour**
- **½ teaspoon salt**
- **2 teaspoons pumpkin pie spice**
- **1 can (16 oz.) mashed cooked pumpkin**
- **1 cup milk**
- **1 (9-inch) Baked Ginger Crumb Crust in glass pie plate, page 124**

1. Combine all ingredients, except baked crust, in medium mixing bowl; beat until smooth and pour into crust.

2. Microwave for 35 to 40 minutes, on SIMMER, or until almost set in center. Let cool and set before serving. 9-Inch Pie

TIP: Extra filling can be cooked separately in individual custard cups.

SIMMER setting microwaves custard pies without overcooking.

PECAN PIE

- **3 tablespoons butter or margarine**
- **3 eggs, slightly beaten**
- **1 cup dark corn syrup**
- **¼ cup packed brown sugar**
- **1½ teaspoons all-purpose flour**
- **1 teaspoon vanilla**
- **1½ cups pecan halves**
- **1 (9-inch) Baked Pastry Shell in glass pie plate, page 124**

1. Place butter in medium glass mixing bowl.

2. Microwave for about 1 minute, on ROAST, or until melted. Stir in remaining ingredients, except Baked Pastry Shell; mix well; pour filling into shell.

3. Microwave for 20 to 25 minutes, on SIMMER, or until almost set in center. Let cool and set before serving. 9-Inch Pie

Pictured: Pecan Pie, recipe at right.

RUBY RED STRAWBERRY PIE

- **¾ cup sugar**
- **3 tablespoons cornstarch**
- **½ cup water**
- **1 package (10 oz.) frozen sliced strawberries, thawed**
- **1 quart fresh strawberries, washed and hulled**
- **1 (9-inch) Baked Pastry Shell, page 124**
- **Whipped cream, if desired**

See convenience food chart, page 25 to thaw frozen fruit.

1. Combine sugar, cornstarch and water in large glass mixing bowl until smooth; stir in strawberries and juice.

2. Microwave for 2 minutes on HIGH. Stir and continue cooking for 2 to 3 minutes, on HIGH, or until thickened (about 190° F.). Cool. Fold whole strawberries into glaze mixture. Pour into baked pastry shell. Chill. Serve with whipped cream. 9-Inch Pie

TIP: Tip whole berries, point-up, for an easy-cutting attractive pie.

RECIPE VARIATION

GLAZED BLUEBERRY PEACH PIE: Substitute 3 cups peeled and sliced fresh peaches and 1 cup fresh blueberries for 1 quart fresh strawberries. Substitute 1 package (10 oz.) frozen sliced peaches, thawed, for strawberries.

FRESH FRUIT PIE

- **1 fresh homemade 2-crust fruit pie, uncooked**

See convenience chart, page 27, for baking frozen, 2-crust pie.

1. Preheat conventional oven to 425° F. Prepare favorite recipe for 2-crust fresh fruit pie. Assemble in 9-inch glass pie plate.

2. Microwave for 7 to 8 minutes, on HIGH, or until juices start bubbling through slits in pie crust. Transfer to preheated 425° F. conventional oven and bake 8 to 10 minutes or until golden brown. 9-Inch Pie

TIP: Microwave a 2-crust 8-inch pie for 6 to 7 minutes; 10-inch pie 8 to 9 minutes.

COUNTRY APPLE PIE

- **6 cups apples, peeled, cored and sliced (about 8 apples)**
- **⅔ cup sugar**
- **¼ cup unsifted all-purpose flour**
- **1 teaspoon cinnamon**
- **Dash salt**
- **1 (9-inch) Baked Pastry Shell in glass pie plate, page 124**
- **¼ cup sliced almonds, if desired**

Topping:

- **¼ cup unsifted all-purpose flour**
- **¼ cup packed brown sugar**
- **2 tablespoons butter or margarine**

One-crust fruit pies are delicious topped with a dollop of whipped cream.

1. Place apples in medium mixing bowl. Combine sugar, flour, cinnamon and salt; mix with apples. Place coated apples in baked pastry shell; sprinkle with Topping.

2. Microwave for 12 to 14 minutes, on HIGH, or until apples are fork tender. Top with sliced almonds. Cool before serving.

3. Topping: Combine flour and brown sugar in small bowl; cut in butter until crumbly. 9-Inch Pie

RECIPE VARIATIONS

CHERRY PIE: Substitute 1 can (21 oz.) cherry pie filling for apples, sugar, flour and salt. Add 1 tsp. grated orange rind to Topping. Microwave for 5 to 7 minutes, on HIGH, or until almost set.

SOUR CREAM BLUEBERRY PIE: Substitute 1 package (16 oz.) unsweetened frozen blueberries, partially thawed, or 3 cups fresh blueberries, 1 carton (8 oz.) sour cream, and 1 egg, beaten, for apples. Omit Topping. Microwave for 24 to 26 minutes on ROAST, or until almost set in center. Let stand 5 minutes. Cool.

PEACH PIE: Substitute 5 cups peeled and sliced fresh peaches or 5 cups frozen sliced peaches, thawed and well drained, for apples. Increase flour to ⅓ cup, substitute ¼ teaspoon nutmeg for cinnamon. Add 3 tablespoons orange-flavored liqueur and ½ teaspoon almond extract when mixing peaches with flour mixture.

BANANA CREAM PIE

Fillings with sensitive ingredients cook on ROAST.

1½ cups milk
⅔ cup sugar
3 tablespoons cornstarch
¼ teaspoon salt
4 egg yolks, slightly beaten
1 tablespoon butter or margarine
1 teaspoon vanilla
2 bananas, sliced
1 tablespoon lemon juice
1 (9-inch) Baked Pastry Shell in glass pie plate, page 124
Banana slices, if desired

1. Combine milk, sugar, cornstarch and salt in medium mixing bowl; beat with rotary beater until smooth.

2. Microwave for 4 minutes on HIGH. Beat well and continue cooking for about 1 minute, on HIGH, or until thickened (about 180° F.); beat well. Beat eggs and a small amount of hot milk in small bowl; beat into milk and sugar.

3. Microwave for 1½ to 2 minutes, on ROAST, or until thickened (about 190° F.). Stir in butter and vanilla. Place banana slices in bottom of baked pastry shell; sprinkle with lemon juice. Pour cream mixture over bananas. Chill in refrigerator until set. Garnish with additional banana slices.

9-Inch Pie

RECIPE VARIATIONS

VANILLA CREAM PIE: Omit bananas and lemon juice. Garnish with orange slices.

COCONUT CREAM PIE: Substitute 1 cup shredded coconut for bananas and fold into cream mixture with butter and vanilla. Omit lemon juice. Top with toasted coconut.

CHOCOLATE CREAM PIE: Substitute 1 package (6 oz.) real chocolate pieces for bananas and stir into cream mixture with butter and vanilla until melted. Omit lemon juice. Top pie with whipped cream and chocolate shavings, if desired.

GRASSHOPPER PIE

Substitute 1 container (4½ oz.) whipped topping for whipped cream.

3 cups miniature marshmallows
½ cup milk
2 tablespoons green crème de menthe
2 tablespoons crème de cacao
1 cup whipping cream, whipped
1 (9-inch) baked Chocolate Cookie Crumb Crust, page 124
Whipped cream, if desired
Chocolate curls, if desired

1. Combine marshmallows and milk in large glass mixing bowl.

2. Microwave for 2 to 2½ minutes, on HIGH, or until marshmallows begin to puff; stir until smooth. Stir in crème de menthe and crème de cacao; mix well. Cool about 30 minutes or until consistency of egg whites. Fold whipped cream into cream mixture. Pour into crust. Refrigerate at least 4 hours or until ready to serve. Garnish with whipped cream and chocolate curls.

9-Inch Pie

TIP: Add 4 to 5 drops green food coloring with liqueurs, if desired.

RECIPE VARIATIONS

BRANDY ALEXANDER PIE: Substitute 3 tablespoons cherry brandy for crème de menthe; decrease crème de cacao to 1 tablespoon. Garnish with whipped cream and filberts.

GALLIANO®-BANANA PIE: Substitute 2 tablespoons Galliano® liqueur and 2 tablespoons banana liqueur for crème de menthe and crème de cacao. Add 4 to 5 drops yellow food coloring with liqueurs, if desired. Garnish with banana slices.

ORANGE CHIFFON PIE

Gelatin pie filling with eggs microwave on ROAST – eggs are sensitive.

4 egg yolks
1 cup orange juice
1 envelope unflavored gelatin
½ cup sugar
¼ teaspoon salt
2 teaspoons grated orange rind
4 egg whites
¼ cup sugar
1 (9-inch) Baked Pastry Shell, page 124
Whipped cream

1. Beat egg yolks in medium glass mixing bowl. Stir in orange juice, gelatin, sugar and salt.

2. Microwave for 4 to 4½ minutes, on ROAST, or until gelatin dissolves (about 160° F.). Stir in grated orange rind. Cool until consistency of unbeaten egg whites. Beat egg whites in small mixer bowl until frothy. Gradually beat in ¼ cup sugar, beating until mixture forms stiff peaks. Fold egg whites into gelatin mixture. Pour into baked pastry shell. Refrigerate at least 4 hours. Garnish with whipped cream before serving.

9-Inch Pie

Poultry

Savory Chicken, Turkey, Goose, Duckling, Game Birds and Pheasant

Here's How — and Why

Thaw Birds Completely: Poultry must be completely thawed before cooking. See defrosting chart, page 31.

Microwave Whole or Cut-up Chicken or Game Hens on HIGH: Use HIGH setting for tender young chicken and Rock Cornish Game Hens — whole birds under 6 pounds, quarters and smaller pieces.

Stew Chicken on HIGH/SIMMER: Stew chickens first on HIGH to heat quickly; then on SIMMER to tenderize the meat with slow moist heat cooking.

Roast Turkey and Capon on HIGH/ROAST: Start microwaving turkeys weighing up to 14 pounds and capon over 6 pounds on HIGH setting to heat birds through; then on ROAST to tenderize, keep meat juicy and cook it evenly. Metal leg clip may be left in birds during cooking.

Cook Turkey Parts on ROAST: Bone-in or boneless turkey breasts and all turkey parts cook evenly and stay deliciously moist on ROAST.

Duckling, Goose and Pheasant Microwave on ROAST: Duckling and goose are fatty birds and ROAST setting keeps rendered fat from spattering during cooking. Drain fat from cooking dish part way through cooking. Pheasant, a naturally dry meat, cooks juicy, tender on ROAST.

Sauces Help Tenderize Poultry Dishes: Poultry parts tenderize well when cooked in a sauce. If sauce contains sensitive ingredients such as cream, mushrooms or cheese, use ROAST setting to prevent separation and curdling.

Microwave Poultry in Flat Glass Dishes: Whole birds and poultry pieces microwave in glass or glass ceramic baking dishes or skillets.

Place Whole Birds on a Rack: Use a microwave roasting rack in the baking dish to keep whole birds above drippings. Improvise a rack, if necessary, by criss-crossing wooden spoons or using an inverted glass saucer.

Arrange Thick Pieces at Edge of Cooking Dish — Turn When Recipe Suggests: Arrange larger pieces and thickest edges of meat at the outside of dish where microwaves penetrate first. Place pieces toward edges of the dish, leaving center open to speed cooking. Most poultry pieces and whole birds weighing 6 pounds or less do not need to be turned over during cooking. Cook this poultry with skin or breast-side-up. The following poultry is turned over once during cooking: Whole birds weighing over 6 pounds; irregular-shaped pieces, such as wings and drumsticks, pheasant halves or Rock Cornish Game Hens; pieces microwaved over rice or vegetables. When poultry is turned, begin cooking it skin or breast-side-down.

Microwave Most Whole Poultry Uncovered: Most whole poultry is cooked uncovered. Small pieces of foil reflect microwaves so may be used to cover wings, legs or top of bird if they appear to dry and start cooking too quickly. Do not allow foil to touch oven interior which causes arcing and pitting. *(Continued, next page.)*

Pictured: Early American Turkey, page 138; Apple-Sausage Stuffing, page 139.

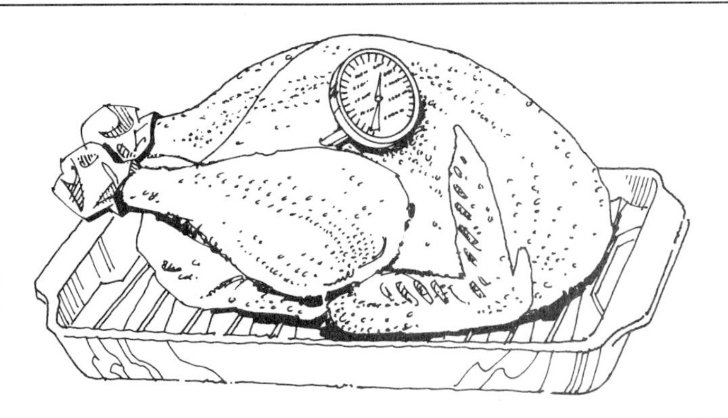

Insert microwave meat thermometer in thickest part of thigh to check doneness of whole bird.

Cover Most Cut-Up Poultry during Cooking: Cover poultry pieces during cooking unless it is crumb coated. Cover with a glass lid or wax paper. Tip cover away from arm when removing from steamy food. Plastic wrap may be used as a cover. Pierce it before removing and allow steam to escape.

Check Meat Carefully to Assure Doneness: When meat cut near the bone is no longer pink (about 180° F.), poultry is done. Check bone areas in breast and both thighs. Use a microwave meat thermometer inserted in thickest part of thigh to check doneness in whole birds. Insert it after bird is turned. Meat is done if thermometer registers 180° F. when bird comes from the oven. DO NOT use a regular meat thermometer in a microwave oven. Pop-out "doneness indicators" will not indicate proper doneness in microwave cooking, but may be left on birds during microwaving. See poultry chart in this chapter for other doneness tests.

How to "Crisp" Skin: Crisp poultry skin by placing it under a conventional oven broiler for a few minutes before standing time.

Standing Time Allows Juices to Set; Thoroughly Heats a Stuffing: Standing time is important with poultry, especially big birds, because it completes cooking and allows juices to "set" so carving is easier. Allow whole birds or pieces totaling 10 pounds or less to stand 5 to 10 minutes after removal from the oven. Poultry over 10 pounds should stand 10 to 15 minutes. Leave covering on poultry parts during standing time. Cover whole roast birds tightly with aluminum foil, dull side out, to hold heat.

Microwave Stuffing in Bird or Glass Casserole: Use stuffing recipe directions as guides to the amount of stuffing needed for various size birds. Stuff poultry just before cooking — remove stuffing right after cooking to assure quality. Cooking time may increase up to 15 minutes when larger birds are stuffed. Assemble and microwave a casserole stuffing as directed in Basic Bread Stuffing Tip.

"ADD-A-" Vegetable, Dessert or Stuffing: Microwave a vegetable, dessert or stuffing along with a dish of poultry pieces or whole poultry weighing up to 5 pounds. The HIGH setting is usually used, even when the food added contains a few sensitive ingredients. The reason? With two dishes of food in the oven, microwave intensity to each one is reduced. When foods contain a large quantity of sensitive ingredients, use ROAST. When another dish of food is cooked with a dish of larger, less tender poultry on ROAST, add the new food near the end of the poultry cooking period and leave the setting on ROAST.

How to Use the Oven Rack When Two Foods Cook: Cook poultry pieces on the upper rack. Use the lower rack for whole birds weighing 3 to 5 pounds. Place the second dish of food on the bottom shelf. Food cooks faster and more evenly if one dish is not placed directly above another.

The " * " Is a Reminder: The " * " in recipe titles reminds you that two settings are used in the recipe. Turning and/or basting are convenient at this time.

Microwave-Conventional Comparison: Poultry cooks quickly in a microwave oven — a quartered 3-pound fryer microwaves in about 20 minutes, takes about 1 hour in a conventional oven. Skin does not crisp and brown on small, fast-cooking poultry. Browning occurs on larger birds that microwave longer because natural fat under skin increases temperature. Fat spatters from rapid heating may make "popping" sounds during cooking.

HOW TO COOK POULTRY

- Poultry should be completely thawed before cooking. A 2 to 3-lb. fryer, for example, thaws in 20 to 25 minutes on DEFROST. See defrosting chart, page 31.
- Wash bird, set aside giblets, then season cavity with salt and pepper before cooking, if desired.
- Metal clip holding drumsticks may be left in place on large whole birds during cooking. Pop-out "doneness indicators" do not indicate doneness but may be left in bird during microwave cooking.
- Place large whole poultry in glass or glass ceramic baking dish; poultry pieces in glass baking dishes or skillets.
- Use a microwave roasting rack in the dish when cooking whole birds.
- Arrange pieces of poultry with thick edges toward outside of dish. As much as possible keep pieces of poultry toward the outside edges of the dish, leaving center of dish open.
- Arrange pieces of poultry skin-side-up; whole poultry breast-side-up. However, if poultry is turned, start it cooking skin or breast-side-down.
- Poultry pieces should be covered during cooking and standing time, unless a crumb coating is used or a crisper surface is desired. Use a glass lid or wax paper.
- Whole poultry is cooked uncovered.
- When two different settings are mentioned, use HIGH during first cooking period; ROAST during the second.
- Most poultry pieces and whole birds weighing 6 pounds or less do not need to be turned over half way through cooking or when setting changes during cooking. The following poultry should be turned over once during cooking: Irregular-shaped pieces such as wings, drumsticks, or pheasants cut in half; Rock Cornish Game Hens; cut-up poultry that is microwaved over rice or vegetables; whole birds over 6 pounds.
- Foil may be used to cover portions of the meat, such as wings or drumsticks, that appear to be drying and darkening during cooking. Do not allow foil to touch oven walls or microwaves will arc and pit oven surfaces.
- Doneness in all microwaved poultry is determined when meat cut near bone is no longer pink (about 180° F.). Check bone areas at both breast and thighs.
- Whole birds are done if a microwave meat thermometer in the thickest part of the thigh registers 180° F. when the bird comes from the oven. When a bird must be turned over, insert thermometer into thick part of thigh after bird is turned. DO NOT use a regular meat thermometer in a microwave oven.
- Other doneness tests: Meat and juices are no longer pink when bird is sliced between leg and body. Leg and thigh meat of small birds is tender when pinched. A conventional meat thermometer inserted in thickest part of thigh meat after bird comes from oven registers 180° F. at the end of cooking time. It is a good idea to check doneness in the breast and both thighs.
- Cooking time may increase up to 15 minutes for birds above 8 pounds.
- Poultry skin may be crisped by placing it under a 450° F. preheated conventional oven broiler for 10 to 15 minutes before standing time.
- Standing time completes cooking of poultry. Allow whole birds or pieces totaling 10 pounds or less to stand 5 to 10 minutes after being taken from oven. Poultry over 10 pounds should stand 10 to 15 minutes.
- Cover whole birds tightly with foil, dull-side-out, during standing time. Cover cut-up poultry with a glass lid or wax paper.
- Duckling and goose are fatty meats. Drain excess fat from dish during cooking to prevent spatters and burning.

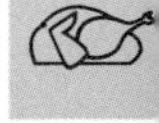

POULTRY	WEIGHT	FIRST SETTING AND TIME	SPECIAL TECHNIQUES	SECOND SETTING AND TIME
CHICKEN				
Whole, fryer	2 to 3-lb.	HIGH 7 min. per lb. (about 180° F.)	—	—
Whole, roasting	3 to 4-lb.	HIGH 8 min. per lb. (about 180° F.)	—	—
Quartered	2 to 3-lb.	HIGH 7 min. per lb. (about 180° F.)	—	—
Parts	1 to 2-lb.	HIGH 7 min. per lb. (about 180° F.)	Turn over wings and drumsticks	—
TURKEY				
Whole *	8 to 10-lb.	HIGH 5 min. per lb.	Turn over	ROAST 4 min. per lb. (about 180° F.)
	10 to 14-lb.	HIGH 5 min. per lb.	Turn over	ROAST 4 min. per lb. (about 180° F.)
Breast, bone-in *	4 to 5-lb.	HIGH 7 min. per lb.	Turn over	ROAST 7 min. per lb. (about 180° F.)
Parts	2 to 3-lb.	ROAST 15 min. per lb. (about 180° F.)	Turn over wings and drumsticks	—

(Continued, next page.)

CAPON Whole *	6 to 8-lb.	HIGH 4 min. per lb.	Turn over	ROAST 3 min. per lb. (about 180° F.)
DUCKLING Whole	4 to 5-lb.	ROAST 9 min. per lb. (about 180° F.)	—	—
GOOSE Whole	9 to 11-lb.	ROAST 9 min. per lb. (about 180° F.)	Turn over	—
PHEASANT Whole	2 to 3-lb.	ROAST 8 min. per lb. (about 180° F.)	—	—
ROCK CORNISH GAME HEN Whole	4 (1-lb. ea.)	HIGH 8 min. per lb. (about 180° F.)	Turn over	—

HOW TO COOK A FEW CHICKEN PIECES

- Microwave 1 tablespoon butter in glass pie plate or flat glass baking dish for about 1 minute, on ROAST, or until melted.
- Roll chicken piece in melted butter, then in seasoned dry bread crumbs.
- Place chicken, skin-side-up, in glass pie plate or flat baking dish.
- Microwave on HIGH until fork tender (about 180° F.). These times may also be used for chicken cooked without a crumb coating.

CHICKEN PIECE	WEIGHT	SETTING	TIME
1 WING OR DRUMSTICK	4-oz.	HIGH	2 to 2½ min. (about 180° F.)
1 THIGH OR BREAST	5 to 6-oz.	HIGH	2½ to 3 min. (about 180° F.)
3 INDIVIDUAL PIECES Assorted	14-oz.	HIGH	5 to 5½ min. (about 180° F.)
1 QUARTER	10-oz.	HIGH	4 to 4½ min. (about 180° F.)
2 QUARTERS	1½-lb.	HIGH	9 to 10 min. (about 180° F.)

BLACKBERRY ROAST CAPON *

7½ to 8-lb. whole capon
Basic Bread Stuffing, page 139

Blackberry Basting Sauce:
1 cup blackberry wine
1 tablespoon cornstarch
2 tablespoons cooking oil
1 tablespoon snipped chives, if desired
½ teaspoon salt

Microwave roasting rack holds bird above pan juices.

1. Wash capon; set aside giblets. Fill neck opening and body cavity with stuffing. Secure openings with toothpicks or metal skewers. Tie legs together and wings to body. Place capon, breast-side-down on microwave roasting rack, in 2-quart (12 x 7) glass baking dish. Brush with ½ of Blackberry Basting Sauce.

2. Microwave for 30 minutes on HIGH. Turn capon over; brush with remaining sauce, and continue cooking for 30 to 35 minutes, on ROAST, or until meat cut near bone is no longer pink (about 180° F.). Let stand, covered with foil, 10 minutes before serving.

3. **Blackberry Basting Sauce:** Combine wine and cornstarch in 4-cup glass measure; beat with rotary beater until smooth. Add remaining ingredients.

4. Microwave for 2 minutes on HIGH. Beat and continue cooking for 2 to 3 minutes or until thickened (about 180° F.). Beat lightly. 8 to 10 Servings

CRANBERRY ROAST CHICKEN

Cook plain roasting chicken as directed in chart, page 131.

5 to 5½-lb. frozen whole roasting chicken, thawed
Salt
Pepper

Cranberry Sauce:
2 tablespoons butter or margarine
1 can (8 oz.) jellied cranberry sauce
2 tablespoons orange juice
2 teaspoons grated orange rind
½ teaspoon onion salt

1. Wash chicken; set aside giblets. Sprinkle body cavity with salt and pepper. Tie chicken legs together and wings to body. Place chicken, breast-side-up on microwave roasting rack, in 2-quart (12 x 7) glass baking dish. Brush with Cranberry Sauce.

2. Microwave for 40 to 45 minutes, on HIGH, or until meat cut near bone is no longer pink (about 180° F.). Let stand, covered with foil, 5 minutes before serving.

3. **Cranberry Sauce:** Place butter in small glass mixing bowl.

4. Microwave for about 1 minute, on ROAST, or until melted. Add remaining ingredients; beat with rotary beater until smooth. 6 to 8 Servings

ADD-A-VEGETABLE: Prepare Cranberry Roast Chicken through Step 1; set aside. Wash 4 medium sweet potatoes and prick skin. Place chicken on lower rack of oven and sweet potatoes on bottom shelf. Microwave both for 45 to 50 minutes, on HIGH, or until meat cut near bone is no longer pink (about 180° F.). Let chicken stand, covered with foil, 5 minutes before serving. Serve sweet potatoes with butter.

SAVORY CHICKEN

Thaw poultry completely before cooking.

2½ to 3-lb. whole frying chicken
Salt
Pepper
1 small onion, chopped
1 stalk celery, chopped

Basting Sauce:
¼ cup butter or margarine
½ teaspoon celery salt
½ teaspoon thyme leaves
¼ teaspoon rubbed sage

1. Wash chicken; set aside giblets. Sprinkle body cavity with salt and pepper. Place onion and celery in cavity. Tie legs together and wings to body. Place chicken, breast-side-up on microwave roasting rack, in 2-quart (12 x 7) glass baking dish. Brush with Basting Sauce.

2. Microwave for 19 to 21 minutes, on HIGH, or until meat cut near bone is no longer pink (about 180° F.). Let stand, covered with foil, 5 minutes before serving.

3. **Basting Sauce:** Place butter in 2-cup glass measure.

4. Microwave for about 1 minute, on ROAST, or until melted. Stir in remaining sauce ingredients. 4 to 6 Servings

ADD-A-VEGETABLE: Prepare Savory Chicken through Step 1; set aside. Place 2 lbs. fresh boiling potatoes, peeled and cut into pieces, and ¼ cup water in 2-quart (8 x 8) glass baking dish; cover with wax paper. Place chicken on lower rack of oven and potatoes on bottom shelf. Microwave both for 28 to 30 minutes, on HIGH, or until meat cut near bone is no longer pink (about 180° F.). Let chicken stand, covered with foil, 10 minutes before serving.

CREAMY CHEESY CHICKEN

Poultry pieces with sensitive ingredients cook on ROAST.

2½ to 3-lb. quartered frying chicken
¼ lb. fresh mushrooms, sliced
1 small onion, chopped
1 cup chicken broth
¼ cup dry white wine

Cheese Sauce:
½ cup light cream
½ cup unsifted all-purpose flour
½ teaspoon garlic salt
1½ cups reserved chicken broth
1 cup shredded Cheddar cheese
2 tablespoons chopped pimento
2 teaspoons dried parsley flakes

1. Place chicken, skin-side-up and thick edges toward outside, in 2-quart (12 x 7) glass baking dish. Sprinkle on mushrooms and onion; pour chicken broth and wine over chicken. Cover with wax paper.

2. Microwave for 22 to 24 minutes, on ROAST, or until meat cut near bone is no longer pink (about 180° F.). Drain, reserving 1½ cups broth; set aside. Let stand, covered, 5 minutes. Pour Cheese Sauce over chicken to serve.

3. **Cheese Sauce:** Combine cream, flour and garlic salt in 4-cup glass measure; beat with rotary beater until smooth. Beat in reserved broth; stir in remaining sauce ingredients.

4. Microwave for 3 minutes on ROAST. Beat and continue cooking for 2 to 2½ minutes, on ROAST, or until thickened (about 170° F.). Beat lightly. 4 to 6 Servings

SEASONED CRUMB CHICKEN

- **¼ cup butter or margarine**
- **¾ cup crushed rich round crackers (about 16 crackers)**
- **½ cup grated Parmesan cheese**
- **1 tablespoon dried parsley flakes**
- **½ teaspoon garlic powder**
- **⅛ teaspoon pepper**
- **2½ to 3-lb. quartered frying chicken**

Microwave crumb-coated poultry uncovered to crisp it. For plain chicken pieces, see chart on page 141.

1. Place butter in 2-quart (12 x 7) glass baking dish.

2. Microwave for about 1 minute, on ROAST, or until melted. Combine remaining ingredients, except chicken, in flat dish. Roll chicken in melted butter, then in seasoned crumbs. Place chicken pieces, skin-side-up and thick edges toward outside, in buttered baking dish. Sprinkle with remaining bread crumbs.

3. Microwave for 19 to 21 minutes, on HIGH, or until meat cut near bone is no longer pink (about 180° F.). Let stand 5 minutes before serving.

4 to 6 Servings

ADD-A-DESSERT: Prepare Seasoned Crumb Chicken through Step 2; set aside. Prepare Old-Fashioned Baked Apples (recipe variation), page 181, through Step 1. Place chicken on upper rack of oven and apples on bottom shelf. Microwave both for 30 to 35 minutes, on HIGH, or until meat cut near bone is no longer pink (about 180° F.). Let both stand for 5 minutes before serving.

RECIPE VARIATIONS

STUFFING CRUMB CHICKEN: Substitute ¾ cup herb seasoned stuffing mix, ½ teaspoon dill weed and ¼ teaspoon salt for crackers, parsley flakes and garlic powder.

SESAME CRUMB CHICKEN: Substitute ¾ cup crushed, crisp rice cereal, 2 tablespoons sesame seeds, 1 teaspoon leaf oregano and 1 teaspoon salt for crackers, cheese, parsley flakes and garlic powder.

NUTTY CRUMB CHICKEN: Add 2 teaspoons soy sauce to melted butter; substitute ½ cup chopped cashews for cheese.

Pictured: Seasoned Crumb Chicken, recipe above, with ADD-A-DESSERT, Old-Fashioned Baked Apples, page 181.

CHICKEN CACCIATORE

Mushrooms are sensitive; cook sauce on ROAST.

- **2½ to 3-lb. quartered frying chicken**
- **1 small onion, thinly sliced and separated into rings**
- **½ medium green pepper, cut into strips**
- **1 can (28 oz.) whole tomatoes**

Mushroom Sauce:

- **2 tablespoons cornstarch**
- **¼ cup water**
- **1 teaspoon sugar**
- **½ teaspoon salt**
- **2 cups reserved chicken broth**
- **1 can (4 oz.) mushroom stems and pieces, drained**

1. Arrange chicken pieces, skin-side-up and thick edges toward outside, in 2-quart (12 x 7) glass baking dish. Place onion, green pepper and tomatoes over chicken. Cover with wax paper.

2. Microwave for 35 to 40 minutes, on HIGH, or until meat cut near bone is no longer pink (about 180° F.). Drain, reserving 2 cups broth; set aside. Let stand, covered, 5 minutes before serving.

3. Mushroom Sauce: Combine all sauce ingredients, except mushrooms and broth, in 4-cup glass measure; beat with rotary beater until smooth. Beat in reserved broth.

4. Microwave for 2 minutes on HIGH. Beat; add mushrooms and continue cooking for 2 to 3 minutes, on ROAST, or until thickened (about 200° F.). Stir well and pour over chicken to serve.

4 to 6 Servings

ADD-A-VEGETABLE: Prepare Chicken Cacciatore through Step 1; set aside. Place 1 can (17 oz.) whole kernel corn, undrained, in 1½-quart glass casserole; cover with glass lid; set aside. Place chicken on upper rack of oven. Microwave for 25 minutes on HIGH. Place corn on bottom shelf of oven and continue cooking for 15 to 20 minutes, on HIGH, or until meat cut near bone is no longer pink (about 180° F.). Drain chicken, reserving 2 cups broth. Let both stand, covered, 5 minutes. Meanwhile, remove rack and prepare sauce for Chicken Cacciatore as directed in Steps 3 and 4 of basic recipe.

ORIENTAL CHICKEN

Arrange poultry pieces with thick edges toward outside of dish.

- **2 tablespoons butter or margarine**
- **⅓ cup chopped green pepper**
- **3 cups cooked rice**
- **1 can (16 oz.) chow mein vegetables, drained**
- **1 can (8 oz.) water chestnuts, drained and sliced**
- **1 teaspoon soy sauce**
- **2½ to 3-lb. quartered frying chicken**

Pineapple Sauce:

- **¼ cup unsweetened pineapple juice**
- **1 tablespoon cornstarch**
- **¼ cup honey**
- **¼ cup dry sherry or additional pineapple juice**
- **1 tablespoon soy sauce**
- **¼ teaspoon ginger**

1. Place butter and green pepper in 2-quart (12 x 7) glass baking dish.

2. Microwave for about 3 minutes, on HIGH, or until green pepper is partly cooked. Stir in remaining chicken ingredients, except chicken; spread in bottom of dish. Place chicken, skin-side-down and thick edges toward outside, over rice. Brush with ½ of Pineapple Sauce; cover.

3. Microwave for 15 minutes on HIGH. Turn chicken pieces over; brush with remaining sauce and continue cooking for 13 to 15 minutes, on HIGH, or until meat cut near bone is no longer pink (about 180° F.). Let stand, covered, 5 minutes before serving.

4. Pineapple Sauce: Combine pineapple juice and cornstarch in 4-cup glass measure until smooth. Stir in remaining sauce ingredients.

5. Microwave for 2 to 3 minutes, on HIGH, or until thickened (about 200° F.). Stir well.

4 to 6 Servings

ADD-A-VEGETABLE: Prepare Oriental Chicken through Step 2; set aside. Place 2 packages (6 oz. each) frozen Chinese pea pods in 1½-quart glass casserole; cover with glass lid; set aside. Place chicken on upper rack of oven. Microwave for 15 minutes on HIGH. Turn chicken pieces over; brush with remaining sauce, and recover. Place pea pods on bottom shelf. Microwave both for 20 to 25 minutes, on HIGH, or until meat cut near bone is no longer pink (about 180° F.). Let both stand, covered, 5 minutes before serving.

CHICKEN FOR BARBECUING

Microwave chicken, then grill, to assure thorough cooking.

- **2½ to 3-lb. quartered frying chicken**

Barbecue Sauce:

- **½ cup bottled barbecue sauce**
- **¼ cup bottled Italian salad dressing**
- **2 teaspoons dried parsley flakes**

1. Place chicken, skin-side-up and thick edges toward outside, in 2-quart (12 x 7) glass baking dish.

2. Microwave for 15 minutes on HIGH. Remove from oven. Brush both sides of each chicken piece with Barbecue Sauce. Place chicken on barbecue grill over hot coals. Grill 20 to 25 minutes; turn occasionally and brush with remaining Barbecue Sauce until chicken is fork tender.

3. Barbecue Sauce: Combine all sauce ingredients in small bowl; mix well.

4 to 6 Servings

TIP: If barbecue grill has a hood, follow manufacturer's directions.

PIZZA CHICKEN THIGHS

A cover speeds cooking – keeps it even.

- **1½ lbs. chicken thighs**
- **1 can (10¾ oz.) condensed tomato soup**
- **1 package (1.5 oz.) dry spaghetti sauce mix**
- **1 can (4 oz.) mushroom stems and pieces, undrained**
- **1 cup shredded Mozzarella cheese**

1. Place thighs, skin-side-up and thick edges toward outside, in 2-quart (8 x 8) glass baking dish. Cover with wax paper.

2. Microwave for 8 minutes on HIGH. Drain. Combine remaining ingredients, except cheese, in small mixing bowl; pour over thighs. Sprinkle with cheese.

3. Microwave for 6 to 8 minutes, on ROAST, or until meat cut near bone is no longer pink (about 180° F.). Let stand 5 minutes. About 4 Servings

ADD-A-SALAD: Prepare Pizza Chicken Thighs through Step 1; set aside. Prepare Hot Apple Slaw, page 146, through Step 1; set aside. Place chicken on upper rack of oven. Microwave for 8 minutes on HIGH. Drain chicken. Combine remaining chicken ingredients, except cheese, in small mixing bowl; pour over chicken. Sprinkle with cheese. Place Hot Apple Slaw on bottom shelf. Microwave both for 8 to 10 minutes, on HIGH, or until meat cut near bone is no longer pink (about 180° F.). Let both stand 5 minutes before serving.

ORANGE CHICKEN WINGS

Irregular-shaped pieces are turned during cooking for fast, even cooking.

- **1½ lbs. chicken wings**
- **3 green onions, sliced**
- **½ cup orange juice**
- **3 to 4 tablespoons orange-flavored liqueur or orange juice**

Orange Sauce:

- **1 can (11 oz.) mandarin oranges**
- **¼ cup packed brown sugar**
- **1 tablespoon cornstarch**
- **¾ cup reserved chicken broth**
- **½ cup macadamia nuts or almonds**

1. Place wings, skin-side-down and thick edges toward outside, in 2-quart (12 x 7) glass baking dish. Sprinkle on onion; pour orange juice and liqueur over wings. Cover with wax paper.

2. Microwave for 10 minutes on HIGH. Turn wings over; recover, and continue cooking for 4 to 6 minutes, on HIGH, or until meat cut near bone is no longer pink (about 180° F.). Drain, reserving ¾ cup broth; set aside. Let stand, covered, 5 minutes before serving. Pour Orange Sauce over wings.

3. Orange Sauce: Drain mandarin oranges, reserving ⅓ cup juice. Set aside mandarin oranges. Combine ⅓ cup reserved juice, brown sugar and cornstarch in 4-cup glass measure; beat with rotary beater until smooth. Add reserved broth; beat well.

4. Microwave for 2 minutes on HIGH. Stir well and continue cooking for 1½ to 2 minutes, on HIGH, or until thickened (about 200° F.). Stir in mandarin oranges and nuts. 4 to 6 Servings

ADD-A-VEGETABLE: Prepare Orange Chicken Wings through Step 1; set aside. Place 1 can (16 oz.) French-style green beans, undrained, in 1½-quart glass casserole; cover with glass lid. Place chicken on upper rack of oven and beans on bottom shelf. Microwave both for 10 minutes on HIGH. Turn wings over; recover, and continue cooking both for 4 to 6 minutes, on HIGH, or until meat cut near bone is no longer pink (about 180° F.). Drain chicken, reserving ¾ cup broth; set aside. Let both stand, covered, 5 minutes. Remove rack and prepare Orange Sauce as directed in basic recipe. Pour over wings to serve.

BACON-GARLIC CHICKEN BREASTS

Poultry is done when meat cut near the bone is no longer pink.

- **¼ cup butter or margarine**
- **1 clove garlic, finely chopped**
- **2 teaspoons dried parsley flakes**
- **1 teaspoon grated lemon rind**
- **¼ teaspoon salt**
- **⅛ teaspoon hot pepper sauce**
- **2 whole chicken breasts (1 lb. each), halved**
- **4 bacon slices, cut in half**

1. Place butter and garlic in 2-quart (12 x 7) glass baking dish.

2. Microwave for about 1 minute, on HIGH, or until garlic is partly cooked. Add remaining ingredients, except chicken breasts and bacon; mix well. Roll chicken breasts in seasoned butter; arrange, skin-side-up and thick edges toward outside, in buttered baking dish. Lay 2 half slices of bacon on each chicken breast.

3. Microwave for 14 to 16 minutes, on HIGH, or until meat cut near bone is no longer pink (about 180° F.). Let stand 5 minutes before serving. 4 Servings

ADD-A-DESSERT: Prepare Bacon-Garlic Chicken Breasts through Step 2; set aside. Prepare Fruit Mélange, page 186, through Step 1. Place chicken on upper rack of oven and fruit on bottom shelf. Microwave both for 18 to 20 minutes, on HIGH, or until meat cut near bone is no longer pink (about 180° F.). Let both stand 5 minutes before serving.

ONION TURKEY THIGH

1½ to 2-lb. frozen turkey thigh, thawed
Garlic salt
¼ cup water
2 carrots, peeled and thickly sliced
1 medium onion, cut into pieces
2 tablespoons dry onion soup mix

ROAST setting keeps turkey meat juicy and more tender.

1. Place thigh in 9-inch round glass baking dish. Sprinkle with garlic salt; add water. Cover with wax paper.

2. Microwave for 20 minutes on ROAST. Place vegetables around thigh; sprinkle with dry onion soup mix. Recover and continue cooking for 20 to 25 minutes, on ROAST, or until meat cut near bone is no longer pink (about 180° F.). Let stand, covered, 5 minutes before serving. 3 to 4 Servings

ADD-A-DESSERT: Prepare Onion Turkey Thigh through Step 1, set aside. Prepare Rhubarb Crisp (recipe variation), page 185, through Step 1. Place thigh on upper rack of oven and dessert on bottom shelf. Microwave both for 20 minutes on ROAST. Place vegetables around thigh; sprinkle with dry onion soup mix; recover. Continue cooking both for 30 to 35 minutes, on ROAST, or until meat cut near bone is no longer pink (about 180° F.). Let both stand 5 minutes before serving.

BARBECUED TURKEY DRUMSTICKS

2 to 2½ lbs. frozen turkey drumsticks, thawed
½ cup chili sauce
¼ cup white vinegar
2 tablespoons cooking oil
¼ cup chopped onion
¼ cup chopped green pepper
2 tablespoons packed brown sugar
1 tablespoon prepared mustard
1 teaspoon salt
½ teaspoon chili powder
⅛ teaspoon pepper

Cover speeds cooking.

1. Place turkey drumsticks, thick end toward outside, in 2-quart (12 x 7) glass baking dish. Combine remaining ingredients in small mixing bowl; mix well. Pour sauce over drumsticks. Cover with wax paper.

2. Microwave for 20 minutes on ROAST. Turn drumsticks over; recover, and continue cooking for 16 to 20 minutes, on ROAST, or until meat cut near bone is no longer pink (about 180° F.). Let stand, covered, 5 minutes before serving. 3 to 4 Servings

ADD-A-VEGETABLE: Prepare Barbecued Turkey Drumsticks through Step 1; set aside. Place 6 ears of fresh corn and ¼ cup water in 3-quart (13 x 9) glass baking dish; cover with wax paper; set aside. Place turkey drumsticks on upper rack of oven. Microwave for 20 minutes on ROAST. Turn drumsticks over; recover. Place corn on bottom shelf and continue cooking both for 25 to 30 minutes, on HIGH, or until meat cut near bone is no longer pink (about 180° F.). Let both stand, covered, 5 minutes before serving.

TURKEY BREAST MADEIRA ✻

4 to 5-lb. frozen bone-in turkey breast, thawed

Madeira Glaze:
½ cup red currant jelly
2 tablespoons Madeira or apple juice

Microwave plain roast turkey breast as directed in chart on page 131.

1. Place turkey breast, top-side-down on microwave roasting rack, in 2-quart (12 x 7) glass baking dish. Brush with ½ of Madeira Glaze.

2. Microwave for 40 minutes on HIGH. Turn breast-side-up; brush with remaining glaze and continue cooking for 35 to 40 minutes, on ROAST, or until meat cut near bone is no longer pink (about 180° F.). Some areas may cook more rapidly than others; cover these with small pieces of foil to slow cooking. Let stand, covered with foil, 10 minutes before serving.

3. **Madeira Glaze:** Combine all glaze ingredients in small mixing bowl; beat with rotary beater until smooth. 8 to 12 Servings

TIP: Thaw turkey breast as defrosting chart, page 31, directs.

ADD-A-STUFFING: Prepare Turkey Breast Madeira through Step 1; set aside. Prepare and double Mushroom-Carrot Stuffing Mix (recipe variation), page 139, through Step 2; add 1 cup chicken broth. Place stuffing in 3-quart (13×9) glass baking dish; cover with wax paper; set aside. Place turkey breast on lower rack of oven. Microwave for 40 minutes on HIGH. Turn breast over; brush with remaining glaze. Place stuffing on bottom shelf. Continue cooking both for 35 to 40 minutes, on ROAST, or until meat cut near bone is no longer pink (about 180° F.). Let turkey stand, covered with foil, 10 minutes before serving.

EARLY AMERICAN TURKEY *

14-lb. frozen turkey, thawed
Salt
Apple-Sausage Stuffing (recipe variation), page 139

Maple-Apple Glaze:
- **½ cup maple-flavored syrup**
- **½ cup applesauce**
- **½ teaspoon salt**
- **¼ teaspoon poultry seasoning**

See chart, page 131, for microwaving plain, roast turkey.

1. Wash completely thawed turkey; set aside giblets. Sprinkle inside of cavity with salt. Stuff cavity and neck opening with Sausage Apple Stuffing. Secure opening with toothpicks or metal skewers. Tie drumsticks together and wings to body with string.

2. Place bird, breast-side-down on microwave roasting rack, in 3-quart (13 x 9) glass baking dish. Brush with ½ of Maple-Apple Glaze.

3. Microwave for 80 minutes on HIGH. Turn breast-side-up; brush with remaining glaze and continue cooking for 70 to 75 minutes, on ROAST, or until meat cut near bone is no longer pink (about 180° F.). Some areas may cook more rapidly than others; cover these with small pieces of foil to slow cooking. Let stand, covered with foil, 10 minutes before serving.

4. Maple-Apple Glaze: Combine all glaze ingredients in small bowl; mix well.

About 14 Servings

TIP: Thaw turkey as directed in defrosting chart, page 31.

APRICOT CORNISH HENS

4 frozen whole Rock Cornish Game Hens (1 to 1½ lb. each), thawed
Salt
Apricot-Nut Stuffing (recipe variation), page 149

Apricot Glaze:
- **1 jar (12 oz.) apricot preserves**
- **2 tablespoons lime juice**
- **1 tablespoon soy sauce**
- **½ teaspoon salt**

Microwave plain Rock Cornish Game Hens as directed in chart, page 132.

1. Wash hens; set aside giblets. Salt body cavities of hens. Fill each with Apricot Nut Stuffing. Tie legs together and wings to body. Arrange, breast-side-down and drumsticks toward center of microwave roasting rack, in 3-quart (13 x 9) glass baking dish. Brush with ½ of Apricot Glaze.

2. Microwave for 15 minutes on HIGH. Turn breast-side-up; brush with remaining Apricot Glaze and continue cooking for 22 to 25 minutes, on HIGH, or until meat cut near bone is no longer pink (about 180° F.). Let stand 5 minutes before serving.

3. Apricot Glaze: Combine all glaze ingredients in small bowl; mix well.

4 Servings

ROAST PLUM GOOSE

9 to 10-lb. frozen domestic goose, thawed
Salt
Prune-Almond Stuffing (recipe variation), page 139

Plum Glaze:
- **1 jar (12 oz.) plum preserves**
- **2 tablespoons teriyaki sauce**
- **¼ cup sweet vermouth or apple juice**

Fat spatters less on ROAST setting.

1. Wash goose; set aside giblets. Sprinkle inside of cavity with salt; stuff with Prune-Almond Stuffing. Secure openings with toothpicks or metal skewers. Tie legs together and wings to body. Place goose, breast-side-down on microwave roasting rack, in 3-quart (13 x 9) glass baking dish. Brush with ½ of Plum Glaze.

2. Microwave for 40 minutes on ROAST. Drain off fat. Turn goose breast-side-up; brush with remaining Plum Glaze, and continue cooking for 40 to 45 minutes, on ROAST, or until meat cut near bone is no longer pink (about 180° F.). Let stand, covered with foil, 10 minutes before serving.

3. Plum Glaze: Combine all ingredients in small mixing bowl; mix well.

About 10 Servings

TIP: Thaw goose as directed in defrosting chart on page 31.

PHEASANT IN CREAM SAUCE

1½ to 2-lb. frozen pheasant, thawed and cut in half
Salt

Cream Sauce:
- **1 package (3 oz.) cream cheese**
- **1 can (10¾ oz.) condensed cream of onion soup**
- **¼ cup dry white wine or water**
- **2 tablespoons milk**
- **½ cup shredded carrot**
- **1 tablespoon dried parsley flakes**
- **1 teaspoon instant beef bouillon**

Sauces help steam and moisten meat.

1. Wash pheasant and place, skin-side-down and thick edges toward outside, in 2-quart (8 x 8) glass baking dish. Sprinkle both sides of pheasant with salt. Cover with wax paper.

2. Microwave for 15 minutes on ROAST. Drain; turn pheasant over, and pour on Cream Sauce. Recover and continue cooking for 15 to 20 minutes, on ROAST, or until meat cut near bone is no longer pink (about 180° F.). Let stand, covered, 5 minutes before serving.

3. Cream Sauce: Place cream cheese in medium glass mixing bowl.

4. Microwave for about 30 seconds, on ROAST, or until softened. Stir in remaining sauce ingredients; mix well.

2 to 3 Servings

DUCKLING WITH PEACH SAUCE

- 4 to 5-lb. frozen young duckling, thawed
- 1 orange, unpeeled and quartered
- 1 small onion, quartered

Peach Glaze and Sauce:

- 1 can (16 oz.) sliced peaches
- ¼ cup water
- ¼ cup orange juice
- ½ cup packed brown sugar
- 1 tablespoon cornstarch
- 1½ teaspoons dry mustard
- ⅛ teaspoon ground cloves

Simple glazes add flavor, enhance appearance.

1. Wash duckling; set aside giblets. Stuff duckling neck and body cavity with orange and onion quarters. Secure openings with toothpicks or metal skewers. Tie legs together and wings to body. Place duckling, breast-side-up on microwave roasting rack, in 2-quart (12 x 7) glass baking dish. Brush with Peach Glaze.

2. Microwave for 45 to 47 minutes, on ROAST, or until meat cut near bone is no longer pink (about 180° F.). Let stand, covered with foil, 10 minutes. Serve Peach Sauce over duckling.

3. **Peach Glaze and Sauce:** Drain peaches, reserving ½ cup juice; set aside peaches. Combine ½ cup reserved juice and remaining glaze ingredients in 4-cup glass measure; beat with rotary beater until smooth.

4. Microwave for 2 minutes on HIGH. Beat and continue cooking for 30 to 60 seconds, on HIGH, or until thickened (about 200° F.). Divide in half; add peach slices to one half for Peach Sauce. Use other half for Peach Glaze.

4 to 6 Servings

BASIC BREAD STUFFING

- ⅔ cup butter or margarine
- ½ cup chopped onion
- 1½ cups chopped celery
- 10 cups day-old soft bread cubes
- 1 tablespoon dried parsley flakes
- 1 teaspoon salt
- ½ teaspoon rubbed sage
- ¼ teaspoon poultry seasoning
- ⅛ teaspoon pepper

Increase or decrease recipes, depending on size bird being stuffed.

1. Place butter, onion and celery in 3-quart glass casserole.

2. Microwave for 4 to 5 minutes, on HIGH, or until vegetables are partly cooked. Stir in remaining ingredients; mix well. Stuff poultry.

Stuffs 8 to 9-lb. Bird

TIP: Microwave a casserole stuffing by blending ¾ to 1 cup chicken broth into basic recipe ingredients. Place in buttered 2-quart glass baking dish or casserole. Cover with glass lid or wax paper. Microwave for 12 to 15 minutes, on SIMMER, or until hot (about 160° F.). Let stand, covered, 5 minutes before serving.

6 to 8 Servings

RECIPE VARIATIONS

PRUNE-ALMOND STUFFING: Decrease onion to ¼ cup and celery to 1 cup. Add 1 cup chopped prunes and ½ cup slivered almonds to basic recipe. **If stuffing a goose,** decrease butter to ¼ cup.

APPLE-SAUSAGE STUFFING: Add 1 package (12 oz.) bulk pork sausage, cooked and crumbled, and 1 small apple, chopped.

Stuffs 14-lb. bird.

WILD RICE STUFFING

- 3 tablespoons butter or margarine
- ¼ cup chopped celery
- ¼ cup chopped onion
- ¼ cup chopped green pepper
- 1 package (6 oz.) white and wild rice mix, cooked

1. Place all ingredients, except rice, in 2-quart glass casserole.

2. Microwave for 3 to 4 minutes, on HIGH, or until vegetables are partly cooked. Stir in cooked rice mix; mix well. Stuff poultry.

Stuffs 4 to 5-lb. Bird

TIP: 3 cups cooked wild rice may be substituted for white and wild rice mix. Season to taste.

RECIPE VARIATION

APRICOT-NUT STUFFING: Add ½ cup sunflower nuts and ½ cup chopped dried apricots with rice in basic recipe.

STUFFING MIX

- ½ cup butter or margarine
- 1 cup water
- 1 package (8 oz.) crushed seasoned stuffing

When this stuffing is cooked in a glass casserole, assemble as recipe directs, cover and cook 8 to 10 minutes, on SIMMER, until hot.

1. Combine butter and water in 2-quart glass casserole.

2. Microwave for 3 to 4 minutes, on HIGH, or until butter is melted. Stir in stuffing mix. Stuff poultry.

Stuffs 5 to 8-lb. Bird

TIP: Recipe may be doubled. Increase microwave time to 5 to 6 minutes.

RECIPE VARIATIONS

CORNBREAD STUFFING: Substitute 1 package (8 oz.) seasoned cornbread stuffing.

MUSHROOM-CARROT STUFFING: Add 1 can (4 oz.) mushroom stems and pieces, drained, ½ cup shredded carrot and 1 tablespoon dried parsley flakes to basic recipe.

Preserving Shortcuts

Jelly Preserves and Pickles— Good as Grandma's

Here's How — and Why

Make Small Batches in a Jiffy: Need a few cups of jelly, preserves, pickles or relish right now? Microwave some. These preserving techniques are designed for small batches of food stored in a refrigerator or freezer for a few days or weeks. *Use only conventional canning methods for processing* all food sealed in jars for shelf storage *and for blanching large batches* of food to be frozen or processed. *Do not* preserve meats or poultry in a microwave oven.

Jelly and Preserves Cook in Minutes on ROAST: Clear, firm jelly and fruity, soft preserves microwave superbly with commercial liquid pectin. Use commercial fruit juice for jelly, fresh or frozen fruit for preserves. Refrigerate microwaved jelly and preserves in covered glass jars or custard cups up to 4 months.

Microwave a Sparkling-Sweet Freezing Syrup on ROAST: Fresh fruits frozen in sugar-water syrup have sparkling flavor plus a sweetness that lets them thaw, table-ready, for compotes or serving over cake, custard and ice cream. Freeze most any fruit in sugar syrup microwaved on ROAST. Always cool syrup before pouring it over fruit. When an anti-darkening agent is needed, add it to cooled syrup, then pour over fruit in containers. Syrup must cover fruit. A small piece of crumpled parchment, wax or other water-resistant paper under the lid prevents floating fruit which darkens.

Pickle and Relish Brines Microwave on HIGH: Refrigerator pickles and relishes are a cinch with brines cooked quickly and easily on Microwave HIGH. And, these microwave condiments cure for zesty eating in 24 hours. Individual recipes specify refrigerator storage life.

Small-Batch Blanch Vegetables — Do It on HIGH: Frozen vegetables are best when picked young and tender, then blanched and frozen right from the garden. This sometimes means small batches — a great time to use fast, microwave blanching for quantities weighing up to ½ pound (about 2 cups). All vegetables, except bell peppers, must be blanched or scalded before freezing to prevent flavor and color changes. Cool all blanched vegetables immediately in cold running water or ice water. When completely cold, drain and pack for the freezer. If vegetables are to be reheated or cooked in a microwave oven, freeze only in boilable, freezer bags as manufacturer directs. Bags must be slit before vegetable is cooked in a microwave oven; remove twister.

Use Quality Fruits and Vegetables: Select good quality fruits at the firm-ripe stage. Use only fresh, young, tender vegetables and prepare them right after picking.

Prepare Food Carefully: Quality preserved fruits and vegetables have been prepared with care — and each type needs some special handling. Canning and freezing guides from the USDA Extension Service or freezing and canning equipment manufacturers spell out, in detail, how to clean and cut food, estimate yields of prepared food from whole, when anti-darkening agents are needed with fruit, plus other preparation specifics.

Remember to Microwave in Glass: Microwave jelly, preserves and pickles in glass bowls, as specified in each recipe. Cover, where directed, with a glass lid or wax paper.

New Microwave Directions Give Fast, Fun Results: These preserving techniques and short cuts are somewhat different than conventional methods. Follow recipe directions carefully.

Pictured from the top: Harvey's Dill Pickles, page 142; Chinese Cauliflower Pickles, page 142; Strawberry Preserves, page 143.

HARVEY'S DILL PICKLES

Pickles cure in a brine for crispness and flavor zing.

24 pickling cucumbers (3 to 4-inch each)
1 sweet red pepper, sliced
2 heads of fresh dill plant
4 cloves garlic
2 teaspoons pickling spices
⅛ teaspoon alum

Brine:
1 cup vinegar
2 cups water
¼ cup pickling salt

1. Wash cucumbers; cut off flower end. Cover with ice water; let stand 2 hours.

2. Divide red pepper, dill, garlic, pickling spices and alum between two 1-quart jars. Pack cucumbers into jars.

3. Combine Brine ingredients in 4-cup glass measure.

4. Microwave 10 to 12 minutes, on HIGH, or until boiling (about 200° F.). Fill jars with hot brine mixture. Cool; cover, and refrigerate for at least 24 hours before serving. Pickles will keep up to 3 months in refrigerator.

2 Quarts Pickles

BABY CARROT PICKLES

Pickles are ready to eat in 24 hours.

2 cans (16 oz. each) baby carrots, drained
2 cinnamon sticks
16 whole cloves
3 cups sugar
2 cups vinegar
1 cup water

1. Divide carrots, cinnamon sticks and cloves between two 1-quart jars; fill jars.

2. Combine remaining ingredients in 2-quart casserole.

3. Microwave for 4 minutes on HIGH. Stir and continue cooking for 4 to 5 minutes, on HIGH, or until boiling (about 200° F.). Pour mixture over carrots while hot. Cool; cover, and refrigerate at least 24 hours before serving. Carrots will keep up to 2 months in refrigerator.

2 Quarts Pickles

CHINESE CAULIFLOWER PICKLES

This versatile oven microwaves two foods at once.

1 medium head cauliflower, broken into flowerettes
¼ cup water

Brine:
1½ cups sugar
1 cup vinegar
1 tablespoon finely chopped onion
1 teaspoon pickling salt
1 teaspoon celery seeds
1 teaspoon mustard seeds
¼ teaspoon pickling spices
1 tablespoon diced pimento

1. Place cauliflower and water in 1½-quart glass casserole. Cover with glass lid; set aside.

2. Combine Brine ingredients, except pimento, in 1-quart glass casserole.

3. Place cauliflower on upper rack in oven and Brine on bottom shelf.

4. Microwave both for 18 to 20 minutes, on HIGH, or until Brine comes to a full boil (about 200° F.). Stir Brine and pour over cauliflower. Stir in pimento. Cool; cover, and refrigerate at least 24 hours before serving. Pickles will keep up to 2 months in refrigerator.

About 1 Quart Pickles

TWO-IN-ONE RELISH

Chopped, seasoned vegetables plus brine create a relish.

12 medium cucumbers, washed and unpeeled
6 medium onions
3 green peppers
3 sweet red peppers
½ cup pickling salt

Sweet Relish Brine:
1½ cups sugar
1 cup vinegar
1 teaspoon celery seeds
1 teaspoon mustard seeds

Curry Relish Brine:
1½ cups packed brown sugar
1¼ cups vinegar
½ cup water
2 teaspoons dry mustard
¼ teaspoon tumeric powder
¼ teaspoon curry powder
Dash cayenne pepper

1. Grind cucumbers, onions and peppers. Place in large mixing bowl; stir in salt. Let stand at least 8 hours. Drain well; divide mixture between 2 medium glass mixing bowls.

2. Combine Sweet Relish Brine ingredients in 4-cup glass measure; set aside.

3. Combine Curry Relish Brine ingredients in 4-cup glass measure.

4. Place both brines on bottom shelf of oven.

5. Microwave about 10 minutes, on HIGH, or until boiling (about 200° F.). Pour Sweet Relish Brine over one bowl of the relish mixture. Cool; cover and refrigerate at least 24 hours before serving.

6. Pour Curry Relish Brine over other bowl of relish mixture; cover. Place Curry Relish mixture in oven.

7. Microwave for 8 to 10 minutes, on HIGH, or until flavors are blended. Cool; cover and refrigerate at least 24 hours before serving. Both relishes will keep up to 1 month in refrigerator.

About 1½ Quarts of Each Relish

TIP: Substitute 2 jars (2½ oz. each) diced pimento for sweet red peppers.

PICKLED MUSHROOMS

An occasional stir assures that brine flavor penetrates all mushrooms.

1 lb. fresh whole small mushrooms

Pickling Brine:
- **⅔ cup cider vinegar**
- **½ cup water**
- **1 tablespoon finely chopped onion**
- **2 teaspoons pickling salt**
- **½ teaspoon dried parsley flakes**
- **½ teaspoon celery seeds**
- **2 bay leaves**
- **12 peppercorns**

1. Clean mushrooms and trim stem ends. Place in glass mixing bowl; set aside.

2. Combine Pickling Brine ingredients in 4-cup glass measure.

3. Microwave for 4 to 5 minutes, on HIGH, or until boiling (about 200° F.). Pour over mushrooms; cool. Cover and refrigerate at least 24 hours before serving. Mushrooms will keep up to 1 week in refrigerator.

About 1 Quart Mushrooms

VEGETABLE BLANCHING TECHNIQUE

Vegetables must be young, tender and fresh-picked.

- **4 cups water**
- **½ lb. fresh vegetable**

1. Place water in 2-quart glass casserole.

2. Microwave about 12 minutes, on HIGH, or until boiling (about 200° F.). Drop vegetables into boiling water.

3. Microwave for ½ of regular cooking time on HIGH — see Vegetable Chart page 172.

4. Chill in ice water immediately. Follow conventional freezing procedures, using only boilable, freezer bags. Check with your USDA Extension Service canning, preserving and freezing guides or freezer equipment manufacturers' guides for proper storage times and the blanching of special foods.

APPLE JELLY

Small batches microwave superbly.

- **3 cups sugar**
- **2 cups commercial apple juice**
- **1 tablespoon lemon juice**
- **½ bottle (6 oz.) liquid pectin**

1. Mix all ingredients except pectin in 1½-quart glass casserole.

2. Microwave for 7 minutes on ROAST. Stir and continue cooking for 7 to 8 minutes, on ROAST, or until boiling. Stir in pectin.

3. Fill glass jars; cool, and cover. Jelly will keep up to 4 months in the refrigerator.

About 3 Cups Jelly

TIP: A drop or two of red food coloring may be added if desired.

RECIPE VARIATION

PORT WINE JELLY: Substitute 2 cups port wine for apple juice in basic recipe.

RASPBERRY PRESERVES

Either fresh fruit or sweetened frozen fruit may be used.

- **4 cups fresh raspberries, cleaned and washed**
- **2½ cups sugar**
- **2 tablespoons lemon juice**
- **¼ bottle (6 oz.) liquid pectin**

1. Combine raspberries, sugar and lemon juice in 1½-quart glass casserole.

2. Microwave for 7 minutes on ROAST. Stir and continue cooking for 8 to 10 minutes, on ROAST, or until bubbly. Stir in pectin.

3. Fill glass jars; cool, and cover. Preserves will keep up to 4 months in refrigerator.

About 2 Cups Preserves

TIP: Substitute 2 packages (10 oz. each) frozen raspberries with sugar for fresh raspberries. Reduce sugar by ¼ cup and increase cooking time 5 to 6 minutes.

RECIPE VARIATION

STRAWBERRY PRESERVES: Substitute 4 cups fresh strawberries for raspberries in basic recipe. Or substitute 2 packages (10 oz. each) frozen strawberries with sugar; reduce sugar by ¼ cup, and increase cooking time 5 to 6 minutes.

SYRUP FOR FREEZING FRUIT

Syrup must cover fruit in containers.

- **3 cups sugar**
- **4 cups water**

1. Combine sugar and water in 2-quart glass casserole.

2. Microwave for about 6 minutes, on ROAST, or until sugar is dissolved (about 160° F.). Cool before using.

About 5½ Cups Syrup

Salads & Dressings

Create Hot and Cold Originals without Fuss

Here's How — and Why

Raw Vegetable Salads Microwave Quickly on HIGH:	Hot and crunchy — that's the ideal heated vegetable salad. Do it quickly and easily on Microwave HIGH.
Salads Made of Cooked Ingredients Microwave on REHEAT:	Many salads are combinations of cooked ingredients. Heat these mixtures on REHEAT.
Microwave Salads Mixed with Mayonnaise on ROAST:	Hot salad mixtures dressed with mayonnaise microwave on ROAST to prevent separation of this sensitive ingredient.
Melt Gelatin Quickly and Smoothly on HIGH:	Simply stir gelatin into water, microwave on HIGH and presto — it's mixed and melted without fussing. Use Raspberry Peach Salad, page 147, as a guide for preparing your own favorite gelatin salads.
Simple Dressings Microwave on HIGH — Use ROAST When Eggs or Cream Are Added:	Simple tart or sweet salad dressings microwave easily and quickly on HIGH. But when sensitive ingredients such as cream, yogurt, mayonnaise or eggs are added, use Microwave ROAST.
Mix and Microwave Salads and Dressings in a Single Bowl:	Cook or heat salads and dressings in glass casseroles, glass measures or glass serving bowls without gold, silver or other metal trim. Often, you can mix right in this cooking dish, too. Do not microwave in wooden bowls which may crack when they heat and dry. Cover cooking dishes with glass lids or wax paper, when called for in a recipe, to hold moisture and speed heating. Tip cover away from arm to avoid hot steam. Plastic wrap may be used as a cover. Pierce it before removing and allow hot steam to escape.
Standing Time Completes Heating:	Follow standing time directions to assure heating throughout a mixture.
The " ✻ " Notes a Setting Change:	Use the " ✻ " in recipe titles to remind yourself that there are two or more settings in the recipe. Stirring or beating is convenient at this time.
Microwave-Conventional Comparison:	Hot salads can be served really hot from a microwave oven without drying or scorching edges because microwaves cook from all directions, not just the bottom. Gelatin dissolves quickly and smoothly. Both salads and dressings can usually be mixed, cooked and served in a single dish.

Pictured: Cardamom Fruit Dressing, recipe below, over fruit salad.

CARDAMOM FRUIT DRESSING

Use on fresh or canned fruit salads.

1 egg, beaten
1 cup orange juice
⅓ cup honey
1 tablespoon cornstarch
¼ teaspoon ground cardamom
2 tablespoons butter or margarine
½ cup whipping cream, whipped

1. Beat egg in 4-cup glass measure with rotary beater. Stir in remaining ingredients, except butter and whipping cream; beat well. Add butter.

2. Microwave for 3 minutes on ROAST. Beat and continue cooking for 2½ to 3 minutes, on ROAST, or until thickened (about 200° F.). Beat lightly. Chill. Fold in whipped cream. Serve over fruit salad.

About 2 Cups Dressing

CLASSIC DRESSING *

Vary this classic dressing for all your green salads.

- **1 cup milk**
- **1 tablespoon cornstarch**
- **2 teaspoons sugar**
- **1 teaspoon dry mustard**
- **1 teaspoon salt**
- **¼ teaspoon paprika**
- **⅛ teaspoon pepper**
- **1 egg yolk, beaten**
- **2 tablespoons vinegar**
- **¼ cup cooking oil**

1. Measure milk in 4-cup glass measure. Add cornstarch, sugar and seasonings; beat with rotary beater until smooth.

2. Microwave for 3 minutes on HIGH. Beat and continue cooking for 1 to 1½ minutes, on HIGH, or until thickened (about 200° F.). Beat well. Add small amount of warm mixture to beaten egg yolk. Stir and combine with remaining hot cream mixture.

3. Microwave for 2 to 3 minutes, on ROAST, or until slightly thickened (about 180° F.). Stir in vinegar and oil. Beat until smooth. Store in the refrigerator up to a week. About 1⅓ Cups Dressing

RECIPE VARIATIONS

GARDEN DRESSING: Add ⅓ cup finely chopped cucmber or zucchini and 1 tablespoon snipped chives with vinegar and oil.

EGG DRESSING: Add 2 chopped hard-cooked eggs and 1 teaspoon dried parsley flakes with vinegar and oil.

CREAMY DRESSING: Add ¼ cup sour cream and 1 teaspoon dried parsley flakes with vinegar and oil.

HOT APPLE SLAW

- **⅓ cup vinegar**
- **¼ cup water**
- **2 tablespoons sugar**
- **1 teaspoon celery seed**
- **1 teaspoon salt**
- **6 cups shredded cabbage**
- **1 small apple, finely sliced**
- **2 tablespoons butter or margarine**

1. Combine vinegar, water, sugar, celery seed and salt in 2-quart glass casserole. Toss with cabbage and apple slices. Dot with butter. Cover with glass lid.

2. Microwave for 4 to 5 minutes, on HIGH, or until heated through. Let stand, covered, 3 minutes. Toss and serve. 3 to 4 Servings

TIP: Serve with cooked ham slices and Swiss cheese.

Pictured: Hot Apple Slaw, recipe above, with sliced ham rolls and Swiss cheese.

CHEESE PEACHES

Sensitive cream and cheese microwave best on ROAST.

- **1 can (16 oz.) peach halves, drained**
- **½ cup shredded Cheddar cheese**
- **¼ cup sour cream**
- **¼ cup chopped pecans**
- **Endive leaves**

1. Arrange peaches, cut-side-up, in 1-quart (9 x 5) glass loaf dish. Combine remaining ingredients, except endive leaves, in small mixing bowl; spoon into peach halves.

2. Microwave for 3 to 3½ minutes, on ROAST, or until peaches are heated through. Serve warm on endive leaves. May also be used as a plate garnish. 4 to 6 Servings

TIP: Substitute 1 can (16 oz.) pear halves, drained, or 3 fresh peaches, peeled, pitted and halved, for canned peaches.

RECIPE VARIATIONS

ALMOND PEACHES: Substitute ½ cup pineapple yogurt, 1 teaspoon sugar and ¼ teaspoon almond extract for cheese, sour cream and pecans. Top filled peaches with sliced almonds.

STRAWBERRY PEACHES: Substitute ½ cup strawberry preserves, 1 to 2 tablespoons orange-flavored liqueur or orange juice and ½ teaspoon grated orange rind for cheese, sour cream and pecans. Combine and spoon into peaches as directed in basic recipe. Microwave for 2½ to 3 minutes, on HIGH, or until peaches are heated through.

HOT GERMAN POTATO SALAD

Cook potatoes as directed on page 165.

- **8 slices bacon**
- **6 green onions, sliced**
- **½ cup chopped green pepper**
- **⅓ cup vinegar**
- **1 teaspoon sugar**
- **1 teaspoon salt**
- **Dash pepper**
- **1 egg, beaten**
- **5 cups sliced cooked potatoes**

1. Arrange bacon in a single layer in 3-quart (13 x 9) glass baking dish.

2. Microwave for 7 to 8 minutes, on HIGH, or until bacon is crisp. Crumble bacon; set aside. Reserve ¼ cup bacon drippings; pour into 2-quart glass casserole. Add onions and green pepper.

3. Microwave for about 2 minutes, on HIGH, or until vegetables are partly cooked. Stir in vinegar and seasonings. Add beaten egg; mix well.

4. Microwave for 1 minute on ROAST. Stir well and continue cooking for about 30 seconds, on ROAST, or until slightly thickened. Stir in potatoes and crumbled bacon. Cover with glass lid.

5. Microwave for 8 to 10 minutes, on ROAST, or until hot. About 6 Servings

TURKEY SALAD BAKE

A microwave oven makes hot, moist, flavorful salads an easy reality.

- **1 cup mayonnaise or salad dressing**
- **2 tablespoons dry white wine, if desired**
- **1 tablespoon lemon juice**
- **½ teaspoon onion salt**
- **5 cups cubed cooked turkey**
- **2 cups finely chopped celery**
- **1 jar (2 oz.) diced pimento, drained**
- **¼ cup slivered almonds**
- **2 green onions, sliced**
- **1 can (3 oz.) French-fried onion rings**

1. Combine mayonnaise, wine, lemon juice and onion salt in 2-quart glass casserole until smooth. Stir in remaining ingredients, except onion rings; mix well.

2. Microwave for 5 minutes on ROAST. Stir well; top with onion rings, and continue cooking for 3 to 4 minutes, on ROAST, or until hot (about 140° F.). Let stand 3 minutes before serving. 6 to 8 Servings

RECIPE VARIATIONS

CHICKEN SALAD BAKE: Substitute 5 cups cubed cooked chicken and ¼ cup chopped cashews for turkey and almonds.

HAM SALAD BAKE: Omit wine and lemon juice. Substitute 2 teaspoons prepared horseradish for onion salt. Substitute 4 cups finely chopped cooked ham for turkey; add 1 cup shredded Swiss cheese. Increase cooking time in basic recipe by 4 minutes. Serve on pineapple rings; garnish with parsley sprig.

CRAB SALAD BAKE: Decrease mayonnaise to ¾ cup and wine to 1 tablespoon. Substitute 1 teaspoon dill weed for onion salt. Substitute 1 can (6½ oz.) crab meat, drained; and 1 can (6½ oz.) tuna, drained, rinsed and flaked, for turkey. Add ½ cup finely chopped cucumber.

RASPBERRY PEACH SALAD

Use this recipe as a guide for preparing other gelatin salads with a microwave oven.

- **1 package (10 oz.) frozen red raspberries**
- **1 package (10 oz.) frozen peaches**
- **Water**
- **1 package (3 oz.) raspberry-flavored gelatin**
- **2 tablespoon sugar**
- **½ cup whipping cream, whipped**

1. Remove lid from frozen raspberry container. Place peaches in 1-quart glass casserole.

2. Microwave both for 7 to 8 minutes, on DEFROST, or until thawed. Drain fruits into a 4-cup glass measure; set aside fruits. Add enough water to make 1½ cups liquid. Stir in gelatin; mix well.

3. Microwave for 4 to 4½ minutes, on HIGH, or until mixture boils (about 200° F.). Divide mixture in half; pour half into medium mixing bowl. Chill both until consistency of unbeaten egg white.

4. Stir raspberries and peaches into half of gelatin; pour into 1½-quart (10 x 6) glass baking dish. Chill until firm.

5. Beat remaining half of gelatin and sugar until foamy with rotary beater; fold in whipped cream. Pour over fruit layer; chill. Cut in squares to serve. 6 to 8 Servings

RECIPE VARIATION

BASIC FRUIT FLAVORED PACKAGED GELATIN: Combine all water called for on gelatin package with gelatin; use cold water. Microwave for 4 to 5 minutes, on HIGH, or until hot (about 200° F.). Stir to dissolve. Pour into metal mold or serving dishes.

Sauces
Measure, Mix and Cook in a Cup

Here's How — and Why

Most Sauces Cook on HIGH: Microwave sauces on HIGH setting unless recipe calls for sensitive ingredients. Microwave 1 cup of sauce about 4 to 4½ minutes; 2 cups of sauce about 5 to 6 minutes. When sauces with eggs, cream, condensed milk, cheese or mushrooms are cooked by themselves in a microwave oven, use Microwave ROAST to prevent separation or popping. Sauces with a few sensitive ingredients cook on HIGH when other foods are also cooking in the oven because each food then absorbs less microwave intensity.

A Single Dish Does It: Mix, measure and cook sauces in a glass measuring cup. Choose a size at least twice as large as the sauce's volume to allow for bubbling — and a cup large enough to hold a rotary beater when necessary.

Sauces Must Boil to Thicken: Any sauce made with flour or cornstarch must reach a boiling point to cook the starch and thicken the sauce. Use the temperature in a recipe, if specified, to indicate when sauce is cooked.

A Beating Smoothes Sauces: Microwaves cook from all directions, so eliminate scorching — and constant stirring. However, flour, cornstarch and other thickenings tend to settle, so an occasional stirring from outside toward center of dish, plus beating with a rotary beater, keeps sauces velvet-smooth.

Overcooking Curdles: Overcooking curdles a sauce. Use an electric mixer or blender to regain smoothness.

The "*" Is a Reminder: Recipes marked with an "*" are a handy reminder that the food is cooked with two or more power settings. Stirring, when suggested, is convenient at this time.

Sauces REHEAT Superbly: Warm a sauce quickly and easily in its glass storage jar on REHEAT setting. Container should be uncovered and no more than half full when placed in the oven. Stir once to heat evenly.

Some Utensils Can Go into the Oven: Wood, plastic, rubber or metal spoons, whisks and scrapers may be left in a sauce during microwave cooking. DO NOT use silver tableware in the oven because it will tarnish.

Microwave-Conventional Comparison: Microwaves do not scorch food, so constant stirring while sauces cook is eliminated. Since no evaporation occurs, less liquid or more thickening is needed than in conventional sauce recipes. Thickenings must be thoroughly blended into microwave sauces to keep them smooth — and must be cooked thoroughly.

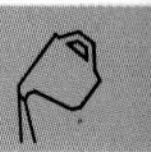

Pictured clockwise from the top: Caramel Sauce, recipe below; Fudge Sauce, page 150; Basic White Sauce, page 151.

CARAMEL SAUCE

Stir and beat for smoothest sauces.

1 cup packed brown sugar
1 tablespoon cornstarch
½ cup light cream
½ cup dark corn syrup
1 teaspoon vanilla
2 tablespoons butter or margarine

1. Combine all ingredients, except butter, in 4-cup glass measure; beat with rotary beater until smooth. Add butter.

2. Microwave for 5 minutes on ROAST. Beat well and continue cooking for about 2 minutes, on ROAST, or until bubbly (about 200° F.). Beat lightly; cool about 10 minutes to thicken, and serve. About 1⅓ Cups Sauce

FUDGE SAUCE

- 1 package (6 oz.) semi-sweet "real" chocolate pieces
- 1 square unsweetened chocolate
- ⅓ cup butter or margarine
- 2 cups powdered sugar
- 2 cans (5 oz. each) evaporated milk
- 1 teaspoon vanilla

Sauces must boil to cook and thicken.

1. Place all chocolate and butter in 4-cup glass measure.

2. Microwave for about 1½ minutes, on ROAST, or until melted. Stir in remaining ingredients; beat with rotary beater until smooth.

3. Microwave for 5 to 6 minutes, on ROAST, or until bubbly (about 200° F.). Serve warm.

About 2 Cups Sauce

RECIPE VARIATIONS

MOCHA FUDGE SAUCE: Add 2 tablespoons dry instant coffee with vanilla in basic sauce.

MINT FUDGE SAUCE: Substitute 1 teaspoon peppermint flavoring for vanilla in basic sauce.

ORANGE SAUCE

- ¼ cup sugar
- 1 tablespoon cornstarch
- Juice of 1 orange plus enough water to make 1 cup liquid
- 1 to 2 teaspoons grated orange rind
- 2 to 4 tablespoons Grand Marnier or other orange-flavored liqueur, if desired

HIGH setting cooks most sauces quickly.

1. Combine all ingredients, except liqueur, in 4-cup glass measure; beat with rotary beater until smooth.

2. Microwave for 2 minutes on HIGH. Beat well and continue cooking for about ½ minute, on HIGH, or until thickened (about 175° F.). Stir in Grand Marnier.

About 1½ Cups Sauce

RECIPE VARIATION

LEMON SAUCE: Substitute juice of 1 lemon and 1 tablespoon grated lemon rind for orange juice and orange rind in basic sauce. Omit Grand Marnier.

PARSLEY BUTTER

- ¼ cup butter or margarine
- 2 tablespoons snipped fresh parsley or 1 tablespoon dried parsley flakes.
- ½ teaspoon lemon juice

Fats attract microwaves. Use ROAST to melt and prevent spattering.

1. Place butter in 1-cup glass measure.

2. Microwave for about 1 minute, on ROAST, or until melted. Stir in parsley and lemon juice.

About ¼ Cup Parsley Butter

TIP: Any time you want to melt butter without seasonings, microwave for about 1 minute, on ROAST, or until melted.

RECIPE VARIATIONS

CHIVE BUTTER: Substitute 1 tablespoon chopped fresh or frozen chives for parsley and lemon juice in basic recipe.

DILL BUTTER: Substitute ½ teaspoon dill weed for parsley and lemon juice in basic recipe.

CHEESY GARLIC BUTTER: Substitute 2 tablespoons grated Parmesan cheese and ¼ teaspoon garlic powder for parsley and lemon juice in basic recipe.

ONION BUTTER: Substitute 1 tablespoon dry onion soup mix for parsley and lemon juice in basic recipe.

HOLLANDAISE SAUCE

- ¼ cup butter or margarine
- ¼ cup light cream
- 1 tablespoon lemon juice or vinegar
- 2 egg yolks, beaten
- ½ teaspoon dry mustard
- ¼ teaspoon salt

Sensitive ingredients cook on ROAST.

1. Place butter in 4-cup glass measure.

2. Microwave for about 1 minute, on ROAST, or until melted.

3. Stir in remaining ingredients, following order listed, then beat with rotary beater until smooth.

4. Microwave for 1 minute on ROAST. Beat well and continue cooking for about 1 minute, on ROAST, or until thickened (about 175° F.). Beat lightly and serve.

About ¾ Cup Sauce

TIP: If sauce curdles, add 1 teaspoon hot water and beat well.

RECIPE VARIATION

BÉARNAISE SAUCE: After adding salt to Hollandaise sauce, stir in all at once 1 tablespoon finely chopped onion, ½ teaspoon tarragon leaves, ½ teaspoon chervil leaves and 1 tablespoon dry white wine. Continue as directed in basic recipe.

About 1 Cup Sauce

GRAVY

Add or subtract liquid to thin or thicken a gravy.

⅓ cup meat or poultry drippings
⅓ cup unsifted all-purpose flour
1¾ cups warm broth or water
Salt
Pepper

1. Combine drippings and flour in 4-cup glass measure. Add broth and beat with rotary beater until smooth. Season to taste.

2. Microwave on HIGH for 2 minutes. Beat well and continue cooking for 1½ to 2 minutes, on HIGH, or until thickened (about 200° F.). Beat lightly and serve. About 2 Cups Gravy

TIP: For additional color, add 1 to 2 teaspoons soy sauce.

BASIC WHITE SAUCE

Proportion of fat to thickening is always equal in white and brown sauces.

1 cup milk
3 tablespoons all-purpose flour
¼ teaspoon salt
⅛ teaspoon pepper
3 tablespoons butter or margarine

1. Combine all ingredients, except butter, in 4-cup glass measure; beat with rotary beater until smooth. Add butter.

2. Microwave for 3 minutes on HIGH. Beat well and continue cooking for 1 to 1½ minutes on HIGH, or until thickened (about 175° F.). Beat lightly and serve. About 1 Cup Sauce

RECIPE VARIATIONS

THIN WHITE SAUCE: Use 2 tablespoons all-purpose flour and 2 tablespoons butter or margarine in basic recipe.

THICK WHITE SAUCE: Use ¼ cup all-purpose flour and ¼ cup butter or margarine in basic recipe.

BÉCHAMEL SAUCE: Add 1 green onion, chopped, and dash nutmeg with butter in basic recipe. About 1 Cup Sauce

EGG SAUCE: Stir in 2 hard-cooked eggs, finely chopped, when basic sauce has been cooked. Microwave for an additional 1 to 1½ minutes, on ROAST, or until hot. About 1½ Cups Sauce

CHEESE SAUCE: Add ½ cup shredded process American cheese and ¼ teaspoon Worcestershire sauce with butter in basic sauce. Microwave for 3 minutes on ROAST. Beat well and continue cooking for 2½ to 3 minutes, on ROAST, or until thickened (about 175° F.). Beat lightly and serve. About 1¼ Cups Sauce

BASIC BROWN SAUCE

Rotary beater smoothes sauces.

1 cup water
3 tablespoons all-purpose flour
¼ teaspoon salt
⅛ teaspoon pepper
3 tablespoons butter or margarine
1 small onion, finely chopped
1 teaspoon instant beef bouillon

1. Combine water, flour and seasonings in 4-cup glass measure; beat with rotary beater until smooth. Add remaining ingredients.

2. Microwave on HIGH for 3 minutes. Beat well and continue cooking for 1 to 1½ minutes, on HIGH, or until thickened, (about 200° F.). Beat lightly and serve. About 1½ Cups Sauce

RECIPE VARIATIONS

BORDELAISE SAUCE: Add ¼ cup red Bordeaux wine and ⅛ teaspoon thyme leaves after first cooking time in basic sauce. Beat well and continue cooking for 2 to 2½ minutes, on HIGH, or until thickened (about 200° F.). Beat lightly and serve. About 1¾ Cups Sauce

CHASSEUR SAUCE*: Add 1 jar (2½ oz.) sliced mushrooms, drained, ¼ cup dry white wine and 1 tablespoon catsup after first cooking time in basic sauce. Beat well and continue cooking for 3½ to 4 minutes, on ROAST, or until thickened (about 200° F.). Beat lightly and serve. About 2 Cups Sauce

MADEIRA SAUCE: Add ¼ cup Madeira or dry sherry, 1 tablespoon catsup and 1 teaspoon dried parsley flakes after first cooking time in basic sauce. Beat well and continue cooking for 2 to 2½ minutes, on HIGH, or until thickened (about 200° F.). Beat lightly and serve. About 1¾ Cups Sauce

Soups & Sandwiches

Super Meals for the No-Time-Cook

Here's How — and Why

Soup Settings: There are three basic soup techniques. First, microwave soups made with raw vegetables on HIGH to retain flavor and color. Second, microwave soups made with uncooked meat or chicken on HIGH for fast heating, then finish on SIMMER to blend flavors into broth and tenderize meat. Also use this HIGH/SIMMER technique to soften and tenderize dried peas, beans and lentils in soup. Third, microwave soups made of cooked meat and/or vegetables on REHEAT so food holds shape and texture. Most canned soups are heated on REHEAT. See charts in this chapter.

Soup Exceptions: Microwave sensitive ingredients such as clams, cream, cheese or mushrooms on ROAST setting or lower to prevent "popping" or curdling.

Sandwich Settings: Microwave uncooked ground beef on HIGH for fast heat penetration. Microwave fillings made with cooked ingredients on REHEAT. Note that several thin slices of cooked meat heat better than 1 thick slice. Microwave fillings with cheese on ROAST to prevent overcooking. Grill sandwiches using a microwave browning grill and the instructions for grilled cheese sandwiches in this chapter.

Sandwich Bread Tips: Bread, rolls and taco shells all make great microwave sandwiches. Toasted bread makes the firmest base for hot sandwiches. Heat bread and rolls just until warm, not hot, or bread toughens. Taco shells freshen nicely when warmed for 15 to 20 seconds on REHEAT.

Cook Soup in a Bowl— A Sandwich on Paper: Microwave soups in glass casseroles, pretty glass or pottery serving bowls without gold, silver or other metal trim. Measure and microwave "instant" soups right in a glass measure. Note that the cooking container must be at least twice the size of ingredient volume so mixture does not boil over. Microwave most sandwiches easily on a paper towel or napkin and wrap thick sandwiches loosely to absorb steam.

What to Cover: Most soups are cooked covered with fitted glass lids or wax paper. Lift lids away from hands or arms to prevent steam burns. Plastic wrap may also be used as a cover. Pierce it and allow steam to escape before removing from hot food. Microwave thin sandwiches, uncovered; wrap thick sandwiches loosely. Standing time, when called, completes cooking.

Soup and Sandwich "ADD-A-" Meals: Microwave soup and sandwiches at the same time and create a super meal in minutes. Oven settings usually increase to HIGH because a large quantity of food is being cooked. When either or both foods contain large amounts of sensitive ingredients, cook both on ROAST setting. When a soup cooks for a longer time on SIMMER, add sandwiches during the last few minutes of cooking and microwave both on SIMMER. When soup is precooked, heat it on the upper rack, place sandwich on bottom shelf. If soup is cooking "from scratch," place soup on bottom shelf, sandwich on upper rack. Specific recipes give accurate guides for cooking times.

The "*" Helps You Remember: The "*" at the end of a recipe title is a reminder that there are two or more power settings. Stirring, when suggested, is convenient at this time.

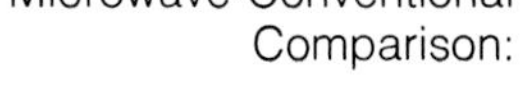

Microwave-Conventional Comparison: Microwaved soups cook quickly and retain fresh food flavors, however broth flavors are not as hearty as those in long-simmered, home-cooked soups. Microwave sandwiches heat right on paper in minutes — however, overcooking toughens bread and makes cheese stringy.

Pictured: Club Hero Sandwich, page 159; Canned Tomato Soup, chart, page 154.

HOW TO COOK DEHYDRATED SOUP MIX

- Pour water into glass casserole or 8-ounce mugs. Add soup mix, if directed on package, and heat. Heat water only, if package directs.
- Cover containers with glass lids, wax paper or plastic wrap.
- Microwave on HIGH until liquid boils (about 200° F.).
- Stir in dry mix, if package specifies that mix is added after water boils, and continue cooking as chart directs.
- Microwave soups with dehydrated rice or noodles on DEFROST until rice or noodles are tender.
- Let stand, covered, 5 minutes before serving.

SOUP	AMOUNT	GLASS CONTAINER	WATER	SETTING	MINUTES
CUP-OF-SOUP Any kind, 1½-oz. pkg. (with 4 envelopes)	1 envelope	1 (8 oz.) mug	⅔ cup	HIGH	2 to 2½ (about 200° F.)
	2 envelopes	2 (8 oz.) mugs	⅔ cup ea.	HIGH	3 to 3½ (about 200° F.)
	4 envelopes	4 (8 oz.) mugs	⅔ cup ea.	HIGH	6 to 7 (about 200° F.)
SOUP MIX Without rice or noodles, 2¾-oz. pkg. (with 2 envelopes)	1 envelope	2-qt. casserole	4 cups	HIGH	8 to 10 (about 200° F.)
				add mix; HIGH	4 to 5 (about 200° F.)
With rice or Noodles, 3½-oz. * pkg. (with 2 envelopes)	1 envelope	2-qt. casserole	3 cups	HIGH	7 to 8 (about 200° F.)
				add mix; DEFROST	5 to 6 (about 200° F.)
5-oz. pkg. *	½ box	2-qt. casserole	5 cups	HIGH	9 to 10 (about 200° F.)
				add mix; DEFROST	10 to 12 (about 200° F.)

HOW TO HEAT CANNED SOUP

- Pour soup into 1½-quart or 2-quart glass casserole.
- Add milk or water as directed on can.
- Cover with glass lid, wax paper or plastic wrap.
- Microwave on REHEAT until hot (about 160° F.) — except mushroom soup which heats on ROAST to prevent "popping."
- Stir when taken from oven.
- Let stand, covered, 3 minutes before serving.

SOUP	SETTING	MINUTES
DILUTED Broth 10½-oz.	REHEAT	3 to 4 (about 160° F.)
Tomato, Cream; Noodle, or Vegetable 10¾-oz.	REHEAT	5 to 6 (about 160° F.)
26-oz.	REHEAT	8 to 9 (about 160° F.)
Mushroom, Bean or Pea 10¾-oz.	ROAST	7 to 8 (about 160° F.)
UNDILUTED Chunk Vegetable, Noodle 10¾-oz.	REHEAT	2½ to 3½ (about 160° F.)
19-oz.	REHEAT	5 to 7 (about 160° F.)

TURKEY BROTH *

Lift covers away from hand to prevent steam burns.

- Turkey gizzard, heart, liver and neck
- 3 cups water
- ½ teaspoon salt
- ⅛ teaspoon pepper
- 1 bay leaf

1. Combine all ingredients in 2-quart glass casserole. Cover with glass lid.
2. Microwave for about 15 minutes on HIGH. Stir well and recover.
3. Microwave for 18 to 20 minutes, on SIMMER, or until flavors are blended (about 200° F.). Remove meat and bay leaf from broth. Use broth for soup or gravy. Let stand, covered, 5 minutes.

About 3 Cups Broth

ONION SOUP WITH DUMPLINGS

Dumplings steam light and tender when cooked with a cover.

- 2 medium onions, thinly sliced
- 2 cans (10½ oz. each) condensed consommé
- 1 cup water
- 2 tablespoons soy sauce
- ½ teaspoon thyme leaves

Cheese Dumplings:

- 1 cup biscuit mix
- ⅓ cup shredded Swiss cheese
- ⅓ cup milk

1. Combine all soup ingredients in 3-quart glass casserole. Cover with glass lid.
2. Microwave for 7 to 8 minutes, on HIGH, or until boiling (about 200° F.). Drop Cheese Dumplings by tablespoonfuls into soup; recover.
3. Microwave for 6 to 7 minutes, on HIGH, or until dumplings are no longer doughy. Let stand, covered, 5 minutes before serving.
4. **Cheese Dumplings:** Combine all ingredients in small mixing bowl; mix with fork until moistened.

About 4 Servings

VICHYSSOISE

Vegetable soups microwave quickly on HIGH.

- 2 medium potatoes, peeled and sliced
- 1½ cups thinly sliced Spanish onions or leeks
- 3 cups chicken broth
- ¼ cup unsifted all-purpose flour
- ½ teaspoon salt
- Dash white pepper
- ¼ cup cold water
- 1 cup light cream

1. Place potatoes, onions and chicken broth in 2-quart glass casserole. Cover with glass lid.
2. Microwave for 13 to 15 minutes, on HIGH, or until potatoes are tender. Purée in electric blender or press through colander; return to casserole. Combine flour, seasonings and water in small bowl until smooth; stir into potato mixture.
3. Microwave 8 to 9 minutes, on HIGH, or until thickened (about 190° F.). Cool slightly and stir in cream. Chill and serve in soup bowls or cups.

4 to 6 Servings

HOME-STYLE SPLIT PEA SOUP *

- 1 package (16 oz.) dried yellow split peas (2 cups)
- 1 to 1½ lbs. ham hocks
- 1 onion, finely chopped
- 1 carrot, sliced
- 1 teaspoon salt
- 1 teaspoon dried parsley flakes
- ½ teaspoon sage
- ¼ teaspoon pepper
- 6 cups water

1. Place peas in 4-quart glass casserole. Soak at least 8 hours in cold water; drain.
2. Combine all ingredients in 4-quart glass casserole. Cover with glass lid.
3. Microwave for 30 minutes on HIGH. Stir well and recover.
4. Microwave for 20 to 25 minutes, on SIMMER, or until peas are soft (about 190° F.).
5. Remove ham hocks from broth; cool. Remove meat from bones and cut into small pieces. Return meat to casserole; mix well and recover.
6. Microwave for 6 to 8 minutes, on REHEAT, or until hot (about 160° F.). Let stand, covered, 5 minutes before serving.

About 10 Servings

FARM-STYLE VEGETABLE SOUP *

Use oven rack when cooking soup and sandwiches together.

- 2 medium potatoes, peeled
- 2 carrots, sliced
- 2 small onions, chopped
- 1 cup shredded cabbage
- 1 can (12 oz.) whole kernel corn, undrained
- 4 cups beef stock
- 1 can (16 oz.) stewed tomatoes
- 1 teaspoon salt
- ½ teaspoon thyme leaves
- ⅛ teaspoon pepper

1. Combine all ingredients in 4-quart glass casserole. Cover with glass lid.
2. Microwave for 20 minutes on HIGH. Stir well and recover.
3. Microwave for 20 to 25 minutes, on SIMMER, or until flavors are blended (about 190° F.). Let stand, covered, 5 minutes before serving.

About 6 Servings

ADD-A-SANDWICH: Place 6 wieners in 6 split hot dog buns and wrap each loosely in paper towel or napkin; set aside. Prepare Farm-Style Vegetable Soup through Step 2. Microwave for 20 minutes on SIMMER. Place oven rack in oven; place hot dogs on upper rack. Continue cooking both for 5 to 6 minutes, on SIMMER, or until soup is hot (about 160° F.).

CREAMY SHRIMP-HAM SOUP

Sauté vegetables in butter on HIGH.

2 tablespoons butter or margarine
½ cup chopped celery
4 green onions, sliced
¼ cup finely chopped green pepper
1 can (10¾ oz.) condensed cream of shrimp soup
2 cups milk
1 can (4½ oz.) broken shrimp, drained
1 cup cubed cooked ham

1. Place butter, celery, green onion and green pepper in 2-quart glass casserole.

2. Microwave for 4 minutes on HIGH. Stir in remaining ingredients. Cover with glass lid.

3. Microwave for 10 to 12 minutes, on REHEAT, or until hot (about 160° F.). Let stand, covered, 5 minutes before serving. 4 to 6 Servings

TOMATO SOUP

¼ cup butter or margarine
1 cup finely chopped celery
1 can (46 oz.) tomato juice
1 teaspoon sugar
½ teaspoon salt
¼ teaspoon celery salt
⅛ teaspoon pepper
Dash hot pepper sauce
Lemon slices

1. Place butter and celery in 2½-quart glass casserole.

2. Microwave for 5 minutes on HIGH. Stir in remaining ingredients, except lemon slices. Cover with glass lid.

3. Microwave for 15 to 17 minutes, on REHEAT, or until hot (about 160° F.). Let stand, covered, 5 minutes before serving. Top each serving with lemon slice. 4 to 6 Servings

ADD-A-SANDWICH: Prepare Hot Tuna Buns, below, through Step 1; set aside. Prepare Tomato Soup through Step 2; place on bottom shelf of oven. Microwave for 14 minutes on REHEAT. Place oven rack in oven; place buns on upper rack. Continue cooking both for 2 to 3 minutes, on REHEAT, or until soup is hot (about 160° F.).

RECIPE VARIATIONS

TOMATO CONSOMMÉ: Substitute 1 jar (32 oz.) tomato juice and 1 can (10½ oz.) condensed consommé for tomato juice in basic recipe. Add 1 tablespoon dry sherry and ½ teaspoon thyme leaves. Reduce final cooking time by about 4 minutes.

CHUNKY TOMATO SOUP: Substitute 1 can (16 oz.) stewed tomatoes for tomato juice in basic recipe. Add 1 can (10¾ oz.) condensed chicken broth, 1 soup can water and 1 tablespoon lemon juice. Reduce final cooking time by 8 to 9 minutes.

HOT TUNA BUNS

Cheese and mayonnaise are sensitive; microwave on ROAST.

1 can (6½ oz.) tuna, drained and flaked
1 cup chopped celery
½ cup shredded Swiss cheese
¼ cup mayonnaise or salad dressing
2 tablespoons catsup
⅛ teaspoon salt
Dash pepper
6 hamburger buns, split and toasted

1. Combine all ingredients, except buns, in small mixing bowl; mix well. Fill split buns with tuna mixture. Wrap each filled bun loosely in paper towel or napkin.

2. Microwave for 2½ to 3 minutes, on ROAST, or until hot (about 140° F.). 6 Sandwiches

ADD-A-SOUP: Prepare Hot Tuna Buns through Step 1; set aside. Measure water into 2-cup glass measure according to package direction on 2 individual packages chicken noodle cup-of-soup. Place water on upper rack of oven. Microwave for 4 minutes on HIGH. Place buns on bottom shelf and continue cooking both for about 3 minutes, on HIGH, or until water boils (about 200° F.). Make soup as directed on package.

TACOS

Uncooked ground beef microwaves on HIGH.

1 lb. ground beef
1½ teaspoons chili powder
½ teaspoon salt
½ teaspoon garlic powder
⅛ teaspoon cayenne pepper
¼ cup water
Taco shells
Cheddar cheese, shredded
Lettuce, shredded
Onion, finely chopped
Tomato, chopped

1. Crumble ground beef into 1½-quart glass casserole. Cover with glass lid.

2. Microwave for 5 minutes on HIGH; drain. Stir in seasonings and water and continue cooking for 3 to 4 minutes, on HIGH, or until meat is well done.

3. Fill each taco shell with about 2 heaping tablespoons of meat filling. Top with remaining ingredients. 10 to 12 Tacos

TIP: Taco shells can be heated for 15 to 20 seconds on REHEAT before filling.

REUBEN SALAD SANDWICH

1 can (12 oz.) corned beef
¾ cup sauerkraut, drained
1 small apple, cored and shredded
1 cup shredded Swiss cheese
2 tablespoons Thousand Island Dressing
1 teaspoon dill weed
2 teaspoons prepared mustard
8 pumpernickel buns

Wrap thick sandwiches loosely in paper towel or napkin.

1. Break up corned beef in medium mixing bowl. Stir in remaining ingredients, except buns; mix well. Spoon ½ cup corned beef mixture into each split bun. Wrap each filled bun loosely in paper towel or napkin.

2. Microwave on ROAST until heated through (about 140° F.):
1 bun — 1 to 1½ minutes.
2 buns — 2 to 2½ minutes.
4 buns — 3½ to 4 minutes.
8 buns — 4 to 4½ minutes.

8 Reuben Salad Sandwiches

TIP: Substitute 8 ounces corned beef, chopped, for canned corned beef.

ADD-A-SOUP: Prepare 4 Reuben Salad Sandwiches through Step 1; set aside. Combine 1 can (10½ oz.) condensed chicken with rice soup and water, as directed on can, in 1½-quart glass casserole; cover with glass lid. Place soup on upper rack of oven. Microwave for 4 minutes on HIGH. Place sandwiches on bottom shelf and continue cooking both for 3 to 4 minutes, on HIGH, or until soup is hot (about 160° F.).

SLICED MEAT SANDWICHES

Butter or margarine
Mayonnaise or salad dressing
Buns
Sliced roast beef

Thinly-sliced meat heats more evenly than thick meat slices.

1. Spread butter and mayonnaise on buns. Place beef slices between split buns. Wrap loosely in paper towel or napkin.

2. Microwave on REHEAT or until hot (about 140° F.).
1 sandwich — 45 to 50 seconds.
2 sandwiches — 1 to 1½ minutes.
4 sandwiches — 2 to 2½ minutes.

ADD-A-SOUP: Prepare Sliced Meat Sandwich through Step 1; set aside. Combine 1 can (10¾ oz.) condensed tomato soup and water, as directed on can, in 1½-quart glass casserole; cover with glass lid. Place soup on upper rack of oven. Microwave for 4 minutes on HIGH. Place sandwiches on bottom shelf and continue cooking both for 2 to 3 minutes, on HIGH, or until soup is hot (about 160° F.).

RECIPE VARIATIONS

MINTED LAMB SANDWICH: Add 1 teaspoon chopped fresh mint or ½ teaspoon dry mint leaves to mayonnaise. Substitute sliced cooked lamb for beef.

TURKEY SUPER STACK: Substitute sliced cooked turkey for beef. Add 1 slice Swiss cheese, 1 tomato slice and 1 onion slice to each sandwich. Microwave for 4 to 5 minutes, on ROAST, or until hot (about 140° F.).

Pictured: Creamy Shrimp-Ham Soup, recipe opposite, garnished with whole green onion; Sliced Meat Sandwich, recipe above, garnished with green pepper slice and cherry tomato.

HIKERS' HOT DOGS

Paper wrapping absorbs extra moisture.

- 1 medium green pepper, chopped
- 1 cup sauerkraut, drained
- ½ cup Russian Dressing
- 8 wieners
- 8 hot dog buns

1. Combine all ingredients, except wieners and buns, in small mixing bowl. Place wieners in split hot dog buns; spoon mixture over wieners. Wrap each filled bun loosely in paper towel or napkin.

2. Microwave 5 to 5½ minutes, on REHEAT, or until hot (about 140° F.).

8 Hot Dogs

RECIPE VARIATION

BARBECUED WIENER DOGS: Omit sauerkraut mixture. Combine ¼ cup chili sauce, ¼ cup catsup, 1 tablespoon prepared mustard and ½ teaspoon Worcestershire sauce in 2-cup glass measure. Microwave for 1½ to 2 minutes, on HIGH, or until hot (about 110° F.). Warm hot dogs as directed on page 121; spoon sauce over warmed hot dogs.

FISH STICK SANDWICHES

- 1 package (8 oz.) frozen fish sticks
- 4 hamburger buns
- 4 tomato slices
- 4 slices process American cheese

Tartar Sauce:

- ⅓ cup mayonnaise or salad dressing
- 2 tablespoons chopped green pepper
- 1 tablespoon chopped onion
- 2 tablespoons chopped sweet pickles
- 1 teaspoon prepared mustard
- 1 teaspoon lemon juice
- ¼ teaspoon salt

1. Place frozen fish sticks on glass plate.

2. Microwave for 3 minutes on DEFROST. Spread Tartar Sauce on buns. Place 2 fish sticks on bottom half of each bun. Top with 1 tomato slice and 1 cheese slice. Place other half of bun on top. Wrap loosely in paper towel or napkin.

3. Microwave on ROAST until hot (about 140° F.).
   1 sandwich — 2½ to 3 minutes.
   2 sandwiches — 3½ to 4 minutes.
   4 sandwiches — 5 to 6 minutes.

4. **Tartar Sauce:** Combine all ingredients in small bowl.

4 Servings

ADD-A-SOUP: Prepare Fish Stick Sandwiches through Step 2; set aside. Prepare 1 can (10¾ oz.) condensed cream of mushroom soup according to directions on can. Fill 2 glass soup bowls ⅔ full; cover, and place on upper rack of oven. Microwave for 4 minutes on ROAST. Place sandwiches on bottom shelf and continue cooking both for 7 to 8 minutes, on ROAST, or until soup is hot (about 160° F.).

BACON-CHEESE OPEN FACED SANDWICHES

Use your favorite breads, English muffins or bagels.

- 4 slices bacon
- 4 green onions, sliced
- 1 jar (5 oz.) sharp process cheese spread
- ½ teaspoon lemon juice
- Dash salt
- 4 slices bread, toasted

Sandwich Garnishes:

- Green pepper, sliced
- Green onion
- Mushrooms, sliced
- Tomato slices
- Avocado slices
- Onion rings
- Olives, sliced
- Bacon wrapped olives
- Cheese, shredded

1. Place bacon slices between paper towels or paper napkins on glass or pottery plate.

2. Microwave for 4 to 4½ minutes, on HIGH, or until crisp; set aside. Combine remaining ingredients, except bread, in small glass mixing bowl.

3. Microwave for 30 seconds on ROAST. Spread cheese mixture on bread slices. Crumble bacon over top. Place each sandwich on paper towel on bottom shelf on oven.

4. Microwave for 1 to 1½ minutes, on ROAST, or until warm. Top with desired garnishes.

4 Sandwiches

RECIPE VARIATIONS

PIMENTO SANDWICH: Add 1 jar (2½ oz.) chopped pimento and ¼ cup chopped green pepper to sandwich mixture.

SWISS SALAD SANDWICH: Substitute ¼ cup mayonnaise or salad dressing, ½ cup shredded Swiss cheese and ¼ cup chopped stuffed olives for cheese-onion mixture. Cut bacon slices in half; wrap around additional stuffed olives and use as garnish.

ITALIAN SANDWICH: Substitute ¼ cup mayonnaise or salad dressing, ¼ cup grated Parmesan cheese, ¼ teaspoon oregano leaves and ¼ teaspoon dried parsley flakes for cheese-onion mixture.

CLUB HERO SANDWICH

Overheated bread toughens.

6 slices bacon
1 loaf (1 lb.) French bread
1 package (3 oz.) sliced smoked turkey
8 slices Swiss cheese
8 slices (¾ oz. each) process American cheese
2 tomatoes, sliced

Dressing:
4 green onions, sliced
1 cup sour cream
¼ cup mustard
½ teaspoon horseradish
¾ teaspoon dill weed

1. Arrange bacon in single layer in 2-quart (12 x 7) glass baking dish.

2. Microwave for 5 to 6 minutes, on HIGH, or until crisp. Slice French bread in half cross-wise, then horizontally in thirds. Spread Dressing on all interior surfaces of bread. Place turkey slices on bottom bread slices; top with Swiss cheese slices and middle bread slices. Top with American cheese slices, tomato slices and bacon strips. Place top of bread slices over bacon strips. Wrap loosely in paper towel or napkin.

3. Microwave for 9 to 10 minutes, on ROAST, or until warm (about 140° F.).

4. Dressing: Combine Dressing ingredients in small mixing bowl.

About 8 Servings

SLOPPY JOE SANDWICHES *

Warm 6 buns 25 to 30 seconds on REHEAT.

1 lb. ground beef
1 medium onion, chopped
1 cup bottled barbecue sauce
2 tablespoons packed brown sugar
1 teaspoon prepared mustard
6 hamburger buns, warmed

1. Crumble ground beef into 2-quart glass casserole. Stir in onion. Cover with glass lid.

2. Microwave for 5 minutes on HIGH; drain. Stir in remaining ingredients, except buns; recover.

3. Microwave for 5 to 6 minutes, on REHEAT, or until hot (about 160° F.). Let stand, covered, 5 minutes before serving. Spoon into warm split hamburger buns.

6 Sandwiches

GRILLED CHEESE SANDWICH

Grill a Reuben Sandwich using this technique.

8 slices bread
4 slices process American cheese
¼ cup butter or margarine, softened

1. Preheat microwave browning grill as directed in manufacturer's instruction book.

2. Place cheese slice between 2 bread slices. Butter outside of sandwiches. Place on preheated grill.

3. Microwave for 1 minute on HIGH. Turn sandwiches over and continue cooking on HIGH until cheese is melted:
    1 sandwich — 15 to 30 seconds.
    2 sandwiches — 30 to 45 seconds.
    4 sandwiches — 1 to 1½ minutes.

1 to 4 Sandwiches

RECIPE VARIATION

DOUBLE DECK GRILLED CHEESE: Add 4 slices bread, 4 slices Swiss cheese and 1 package (3 oz.) cream cheese, softened, to basic recipe. Top each of 4 bread slices with 1 slice process American cheese. Spread cream cheese over American cheese; top with bread slice. Spread cream cheese on bread, top with Swiss cheese slice and remaining bread slice. Butter outside of sandwiches. Microwave as directed in basic recipe, increasing cooking time for second side by 30 seconds.

GRILLED FRIJOLE SANDWICH

1 can (16 oz.) refried beans
1 can (4 oz.) chopped green chilies
½ cup chopped green pepper
1 tablespoon chopped onion
½ teaspoon chili powder
½ teaspoon salt
16 slices bread
2 cups shredded Cheddar cheese
⅓ cup butter or margarine, softened

1. Combine beans, chilies, green pepper, onion and seasonings in small mixing bowl. Spread about ¼ cup mixture on each of 8 bread slices. Top with shredded cheese and second bread slice. Butter outside of sandwiches.

2. Preheat microwave browning grill as directed in manufacturer's instruction book. Place 4 sandwiches on preheated grill.

3. Microwave for 1 minute on HIGH. Turn sandwiches over and continue cooking for 1½ to 2 minutes, on HIGH, or until cheese is melted. Repeat with remaining sandwiches.

8 Sandwiches

Vegetables

Full-Flavored, Nutritious and Tender-Crisp

Here's How — and Why

HIGH Setting Cooks Fresh and Frozen Vegetables:	Vegetables cook quickly on Microwave HIGH and reach the table tender-crisp, with top flavor and nutrition.
REHEAT Canned Vegetables:	Canned vegetables are cooked — use REHEAT to prevent mushing.
Microwave Creamed Vegetable Mixtures on ROAST:	Vegetable mixtures made with sour cream, cheese, eggs, cream, condensed cream of mushroom soup or condensed cheese soup cook on Microwave ROAST. This slightly lower setting helps prevent separation and preserves tender texture throughout mixtures.
Cook in Glass Dish or Plastic Pouch:	Cook vegetables in a glass baking dish or casserole without gold, silver or other metal trim. Pouches of frozen vegetables must be slit and may be placed in a glass baking dish or directly on oven's bottom shelf to cook. Cover dishes, when called for in a recipe, using glass lids or wax paper. Tip lids away from arm when lifting off of steamy food. Plastic wrap may be used as a cover. Pierce it and allow steam to escape before removing.
Just a Little Water Steams — Holds Nutrients:	Fresh vegetables need only enough moisture to steam tender-crisp quickly — about ¼ cup water for ½ to 1 lb. Add another ¼ cup water for softer vegetables. Fresh corn-on-the-cob and whole, unpeeled vegetables need no water to cook. Frozen vegetables cook icy-side-up and usually have enough moisture in the package. Stir vegetables once during cooking to help distribute moisture from dish bottom and assure even tenderness.
Important! Pierce Whole, Unpeeled Vegetables:	Whole, unpeeled vegetables, such as eggplant, squash, sweet potatoes, baking or boiling potatoes, should be pierced or pricked before placing in the oven. Piercing makes tiny vents through which steam escapes during cooking, prevents "popping" and a messy oven. Note: Oven may be steamy while whole, unpeeled vegetables cook.
Arrangement Key to Even Cooking:	Arrange fresh spear vegetables, such as broccoli, so the parts that take longer to cook (stalk) are toward outside of dish.
How to Salt:	It is most convenient to add salt before cooking. However, salt tends to dehydrate so you may prefer to add it at the end of cooking. Test and see.
Vegetables Usually Cook on the Bottom Shelf:	Remove rack and cook vegetables on the oven's bottom shelf unless otherwise specified in a recipe.
Standing Time Finishes Cooking:	Microwaves continue to cook, by conduction, after food comes from the oven — especially unpeeled vegetables because skins hold heat. When a recipe calls for a standing period, follow directions carefully.
Look for the "✱" Reminder:	Recipes marked with an "✱" are a handy reminder that food is cooked with two or more power settings. Stir at this time, when suggested.
Microwave Vegetables and Meats Together:	See the chapters on Oven Meals, Main Dishes and Stews, Fish and Seafood, Poultry and Game Birds for ways to microwave vegetables and meat or fish dishes at the same time.
Microwave-Conventional Comparison:	Microwaved vegetables are steam-cooked and so tender-crisp — firm to the touch when removed from the oven. Standing time finishes cooking. Speed-cooking plus minimal liquid preserve water-soluble vitamins in the vegetables. When adapting a conventional recipe, reduce liquids and cook as specified in a similar recipe in this chapter.

Pictured: Baked Potato with butter, chart, page 165.

HOW TO MICROWAVE FRESH AND FROZEN VEGETABLES

- Check the cooking guidelines at the beginning of this chapter.
- Wash and prepare fresh vegetables as outlined in the chart.
- Pierce or prick whole, unpeeled fresh vegetables such as baking or boiling potatoes, sweet potatoes, squash or eggplant before placing in the oven.
- Slit the center of all frozen vegetable pouches.
- Place vegetables in a glass baking dish or casserole. A frozen pouch may be placed in a glass baking dish or directly on oven's bottom shelf.
- Arrange spear vegetables with stalk end toward outside of cooking dish.
- Add ¼ cup water when cooking fresh vegetables, except baked potatoes, squash or ears of corn.
- When vegetables are frozen in a sauce without a pouch, place in a 1½-quart glass casserole and add liquid as directed by manufacturer.
- Cover dish with glass lid or wax paper.
- Microwave all fresh and frozen vegetables on HIGH setting until tender-crisp. Stirring helps hasten cooking.
- Vegetables may seem firm when oven cooking is completed. But cooking continues after food is removed from the oven. Therefore, allow vegetables to stand 2 to 5 minutes after cooking, depending on amount and density of the food.

VEGETABLE	PREPARATION FOR FRESH VEGETABLES	AMOUNT	MINUTES	SAUCES AND SEASONINGS
ARTICHOKES	Wash thoroughly. Cut 1 inch off top, straight across. Remove any loose leaves around bottom. Remove thorns on each outer leaf by clipping about ½ inch off tips. Dip cut edges in lemon juice to prevent darkening. After cooking, remove prickly core with spoon.	**Fresh, 3½ inches in diameter**		Sauces: Hollandaise, Béarnaise, Mornay, Seasoned Butters
		1	4 to 5	
		2	7 to 8	
		3	9 to 10	Seasonings: Butter, Lemon Juice, Nutmeg
		4	11 to 12	
		Frozen hearts		
		10-oz. pkg.	5 to 6	
ASPARAGUS: SPEARS, CUT	Wash thoroughly to remove dirt and sand. Snap off tough stalk discarding base. Leave spears whole, cut or break into 1 to 2-inch pieces.	Fresh		Sauces: Béchamel, Cheese, Egg, Hollandaise, Seasoned Butters
		¾ lb.	5 to 6	
		1½ lbs.	9 to 10	
		Frozen		
		9-oz. pouch	6 to 7	Seasonings: Butter, Lemon Juice, Toasted Almonds
		10-oz. pkg.	8 to 9	
BEANS: GREEN AND WAX	Wash green and wax beans thoroughly; remove ends. Leave whole, cut lengthwise into strips, break or cut into 1 to 2-inch pieces. Add about ¼ cup more water for softer beans.	Fresh		Sauces: Cheese, Mustard
		1 lb.	12 to 14	
		2 lbs.	16 to 18	Seasonings: Butter, Cheese, Chives, Crumbled Bacon, Mushrooms, Nutmeg, Toasted Almonds, Water Chestnuts
		Frozen, French style or cut		
		9-oz. pkg.	8 to 9	
		10-oz. pouch	7 to 8	
BEANS: LIMA	Remove beans from shell; wash thoroughly.	Fresh		Sauces: Cheese, Seasoned Butters
		1 lb.	10 to 12	
		2 lbs.	14 to 16	
		Frozen		Seasonings: Butter, Chopped Ham, Crumbled Bacon
		10-oz. pkg.	6 to 7	
		10-oz. pouch	7 to 8	
BEETS	Scrub beet with brush to remove dirt. Leave 1 inch of top attached to beet. Peel and cut off stem after beets are cooked.	**Fresh, whole**		Seasonings: Butter, Orange Juice Concentrate, Orange Marmalade
		4 medium	14 to 16	
BROCCOLI	Wash carefully, removing large outer leaves and tough portion of stalk. Slit stem ends to speed cooking.	Fresh		Sauces: Cheese, Egg, Mustard, Hollandaise, Mornay
		1½ lbs.	10 to 12	
		Frozen		
		10-oz. pkg.	8 to 9	
		10-oz. pouch	8 to 9	

Microwave all fresh and frozen vegetables on HIGH setting.

VEGETABLE	PREPARATION FOR FRESH VEGETABLES	AMOUNT	MINUTES	SAUCES AND SEASONINGS
BRUSSELS SPROUTS	Discard wilted outer leaves, wash thoroughly. Cut off stem.	**Fresh** ½ lb. 1 lb. **Frozen** 8-oz. pkg. 10-oz. pouch	 5 to 7 7 to 8 6 to 7 6 to 7	Sauces: Mustard, Hollandaise, Béarnaise Seasonings: Butter
CABBAGE	Wash and remove any wilted outside leaves. Add a little vinegar or lemon juice to red cabbage to retain color	**Fresh, shredded** ½ medium 1 medium	 5 to 6 8 to 9	Sauces: Cheese, Béchamel, Mustard Seasonings: Butter, Crumbled Bacon, Nutmeg
CARROTS	Scrape or peel with vegetable peeler to remove thin layer of outer skin. Cut off tops and tips. Leave whole, slice, dice or sliver. Fresh, young, tender carrots microwave best.	**Fresh, sliced, diced, slivered** 2 medium 4 medium 6 medium **Fresh, whole** 2 medium 4 medium 6 medium **Frozen, diced or whole** 10-oz. pouch	 4 to 5 7 to 9 9 to 11 5 to 6 8 to 10 10 to 12 8 to 9	Sauces: Béchamel, Onion, Seasoned Butters Seasonings: Butter, Cinnamon, Cloves, Ginger, Crumbled Bacon, Nutmeg, Parsley
CAULIFLOWER	Remove outer leaves and excess part of stem. Wash thoroughly. Leave whole or cut into flowerettes.	**Fresh, broken into flowerettes** 1 medium **Fresh, whole** 1 medium 1 large **Frozen** 10-oz. pkg.	 7 to 8 8 to 9 12 to 14 8 to 9	Sauces: Cheese, Hollandaise, Béarnaise Seasonings: Butter, Chives, Nutmeg, Thousand Island Dressing
CELERY	Separate stalks and wash thoroughly. Cut off base and any blemishes. Slice or cut into strips.	**Fresh, 1-inch slices or strips** 6 stalks	 8 to 10	Sauces: Cheese, Mornay Seasonings: Bouillon, Brown Gravy Mix, Butter
CORN, KERNEL	Remove husk and silk; trim ends. Wash thoroughly. Cut corn off cob using sharp knife.	**Fresh, cut from cob** 1½ cups 3 cups **Frozen** 10-oz. pkg. 10-oz. pouch	 6 to 7 7 to 8 6 to 7 5 to 6	Sauces: Mornay, Seasoned Butters Seasonings: Butter, Cream Cheese, Crumbled Bacon, Chopped Green Peppers and Pimento, Onion Dip, Parmesan Cheese
CORN ON THE COB	Husk, wash and trim corn. Place cobs in glass baking dish and cover, or wrap individually in wax paper and place directly on oven's bottom shelf. Or, pull husk back enough to remove silk from corn; wash corn thoroughly. Rewrap husk around corn and cook directly on oven's bottom shelf.	**Fresh** 2 4 6 **Frozen** 2 4	 4 to 5 7 to 8 9 to 10 6 to 8 10 to 12	Seasonings: Butter, Chive Butter, Onion Butter

(Continued, next page.)

Microwave all fresh and frozen vegetables on HIGH setting.

VEGETABLE	PREPARATION FOR FRESH VEGETABLES	AMOUNT	MINUTES	SAUCES AND SEASONINGS
EGGPLANT	Wash and peel tough skin areas. Cut off stem. Leave whole, slice or dice. IMPORTANT! Pierce or prick skin if cooked whole.	**Fresh, sliced or diced** 1 medium **Fresh, whole** 1 medium	 5 to 6 6 to 7	Seasonings: Italian Seasonings, Oregano, Parmesan Cheese
OKRA	Wash thoroughly and cut off stems.	**Fresh, whole** ½ lb. **Fresh, sliced** ½ lb. **Frozen** 10-oz. pkg.	 4 to 5 3 to 4 7 to 8	Seasonings: Butter, Crumbled Bacon, Parmesan Cheese
ONIONS	Peel and quarter.	**Fresh, quartered** 8 small 2 large 4 large **Frozen, in cream sauce** 10-oz. pouch	 6 to 7 6 to 7 8 to 9 6 to 7	Sauces: Béchamel, Velouté Seasonings: Butter, Currant Jelly, Nutmeg
PARSNIPS	Scrape or peel with vegetable peeler to remove thin layer of outer skin. Quarter.	**Fresh, quartered** 4	 8 to 9	Sauces: Béchamel Seasonings: Bacon Drippings, Brown Sugar Glaze, Butter
PEAS, GREEN	Shell peas, removing peas from pods. Wash thoroughly.	**Fresh** 2 lbs. 3 lbs. **Frozen** 10-oz. pkg. 10-oz. pouch **Frozen, pods** 6-oz. pkg.	 8 to 9 10 to 11 6 to 7 6 to 7 3 to 4	Sauces: Béchamel, Seasoned Butters Seasonings: Butter, Chives, Cream, Green Onions, Mint, Mushrooms, Onion Dip, Orange Marmalade
PEAS AND CARROTS		**Frozen** 10-oz. pkg.	 7 to 8	Sauces: Mornay, Onion Seasonings: Butter, Chives, Crumbled Bacon
PEAS, BLACK-EYED		**Frozen** 10-oz. pkg.	 9 to 10	Sauces: Tomato, Seasoned Butters Seasonings: Bacon Drippings, Butter, Ham
POTATOES, SWEET OR YAMS	Wash and scrub thoroughly. IMPORTANT! Pierce or prick skin before cooking. Potatoes will feel firm before standing time.	**Fresh** 1 medium 2 medium 4 medium 6 medium	 4 to 4½ 6 to 7 8 to 9 10 to 11	Seasonings: Brown Sugar Glaze, Butter, Crumbled Bacon, Maple Syrup Glaze, Miniature Marshmallows, Pineapple Glaze

Microwave all fresh and frozen vegetables on HIGH setting.

VEGETABLE	PREPARATION FOR FRESH VEGETABLES	AMOUNT	MINUTES	SAUCES AND SEASONINGS
POTATOES, WHITE	Wash and scrub thoroughly. To bake: IMPORTANT! Pierce or prick skins of whole, unpeeled potatoes before cooking. Cook directly on oven's bottom shelf. Use only fresh potatoes and do not overcook as extreme dehydration may cause smoke or fire. Potatoes feel firm when taken from oven. To boil: Cook, peeled or unpeeled quartered potatoes in covered glass baking dish. Potatoes will feel firm before standing time.	**Fresh, baking** 1 medium 2 medium 4 medium 6 medium 8 medium **Fresh, boiling, quartered** 2 medium 4 medium	 4 to 4½ 7 to 8 10 to 12 16 to18 22 to 24 10 to 11 18 to 20	Seasonings: Butter, Cheese, Chives, Crumbled Bacon, Parsley, Green Onions, Onion Soup Dip, Paprika, Sour Cream, Toasted Almonds, Whipped Cream Cheese Sauces: Cheese, Onion Seasonings: Bouillon, Butter, Chives, Green Onions, Onion Soup Mix, Paprika, Parsley
SPINACH	Wash leaves, removing any wilted leaves or tough stems.	**Fresh** 1 lb. **Frozen, leaf or chopped** 10-oz. pkg. 10-oz. pouch	 6 to 7 8 to 9 7 to 8	Sauces: Cheese, Egg, Mornay Seasonings: Butter, Crumbled Bacon, Lemon Juice, Nutmeg, Onion Dip, Sliced Raw Onion, Vinegar
SQUASH, ACORN OR BUTTERNUT	Leave whole until cooked, cut and remove seeds before serving. IMPORTANT! Remember to pierce or prick unpeeled squash before cooking.	**Fresh, whole** 1 medium 2 medium	 8 to 9 12 to 14	Sauces: Cranberry Seasonings: Brown Sugar Glaze, Honey Glaze, Butter, Cinnamon, Nutmeg, Cooked Apples or other fruit, Maple Syrup, Sausage
SQUASH, HUBBARD	Wash and cut into serving pieces. Peel either before or after cooking.	**Fresh** 6 x 6-inch piece **Frozen** 12-oz. pkg.	 8 to 9 6 to 7	Seasonings: Brown Sugar Glaze, Butter, Maple Syrup, Mashed with Ginger or Nutmeg, Orange Marmalade, Pineapple
SQUASH, ZUCCHINI	Wash and slice thinly. Do not peel.	**Fresh, ¼-inch slices** 2 medium or 3 cups	 7 to 8	Sauces: Mornay, Egg Seasonings: Butter, Chives, Sour Cream, Parmesan Cheese
TURNIPS OR RUTABAGA	Peel off thick outer skin. Wash; slice or cube. Tops may be cooked as greens.	**Fresh, cut in eighths** 4 medium	 12 to 14	Sauces: Seasoned Butters Seasonings: Butter, Chives, Lemon Juice
TURNIP GREENS	Wash leaves, removing any wilted leaves or tough stems.	**Fresh** 1 lb. **Frozen** 10-oz. pkg.	 6 to 7 7 to 8	Sauces: Egg, Cheese Seasonings: Crumbled Bacon, Lemon Juice, Butter
VEGETABLES, MIXED		**Frozen** 10-oz. pkg. 10-oz. pouch	 6 to 7 6 to 7	Sauces: Béchamel, Cheese, Onion Seasonings: Butter, Crumbled Bacon

HOW TO HEAT A CAN OF VEGETABLES

- Empty vegetables into 1-quart glass casserole and cover with glass lid.
- Microwave canned vegetables either undrained or drained.
- Microwave canned vegetables on REHEAT (about 150° F., undrained).
- Let stand, covered, 2 to 3 minutes to heat through.

CANNED VEGETABLE	SETTING	MINUTES UNDRAINED	MINUTES DRAINED
VEGETABLES, All kinds 8-oz.	REHEAT	2 to 2½ (about 150° F.)	1½ to 2
15-oz.	REHEAT	3 to 4 (about 150° F.)	2½ to 3
17-oz.	REHEAT	4 to 5 (about 150° F.)	3 to 3½

ARTICHOKES AND HERB-CREAM SAUCE

4 fresh artichokes, cleaned and trimmed
¼ cup water

Herb-Cream Sauce:
1 package (3 oz.) cream cheese with chives
2 tablespoons milk
1 tablespoon lemon juice
½ teaspoon celery salt
½ teaspoon dill weed

A sensitive cheese sauce microwaves well on HIGH when cooked with another dish of food, because less energy goes to each food.

1. Place artichokes and water in 2-quart (12 x 7) glass baking dish. Cover with wax paper; set aside.

2. Place cream cheese in 2-cup glass measure.

3. Place artichokes on upper rack in oven and cream cheese on bottom shelf.

4. Microwave both for about 5 minutes, on HIGH, or until cream cheese is warm (about 100° F.). Remove cream cheese and continue cooking artichokes for 7 to 8 minutes, on HIGH, or until tender-crisp. Let stand, covered, 5 minutes.

5. Meanwhile, stir remaining Herb-Cream Sauce ingredients into warm cheese. Serve as a dipping sauce with artichokes. About 4 Servings

TIP: Try other sauces as artichoke dips — Hollandaise Sauce, page 150, Béarnaise Sauce, page 150, or Seasoned Butters, page 150.

CHEESY ASPARAGUS

1½ lbs. fresh asparagus spears
¼ cup water

Cheesy Sauce:
1 jar (8 oz.) process cheese spread
1 jar (2½ oz.) sliced mushrooms, drained
2 green onions, sliced
1 teaspoon lemon juice

Mushrooms and cheese are sensitive; microwave on ROAST to prevent "popping" or curdling.

1. Arrange asparagus in 2-quart (12 x 7) glass baking dish with stalks toward outside of dish. Add water. Cover with wax paper; set aside.

2. Place Cheesy Sauce ingredients in 2-cup glass measure.

3. Place asparagus on upper rack in oven and sauce on bottom shelf.

4. Microwave both for 12 to 14 minutes, on ROAST, or until asparagus is tender-crisp and sauce is hot (about 160° F.). Stir sauce and drain asparagus; let stand, covered, 2 minutes. Pour sauce over asparagus to serve. 4 to 6 Servings

TIP: Substitute 2 packages (10 oz. each) frozen asparagus spears for fresh asparagus. Omit water.

BEANS VINAIGRETTE

1 package (9 oz.) frozen cut green beans
1 package (9 oz.) frozen cut wax beans

Vinaigrette:
¼ cup cooking oil
¼ cup tarragon vinegar or white vinegar plus dash tarragon
¼ cup grated Parmesan cheese
2 teaspoons snipped chives
½ teaspoon sugar
½ teaspoon salt
¼ teaspoon pepper
Pimento strips, if desired

Beans may be stored covered in refrigerator up to one week.

1. Place beans in medium glass mixing bowl. Cover with wax paper.

2. Microwave for about 10 minutes, on HIGH, or until tender-crisp; drain. Pour Vinaigrette over beans; toss to combine; cover. Chill about 8 hours, stirring occasionally. Garnish with pimento strips.

3. **Vinaigrette:** Combine all ingredients in 1-cup glass measure. 4 to 6 Servings

SPANISH BARBECUE BEANS

Warm covered baked beans on REHEAT.

- **2 cans (16 oz. each) pork and beans in tomato sauce**
- **4 slices bacon, diced**
- **1 medium onion, chopped**
- **¼ cup bottled barbecue sauce**
- **2 tablespoons packed brown sugar**
- **2 tablespoons prepared liquid black coffee**
- **1 teaspoon prepared mustard**

1. Combine all ingredients in 1½-quart glass casserole. Cover with glass lid.

2. Microwave for 10 to 12 minutes, on REHEAT, or until heated through (about 150° F.). Let stand, covered, 2 minutes before serving.

4 to 6 Servings

TANGY GREEN BEANS *

A covered dish holds steam for fast cooking.

- **2 cups cut fresh green beans**
- **¼ cup water**
- **1 can (10¾ oz.) condensed cream of celery soup**
- **½ cup sour cream**
- **1 can (8 oz.) water chestnuts, drained and sliced**
- **2 tablespoons chopped pimento**
- **½ teaspoon salt**
- **¼ teaspoon pepper**
- **½ cup chow mein noodles**

1. Place green beans and water in 1½-quart glass casserole. Cover with glass lid.

2. Microwave for 7 minutes on HIGH; drain. Stir in remaining ingredients, except noodles; sprinkle with chow mein noodles.

3. Microwave for 7 to 8 minutes, on ROAST, or until heated through (about 150° F.). Let stand 2 minutes before serving. 4 to 5 Servings

RUSSIAN BEETS

- **5 medium uncooked beets, diced**
- **3 tablespoons butter or margarine**
- **2 tablespoons vinegar**
- **½ teaspoon dill weed**
- **½ teaspoon salt**
- **¼ teaspoon pepper**
- **3 tablespoons all-purpose flour**
- **½ cup milk**

1. Place all ingredients, except flour and milk, in 1½-quart glass casserole. Cover with glass lid.

2. Microwave for 8 minutes on HIGH. Combine flour and milk in small bowl until smooth; stir into beets, and continue cooking for 4 to 6 minutes, on HIGH, or until thickened. Let stand, covered, 2 minutes before serving.

4 to 6 Servings

TIP: Substitute 2 cans (16 oz. each) beets, drained, for fresh beets in basic recipe. Microwave for 6 minutes on REHEAT. Combine flour and milk in small bowl until smooth; stir into beets, and continue cooking for 5 to 6 minutes, on REHEAT, or until thickened. Let stand, covered, 2 minutes before serving.

BUTTER-CRUNCH BROCCOLI

Dense stalks need most cooking; arrange at outer edge of dish.

- **1½ lbs. fresh broccoli**
- **¼ cup water**

Butter-Crunch Sauce:

- **1 cup water**
- **1 tablespoon cornstarch**
- **1 teaspoon instant chicken bouillon**
- **2 teaspoons dried parsley flakes**
- **¼ teaspoon salt**
- **¼ cup butter or margarine**
- **¼ cup chopped cashews**

1. Arrange broccoli in 2-quart (12 x 7) glass baking dish with stalks toward outside of dish. Add ¼ cup water. Cover with wax paper; set aside.

2. Combine remaining ingredients, except butter and cashews, in 1½-quart glass casserole; beat with rotary beater until smooth. Add butter.

3. Place broccoli on upper rack in oven and sauce on bottom shelf.

4. Microwave both for 10 minutes on HIGH. Beat sauce and continue cooking for 8 to 10 minutes, on HIGH, or until broccoli is tender-crisp and sauce has thickened (about 175° F.). Stir cashews into sauce. Let stand 2 minutes; pour sauce over broccoli to serve. About 4 Servings

TIP: Substitute 2 packages (10 oz. each) frozen broccoli spears for fresh broccoli and omit ¼ cup water in basic recipe. Decrease final cooking time by about 8 minutes.

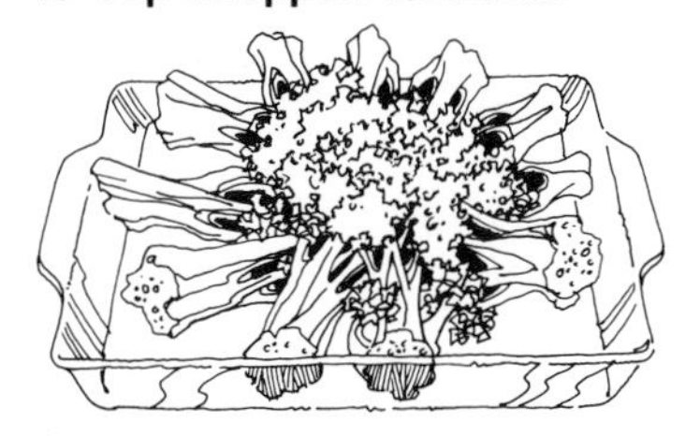

Microwaves first cook outer edges of food. Arrange denser food toward outside of dish.

BROCCOLI SOUFFLE *

Use gentle SIMMER setting for light, tender soufflé.

- **1 package (10 oz.) frozen chopped broccoli**
- **2 eggs, slightly beaten**
- **2 tablespoons all-purpose flour**
- **1½ cups shredded Brick cheese**
- **1 cup creamed cottage cheese**
- **½ teaspoon salt**
- **⅛ teaspoon pepper**

1. Place broccoli in 1½-quart glass casserole. Cover with glass lid.

2. Microwave for 6 minutes on HIGH. Drain well.

3. Combine eggs and flour in medium mixing bowl until smooth. Stir in remaining ingredients and broccoli. Pour into glass casserole.

4. Microwave for 22 to 24 minutes, on SIMMER, or until almost set in center (about 200° F.). Let stand 5 minutes before serving. About 4 Servings

RECIPE VARIATION

SPINACH SOUFFLÉ: Substitute 1 package (10 oz.) frozen chopped spinach for broccoli. Increase final cooking time by 8 to 10 minutes.

BRUSSELS SPROUTS AU GRATIN

Process cheese slices melt the best.

- **1 package (10 oz.) frozen brussels sprouts**
- **1 small onion, thinly sliced**
- **½ medium green pepper, cut into strips**
- **1 can (4 oz.) mushroom stems and pieces, drained**
- **½ teaspoon salt**
- **4 slices process American cheese**

1. Combine vegetables and salt in 1½-quart glass casserole. Cover with glass lid.

2. Microwave for 10 minutes on ROAST. Lay cheese slices over vegetables; recover, and continue cooking for about 3 minutes, on ROAST, or until cheese melts. Stir in cheese. Let stand, covered, 2 minutes before serving. About 4 Servings

CHEESY DILL CABBAGE *

One medium head cabbage equals four cups, shredded.

- **4 cups shredded cabbage**
- **¼ cup water**
- **1 package (3 oz.) cream cheese**
- **1 teaspoon dill seeds**
- **½ teaspoon salt**
- **¼ teaspoon pepper**

1. Place cabbage and water in 1½-quart glass casserole. Cover with glass lid.

2. Microwave for 8 minutes on HIGH. Stir in remaining ingredients; recover.

3. Microwave for about 2 minutes, on ROAST, or until heated through. Stir and let stand, covered, 2 minutes before serving. 4 to 6 Servings

GERMAN RED CABBAGE

A stir distributes hot liquid – speeds and evens cooking.

- **3 tablespoons lard or bacon drippings**
- **6 cups shredded red cabbage**
- **2 medium cooking apples, peeled and chopped**
- **⅓ cup finely chopped onion**
- **¼ cup packed brown sugar**
- **⅓ cup wine vinegar**
- **¼ cup water**
- **1½ teaspoons salt**
- **1 teaspoon caraway seed**
- **¼ teaspoon pepper**

1. Combine all ingredients in 2½-quart glass casserole. Cover with glass lid.

2. Microwave for 8 minutes on HIGH. Stir well and continue cooking for 8 to 9 minutes, on HIGH, or until cabbage is tender-crisp. Let stand, covered, 2 minutes before serving. About 6 Servings

CREAMY DILLED CARROTS

Remember to slit pouches before cooking.

- **2 packages (10 oz. each) carrot nuggets frozen in butter sauce**
- **1 tablespoon all-purpose flour**
- **⅓ cup milk**
- **½ teaspoon dill weed**

1. Place carrot pouches directly on bottom shelf of oven or in 1½-quart glass casserole. Slit pouches.

2. Microwave for 8 minutes on HIGH. Empty carrot pouches into 1½-quart glass casserole. Combine remaining ingredients in small bowl until smooth; stir into carrots. Cover with glass lid.

3. Microwave for 3 to 4 minutes, on HIGH, or until sauce thickens (about 150° F.). Let stand, covered, 2 minutes before serving. About 6 Servings

Pictured: Tangy Mustard Cauliflower, page 170, shown with fresh, frozen and canned vegetables.

TANGY MUSTARD CAULIFLOWER *

Mayonnaise and cheese need lower ROAST setting.

- 1 medium head cauliflower
- ¼ cup water
- ½ cup mayonnaise or salad dressing
- 1 teaspoon finely chopped onion
- 1 teaspoon prepared mustard
- ¼ teaspoon salt
- ½ cup shredded Cheddar cheese

1. Place cauliflower and water in 1½-quart glass casserole. Cover with glass lid.

2. Microwave for 9 minutes on HIGH. Drain. Combine mayonnaise, onion, mustard and salt in small mixing bowl. Spoon mustard sauce on top of cauliflower. Sprinkle with cheese.

3. Microwave for 1½ to 2 minutes on ROAST to heat topping and melt cheese. Let stand 2 minutes before serving.

6 to 8 Servings

CORN 'N OKRA MEDLEY

- 6 slices bacon
- ¼ cup finely chopped onion
- 1 can (15½ oz.) cut okra, drained
- 1 can (12 oz.) whole kernel corn with sweet peppers, drained
- 1 can (7½ oz.) tomatoes, broken up

1. Arrange bacon in single layer in 2-quart glass casserole.

2. Microwave for 5 to 6 minutes, on HIGH, or until crisp. Drain, reserving 1 tablespoon fat in casserole. Crumble bacon into casserole. Stir in remaining ingredients. Cover with glass lid.

3. Microwave for 7 to 8 minutes, on REHEAT, or until heated through (about 150° F.). Let stand, covered, 2 minutes before serving.

6 to 8 Servings

RECIPE VARIATION

CORN 'N OKRA IN TOMATOES: Wash 6 medium-large tomatoes. Cut about ½ inch off tops and hollow out inside. Save tomato pulp for soup. Omit can of tomatoes; stir together remaining ingredients in basic recipe. Fill tomatoes with vegetable mixture. Sprinkle with grated Parmesan cheese. Place on glass serving platter. Microwave for 6 to 7 minutes, on HIGH, or until heated through. Let stand 5 minutes before serving.

About 6 Servings

ONION PIE

SIMMER setting prevents separation.

- ¼ cup butter or margarine
- 1 cup soda cracker crumbs
- 1 tablespoon butter or margarine
- 2 medium onions, thinly sliced and separated into rings
- 1 cup shredded Swiss cheese
- 1 cup milk
- 2 eggs
- 2 teaspoons dried parsley flakes
- 1 teaspoon salt
- Parsley sprigs, if desired

1. Place ¼ cup butter in 9-inch glass pie plate.

2. Microwave for about 1 minute, on ROAST, or until melted. Stir in cracker crumbs; press mixture into bottom and up sides of pie plate.

3. Place 1 tablespoon butter and onions in medium glass mixing bowl.

4. Microwave for about 4 minutes, on HIGH, or until tender. Arrange onions in pie shell; sprinkle with cheese. Beat together milk, eggs, parsley and salt; pour over cheese-onion mixture.

5. Microwave for 30 to 35 minutes, on SIMMER, or until almost set in center (about 200° F.). Let stand 5 minutes before serving. Garnish with parsley.

5 to 6 Servings

SAVORY BLACK-EYED PEAS

Cook frozen vegetables icy side up.

- 1 package (10 oz.) frozen black-eyed peas
- 3 slices bacon, diced
- 1 medium onion, chopped
- ½ medium green pepper, chopped
- 1 can (10½ oz.) condensed tomato soup
- ¼ cup water
- ½ teaspoon salt
- ⅛ teaspoon cayenne pepper

1. Place all ingredients in a 1½-quart glass casserole. Cover with glass lid.

2. Microwave for 15 to 16 minutes, on HIGH, or until peas are tender (about 150° F.). Stir and let stand, covered, 2 minutes before serving.

4 to 6 Servings

EASY POTATO BAKE *

Slit a package before cooking so steam doesn't build up.

- 1 lb. frozen diced hash brown potatoes
- 1 can (10½ oz.) condensed cream of potato soup
- ½ cup sour cream
- 2 green onions, sliced
- ½ teaspoon salt
- ¼ teaspoon pepper
- Paprika

1. Place frozen potatoes in 1½-quart glass casserole. Cover with glass lid.

2. Microwave for 5 minutes on HIGH. Stir in remaining ingredients, except paprika. Sprinkle with paprika; recover.

3. Microwave for 12 to 14 minutes, on ROAST, or until hot (about 150° F.). Let stand, covered, 5 minutes before serving. About 6 Servings

RECIPE VARIATIONS

PARTY POTATOES: Add 2 tablespoons chopped pimento and 2 tablespoons chopped green pepper to potato mixture in basic recipe.

MUSHROOM POTATO: Add 1 jar (2½ oz.) sliced mushrooms, drained, and 2 teaspoons dried parsley flakes to potato mixture in basic recipe.

MASHED POTATO PUFF

Switch to ROAST setting when sensitive ingredients are added.

- 1½ cups water
- 2 tablespoons butter or margarine
- ½ cup milk
- 1½ cups instant potato flakes
- 1 cup creamed cottage cheese
- 1 cup shredded process American cheese
- 3 green onions, sliced
- 2 teaspoons prepared mustard
- ¼ teaspoon garlic salt
- 2 eggs, separated
- ¼ cup buttered dry bread crumbs

1. Place water and butter in 1½-quart glass casserole.

2. Microwave for about 2 minutes, on HIGH, or until hot. Add milk; stir in remaining ingredients, except egg whites and crumbs. Beat well.

3. Beat egg whites in small mixing bowl until stiff peaks form; fold into potato mixture. Sprinkle with bread crumbs.

4. Microwave for about 20 minutes, on ROAST, or until set (about 160° F.). Let stand 5 minutes before serving. 4 to 6 Servings

TIP: Buttered Bread Crumbs — Place 2 tablespoons butter or margarine in 1-cup glass measure. Microwave on ROAST for about 1 minute. Stir in ¼ cup dry bread crumbs.

STUFFED BAKED POTATO

Always pierce or prick whole, unpeeled vegetables before cooking.

- 4 medium baking potatoes
- 2 tablespoons butter or margarine
- ½ cup milk
- ¼ teaspoon salt
- Dash pepper
- ½ cup shredded process American cheese

1. Prick potatoes and place in oven.

2. Microwave for 10 to 12 minutes, on HIGH, or until tender. Cut potatoes in half. Carefully scoop cooked potato out of shells and place in medium mixing bowl. Add butter, milk and seasonings; mash until lump-free. Fill potato shells; top with cheese and place on glass serving platter. Continue cooking for 4 to 5 minutes, on ROAST, or until hot (about 150° F.). Let stand 3 minutes before serving. 4 to 8 Servings

TIP: Prepare stuffed potatoes ahead of meal, arrange on serving platter and refrigerate. Microwave on ROAST for 6 to 8 minutes during final cooking period in basic recipe.

RECIPE VARIATIONS

ZIPPY BACON POTATOES: Stir ¼ cup process Cheddar-type cheese spread with bacon and ½ teaspoon prepared horseradish into mashed potato mixture. Fill potato shells; omit shredded cheese topping. Microwave for 6 to 7 minutes, on ROAST, during final cooking period in basic recipe.

BLEU CHEESE-ONION POTATOES: Stir ⅓ cup crumbled Bleu cheese and 1 tablespoon chopped green onion into mashed potato mixture. Fill potato shells, omit shredded cheese topping. Microwave for 8 to 9 minutes on ROAST during final cooking period in basic recipe.

CREAMY PIMENTO POTATOES: Stir 1 package (3 oz.) cream cheese with pimento into mashed potato mixture. Fill potato shells; omit shredded cheese topping. Microwave for 6 to 7 minutes on ROAST during final cooking period in basic recipe.

SOUR CREAM-CHIVE POTATOES: Stir ½ cup sour cream and 2 tablespoons snipped chives into mashed potato mixture. Fill potato shells; omit shredded cheese topping. Microwave for 6 to 7 minutes on ROAST during final cooking period in basic recipe.

SCALLOPED POTATOES

- 1½ cups Basic White Sauce, page 151
- ½ teaspoon salt
- 4 medium potatoes, peeled and thinly sliced
- ¼ cup buttered dry bread crumbs, if desired

Basic White Sauce and vegetables cook well together on HIGH.

1. Combine all ingredients, except crumbs, in 1½-quart glass casserole.

2. Microwave for 9 minutes on HIGH. Stir; sprinkle with bread crumbs, and continue cooking for 9 to 10 minutes, on HIGH, or until potatoes are tender (about 150° F.). Let stand 2 minutes before serving. About 6 Servings

TIP: Buttered Bread Crumbs — Place 2 tablespoons butter or margarine in 1-cup glass measure. Microwave for about 1 minute on ROAST. Stir in ¼ cup dry bread crumbs.

RECIPE VARIATIONS

AU GRATIN POTATOES: Substitute 1½ cups Cheese Sauce, page 161, for white sauce in basic recipe. Microwave on ROAST for 12 minutes. Stir; sprinkle with bread crumbs, and continue cooking for 13 to 15 minutes, on ROAST, or until potatoes are tender (about 150° F.). Let stand 2 minutes.

MUSHROOM SCALLOPED POTATOES: Substitute 1 can (10¾ oz.) condensed cream of mushroom soup and ¼ cup milk for Basic White Sauce in basic recipe. Microwave as directed in AuGratin Potatoes.

SWEET POTATO PECAN BALLS

- 3 medium sweet potatoes, peeled and quartered
- ¼ cup water
- ½ teaspoon salt
- ½ teaspoon nutmeg
- 1 egg, beaten
- 1¼ cups finely chopped pecans
- ¼ cup butter or margarine
- ½ cup packed brown sugar
- 3 tablespoons light corn syrup

Three medium sweet potatoes yield about 2 cups mashed.

1. Place sweet potatoes in 1½-quart glass casserole. Add water; cover with glass lid.

2. Microwave for 7 to 8 minutes, on HIGH, or until tender. Drain; mash to give 2 cups. Stir in seasonings. Shape mixture into 10 (2-inch) balls. Dip each into beaten egg; roll in chopped nuts, and arrange in 2-quart (12 x 7) glass baking dish.

3. Place butter in 2-cup glass measure.

4. Microwave for about 1 minute, on ROAST, or until melted. Stir in brown sugar and corn syrup. Pour over potato balls.

5. Microwave for 4 to 5 minutes, on HIGH, or until hot. Let stand 2 minutes before serving. About 4 Servings.

BUTTERED RUTABAGA

- 1 medium rutabaga, cut into ½-inch cubes
- ¼ cup butter or margarine
- 1 green onion, sliced
- 1 tablespoon sesame seeds
- ½ teaspoon Worcestershire sauce
- ½ teaspoon salt

1. Combine all ingredients in 1½-quart glass casserole. Cover with glass lid.

2. Microwave for 6 minutes on HIGH. Stir and continue cooking for 6 to 8 minutes, on HIGH, or until tender. Let stand, covered, 2 minutes before serving. About 4 Servings

ONION-FILLED SQUASH

- 2 medium acorn squash
- 1 package (10 oz.) frozen small onions in cream sauce
- Salt
- ¼ cup bacon-flavored bits or 2 slices bacon, crisply fried and crumbled
- ¼ cup chopped green pepper
- ¼ cup buttered bread crumbs

1. Pierce whole squash and set aside.

2. Place slit pouch of frozen onions in 1½-quart glass casserole.

3. Place squash on upper rack in oven and onions on bottom shelf.

4. Microwave both for 6 minutes on HIGH. Remove onions and continue cooking squash for 4 minutes on HIGH.

5. Cut squash in half; remove seeds. Place, cut-side-up, in 2-quart (8 x 8) glass baking dish; sprinkle with salt. Empty onion pouch into casserole; stir in bacon and green pepper. Fill centers of squash with onion mixture; sprinkle with bread crumbs. Remove rack from oven.

6. Microwave squash for 10 to 11 minutes, on HIGH, or until tender. Let stand 5 minutes before serving. 4 Servings

TIP: Buttered Bread Crumbs — Place 2 tablespoons butter or margarine in 1-cup glass measure. Microwave on ROAST for about 1 minute. Stir in ¼ cup dry bread crumbs.

GARDEN SUCCOTASH

Vegetables of similar density microwave well together.

- **1 package (10 oz.) frozen baby lima beans**
- **1 package (10 oz.) frozen corn**
- **2 tablespoons butter or margarine**
- **¼ cup light cream**
- **1 teaspoon sugar**
- **1 teaspoon salt**
- **¼ teaspoon pepper**

1. Combine all ingredients in 1½-quart glass casserole. Cover with glass lid.

2. Microwave for 10 to 12 minutes, on ROAST, or until tender-crisp. Stir and let stand, covered, 2 minutes before serving. 6 to 8 Servings

GARDEN VEGETABLE MARINADE

A great appetizer! Store, covered, in refrigerator up to one week.

- **½ lb. fresh broccoli, cut into 1-inch pieces**
- **1 small head cauliflower, broken into flowerettes**
- **½ cup water**
- **1 package (10 oz.) frozen artichoke hearts**
- **1 pint cherry tomatoes**
- **2 cans (4 oz. each) button mushrooms, drained**

Marinade:

- **½ cup cooking oil**
- **¾ cup wine vinegar**
- **1 tablespoon dried parsley flakes**
- **1 tablespoon marjoram leaves**
- **2 teaspoons rosemary leaves**
- **2 teaspoons salt**
- **1 teaspoon pepper**
- **½ teaspoon garlic powder**

1. Place broccoli, cauliflower and water in 3-quart glass casserole. Cover with glass lid.

2. Microwave for 12 minutes on HIGH. Stir; add artichoke hearts; recover, and continue cooking for about 8 minutes, on HIGH, or until vegetables are tender-crisp. Drain; stir in tomatoes and mushrooms. Pour Marinade over vegetables; toss to combine. Cover; chill overnight.

3. Marinade: Combine all ingredients in 2-cup glass measure. 8 to 10 Servings

TASTY VEGETABLE COMBO *

Sensitive ingredients microwave on ROAST.

- **1 package (10 oz.) frozen chopped broccoli**
- **2 cups frozen sliced carrots**
- **1 can (16 oz.) creamed corn**
- **1 cup shredded Cheddar cheese**
- **½ teaspoon salt**
- **¼ teaspoon pepper**
- **1 can (3 oz.) French-fried onion rings**

1. Place broccoli and carrots in 1½-quart glass casserole. Cover with glass lid.

2. Microwave for 10 minutes on HIGH. Stir in corn, cheese and seasonings; sprinkle with onion rings.

3. Microwave for 5 to 6 minutes, on ROAST, or until heated through (about 150° F.). Let stand 2 minutes before serving. 6 to 8 Servings

ZUCCHINI CASSEROLE

Bacon cooks quickly, crisply on HIGH.

- **6 slices bacon**
- **1 cup chopped onion**
- **½ cup chopped green pepper**
- **3 medium zucchini, sliced**
- **¾ cup catsup**
- **½ teaspoon salt**
- **⅛ teaspoon pepper**
- **2 tablespoons grated Parmesan cheese**

1. Arrange bacon slices in single layer in 2-quart (12 x 7) glass baking dish.

2. Microwave for 5 to 6 minutes, on HIGH, or until crisp. Remove bacon; crumble, and set aside. Add onion and green pepper to bacon fat.

3. Microwave for about 3 minutes, on HIGH, or until onion is partly cooked. Combine sautéd vegetables and crumbled bacon.

4. Assemble in 2-quart glass casserole by layers: ⅓ of sautéd vegetable mixture, ½ of sliced zucchini and ½ of catsup. Sprinkle with ½ of salt and pepper. Repeat layers, ending with last ⅓ of sautéd vegetable mixture.

5. Sprinkle with Parmesan cheese. Cover with glass lid. Microwave for 7 to 8 minutes, on HIGH, or until zucchini is tender-crisp. Let stand, covered, 5 minutes before serving. About 6 Servings

GARDEN SUCCOTASH

- 1 package (10 oz.) frozen baby lima beans
- 1 package (10 oz.) frozen corn
- 2 tablespoons butter or margarine
- ¼ cup light cream
- 1 teaspoon sugar
- 1 teaspoon salt
- ¼ teaspoon pepper

Vegetables of similar density microwave well together.

1. Combine all ingredients in 1½-quart glass casserole. Cover with glass lid.

2. Microwave for 10 to 12 minutes, on ROAST, or until tender-crisp. Stir and let stand, covered, 2 minutes before serving. 6 to 8 Servings

GARDEN VEGETABLE MARINADE

- ½ lb. fresh broccoli, cut into 1-inch pieces
- 1 small head cauliflower, broken into flowerettes
- ½ cup water
- 1 package (10 oz.) frozen artichoke hearts
- 1 pint cherry tomatoes
- 2 cans (4 oz. each) button mushrooms, drained

Marinade:

- ½ cup cooking oil
- ¾ cup wine vinegar
- 1 tablespoon dried parsley flakes
- 1 tablespoon marjoram leaves
- 2 teaspoons rosemary leaves
- 2 teaspoons salt
- 1 teaspoon pepper
- ½ teaspoon garlic powder

A great appetizer! Store, covered, in refrigerator up to one week.

1. Place broccoli, cauliflower and water in 3-quart glass casserole. Cover with glass lid.

2. Microwave for 12 minutes on HIGH. Stir; add artichoke hearts; recover, and continue cooking for about 8 minutes, on HIGH, or until vegetables are tender-crisp. Drain; stir in tomatoes and mushrooms. Pour Marinade over vegetables; toss to combine. Cover; chill overnight.

3. Marinade: Combine all ingredients in 2-cup glass measure. 8 to 10 Servings

TASTY VEGETABLE COMBO *

- 1 package (10 oz.) frozen chopped broccoli
- 2 cups frozen sliced carrots
- 1 can (16 oz.) creamed corn
- 1 cup shredded Cheddar cheese
- ½ teaspoon salt
- ¼ teaspoon pepper
- 1 can (3 oz.) French-fried onion rings

Sensitive ingredients microwave on ROAST.

1. Place broccoli and carrots in 1½-quart glass casserole. Cover with glass lid.

2. Microwave for 10 minutes on HIGH. Stir in corn, cheese and seasonings; sprinkle with onion rings.

3. Microwave for 5 to 6 minutes, on ROAST, or until heated through (about 150° F.). Let stand 2 minutes before serving. 6 to 8 Servings

ZUCCHINI CASSEROLE

- 6 slices bacon
- 1 cup chopped onion
- ½ cup chopped green pepper
- 3 medium zucchini, sliced
- ¾ cup catsup
- ½ teaspoon salt
- ⅛ teaspoon pepper
- 2 tablespoons grated Parmesan cheese

Bacon cooks quickly, crisply on HIGH.

1. Arrange bacon slices in single layer in 2-quart (12 x 7) glass baking dish.

2. Microwave for 5 to 6 minutes, on HIGH, or until crisp. Remove bacon; crumble, and set aside. Add onion and green pepper to bacon fat.

3. Microwave for about 3 minutes, on HIGH, or until onion is partly cooked. Combine sautéd vegetables and crumbled bacon.

4. Assemble in 2-quart glass casserole by layers: ⅓ of sautéd vegetable mixture, ½ of sliced zucchini and ½ of catsup. Sprinkle with ½ of salt and pepper. Repeat layers, ending with last ⅓ of sautéd vegetable mixture.

5. Sprinkle with Parmesan cheese. Cover with glass lid. Microwave for 7 to 8 minutes, on HIGH, or until zucchini is tender-crisp. Let stand, covered, 5 minutes before serving. About 6 Servings

Oven Meals

60 Menus Show How to Microwave Two or Three Foods Together

Here Are 60 Oven Meal Menus—Ready to Use: This chapter includes 60 kitchen-tested meals for you to prepare. All cooking times and oven settir gs have been worked out — including an oven diagram showing where each food goes. The 15 different types of basic meals — each with three variations that microwave in a similar way — are guides. Once you've tried several of these menus, create some of your own. Complete directions for developing Oven Meals start on page 196.

Benefits of Oven Meals: Now you can prepare a whole, two or three dish meal in a microwave oven. Cook it all at once. Serve it all at once — hot and savory. Amazing! Convenient! Fun! This versatile oven has been especially designed to cook three different foods together. Microwaves enter from both sides, evenly surrounding the food for superior cooking results. The metal rack enables you to microwave a number of recipes at the same time. In this large capacity oven, you can experience the ease of preparing complete meals — as much as 50% faster than with a conventional range.

Food Symbols Defined for Meal Cooking: Foods are marked with the following words and abbreviations to show their cooking times compared to other foods in the meal: Long (L) — foods that generally go on the rack. Short (S) — foods that generally go on the glass bottom shelf. Extra Short (XS) — foods added part way through cooking. Extremely Short (XXS) — rolls, breads, pastries or frozen brownies added during last 1 or 2 minutes meal cooks. Microwave Browning Grill (Mw. Grill) which uses entire bottom shelf — other two foods go on rack. Root Vegetables (Root Veg.) such as dense, fresh, uncooked potatoes that always cook on upper rack. Oven Meals marked by an * indicate that one food will be added part way through cooking.

Where Does Food Go in the Oven?

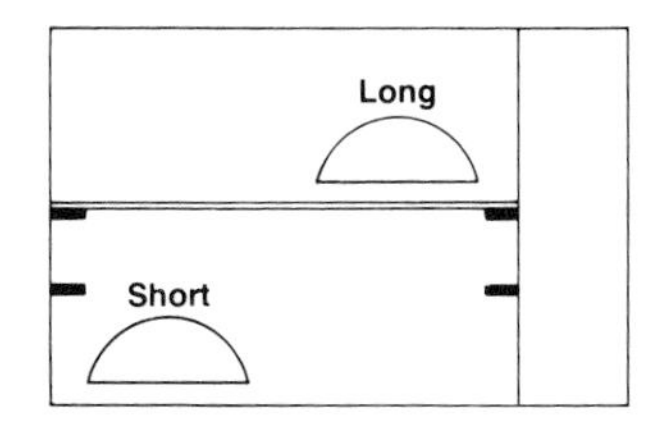

In general, dense or long-cooking foods are placed on the oven's upper rack where they receive most microwave energy when several foods are cooking at once. Foods that cook or heat quickly are placed on the glass bottom shelf where there is less energy and cooking is more gentle. Stagger food in the oven whenever possible as you do in conventional cooking. It does not matter whether the longer cooking item is on the right or the left of the rack as long as it is not placed directly over the shorter cooking item.

When is Food Done? Total Oven Meal cooking time is usually based on the longest cooking (L) food. Foods for some meals include doneness temperatures to use with a food sensor or microwave food thermometer. Since foods cook at slightly different rates when more than one dish is cooking, one food may need to cook a few extra minutes after others have been removed. Continue cooking it alone at the chosen meal setting. Experiment to determine when to add dishes.

Pictured: Gala Feast Oven Meal, page 186 – Beef Standing Rib Roast, New Red Potatoes with Parsley Butter, Fruit Mélange.

Guide to Reading Oven Meals

This EXAMPLE page explains where to find information on the 60 Oven Meals.

MENU

Scrambled Eggs, 6 eggs, chart [illegible]
[illegible]
Bacon, 6 slices, page 97 (Long)
Sweet Rolls, 4 bakery rolls

PREPARATION DIRECTIONS

[illegible]
[illegible]
3. Place sweet rolls on paper towel on glass or pottery plate.

Directions for creating your own Oven Meals start on page 194.

MICROWAVE DIRECTIONS

[illegible]

Step 1: Oven setting HIGH

Step 2: Place bacon on upper rack and eggs on bottom shelf. Rolls (XXS) will be added to bottom shelf during last 1 to 1½ minutes of cooking.

Step 3: Microwave bacon and eggs for 8 minutes on HIGH. Stir eggs; recover. Add rolls to bottom shelf. Continue cooking 1 to 1½ minutes on HIGH or until eggs are almost set in center. Stir eggs to scramble. Let all stand 3 minutes before serving. If crisper bacon is desired, continue cooking bacon for 1 to 2 minutes, on HIGH, while eggs are standing.

4 to 6 Servings

FOOD PLACEMENT DIAGRAM

Long

Short

XX-Short

Meal Variations

MEAL VARIATION EXPLANATION

The three menus below can be microwaved using techniques and oven positions in the basic Oven Meal above. See the Special Techniques column for helpful tips or changes in the basic meal technique. Note that XXS foods such as bakery rolls, muffins, refrigerated French toast or doughnuts go in the last minute of total meal cooking time.

CHART OF 3 OVEN MEAL VARIATIONS

[illegible]			SPECIAL TECHNIQUES
Scrambled Eggs (S), 5 eggs	**Grapefruit with Sherry (L)**, recipe, below, through Step 2	**Reheat Doughnuts (XXS)**, 4 bakery doughnuts	**TOTAL COOKING TIME: 12 to 14 min. on HIGH.** Stir eggs and add doughnuts for last min.
Omelet (S), page 77, through Step 2	**Canadian Bacon (L)**, 4 slices	**Reheat Sweet Rolls (XXS)**, 4 to 6 bakery rolls	**TOTAL COOKING TIME: 6 to 7 min. on HIGH.** Place Canadian Bacon on glass plate. Stir omelet after [illegible] min.; add rolls for last min.
Scrambled Eggs (S), 6 eggs	**Bacon (L)**, 6 slices, page 97	**Reheat Blueberry Muffins (XXS)**, 4 to 6 muffins	**TOTAL COOKING TIME: 10 to 10½ min. on HIGH.**

RECIPE

GRAPEFRUIT WITH SHERRY

Microwave in glass or pottery serving dishes without metal trim.

2 large grapefruit
3 tablespoons sugar
1 teaspoon cinnamon
2 teaspoons butter or margarine
4 to 6 teaspoons dry sherry or orange juice
Mint leaves, if desired

1. Cut grapefruit in half and cut around sections. Place each half in a glass serving bowl.

2. Combine sugar and cinnamon, sprinkle over grapefruit; dot with butter. Pour 1 teaspoon sherry over each half.

3. Microwave for 5 to 7 minutes on HIGH, or until warm. Garnish with mint leaves.

4 Servings

Early Morning Breakfast*

Scrambled Eggs, 6 eggs, chart, page 66 (Short)
Bacon, 6 slices, page 97 (Long)
Sweet Rolls, 4 bakery rolls (XX-Short)

1. Place eggs in 1-quart glass casserole; cover.
2. Arrange bacon in 2-quart (12 x 7) glass baking dish.
3. Place sweet rolls on paper towel on glass or pottery plate.

Directions for creating your own Oven Meals start on page 196.

MICROWAVE USING DIAGRAM AT LEFT:

Step 1: Oven setting HIGH.

Step 2: Place bacon on upper rack and eggs on bottom shelf. Rolls (XXS) will be added to bottom shelf during last 1 to 1½ minutes of cooking.

Step 3: Microwave bacon and eggs for 8 minutes on HIGH. Stir eggs; recover. Add rolls to bottom shelf. Continue cooking all for 1 to 1½ minutes on HIGH or until eggs are almost set in center. Stir eggs to scramble. Let all stand 3 minutes before serving. If crisper bacon is desired, continue cooking bacon for 1 to 2 minutes, on HIGH, while eggs are standing.

About 4 Servings

Meal Variations

The three meals, below, can be microwaved using techniques and oven positions in the basic Oven Meal above. See the Special Techniques column for helpful tips or changes in the basic meal technique. Note that XXS foods such as bakery rolls, muffins, refrigerated French toast or doughnuts go in the last minute of total meal cooking time.

OVEN MEAL VARIATIONS			SPECIAL TECHNIQUES
Scrambled Eggs (S), 6 eggs	**Grapefruit with Sherry (L),** (recipe, below, through Step 2)	**Reheat Doughnuts (XXS),** 4 bakery doughnuts	**TOTAL COOKING TIME: 12 to 14 min. on HIGH.** Stir eggs and add doughnuts for last min.
Omelet (S), page 77, through Step 2	**Canadian Bacon (L),** 4 slices	**Reheat Sweet Rolls (XXS),** 4 to 6 bakery rolls	**TOTAL COOKING TIME: 6 to 7 min. on HIGH.** Place Canadian Bacon on glass plate. Stir omelet after 3 min., add rolls for last min.
Scrambled Eggs (S), 6 eggs	**Bacon (L),** 6 slices, page 97	**Reheat Blueberry Muffins (XXS),** 4 to 6 muffins	**TOTAL COOKING TIME: 10 to 10½ min. on HIGH.**

GRAPEFRUIT WITH SHERRY

Microwave in glass or pottery serving dishes without metal trim.

2 large grapefruit
3 tablespoons sugar
1 teaspoon cinnamon
2 teaspoons butter or margarine
4 to 5 teaspoons dry sherry or orange juice
Mint leaves, if desired

1. Cut grapefruit in half and cut around sections. Place each half in a glass serving bowl.
2. Combine sugar and cinnamon; sprinkle over grapefruit; dot with butter. Pour 1 teaspoon sherry over each half.
3. Microwave for 6 to 7 minutes, on HIGH, or until warm. Garnish with mint leaves.

4 Servings

*Stick-to-the-Ribs Breakfast**

Oatmeal, 4 servings, chart, page 120 (Long)
Easy Caramel Rolls, recipe below (X-Short)
Coffee, 4 cups, 6-oz. ea. (Beverage)

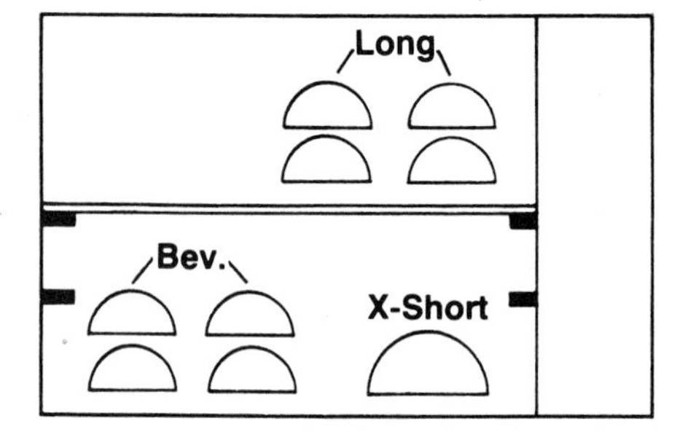

1. Place cereal ingredients in 4 glass or pottery serving bowls; mix well.
2. Prepare Easy Caramel Rolls through Step 2.
3. Place coffee to reheat in 4 cups (6 oz. ea.)

Directions for creating your own Oven Meals start on page 196.

MICROWAVE USING DIAGRAM AT LEFT:

Step 1: Oven setting HIGH.

Step 2: Place cereal on upper rack and coffee on bottom shelf. Rolls (XS) will be added to bottom shelf after 5 minutes of cooking.

Step 3: Microwave cereal and coffee for 5 minutes on HIGH. Add rolls to bottom shelf. Continue cooking all for 8 to 10 minutes, on HIGH, or until cereal is cooked. Let all stand 2 minutes before serving. If making instant coffee, heat water in cups and continue cooking for about 2 minutes, on HIGH, or until boiling. About 4 Servings

Meal Variations

The three meals, below, can be microwaved using techniques and oven positions in the basic Oven Meal above. See the Special Techniques column for helpful tips or changes in basic meal technique. Beverages always go on the bottom shelf.

OVEN MEAL VARIATIONS			SPECIAL TECHNIQUES
Grits, Quick-cooking (L), page 120	**Ham (S),** 4 slices	**Reheat coffee (Beverage),** 4 cups, 6-oz. ea.	**TOTAL COOKING TIME: 14 to 16 min. on HIGH.**
Apricot Oatmeal (L), page 120	**French Toast (XS),** 6 slices, frozen	**Syrup, maple-flavored (S),** 1 cup	**TOTAL COOKING TIME: 12 to 14 min. on HIGH.** Add toast after 7 min.
Raisin Oatmeal (L), page 120	**Reheat Doughnuts (XXS),** 4 doughnuts	**Cocoa (Beverage),** 4 mugs, 8-oz. ea.	**TOTAL COOKING TIME: 12 to 14 min. on HIGH.** Add doughnuts in last 2 min. of cooking time.

EASY CARAMEL ROLLS

- **¼ cup honey**
- **2 tablespoons butter or margarine**
- **1 teaspoon cinnamon**
- **½ cup chopped nuts**
- **¼ cup raisins**
- **1 can (8 oz.) refrigerator biscuits**

1. Combine all ingredients, except biscuits, in (9 x 5) glass loaf dish.

2. Microwave for about 1 minute, on HIGH, or until butter is melted. Stir well. Open and separate biscuits; place in sugar mixture, turning to coat. Arrange biscuits on their sides.

3. Microwave for 3 minutes on SIMMER.

4. Microwave for 1 to 1½ minutes, on HIGH, or until biscuits are no longer doughy. Let stand 2 minutes. Invert onto serving plate.

About 6 Servings

Party Luncheon

Quiche Lorraine, page 68 (Custard Pie)
Wilted Lettuce Salad, recipe below (Short)
Cherries Jubilee, a recipe variation, page 60 (Long)

1. Prepare Quiche Lorraine through Step 2.
2. Prepare Wilted Lettuce Salad through Step 2.
3. Prepare Cherries Jubilee through Step 1.

Directions for creating your own Oven Meals start on page 196.

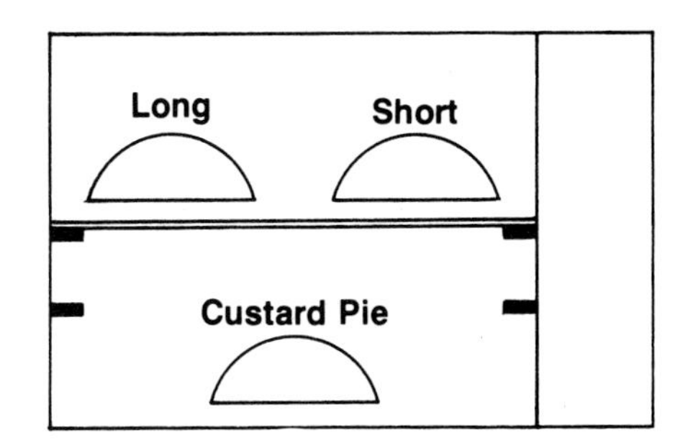

MICROWAVE USING DIAGRAM AT LEFT:

Step 1: Oven setting ROAST.

Step 2: Place salad dressing and dessert on upper rack and quiche on bottom shelf.

Step 3: Microwave for 25 to 30 minutes, on ROAST, or until quiche is almost set in center. Let quiche and dessert stand 5 minutes before serving. Prepare salad during standing time. 4 to 5 Servings

Meal Variations

The three meals, below, can be microwaved using techniques and oven positions in the basic Oven Meal above. Use the Special Techniques column for helpful tips in basic meal technique. Egg custard pies, such as Quiche Lorraine or Onion Pie, are microwaved alone on the bottom shelf for gentle cooking. The dishes above it block some microwaves and allow more gentle heat on bottom shelf at the ROAST setting.

OVEN MEAL VARIATIONS			SPECIAL TECHNIQUES
Quiche Mexican (Custard Pie), recipe variation, page 68, through Step 2	**Wilted Spinach Salad (S),** recipe variation, below, through Step 2	**Fruit Mélange (L),** page 186, through Step 1	**TOTAL COOKING TIME: 25 to 30 min. on ROAST.**
Quiche Salmon (Custard Pie), recipe variation, page 68, through Step 2	**Strawberry Peaches (S),** recipe variation, page 146, through Step 1	**Apricot Jubilee (L),** recipe variation. page 60, through Step 1	**TOTAL COOKING TIME: 25 to 30 min. on ROAST.**
Onion Pie (Custard Pie), page 170, through Step 5	**Wilted Lettuce Salad (S),** recipe, below, through Step 2	**Hot Pink Pears (L),** page 60, through Step 1	**TOTAL COOKING TIME: 28 to 32 min. on ROAST.** Turn and baste pears after 20 min., recover.

WILTED LETTUCE SALAD

- **5 slices bacon**
- **¼ cup vinegar**
- **1 tablespoon sugar**
- **2 tablespoons water**
- **½ teaspoon salt**
- **¼ teaspoon dry mustard**
- **⅛ teaspoon pepper**
- **1 head leaf lettuce, torn apart**
- **2 green onions, finely sliced**

1. Arrange bacon slices in single layer in 2-quart (12 x 7) glass baking dish.

2. Microwave for 4 to 5 minutes, on HIGH, or until bacon is crisp. Drain bacon, reserving 2 tablespoons bacon drippings; crumble, and set aside. Combine reserved bacon drippings and remaining ingredients, except lettuce and onion, in small glass mixing bowl; mix well.

3. Microwave for 2 to 3 minutes, on HIGH, or until hot (about 200° F.). Place lettuce and onion in salad bowl. Pour on hot dressing. Toss lightly to coat lettuce leaves. Sprinkle bacon over top; serve. 6 to 8 Servings

TIP: Add 2 chopped hard-cooked eggs when salad is tossed.

RECIPE VARIATION

WILTED SPINACH SALAD: Substitute 1 tablespoon brown sugar for sugar. Substitute 1-lb. fresh spinach, washed and torn apart, for leaf lettuce.

Saturday Super-Lunch*

Macaroni and Cheese, page 121 (Long)
Spicy-Topped Tomatoes, recipe below (Short)
Fruit, 1 package, 10-oz. frozen (X-Short)

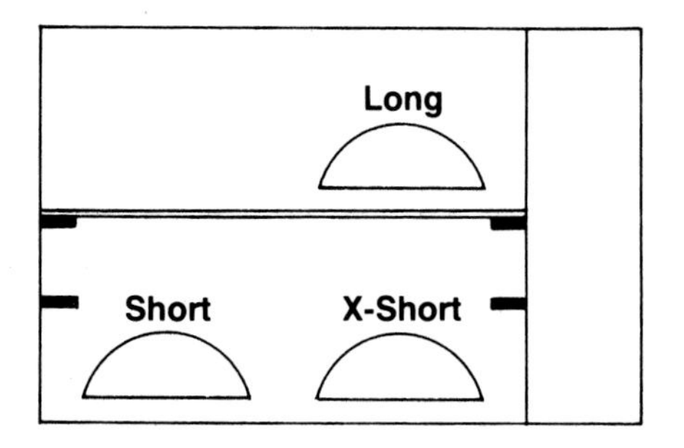

1. Prepare Macaroni and Cheese through Step 1.
2. Prepare Spicy-Topped Tomatoes through Step 1.
3. Place frozen fruit in 2-quart (8 x 8) glass baking dish; slit plastic pouch.

Directions for creating your own Oven Meals start on page 196.

MICROWAVE USING DIAGRAM AT LEFT:
Step 1: Oven setting HIGH.

Step 2: Place casserole on upper rack and tomatoes on bottom shelf. Fruit (XS) will be added to bottom shelf after 10 minutes of cooking.

Step 3: Microwave casserole and tomatoes for 10 minutes on HIGH. Add fruit to bottom shelf. Continue cooking for 10 to 12 minutes, on HIGH, or until casserole is hot (about 150° F.). About 4 Servings

Meal Variations

The three meals, below, can be microwaved using techniques and oven positions in the basic Oven Meal above. See the Special Techniques column for helpful tips or changes in basic meal technique.

OVEN MEAL VARIATIONS			SPECIAL TECHNIQUES
Cheesy Beef Hot Dish (L), page 85, through Step 2	**Asparagus (S),** 1 can, 16-oz.	**Caramel Apples (XS),** 4 apples with caramel sheets	**TOTAL COOKING TIME: 28 to 30 min. on ROAST.** Add caramel apples in last 4 to 5 min. of cooking time.
Hamburger Main Dish Mix (L), 1 pkg. mix 7-oz.	**Reheat Coffee (Beverage),** 4 cups, 6-oz. ea.	**Cheese Peaches (XS),** page 146, through Step 1	**TOTAL COOKING TIME: 20 to 25 min. on ROAST.** After 10 min., stir main dish; recover, and add peaches. (Use only potato or rice hamburger main dish mix.)
Tuna Noodle Casserole (S), page 90, through Step 2	**Chocolate Pudding (L),** 1 pkg. mix, 3¼-oz.	**Reheat Rolls (XXS),** 4 rolls	**TOTAL COOKING TIME: 16 to 18 min. on HIGH.** Place pudding on upper rack of oven and casserole on bottom shelf. Add rolls in final 1 to 1½ min. of cooking time.

SPICY-TOPPED TOMATOES

- **4 medium tomatoes**
- **½ cup mayonnaise or salad dressing**
- **2 green onions, sliced**
- **1 tablespoon prepared mustard**
- **½ teaspoon salt**
- **⅛ teaspoon basil leaves**
- **2 tablespoons crushed unsweetened cereal flakes**

Mayonnaise and salad dressing are sensitive, cook on ROAST.

1. Slice each tomato into 3 slices; arrange in bottom of 3-quart (13 x 9) glass baking dish. Combine remaining ingredients, except cereal flakes, in small bowl. Spread about 1 tablespoon mixture on each tomato slice; sprinkle with crushed cereal flakes.

2. Microwave for 4 to 5 minutes, on ROAST, or until tomatoes are tender. Let stand 2 minutes before serving. 4 to 6 Servings

Hearty Noon Treat*

Chili, 1 can, 40-oz. (Short)
Rolls, 4 rolls (XX-Short)
Old-Fashioned Baked Apples, a recipe variation, below (Long)

1. Place chili in 2-quart glass casserole; cover.
2. Place rolls on paper towel on glass or pottery serving plate.
3. Prepare apples through Step 1.

Directions for creating your own Oven Meals start on page 196.

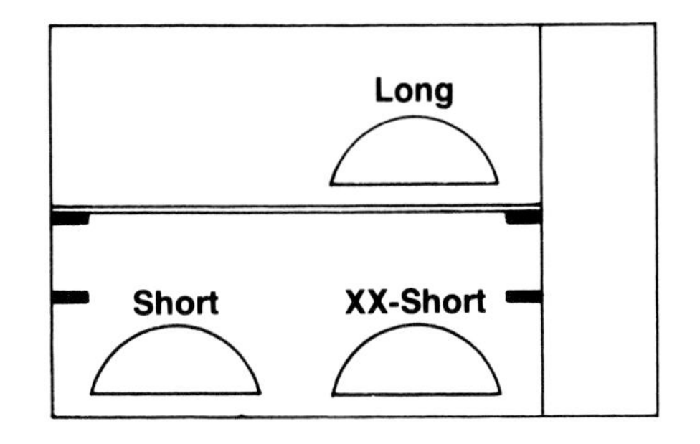

MICROWAVE USING DIAGRAM AT LEFT:
Step 1: Oven setting HIGH.

Step 2: Place apples on upper rack and chili on bottom shelf. Rolls (XXS) will be added to bottom shelf during last 1½ to 2 minutes of cooking.

Step 3: Microwave apples and chili for 18 minutes on HIGH. Stir chili; add rolls to bottom shelf. Continue cooking all for 1½ to 2 minutes, on HIGH, or until apples are tender. Let all stand 5 minutes before serving.
About 4 Servings

Meal Variations

The three meals, below, can be microwaved using techniques and oven positions in the basic Oven Meal above. See the Special Techniques column for helpful tips or changes in basic meal technique.

OVEN MEAL VARIATIONS			SPECIAL TECHNIQUES
Stew (S), 1 can, 40-oz.	**Reheat Rolls (XXS),** 4 rolls	**Applesauce (L),** page 188, through Step 1	**TOTAL COOKING TIME: 20 to 22 min. on HIGH.** Add rolls in last 1½ to 2 min.
Undiluted Chunk Soup (L), 2 cans, 18¾-oz. ea.	**Reheat Muffins (XXS),** 6 muffins	**Cake and Frosting Mix (Cake),** 13.5-oz. pkg. mix	**TOTAL COOKING TIME: 14 to 16 min. on HIGH.** Add muffins in last 2 min. Cake may need additional 1 to 2 min. on HIGH.
Spaghetti (L), 1 can, 26¼-oz.	**Reheat Garlic Bread (XXS),** ½ lb.	**Cupcakes (Cake),** 1 pkg. cake mix, 9-oz.	**TOTAL COOKING TIME: 11 to 12 min. on HIGH.** Add bread in last 3 min.; remove cupcakes as they are done. Cupcakes may need additional 2 min. on HIGH.

SHERRIED BAKED APPLES

6 medium cooking apples, washed and cored
½ cup raisins
½ cup packed brown sugar
½ teaspoon cinnamon
½ cup dry sherry or apple juice

1. Cut off top third of each apple. Place bottoms of apples in 2-quart (8 x 8) glass baking dish. Fill center with raisins. Combine brown sugar and cinnamon in small bowl; sprinkle over raisins. Place tops of apples over sugar mixture. Pour sherry over apples; cover with wax paper.

2. Microwave for 10 to 12 minutes, on HIGH, or until tender. Let stand, covered, 3 minutes before serving.
6 Servings

RECIPE VARIATIONS

BAKED APPLE WITH MINCEMEAT: Substitute 1 can (22 oz.) mincemeat pie filling for raisins, brown sugar and cinnamon. Use port wine or Madeira instead of sherry.

OLD-FASHIONED BAKED APPLE: Substitute 3 tablespoons butter or margarine for raisins and sherry; reduce brown sugar to 6 tablespoons. Omit Step 1 in basic recipe. Place apples in 2-quart (8 x 8) glass baking dish; place 1 tablespoon brown sugar and ½ tablespoon butter in center of each apple. Sprinkle with cinnamon.

Kid-Pleasing Lunch*

Hot Dogs, 4 hot dogs (X-Short)
Chunk Vegetable Soup, 2 cans, 10-¾ oz. ea. (Long)
Brownies, 1 package, 13-oz., frozen (XX-Short)

1. Place 4 wieners in 4 split hot dog buns, wrap each in paper towel or napkin.

2. Place soup in 1½-quart glass casserole; add water as directed on can; cover.

3. Remove lid from tray of frozen brownies.

Directions for creating your own Oven Meals start on page 196.

MICROWAVE USING DIAGRAM AT LEFT:

Step 1: Oven setting HIGH.

Step 2: Place soup on upper rack. Hot dogs (XS) will be placed on bottom shelf after 3 minutes of cooking. Brownies (XS) will be added to bottom shelf for last 1 to 2 minutes of cooking.

Step 3: Microwave soup for 3 minutes on HIGH. Add hot dogs to bottom shelf. Continue cooking both for 4 minutes on HIGH. Add brownies to bottom shelf and continue cooking all for 1 to 2 minutes, on HIGH, or until wieners are heated through and soup is hot (about 160° F.). Let stand 5 minutes before serving. About 4 Servings

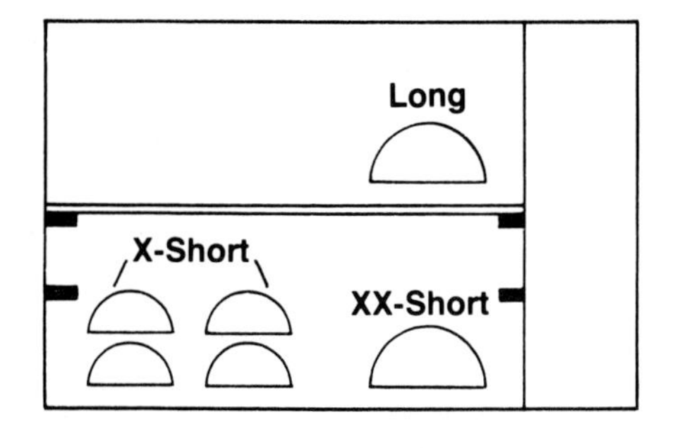

Meal Variations

The three meals, below, can be microwaved using techniques and oven positions in the basic Oven Meal above. See the Special Techniques column for helpful tips or changes in basic meal technique.

OVEN MEAL VARIATIONS			SPECIAL TECHNIQUES
Sliced Meat Sandwich (XS), page 167, through Step 1	**Tomato Soup (S),** 1 can condensed, 10¾-oz.	**Vanilla Pudding (L),** 1 pkg. mix, 3¼-oz.	**TOTAL COOKING TIME: 16 to 18 min. on HIGH.** Place pudding on upper rack of oven and soup on bottom shelf. After 12 min. add sandwiches to bottom shelf; beat pudding and recover.
Tacos (L), page 166, through Step 1	**Reheat Coffee (Beverage),** 4 cups	**Coconut Pudding (L),** 1 pkg. mix, 3¼-oz.	**TOTAL COOKING TIME: 18 to 20 min. on HIGH.** Place ground beef and pudding on upper rack of oven and coffee on bottom shelf. After 10 min., drain ground beef; add seasonings and water; recover. Beat pudding; recover.
Quick Pizza (L), page 95, through Step 1	**Wilted Lettuce Salad (S)** page 25, through Step 2	**Banana Boats (S),** recipe, below, through Step 1	**TOTAL COOKING TIME: 6 to 8 min. on HIGH.** Place pizza on upper rack of oven and salad dressing and bananas on bottom shelf.

BANANA BOATS

- **4 firm bananas**
- **2 tablespoons lemon juice**
- **2 bars (1.2 oz. each) milk chocolate, broken into pieces**
- **½ cup miniature marshmallows**

Whole fruit holds its shape when cooked uncovered.

1. Make a lengthwise cut, about ½-inch deep, down top of each unpeeled banana. Brush each banana with lemon juice. Divide chocolate pieces and marshmallows evenly among bananas and fill each split in each banana. Place in individual glass serving bowls.

2. Microwave for about 3 minutes, on HIGH, or until chocolate melts. 4 Servings

Pictured: Kid-Pleasing Lunch, meal opposite – Hot Dogs, Chunk Vegetable Soup, Brownies.

Sunday Chicken Dinner*

Whole Chicken, 2½ to 3-lb., chart, page 141 (Long)
Boiled Potatoes, 1½ lbs. (Root Vegetable)
Peas, 2 packages, 10-oz. ea., frozen (Short)
Chicken Gravy, recipe below

Root Veg.
Long
Short

1. Place chicken, breast-side-down, on microwave roasting rack in 2-quart (12 x 7) glass baking dish; brush with melted butter, if desired.
2. Place potatoes and ¼ cup water in (9 x 5) glass loaf dish; cover.
3. Place frozen peas in 2-quart (8 x 8) glass baking dish; cover.

Directions for creating your own Oven Meals start on page 196.

MICROWAVE USING DIAGRAM AT LEFT:
Step 1: Oven setting HIGH.

Step 2: Place chicken and potatoes on lower rack and peas on bottom shelf.

Step 3: Microwave for 20 minutes. Turn chicken over. Stir potatoes; recover. Continue cooking for 15 to 20 minutes, on HIGH, or until meat cut near bone is no longer pink (about 180° F.) and potatoes are tender. Drain chicken drippings into 4-cup glass measure and make gravy, recipe below. Let chicken stand, covered with foil, 5 minutes before serving.
About 4 Servings

Meal Variations

The three meals, below, can be microwaved using techniques and oven positions in the basic Oven Meal above. See the Special Techniques column for helpful tips or changes in basic meal technique. Use food sensor in poultry to determine when meat is done.

OVEN MEAL VARIATIONS			SPECIAL TECHNIQUES
Seasoned Crumb Chicken (L), page 134, through Step 2	**Rice (S),** 2 pkgs., frozen pouches, 11-oz. ea., chart, page 27	**Broccoli (S),** 1 pkg. frozen, chopped, 10-oz.	**TOTAL COOKING TIME: 30 to 35 min. on HIGH.** Start chicken skin-side-down. After 15 min., turn chicken over; stir rice, and recover. Rice may need an additional 4 to 5 min. on HIGH.
Rock Cornish Game Hens (L), 4 hens, 1-lb. ea., chart, page 132	**Stuffing (XS),** 4 cups prepared	**Fresh Strawberry Shortcake (XS),** page 50, through Step 1	**TOTAL COOKING TIME: 40 to 45 min. on HIGH.** After 15 min., turn hens over; add stuffing and shortcake to bottom shelf. Shortcake may need an additional 1 to 2 min. on HIGH.
Duckling (L), 4 to 5-lb., chart, page 132	**French-style Green Beans (XS),** 2 pkgs., frozen, 10-oz. ea.	**Mincemeat Pie (XS),** page 124, through Step 1	**TOTAL COOKING TIME: 35 to 40 min. on HIGH.** After 15 min., add beans and pie to bottom shelf. Continue cooking beans for 5 min., on HIGH, while duck stands.

CHICKEN GRAVY

⅓ cup chicken drippings (from whole frying chicken, above)
⅓ cup unsifted all-purpose flour
½ teaspoon salt
2 teaspoons dried parsley flakes
¼ teaspoon poultry seasoning
Dash pepper
1¾ cups warm chicken broth

1. Combine chicken drippings, flour and seasonings in 4-cup glass measure; beat with rotary beater until smooth. Beat in chicken broth.

2. Microwave for 2 minutes on HIGH. Beat and continue cooking for ½ to 1 minute, on HIGH, or until thickened (about 180° F.). Beat lightly.
About 2 Cups Gravy

TIP: Use 1¾ cups boiling water and 2 teaspoons instant chicken bouillon for chicken broth.

Dinner in a Rush

Fish Sticks, 1 pkg. 9-oz. frozen, breaded (Short)
Corn, 1 can, 16-oz. whole kernel (Short)
Crunchy Apple Crisp, recipe below (Long)

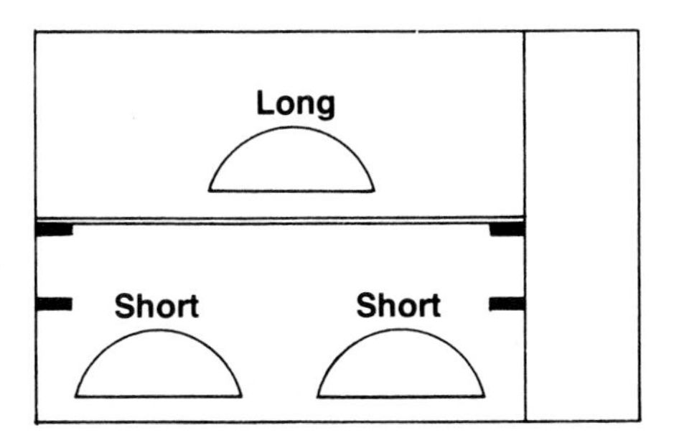

1. Place frozen fish sticks on glass plate.
2. Place corn in 1½-quart glass casserole; cover.
3. Prepare Apple Crisp through Step 1.

Directions for creating your own Oven Meals start on page 196.

MICROWAVE USING DIAGRAM AT LEFT:

Step 1: Oven setting HIGH.

Step 2: Place dessert on upper rack and corn and fish sticks on bottom shelf.

Step 3: Microwave for 20 to 25 minutes, on HIGH, or until apple crisp is tender. Let all stand 5 minutes before serving. About 4 Servings

Meal Variations

The three meals, below, can be microwaved using techniques and oven positions in the basic Oven Meal above.

OVEN MEAL VARIATIONS			SPECIAL TECHNIQUES
Walleye Pike (S), 1 pkg. frozen, 14-oz., thawed	**Cherry Crisp (L),** recipe variation, below, through Step 1	**Green Beans (S),** 1 can, 16-oz.	**TOTAL COOKING TIME: 22 to 24 min. on HIGH.** Dip fish in seasoned coating mix for fish; place in (9 x 5) glass loaf dish.
Fish Fillets (L), 1 pkg. frozen breaded, 14-oz.	**Spinach (L),** 1 pkg. frozen, 10-oz.	**Cake Mix (Cake),** 1 pkg., 9-oz., chart, page 46	**TOTAL COOKING TIME: 18 to 20 min. on HIGH.** Place fish and spinach on upper rack of oven and cake on bottom shelf
Corn Dogs (S), 4 frozen	**Potato Tots (L),** 1 pkg. frozen, 16-oz.	**Mixed Vegetables (L),** 1 pkg. frozen, 10-oz.	**TOTAL COOKING TIME: 18 to 20 min. on HIGH.** Place Potato Tots and vegetable on upper rack of oven and corn dogs on bottom shelf.

CRUNCHY APPLE CRISP

- **6 cups peeled, cored and sliced cooking apples**
- **⅔ cup quick-cooking rolled oats**
- **⅓ cup unsifted all-purpose flour**
- **¾ cup packed brown sugar**
- **½ teaspoon nutmeg**
- **½ teaspoon cinnamon**
- **¼ cup butter or margarine**

Crumb-topped mixtures microwave best uncovered.

1. Place apple slices in 2-quart (8 x 8) glass baking dish. Combine remaining ingredients, except butter, in medium mixing bowl. Cut in butter until crumbly. Sprinkle evenly over apples.
2. Microwave for 12 to 14 minutes, on HIGH, or until apples are tender. About 6 Servings

RECIPE VARIATIONS

CHERRY CRISP: Substitute 1 can (21 oz.) cherry pie filling for apples.

RHUBARB CRISP: Substitute 3 cups diced, fresh or frozen rhubarb and ⅓ cup sugar for apples.

AMBROSIA CRISP: Substitute 6 medium oranges, peeled and sectioned, 3 medium bananas, sliced, ¾ cup flaked coconut, 2 tablespoons lemon juice and 2 tablespoons all-purpose flour for apples.

PEACH CRISP: Substitute 1 can (21 oz.) peach pie filling for apples. Combine 2 tablespoons sugar and ½ teaspoon cinnamon; stir into peach pie filling. Sprinkle topping over fruit as directed in basic recipe.

Gala Feast*

Standing Rib Roast, 4 to 5-lb. (Long)
Parsley-Butter New Potatoes, 2 lbs. potatoes (Root Vegetable)
Fruit Mélange, recipe below (X-Short)

1. Sprinkle roast with 2 tablespoons cracked peppercorns, if desired; rub into roast with heel of hand. Place roast, fat-side-down, on microwave roasting rack in 2-quart (12 x 7) glass baking dish.

2. Place potatoes, with ½-inch peel removed around center, and ½ cup water in (9 x 5) glass loaf dish; cover.

3. Combine Fruit Mélange ingredients in 2-quart (8 x 8) baking dish.

Directions for creating your own Oven Meals start on page 196.

MICROWAVE USING DIAGRAM AT LEFT:

Step 1: Oven setting HIGH.

Step 2: Place roast and potatoes on lower rack. Fruit Mélange (XS) will be placed on bottom shelf after 25 minutes of cooking.

Step 3: Microwave roast and potatoes for 25 minutes on HIGH. Turn meat fat-side-up; rearrange potatoes and recover. Add Fruit Mélange to bottom shelf. Continue cooking all for 20 to 25 minutes, on HIGH, or until roast reaches rare doneness (about 125°F.). Let roast stand, covered with foil, 10 minutes. Serve potatoes with Parsley Butter, page 150.

About 4 Servings

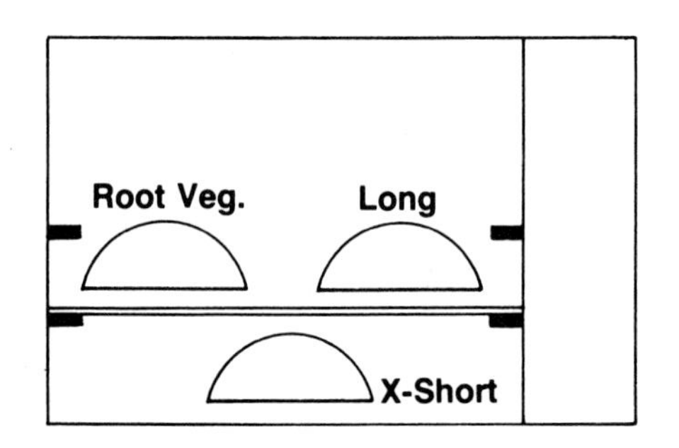

Meal Variations

The three meals, below, can be microwaved using techniques and oven positions in the basic Oven Meal above. Note, sweet potatoes are a root vegetable which go on upper rack, but go into oven part way through cooking.

OVEN MEAL VARIATIONS			SPECIAL TECHNIQUES
Pork Loin Center Rib Roast (L), 4 to 5-lb., chart, page 100	**Potatoes (Root Veg.),** 1½ lbs. boiling, chart, page 165	**Cheesy Dill Cabbage (S),** page 168, through Step 1	**TOTAL COOKING TIME: 50 to 55 min. on HIGH.** After 25 min., turn roast over and add cabbage. During standing time of roast, stir cream cheese into cabbage and continue cooking with potatoes about 3 min.
Lamb Leg Roast (L), 4 to 4½-lb., chart, page 100	**Carrots (Root Veg.),** 6 medium fresh, chart, page 163	**Peach Crisp (S),** recipe variation, page 185, through Step 1	**TOTAL COOKING TIME: 50 to 55 min. on HIGH.**
Ham (L), 4 to 5-lb., fully cooked, chart, page 98	**Sweet Potatoes (Root Veg.),** 4 medium, chart, page 164	**Asparagus (XS),** 2 pkgs. frozen, 10-oz. ea.	**TOTAL COOKING TIME: 50 to 55 min. on HIGH.** After 25 min., turn ham over; add potatoes and asparagus. During standing time of ham, continue cooking potatoes and asparagus about 4 min.

FRUIT MELANGE

1 jar (10 oz.) orange marmalade
¼ cup orange-flavored liqueur
⅓ cup water
1 cup pitted prunes
½ cup flaked coconut
1 can (20 oz.) pineapple chunks, drained
1 can (16 oz.) apricot halves, drained
1 jar (6 oz.) maraschino cherries, drained

When fruit is precooked, microwave on REHEAT.

1. Combine all ingredients in 2-quart glass casserole.

2. Microwave for 8 to 9 minutes, on REHEAT, or until heated through (about 130° F.).

6 to 8 Servings

Grandma's Dinner Favorite

Swiss Steak, page 106 (Long)
Parsley Butter Vegetables, recipe below (Short)
Old-Fashioned Bread Pudding, page 63 (Egg Custard)

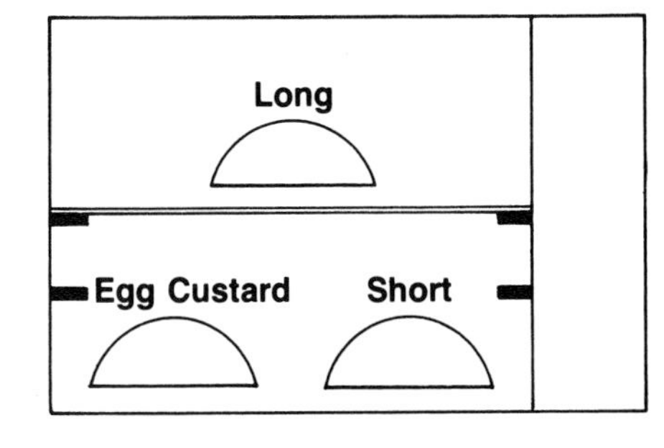

1. Prepare Swiss Steak through Step 1.
2. Prepare Parsley Butter Vegetables through Step 1.
3. Prepare Old-Fashioned Bread Pudding through Step 1.

Directions for creating your own Oven Meals start on page 196.

MICROWAVE USING DIAGRAM AT LEFT:
Step 1: Oven setting ROAST.

Step 2: Place meat on upper rack and vegetables and bread pudding on bottom shelf.

Step 3: Microwave for 35 to 40 minutes, on ROAST, or until meat is fork tender. Dessert may need an additional 8 to 10 minutes, on ROAST, or until almost set in center.
4 Servings

Meal Variations

The three meals, below, can be microwaved using techniques and oven positions in the basic Oven Meal above. See the Special Techniques column for helpful tips in basic meal technique. When a recipe calls for braising meat on HIGH/SIMMER, change the meal setting to ROAST.

OVEN MEAL VARIATIONS			SPECIAL TECHNIQUES
Chuck Roast (L), 2 to 2½-lb., chart, page 99	**Mashed Potatoes (S),** 4 servings, instant	**Carrots (XS),** 2 cups frozen	**TOTAL COOKING TIME: 40 to 45 min. on ROAST.** After 20 min., turn roast over. Add carrots to bottom shelf.
Swiss Steak (L), page 106, through Step 1	**Mashed Potatoes (S),** 4 servings, instant	**Corn (XS),** 1 pkg. frozen, 10-oz.	**TOTAL COOKING TIME: 35 to 40 min. on ROAST.** After 20 min, add corn to bottom shelf.
Pork Blade Steak (L), 1 to 1½ lbs., chart page 101, through Step 1	**Mashed Potatoes (S),** 4 servings, instant	**Lima Beans (S),** 1 pkg. frozen, 10-oz.	**TOTAL COOKING TIME: 25 to 30 min. on ROAST.**

PARSLEY BUTTER VEGETABLES

- **1 can (16 oz.) sliced potatoes, drained**
- **1 can (16 oz.) diced carrots, drained**
- **3 tablespoons butter or margarine**
- **1 small onion, chopped**
- **1 tablespoon dried parsley flakes**
- **½ teaspoon salt**
- **¼ teaspoon pepper**

1. Combine all ingredients in 1½-quart glass casserole. Cover with glass lid.

2. Microwave for about 5 minutes, on REHEAT, or until heated through. Toss to coat vegetables. Let stand, covered, 2 minutes before serving.
About 4 Servings

Springtime Dinner

Ham Slice, 1½ to 2-lb., chart, page 98 (Short)
Mushroom Scalloped Potatoes, recipe variation, page 172 (Root Vegetable)
Rhubarb-Orange Sauce, recipe variation below (Short)

1. Place ham in 2-quart (12 x 7) glass baking dish; cover.
2. Prepare Mushroom Scalloped Potatoes through Step 1.
3. Prepare Rhubarb-Orange Sauce through Step 1 in medium bowl.

Directions for creating your own Oven Meals start on page 196.

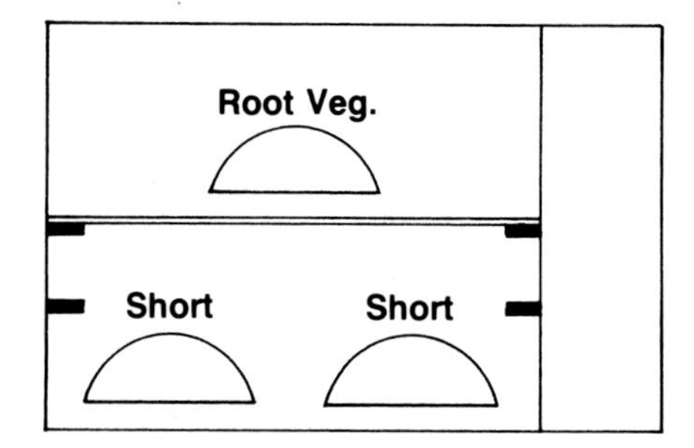

MICROWAVE USING DIAGRAM AT LEFT:
Step 1: Oven setting HIGH.

Step 2: Place potatoes on upper rack and ham and sauce on bottom shelf.

Step 3: Microwave for 25 minutes on HIGH. Stir potatoes; top with buttered bread crumbs. Continue cooking all for 15 to 20 minutes on HIGH. Let all stand 5 minutes before serving. About 4 Servings

Meal Variations

The three meals, below, can be microwaved using techniques and oven positions in the basic Oven Meal above. See the Special Techniques column for helpful tips or changes in basic meal technique.

OVEN MEAL VARIATIONS			SPECIAL TECHNIQUES
Saucy Luncheon Meat (L), recipe variation, page 111, through Step 1	**Mashed Potatoes (S),** 4 servings, instant	**Butterscotch Pudding (L),** 1 pkg. mix, 3⅝-oz., chart, page 60	**TOTAL COOKING TIME: 14 to 16 min. on HIGH.** Place water and salt for potatoes as directed on pkg. in 1-qt. glass casserole; cover. Place luncheon meat and pudding on upper rack and water on bottom shelf.
Ring Bologna (S), 1½ lbs., chart, page 101	**Potatoes (Root Veg.),** 1½ lbs. boiling with Parsley Butter, page 150	**Sauerkraut (S),** 1 can, 16-oz.	**TOTAL COOKING TIME: 10 to 14 min. on HIGH.** Remove bologna after 10 min. to stand; continue cooking potatoes and sauerkraut for 3 to 4 min.
Ham Slice (S), 1½ to 2-lb., chart, page 98	**Acorn Squash (L),** 2 medium, chart, page 165	**Applesauce (L),** recipe below, through Step 1	**TOTAL COOKING TIME: 32 to 34 min. on HIGH.** Squash may need an additional 2 to 4 min. while ham and sauce stand.

APPLESAUCE

- **6 cups peeled, cored and sliced cooking apples**
- **½ cup water**
- **1 tablespoon lemon juice**
- **½ cup sugar**
- **½ teaspoon cinnamon, if desired**

One medium apple equals about 1 cup sliced.

1. Combine apples, water and lemon juice in 2-quart glass casserole. Cover with glass lid.
2. Microwave for 10 to 12 minutes, on HIGH, or until apples are tender (about 200° F.). Stir in remaining ingredients. 4 to 6 Servings

RECIPE VARIATIONS

RHUBARB-ORANGE SAUCE: Substitute 4 cups diced fresh rhubarb for apples and ¼ cup orange juice for water and lemon juice in basic recipe. Increase sugar to ¾ cup and substitute nutmeg for cinnamon.

FOAMY APPLESAUCE: Microwave Applesauce as directed in basic recipe. Puree in blender; cool. Beat 2 egg whites with 2 tablespoons sugar until soft peaks form. Fold into applesauce.

STRAWBERRY-RHUBARB SAUCE: Substitute 1 pint strawberries, washed, hulled and sliced, and 3 cups diced fresh rhubarb for apples in basic recipe. Reduce water to ¼ cup. Increase sugar to 1 cup and substitute nutmeg for cinnamon.

All-American Meatloaf Meal*

Meatloaf, page 108 (Long)
Quick-Bake Potatoes, recipe below (Root Vegetables)
Fruit, 1 package, 10-oz., frozen fruit (X-Short)

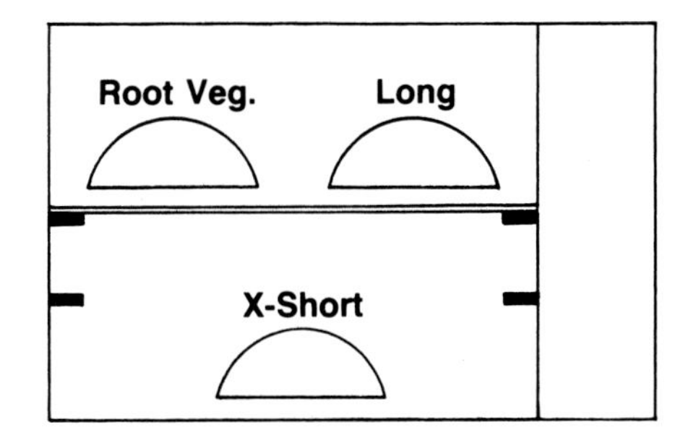

1. Prepare Mother's Meatloaf, page 108, through Step 1.
2. Prepare Quick-Bake Potatoes through Step 3.
3. Place frozen fruit in 2-quart (8 x 8) glass baking dish; slit plastic pouch.

Directions for creating your own Oven Meals start on page 196.

MICROWAVE USING DIAGRAM AT LEFT:
Step 1: Oven Setting HIGH.

Step 2: Place meatloaf and potatoes on upper rack. Fruit (XS) will be placed on bottom shelf after 25 minutes of cooking.

Step 3: Microwave meatloaf and potatoes for 25 minutes on HIGH. Rearrange potatoes; add fruit to bottom shelf. Continue cooking all for 8 to 10 minutes, on HIGH, or until meatloaf is well done in center (about 140° F.) and potatoes are tender. Let all stand 5 minutes before serving. Serve fruit over ice cream, pudding or cake. About 4 Servings

Meal Variations

The three meals, below, can be microwaved using techniques and oven positions in the basic Oven Meal above. See the Special Techniques column for helpful tips or changes in basic meal technique.

OVEN MEAL VARIATIONS			SPECIAL TECHNIQUES
Meatballs (L), page 107, through Step 2	**Mashed Potatoes (S)** 4 servings instant	**Mixed Vegetables (S),** 1 can, 16-oz.	**TOTAL COOKING TIME: 16 to 18 min. on HIGH.** Place water and salt for potatoes as directed on package in 1-quart glass casserole; cover. After 10 min. on HIGH, add cornstarch and water to meatballs; recover.
Stuffed Peppers (L), page 108, through Step 1	**Cherry Crisp (S),** recipe variation, page 185	**Reheat Dinner Rolls (XXS),** 6 rolls	**TOTAL COOKING TIME: 32 to 34 min. on HIGH.** Add rolls in last min. of cooking time.
Salmon Loaf (S), page 75, through Step 2	**Broccoli Spears (L),** 1 pkg. frozen, 10-oz.	**Lemon Sauce (S),** recipe variation, page 150, through Step 1	**TOTAL COOKING TIME: 20 to 22 min. on HIGH.** Place sauce in 1-quart glass casserole. After 14 min., beat sauce. Sauce may need an additional 1 to 2 min. on HIGH during standing time of salmon and broccoli.

QUICK-BAKE POTATOES

2 tablespoons butter or margarine
¼ cup grated Parmesan cheese
1 teaspoon dried parsley flakes
½ teaspoon salt
¼ teaspoon pepper
4 medium baking potatoes

1. Place butter in small glass mixing bowl.
2. Microwave for about 1 minute, on ROAST, or until melted. Combine cheese and seasonings in shallow dish.
3. Cut potatoes in half lengthwise. Dip cut side of each half into melted butter, then into cheese mixture. Place cut-side-up in 2-quart (12 x 7) glass baking dish.
4. Microwave for 10 to 12 minutes, on HIGH, or until tender. Let stand 5 minutes before serving. 4 to 6 Servings

RECIPE VARIATION

CORNFLAKE-BAKE POTATOES: Substitute ⅓ cup cornflake crumbs for Parmesan cheese.

Ranch Barbecue

Barbecued Country Style Ribs, recipe below (Long)
AuGratin Potatoes, 1 package mix, 5.5-0z. (Short)
Brussels Sprouts, 2 packages, 10-oz. ea., frozen (Short)

Long
Short Short

1. Prepare ribs through Step 1.

2. Prepare potatoes, according to package directions, in 1½-quart glass casserole; cover.

3. Place Brussells sprouts in (9 x 5) glass loaf dish; cover.

Directions for creating your own Oven Meals start on page 196.

MICROWAVE USING DIAGRAM AT LEFT:

Step 1: Oven setting HIGH.

Step 2: Place ribs on upper rack and potatoes and vegetable on bottom shelf.

Step 3: Microwave for 20 minutes on HIGH. Drain ribs; combine remaining rib ingredients and brush over ribs; recover. Stir potatoes; recover. Stir Brussels sprouts; recover. Continue cooking all for 20 to 25 minutes, on HIGH, or until meat is fork tender. Let all stand 5 minutes before serving.
About 4 Servings

Meal Variations

The three meals, below, can be microwaved using techniques and oven positions in the basic Oven Meal above. See the Special Techniques column for helpful tips or changes in basic meal technique. Packaged potato mixes are not raw potatoes and therefore do not take special oven placement as do fresh, uncooked root vegetables.

OVEN MEAL VARIATIONS			SPECIAL TECHNIQUES
Pork Spareribs (L), 2 to 2½ lbs., chart, page 99	**Baked Potatoes** (Root Veg.), 4 potatoes, chart, page 165	**Corn-on-the-Cob (S),** 6 ears, chart, page 163	**TOTAL COOKING TIME: 45 to 50 min. on HIGH.** After 25 min., drain ribs; brush with bottled barbecue sauce and recover.
Pork Chops with Walnut Sauce (L), page 109, through Step 1	**Cauliflower (S),** 2 pkgs. frozen, 10-oz. ea.	**Stuffing (XS),** 2 cups prepared	**TOTAL COOKING TIME: 40 to 45 min. on HIGH.** After 20 min., add stuffing to bottom shelf.
Barbecued Country Style Ribs (L), recipe below, through Step 1	**Scalloped Potatoes (S),** 1 pkg. mix, 5.5 oz.	**Peas (S),** 1 can, 16-oz.	**TOTAL COOKING TIME: 40 to 45 min. on HIGH.** After 20 min., drain ribs and brush with barbecue sauce. Add peas to bottom shelf.

BARBECUED RIBS

2½ to 3 lbs. country-style pork ribs
½ cup bottled barbecue sauce
¼ cup bottled Italian salad dressing
1 teaspoon dried parsley flakes

1. Place ribs in 3-quart (13 x 9) glass baking dish; cover with wax paper.

2. Microwave for 25 minutes on ROAST. Drain; combine remaining ingredients, and brush over ribs. Recover and continue cooking for 30 to 35 minutes, on ROAST, or until meat is fork tender (about 170° F.). Let stand, covered, 5 minutes.
4 to 6 Servings

Pictured: Ranch Barbecue, meal opposite – Barbecued Country Style Ribs, Au Gratin Potatoes, Brussels Sprouts.

Company Dinner*

Steak, 1 to 1½ lbs. rib-eye steaks (Microwave Browning Grill)
Baked Potatoes, 4 medium baking potatoes (Root Vegetable)
Chocolate Fondue, recipe below (X-Short)

1. Season steaks as desired.
2. Wash and pierce 4 baking potatoes.
3. Prepare Chocolate Fondue through Step 1.

Directions for creating your own Oven Meals start on page 196.

MICROWAVE USING DIAGRAM AT LEFT:
Step 1: Oven setting HIGH.

Step 2: Place potatoes on upper rack and (14 x 11) microwave browning grill on bottom shelf. Fondue (XS) will be added to upper rack after 26 minutes of cooking.

Step 3: Microwave potatoes and browning grill for 18 minutes on HIGH. Microwave browning grill preheats while potatoes begin baking. Place steaks on grill. Microwave both for 8 minutes on HIGH. Turn steaks over. Add fondue to upper rack. Continue cooking all for 5 to 6 minutes, on HIGH, or until meat is done. Let meat and potatoes stand 2 minutes. Beat fondue until smooth and keep warm in fondue pot. About 4 Servings

Meal Variations

The three meals, below, can be microwaved using techniques and oven positions in the basic Oven Meal above.

OVEN MEAL VARIATIONS			SPECIAL TECHNIQUES
Hamburgers (Mw. Grill), 4 patties about 1 lb.	**Potato Tots (L),** 1 pkg. frozen, 16-oz.	**Green Beans (XS),** 1 can, 16-oz.	**TOTAL COOKING TIME: Grill preheat time plus 16 to 18 min. on HIGH.** Preheat grill according to manufacturer's directions. Place Potato Tots on upper rack and meat on grill. After 7 min., turn meat over and add green beans.
Cubed Steaks (Mw. Grill), 2 steaks, ½ lb. ea.	**Cauliflower (L),** 1 pkg. frozen, 10-oz.	**Fruit (XS),** 1 pkg. frozen, 10-oz.	**TOTAL COOKING TIME: Grill preheat time plus 14 to 16 min. on HIGH.** Preheat grill according to manufacturer's directions. Place cauliflower on upper rack and meat on grill. After 6 min., turn steaks over and add fruit.
T-Bone Steaks (Mw. Grill), 2 steaks, ½ lb. ea.	**Corn-on-the-Cob (L),** 4 ears	**Chocolate Fondue (XS),** recipe below	**TOTAL COOKING TIME: Grill preheat time plus 14 to 16 min. on HIGH.** Preheat grill according to manufacturer. Place corn on upper rack and steaks on grill. After 6 min., turn steaks over and add fondue.

CHOCOLATE FONDUE

This is a sauce cooked on ROAST because of sensitive ingredients.

- **½ cup light cream**
- **2 tablespoons orange liqueur**
- **2 bars (4 oz. each) German chocolate, broken into pieces**

1. Combine cream and liqueur in 1-quart glass casserole; stir in chocolate.
2. Microwave 2½ to 3 minutes, on ROAST, or until warmed (about 140° F.). Beat well until ingredients combine and mixture is smooth.

About 1 Cup Sauce

RECIPE VARIATION

SPICED CHOCOLATE FONDUE: Substitute 2 tablespoons orange juice for orange liqueur and add ¼ teaspoon cinnamon and ⅛ teaspoon ground cloves.

Jiffy Supper*

Hamburgers, 1 lb. ground beef (Short)
Glazed Carrots, recipe below (Root Veg.)
Hamburger Buns, 4 buns (XX-Short)

1. Form ground beef into 4 patties and season; place in 2-quart (8x8) glass baking dish.
2. Prepare Glazed Carrots through Step 1.
3. Place buns on paper towel on glass or pottery plate.

Directions for creating your own Oven Meals start on page 196.

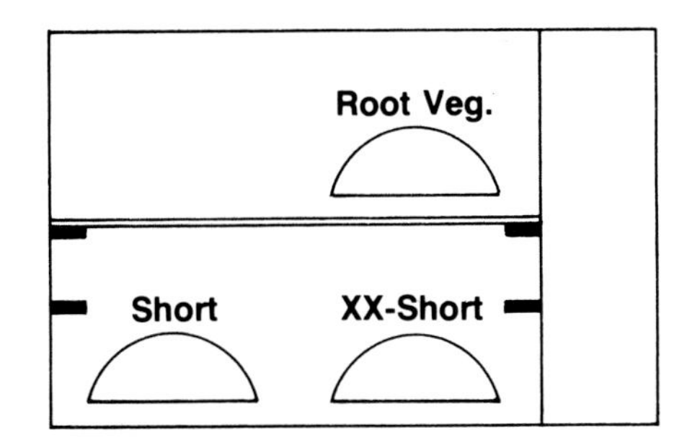

MICROWAVE USING DIAGRAM AT LEFT:
Step 1: Oven Setting HIGH

Step 2: Place carrots on upper rack and hamburgers on bottom shelf. Buns (XXS) will be placed on bottom shelf after 12 minutes of cooking.

Step 3: Microwave both for 12 minutes on HIGH. Turn meat patties over; stir carrots. Add buns to bottom shelf and continue cooking all for 2 to 2½ minutes on HIGH. Let all stand 5 minutes before serving. Place cooked patties in split buns.
About 4 Servings

Meal Variations

The three Oven Meals, below, can be microwaved using techniques and oven positions in the basic Oven Meal. See the Special Techniques column for helpful tips or changes in basic meal technique.

OVEN MEAL VARIATIONS			SPECIAL TECHNIQUES
Cheeseburgers (L) (Hamburger recipe, above)	**Baked Beans (L)** (1 can pork and beans, 31-oz.)	**Hot Apple Slaw (XS)** (page 146, through Step 1)	**TOTAL COOKING TIME: 14 to 16 min. on HIGH** After 10 min., turn meat patties over and add salad to bottom shelf. Place 1 slice cheese on each patty in last min. of cooking.
Lamb Patties (L) (4 patties, 1 lb. ground lamb)	**Spicy-Topped Tomatoes (S)** (page 180, through Step 9)	**Reheat Coffee (B)** (2 cups, 6 oz. ea.)	**TOTAL COOKING TIME: 16 to 18 min. on HIGH**
Tuna Fish Cakes (L) (page 76, through Step 2)	**Peas (S)** (1 can, 16-oz.)	**Buns (XXS)** (4 hamburger buns)	**TOTAL COOKING TIME: 10 to 12 min. on HIGH** Add buns in last min. of cooking time; place cooked tuna in split buns.

GLAZED CARROTS

Standing time completes cooking.

4 medium carrots, peeled and sliced
2 tablespoons butter or margarine
3 tablespoons packed brown sugar
1 tablespoon snipped chives
¼ teaspoon salt

1. Combine all ingredients in 1-quart glass casserole. Cover with glass lid.
2. Microwave for 5 minutes on HIGH. Stir and continue cooking for 2 to 3 minutes, on HIGH, or until tender-crisp. Let stand, covered, 5 minutes before serving.
2 to 3 Servings

RECIPE VARIATION

MAPLE-GLAZED CARROTS: Substitute 2 tablespoons maple-flavored syrup for brown sugar and 2 teaspoons dried parsley flakes for snipped chives.

Mix & Match Oven Meals

Create Your Own Oven Meals: Now that you feel at home with basic microwave cooking and have also become familiar with the menu plans we developed for you, here are some general guidelines to help you create your own Oven Meals — to put together those foods that you and your family particularly like. Just use your common cooking sense; you don't have to learn to cook all over.

Cooking a Meal for Two: If you are cooking for two rather than the four or six people that the recipes in this cookbook were primarily designed for, you can prepare less food. However, do remember that 50% less food does not necessarily mean 50% less time. Again, rely on your own common cooking sense and taste judgment. And use the meal placement and time charts that follow.

Mix 'n Match Chart: The following chart is a reference for frequently cooked food combinations for a family of 4 to 6 members. You will also want to use your cookbook recipes as a guide. Check food at the minimum cooking time and add more time if necessary. Remember, most meals microwave on HIGH setting.

FOOD	RACK	BOTTOM SHELF	APPROX. TIME	COMMENTS
Bacon	Rack		6-9 min.	Stir eggs before they are done. Add more cooking time for bacon if necessary.
Plus Scrambled Eggs		Shelf		
Baked Potatoes (4)	Rack		14-20 min.	Place small amount of meat in oven during cooking.
Plus Reheating Meat		Shelf		
Baked Potatoes (4)	Rack		14-20 min.	
Plus Vegetable		Shelf		
Beef Short Ribs	Rack		50-60 min.	Add noodles when water boils.
Plus Hot Water for Noodles		Shelf		
Cake (2 Layers)		Shelf	15-17 min.	Gentle cooking required for cakes and breads.
Casserole	Rack		15-25 min.	
Plus Vegetable		Shelf		
Chicken		Shelf	30-40 min.	Potatoes will be done first. Remove and microwave chicken alone for a few more minutes.
Plus Baked Potatoes	Rack			
Chicken	Rack		30-40 min.	
Plus Baked Potatoes	Rack			
Plus Vegetable		Shelf		
Chicken	Rack		30-40 min.	
Plus Rice		Shelf		
Chops	Rack		35-45 min.	
Plus Potatoes	Rack			
Plus Vegetable		Shelf		

FOOD	RACK	BOTTOM SHELF	APPROX. TIME	COMMENTS
Fish		Shelf	15-25 min.	Fish is easily done in microwave.
Plus Vegetable	Rack			
Fish		Shelf	15-25 min.	
Plus Vegetable	Rack			
Plus Baked Potatoes	Rack			
Ham Slice		Shelf	30-35 min.	
Plus Scalloped Potatoes	Rack			
Ham Slice		Shelf	30-40 min.	If potatoes are not done, finish alone on rack for a few minutes.
Plus Sweet Potatoes	Rack			
Leftovers (2 Plates)	Rack	Shelf	5-10 min.	Plate on rack will heat faster. Remove and microwave other for a few more minutes.
Meatloaf		Shelf	35-45 min.	Potatoes go on rack and will be done first. Remove and microwave meatloaf for a few more minutes.
Plus Baked Potatoes	Rack			
Meatloaf	Rack		35-45 min.	
Plus Baked Potatoes	Rack			
Plus Vegetable		Shelf		
Pork Ribs	Rack		35-45 min.	Scalloped potatoes made from a mix go on bottom shelf.
Plus Scalloped Potatoes	Rack			
Plus Vegetable		Shelf		
Roast	Rack		50-60 min.	Roast will fit on lower rack.
Plus Vegetable		Shelf		
Roast	Rack		50-60 min.	Baked potatoes and other root vegetables such as beets, carrots, turnips, etc. go on rack.
Plus Vegetable		Shelf		
Plus Baked Potatoes	Rack			
Sausage		Shelf	10-18 min.	Add preheating time for microwave grill.
Plus Instant Grits in Bowl	Rack			
Soup	Rack		4-7 min.	Start soup alone, then add sandwich for the last 1-2 minutes of cooking.
Plus Sandwich		Shelf		
Steak		Shelf	14-18 min.	Add preheating time for microwave grill. Always place on shelf.
Plus Baked Potatoes	Rack			
TV Dinners (2 Trays)		Shelf	14-18 min.	
TV Dinners (4 Trays)	Rack	Shelf	18-20 min.	Check doneness after 14 minutes. Remove trays as they are done.
Vegetable	Rack		7-10 min.	If there's a small amount of food on plate, add part way through cooking.
Plus Reheating Plate of Food		Shelf		

Rule of Thumb

For Basic Two- Or Three-Food Meals

This Rule of Thumb is just a guideline for you to design your own Oven Meals. Check foods at shortest cooking time, remove those foods that are done and add more time for foods that need to continue cooking.

Three Steps to Oven Meals

Decide where food goes in the oven— and when.

Decide oven setting— usually HIGH.

Decide cooking time.

STEP

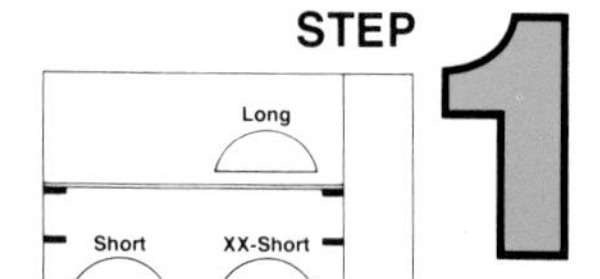

Decide Where Food Goes — and When:

Generally, put the food that takes the longest to cook, the more dense food, on the upper rack. Put the food that takes the shorter time, the quick-cooking or porous food, on the bottom shelf. More microwave energy reaches the food on the upper rack. Foods cook more evenly if they are not placed directly over one another.

Food	Rack	Bottom Shelf	Comments
Long (L)	Rack		Food items in meal requiring the longest cooking time.
Short (S)		Shelf	Food items in meal requiring shorter cooking time.
Baked Goods, Extremely Short (XXS)		Shelf	Rolls, breads, pastries added during last 1 or 2 min. of total meal cooking.
Beverages		Shelf	Best balance for cups, mugs.
Cakes		Shelf	Need gentle cooking.
Custards		Shelf	Need gentle cooking, alone, on bottom shelf. Always place other two foods on rack.
Food added part way through cooking— Extra Short (XS)		Shelf	Extra Short Foods are reheated precooked foods or food that cooks for a very short time in relation to other foods.
Microwave Browning Grill (Mw. Grill)		Shelf	Cook, alone, on bottom shelf. Always place other two foods on rack.
Root Vegetables, dense (Root Veg.)	Rack		Fresh, uncooked beets, carrots, parsnips, white and sweet potatoes, rutabagas, turnips.

STEP

Decide Oven Setting — Usually HIGH:

Generally, set the variable power on HIGH because the increased quantity of food cuts the microwave energy available to each food. Exceptions are foods that contain a lot of sensitive ingredients, foods that pop and the less tender cuts of meat. These foods use a lower setting, ROAST, just as you would on the conventional range.

STEP 3

Decide Cooking Time:

General Rule: When preparing to cook a meal including 2 to 3 foods, look at the individual cooking times of each food.

If the longest cooking time is less than 15 minutes, add all the cooking times together for the total oven meal time. Example: 6 Scrambled Eggs (6 minutes), 6 Strips of Bacon (5 minutes), Reheated Rolls (1 minute) — Total time 11 to 12 minutes.

If the longest cooking time is between 15 and 35 minutes, add all the cooking times together and subtract 5 for the total oven meal time. Example: Seasoned Chicken Parts (19 to 21 minutes), 2 pkgs. Frozen Rice (11 minutes), 1 pkg. Frozen Broccoli (8 to 9 minutes) — Total time 33 to 36 minutes.

If the longest cooking time is over 35 minutes, cook all foods for that longest cooking time. Example: 4 to 5 lb. Rib Roast (40 to 45 minutes), 2 lbs. Potatoes (16 to 18 minutes), 2 packages Frozen Asparagus (15 minutes) — Total time 40 to 45 minutes.

In the box below are some typical foods you might prepare as a main dish in a meal. Follow steps 1, 2, 3 above and also use the cooking time ranges in the box below as a guide to making your own microwave oven meals. The cooking time ranges shown take into consideration the fact that you will be cooking vegetables, desserts, etc., along with the main dish. Most meals cook on HIGH setting.

General Cooking Times for Two-or Three-Food Meals

Check foods at first time given, remove those that are done and add more time for foods that need to continue cooking.

Meals	Microwave Time Range
Casserole Meals	15 to 25 minutes
Chicken Meals	30 to 40 minutes
Fish Meals	15 to 25 minutes
Meatloaf/Meatball Meals	35 to 45 minutes
Rib/Chop Meals	35 to 45 minutes
Roast Meals	50 to 60 minutes
Steak Meals	14 to 18 minutes, plus preheating time for microwave grill

Kitchen Metrics

Since the United States is in the process of changing to metric measure, the charts and recipe on this page are designed to show how recommended U.S. metric measuring units compare with the U.S. Standard weights and measures now used in the kitchen.

Temperature will be measured in Degrees Celsius; length, width and thickness will be measured in centimeters (1/100 of a meter). You will buy food such as butter, sugar and flour by gram or kilogram (about 2.2 pounds) weight. A metric cup is 250 milliliters, slightly larger than the 8 fluid ounce cup. Time continues in minutes and hours. U.S. metric recipes will use volume (cups and spoons) as they do now.

Metric recipe yield is slightly greater (about 10%) than the U.S. standard yield, but proportions are the same. IMPORTANT: Measure a recipe using either metric or U.S. Standard weights and measures — do not mix the two.

LENGTH, WIDTH AND THICKNESS

The meter (m) is the metric measure for length. It's a little over 1 yard long. Since recipes talk about food cut into inches, you will be dealing with metric centimeters (cm) which are 1/100 of a meter. There are about 2.5 centimeters to 1 inch. The graph on the side of this page shows the camparison.

DRY AND LIQUID VOLUME

The metric volume measure is a liter. It's a little larger than 1 quart. The smaller milliliter (ml), however, is used more often in the kitchen. There are 1000 milliliters in a liter. The new metric cup of milk or flour is 250 ml,* slightly more than the measuring cup now standard in the U. S.

Current U.S. Standards	Exact Conversion to Metric	Recommended U.S. Metric
4 cups (1 qt. or 32 fl. oz.)	946 ml	4 cups (1 liter or 1000 ml)
1 cup (8 fl. oz.)	237 ml	1 cup (250 ml)
½ cup (4 fl. oz.)	118 ml	½ cup (125 ml)
⅓ cup (2⅔ fl. oz.)	79 ml	⅓ cup (80 ml)
¼ cup (2 fl. oz.)	59 ml	¼ cup (60 ml)
1 tablespoon	14.8 ml	1 tablespoon (15 ml)
1 teaspoon	4.9 ml	1 teaspoon (5 ml)
½ teaspoon	2.45 ml	½ teaspoon (2.5 ml)
¼ teaspoon	1.225 ml	¼ teaspoon (1.25 ml)

*U.S. kitchen volume measures for both dry and liquid ingredients are based on the 8-fluid-ounce cup.

WEIGHTS

Metric weights are measured in grams (g) and kilograms (kg). There are 1000 grams in a kilogram. A kilogram weighs a little over 2 pounds so, for example, a ½ kilogram package of butter will be slightly larger than the pound package you now buy.

Current U.S. Standard	Exact Conversion to Metric	Recommended U.S. Metric
½ oz.	14.18 g	15 g
1 oz.	28.35 g	30 g
2 oz.	56.70 g	60 g
4 oz. (¼ lb.)	113.40 g	125 g
12 oz. (¾ lb.)	340.20 g	375 g
16 oz. (1 lb.)	453.60 g	500 g (½ kg)
32 oz. (2 lb.)	907.20 g	1000 g (1 kg)

TEMPERATURE

Water on the Celsius temperature scale freezes at 0 C and boils at 100 C. The conversion formula from Fahrenheit is °C = (°F − 32) X 5/9. A conversion chart to match your Fahrenheit microwave oven thermometer, food sensor or conventional oven temperature control looks like this chart.

DEGREES FAHRENHEIT	DEGREES CELSIUS
250° F.	120° C.
300° F.	150° C.
325° F.	160° C.
350° F.	175° C.
375° F.	190° C.
400° F.	200° C.
425° F.	220° C.
450° F.	230° C.

CHECK OUT A MICROWAVE RECIPE IN METRIC

Macaroni and Cheese, page 121, is printed below with both U.S. Standard and the new recommended U.S. Metric measures. Note that the total ingredient volume will be slightly more using metric measuring cups and spoons (now available in housewares departments).

MACARONI AND CHEESE

INGREDIENTS	U.S. STANDARD	RECOMMENDED METRIC
Macaroni, cooked	**1 package (7 oz.)**	**225 g**
Condensed Cheddar cheese soup	**1 can (11 oz.)**	**305 g**
Process American cheese, shredded	**1 cup (8 oz.)**	**250 ml**
Green onions, sliced	**3**	**3**
Salt	**½ teaspoon**	**2.5 ml**
Pepper	**⅛ teaspoon**	**.6 ml**
Milk	**½ cup**	**125 ml**

23 cm or 9 in.
20 cm or 8 in.
18 cm or 7 in.
15 cm or 6 in.
13 cm or 5 in.
10 cm or 4 in.
8 cm or 3 in.
6 cm or 2½ in.
5 cm or 2 in.
4 cm or 40 mm or 1½ in.
2.5 cm or 25 mm or 1 in.
2.0 cm or 20 mm or ¾ in.
1.2 cm or 12 mm or ½ in.
6 mm or ¼ in.
3 mm or ⅛ in.
0

Index

How to Use This Index: Recipes are found under various headings. As an example let's look for Chicken and Green Bean Stew. You'll find it listed under S for stew, C for chicken and G for green beans.

A

B

C

D

E

F

G

H

I

J-K

L

M

N

O

P

Q-R

S

T

U-V

W

Y-Z